VIRGINIA
MEDICAL LAW

Fourth Edition

RODNEY K. ADAMS, ESQUIRE

ISBN: 978-1-4834-6189-2 (sc)
ISBN: 978-1-4834-6190-8 (hc)
ISBN: 978-1-4834-6188-5 (e)

Library of Congress Control Number: 2016919768

Lulu Publishing Services rev. date: 12/22/2016

About The Fourth Edition

Prior to the *First Edition*, health care providers did not have a good starting point for becoming acquainted with Virginia law. Statutes, regulations, and court decisions had not been collected in any organized manner from a health care provider's perspective. Even most attorneys were not familiar with the often obscure laws that may affect Virginia health care providers.

With all of this in mind, the *First Edition* was intended to be a better resource on Virginia law for the health care professional or administrator. Then the *Second Edition* and *Third Edition* continued the journey. The *Fourth Edition* is a further refinement after each chapter was revisited while teaching Master of Health Administration students. While the textbook is a bare-bones discussion of general legal concepts, it has benefited from the input of readers throughout the Commonwealth over the past many years. The author appreciates any corrections, suggestions or other comments to improve future editions of the book.

Virginia Medical Law, Fourth Edition should be read with the understanding that it is for informational purposes only. It is not intended to be legal advice. The law at the federal and state levels is ever changing and subject to interpretation. Staying current on all aspects of health care law is virtually impossible. Applying the law to a particular fact situation is often extremely challenging. Therefore, consultation with an attorney specializing in health care law is very important to assure that the points made in this book are correct and apply to the situation at hand.

Dedication – Fourth Edition

Four years have flown by since the last edition of *Virginia Medical Law*. Thanks to my clients, colleagues and students, every day brings a new question to be answered from an unexpected perspective. For that, I am very grateful.

Ruma and I have been blessed with wonderful children who always keep it real for me. Kara challenges me with her experiences in psychology and correctional services while Kyle wrestles with the study of classical ethics and aspirations of a career in business. The laughter that they bring to my life can never be replaced, and I will forever love them.

R. Adams

Dedication – Third Edition

Another half decade has flown by as I continue to be blessed with wonderful clients who continually challenge me with interesting issues. I appreciate their sense of humor as we work together to find a solution.

The indulgence of my family and law partners permits the luxury of reflecting on a day's work and how to better approach it tomorrow. Not only my children but also LeClairRyan has grown exponentially over the past few years, and I marvel at being surrounded by such talented lawyers now scattered across the country.

R. Adams

Dedication – Second Edition

Stealing time away to work on the *Second Edition* has been ever more challenging as my children have gotten older. They have learned where to find me and inflict the exquisite jab of guilt in the most innocent of comments. To Kara and Kyle as well as my wife Ruma, I will always be indebted for keeping me somewhat involved in reality and away from work.

My clients always provide the best material from which I have drawn to expand the *Second Edition*. I have often joked with my clients that one cannot make up the facts of the situations that occur in health care. That is what keeps me intrigued by the subject of health law.

I also appreciate the tremendous support from the attorneys and staff at LeClairRyan. The Firm has many of the best lawyers in a wide range of specialties. Several have given freely of their time and insights to make the *Second Edition* a success.

R. Adams

Dedication – First Edition

Writing this book has been very easy in some respects. Drafting the outline for the text merely required me to organize the multitude of questions I receive on a daily basis from physicians, health care administrators, and medical malpractice insurers. For these never-predictable scenarios that make my practice so interesting, I am very grateful to my loyal clients. We have worked through some of the most challenging situations together, and still remained friends. Maybe one day I will write a book about these episodes.

Prior to moving to Virginia, I had several very good mentors who had major impacts on my life. Richard Hopp in my native Decatur, Illinois let me follow him around while I was in college and law school to see what a real trial lawyer did. He taught me the importance of getting out and talking to witnesses and preparing a case. Command of the facts and law determine the winning lawyer in so many cases. Richard also made sure that I was admitted to his alma mater law school, which opened the doors of big-city law firms when I went looking for a job, though I will always wonder what it would have been like to practice with Richard. David Slawkowski took me under his wing at Lord Bissell & Brook in Chicago. He tortured me into writing better and learning the medicine of a case. He deputized me as his protégé "utility infielder" of medical law. This is the lawyer that a hospital administrator calls when something unusual is about to happen or has happened and quick answers are needed. Often these incidents have no black or white answer. (How often do you have a man with a .357 magnum in the pediatric ICU taking his son off a ventilator?) All a lawyer can do is recommend the "better course," as my favorite University of Illinois law professor Wayne LaFave frequently said.

The people of LeClairRyan, A Professional Corporation, have made this book possible. My fellow attorneys frequently give me valuable insight on legal analysis of a situation. The legal assistants and paralegals continually do the heavy work for me and bring me back to reality. The research of the text was funded by LeClairRyan's "self-improvement allowance" program.

Last but not least is my indulgent family who has watched me work in the evenings and weekends. To their sacrifice, I dedicate this book.

R. Adams

Special Thanks to the Review Team – Third Edition

In addition to the wonderful folks that helped review the *First Edition* and *Second Edition*, I appreciate all of the diligence and insights of the following people in reviewing the *Third Edition* before it went to print:

Maureen E. Burke, RN, MSN, CPHRM
Director of Risk Management
Inova Health System
Falls Church, VA

Rhonda Coor
Chief Operating Officer
OrthoVirginia
Richmond, VA

Jody Friend
Director, Risk Management
Riverside Health System
Newport News, VA

L. Inez Lifsey
Claims Representative
Professionals Advocate
Richmond, VA

Bruce Lo, MD, RDMS, FACEP
Chief, Emergency Services
Sentara Norfolk General Hospital
Norfolk, VA

Patti Love
Director, Risk Management
Carilion Health System
Roanoke, VA

Rhonda McGlothlin
Director, Risk Management & Insurance Operations
Centra Health, Inc.
Lynchburg, VA

Cynthia Smith
Risk Manager – Physicians
Sentara Healthcare
Virginia Beach, VA

Betty Svoysky
Asst. Vice President – Risk
Management
Professionals Advocate
Hunt Valley, MD

Jay Sweeney
Claims Manager
Sentara Healthcare
Virginia Beach, VA

Sandy Underhill, FASHRM,
CPHRM, CPHQ
Director, Risk Management
Chippenham / Johnston-Willis
Hospital
Richmond, VA

Special Thanks to the Review Team – Second Edition

In addition to the wonderful troop that helped review the *First Edition*, I appreciate all of the time and thoughtfulness of the following people in reviewing the *Second Edition* before it went to print:

Thomas Cox
President
Bluewater Solutions, LLC
Henrico, VA

Lynne J. Fiscella, Esq.
Corporate Counsel
Riverside Health System
Newport News, VA

Warren Koontz, Jr., MD
Past Executive Director
Virginia Board of Medicine
Richmond, VA

Joseph Atkins Leming, MD, FAAFP
Past President
Virginia Board of Medicine
Prince George County, VA

Russell C. Libby, MD, FAAP
President
Virginia Pediatric Group, Ltd.
Fairfax, VA

Jacque L. Mitchell
Risk Manager
Sentara Norfolk General Hospital
Norfolk, VA

Lucien W. Roberts III, MHA, FACMPE
Vice President
Pulse Systems
Glen Allen, VA

Anne G. Scher, Esq.
Director, Dept of Professional Liability
VCU Health System
Richmond, VA

Abraham Segres
Director, Risk Management
UVA Health System
Charlottesville, VA

Special Thanks to the Review Team – First Edition

I appreciate very much the following individuals who gave so freely of their time and thoughts to critique *Virginia Medical Law* while it was being drafted:

R. V. Bennett
Legal Department
Medical Protective Company
Richmond, VA

George W. Burke, III, MD
Pulmonary Associates of
Richmond
Richmond, VA

Bradley S. Butterfield
Claims Manager
Professionals Advocate
Insurance Co.
Richmond, VA

Betty Cochran, RN
Long-Term Care Consultant
Richmond, VA

Jeffrey Custer
Administrator
Cardiovascular Associates of
Virginia
Richmond, VA

John Glander
President
Professional Risk Associates, Inc.
Midlothian, VA

Barbara A. Jackman
Chief Operating Officer
Memorial Hospital of
Martinsville & Henry County
Martinsville, VA

Wendy S. Klein MD
Associate Professor
Dept. of Internal Medicine
VCU Health System
Richmond, VA

Mitchell Miller, MD
Family Practice
Virginia Beach, VA

Fred Schriever
Sentara Risk Management
Virginia Beach, VA

Beverley Soble
Vice President of Regulatory
Affairs
Virginia Health Care Association
Richmond, VA

Rose Tate
Director of Risk Management
Medical College of Hampton
Roads
Norfolk, VA

J. Corbett Talton, DDS
Richmond, VA

Robert F. Yeoman
Administrator
Riverside Convalescent Center
Smithfield, VA

About the Author

Rodney K. Adams is a health care trial attorney at LeClairRyan. He has been advising and defending health care providers for over thirty years. Mr. Adams has a unique niche in patient care issues and has published two books on various aspects of the topic, *Virginia Medical Law* (now in its fourth edition) and *Clinical Trials and Human Research: A Practical Guide to Compliance* (co-authored with F. Rozovsky). Mr. Adams also contributed to Rozovsky & Woods, *The Handbook of Patient Safety Compliance: A Practical Guide for Health Care Organizations.* His guidance, whether during a strategic discussion or during a crisis, is based on practical experience before juries and government boards.

Mr. Adams represented several large hospitals and medical colleges in Chicago before moving to Richmond in 1991. He currently counsels and defends hospitals, nursing homes, physicians, dentists, nurses, and other health care providers in court and administrative forums throughout the Commonwealth. Mr. Adams is annually included in lists of prominent attorneys such as *Virginia Business* Magazine's "Legal Elite," *Super Lawyers, Benchmark* and *The Best Lawyers in America. Virginia Lawyers Weekly* has repeatedly recognized his work in its annual "Largest Defense Verdicts." Mr. Adams is certified by the National Board of Trial Advocacy in Civil Trial Practice.[1]

Mr. Adams is an adjunct professor at William and Mary Law School (medical malpractice trial advocacy) and at Virginia Commonwealth University, School of Health Administration (bioethics and health law). Previously, he taught health law at Kent College of Law and trial

---

[1]   Virginia does not have a process for determining specialty accreditation.

advocacy at University of Richmond School of Law. He graduated from Millikin University; the University of Glasgow, Scotland (L.L.M. in Forensic Medicine); and the University of Illinois College of Law. Mr. Adams is admitted to the state and federal courts of Virginia and Illinois.

For more than five years, Mr. Adams co-chaired an ABA sub-committee on medical ethics. He is a member of the American Health Lawyers Association and the Virginia Association of Defense Attorneys. Mr. Adams has served on a hospital system bioethics committee and on the board of directors for non-profit organizations providing assisted living, free medical care, funding for human research, and home health services. He is a frequent speaker at state and national health care meetings.

Rodney K. Adams
804 / 343-4173
LeClairRyan
Rodney.Adams@LeClairRyan.com
919 E. Main Street, 24th Floor
Richmond, VA 23219

Summary of Contents

I. Patient Care

A. Access to Health Care

1. Office Practice

a. Formation of the Physician-Patient Relationship

Determining when a doctor-patient relationship is formed is a fact-specific inquiry. The Supreme Court of Virginia, on one occasion, has gone so far as to say that the relationship may be formed, and there may be a duty to treat, when an individual makes an appointment after describing her symptoms to the office staff.[2] This begs the question as to whether the relationship could be stretched back even further by the Court. For example, a patient may choose a primary care physician from a managed care company's list without ever contacting the physician. Has the relationship been formed at that point? In other cases where the relationship has been discussed, the Court has more reasonably described the "consensual relationship"[3] that "exists if a patient entrusts his treatment to the physician and the physician accepts the case."[4] The physician, said the Court, must "personally engage in some affirmative act amounting to a render[ing of] services to another."[5]

The Supreme Court of Virginia has rarely directly dealt with the issue of when the physician-patient relationship is formed. The facts of one case[6] led to broad statements that may be troublesome to a physician. The Court was determining whether a physician had

---

[2]   Lyons v. Grether, 218 Va. 630 (1977) Also see George v. Kaiser Found. Health, 15 Va. Cir. 327 (1989); Schurman v. Brock, 31 Va. Cir. 298 (1993); and Vann v. Harden, 187 Va. 555

[3]   Washburn v. Klara, 263 Va. 586, 590 (2002)

[4]   Prosise v. Foster, 261 Va. 417, 421 (2001)

[5]   Fruiterman v. Granata, 276 Va. 629 (2008)

[6]   Lyons, 218 Va. 630

violated the White Cane Act when he refused to see a patient who arrived at his office with her guide dog. The patient had stated on the telephone that she needed to be seen for a vaginal infection, and the physician's staff had scheduled her for an appointment. The Court held that the physician had violated the statute, a forerunner of the Americans with Disabilities Act, because a doctor-patient relationship had been formed. However, in reaching its decision, the court stated that:

> [i]n the absence of a statute, a physician has no legal obligation to accept as a patient everyone who seeks his services. A physician's duty arises only upon the creation of a physician-patient relationship; that relationship springs from a consensual transaction, a contract, express or implied, general or special, and a patient is entitled to damages resulting from a breach of a physician's duty.[7]

The more difficult question then becomes whether the contact in question has risen to the level of that "consensual transaction" or the express, implied, general or special contract. Again, Lyons provides the following about that determination:

> Whether a physician-patient relationship is created is a question of fact, turning upon a determination whether the patient entrusted his treatment to the physician and the physician accepted the case.[8]

In language that is somewhat helpful, the court wrote that:

> [s]tanding alone, plaintiff's allegation that she "had an appointment with defendant" would be insufficient,

---

[7]   Lyons, 218 Va. 630, 633 (citations omitted)

[8]   Lyons v. Grether, 218 Va. 630 (1977)

for it connotes nothing more than that defendant had agreed to see her.[9]

From this, the reasonable assertion is that simply making an appointment to see a doctor would be insufficient as a matter of law to establish a physician/client relationship.[10] It is at this first threshold, the physician can begin to assert control over the process to strengthen the argument that what is happening at the initial stage is simply a general appointment being made. Some form of routine disclaimer that limits the telephone contact to scheduling only is critical to strengthening a factual assertion that this is clearly not a consensual transaction establishing a contract to treat the prospective patient.

One part of the disclaimer could include routine language stating unequivocally that if the patient arrives without a referral, the physician will not provide treatment or even more specifically, will not enter into a contract to treat the patient. This would strengthen the physician's assertion, in the case of a specialty practice, that the physician-patient relationship was contingent on the patient obtaining a referral. Oral disclaimers or qualifiers would suffice if they were given habitually and routinely but certainly, for evidentiary reasons, some written form of qualifier would be preferable.

The Lyons decision was limited to resolving the question of whether the plaintiff alleged sufficient facts to present a question of a physician-patient relationship. The Court did not rule that as a matter of law where the patient alleged not only an appointment, but also "that the appointment she had been given was 'for treatment of a [specific] infection,'" proved the relationship. The Court merely held that the plaintiff's allegations created a question of fact for a jury to decide. Interestingly, it seems the less the patient reveals to the physician's staff in making the initial appointment, the stronger the

---

9   Lyons v. Grether, 218 Va. 630 (1977)
10   The determinative fact in the Lyons case was that the patient had given a specific complaint and the office agreed to see her for it.

argument against creation of a physician-patient relationship. For example, the Court went on to observe that: [11]

> [t]he unmistakable implication is that plaintiff had sought and defendant had granted an appointment at a designated time and place for the performance of a specific medical service, one within defendant's professional competence, viz., treatment of a particular ailment.

Again, it should be noted that the Court did not set these facts as the threshold determination for establishing the relationship; it merely said these facts were sufficient to put the question to a jury. The Court reinforced this standard in a subsequent decision when it ruled that physician-patient relationship is a "consensual relationship in which the patient's care [is] entrusted to the physician and the physician [accepts] the case."[12] The more recent language counsels the use of appointment procedures that make acceptance of the patient contingent on certain conditions being met such as a valid referral from an HMO or primary care physician.

The key point of this discussion is that a jury will likely make the decision in a medical malpractice lawsuit unless a plaintiff's lawyer is so unimaginative as to present an allegation wherein only a bare general appointment exists. If the circumstance is one in which there is *only* a general appointment, then the trial judge ought to find as a matter of law that no physician-patient relationship exists. If no duty exists, then the case should end quickly. But if the judge finds that it is a question of fact as to whether a relationship exists, then the physician will need to rely on other factors that argue for a contingent contract, one that only arises upon presentation of the requisite referral or other event.

Virginia legislation has more clearly defined the physician-patient

---

[11] Lyons v. Grether, 218 Va. 630 (1977)
[12] Prosise v. Foster, 261 Va. 417, 424, 544 S.E.2d 331, 334 (2001) citing Lyons

relationship for purposes of what is required in order to prescribe medications: [13]

> [A] bona fide practitioner-patient relationship means that the practitioner shall:
>
> (i) ensure that a medical or drug history is obtained;
>
> (ii) provide information to the patient about the benefits and risks of the drug being prescribed;
>
> (iii) perform or have performed an appropriate examination of the patient, either physically or by the use of instrumentation and diagnostic equipment through which images and medical records may be transmitted electronically; except for medical emergencies, the examination of the patient shall have been performed by the practitioner himself, within the group in which he practices, or by a consulting practitioner prior to issuing a prescription; and
>
> (iv) initiate additional interventions and follow-up care, if necessary, especially if a prescribed drug may have serious side effects.

Virginia courts have not been asked to consider whether this degree of involvement between physician and patient is required to establish the physician-patient relationship in the context of creating a duty of care toward a patient.[14] The better course, though not adopted by the Virginia courts, would be to hold that the doctor-patient relationship does not form until a patient and a physician discuss

---

[13]   Va. Code 32.1-3303

[14]   One Circuit Court has held that supervision of a nurse practitioner does not create a physician-patient relationship giving rise to liability for the physician. Monahan v. Obici Med. Mgmt. Servs., Inc., 59 Va. Cir. 307 (2002), citing Prosise, 261 Va. at 423

the patient's condition and the physician explicitly agrees to accept the patient. This would avoid the all too common situation of where a person presents with problems that a physician is ill-equipped to handle yet feels obligated to do so because the person is now a patient.

A frequent concern for a physician is when a patient is seen in an emergency department and is told to follow up with the physician. Is there an obligation to treat that patient? Is the physician responsible for the patient, even if the patient does not come for follow up? The better course is to not look at what referral was made by an emergency department but what course of action was taken by a patient. For numerous reasons, a patient may elect not to follow up with the suggested physician. No physician-patient relationship can form in the absence of consent. Likewise, a physician has the option of accepting a new patient or not for numerous reasons. A different answer might be reached if the physician is contacted and agrees to schedule an appointment for the patient.

Under certain circumstances, a physician may owe a duty of care to non-patients, such as other family members in genetic counseling.[15] A physician has a "limited physician-patient relationship" when performing a court-ordered examination of a plaintiff, but the physician's sole obligation is to use the applicable standard of care so as to do no harm.[16]

b. The Obligation to Treat

Once a physician-patient relationship is formed, a physician is obligated to render care to the patient. This broad principle is

---

[15]   Didato v. Strehler, 262 Va. 617 (2001); Khadim v. Laboratory Corporation of America, (WD Va. 2011) VLW 011-3-604

[16]   Harris v. Kreutzer, 271 Va. 188 (2006). One might argue that the Supreme Court of Virginia stretched in its determination that the relationship was consensual and that the court-ordered examination was the rendering of health care. The Supreme Court recognized that other state supreme courts have reached the opposite conclusion.

challenging to apply. However, failure of a physician to diligently treat a patient may leave the physician exposed to allegations of abandoning his patient.[17]

The Americans with Disabilities Act (ADA) has placed new restrictions on health care providers. For example, a physician cannot generally refuse to treat an HIV-positive patient.[18] A health care provider must rely on scientific evidence as opposed to personal belief or bias in determining whether or not he will treat a person suffering HIV. A health care provider cannot refuse to examine or treat a person suffering HIV solely based on the patient's infectious status.[19] The ADA also requires health care providers to make reasonable accommodation for disabled patients, such as the blind or hearing impaired.[20]

Generally, a physician is not liable for failing to act on a laboratory result that she did not order, unless the patient presents the report to the physician with a request for consultation.[21] Unfortunately, the Supreme Court of Virginia in 2005 narrowed this simple statute by presuming that the General Assembly did not mean what it stated. In reversing its own prior decision,[22] the Court held that a physician can be liable for not reviewing studies that were ordered by other physicians for his patient.[23] Three of the Justices in a strong dissent pointed out that the majority failed to articulate a compelling argument that the prior unanimous opinion of the Court was a mistake. The statute is not ambiguous, wrote the dissenters, but merely provides an immunity that the majority of the Court does not

---

[17] Vann v. Harden, 187 Va. 555 (1948); George v. Kaiser Found. Health, 15 Va. Cir. 327 (1989)

[18] Americans with Disabilities Act, 42 U.S.C.A. 12112(d)

[19] Bragdon v. Abbott, 524 U.S. 624, 118 S. Ct. 2196, 141 L. Ed. 2d 540 (1998)

[20] Title II and III of Americans with Disabilities Act, 42 U.S.C.A. 12101 (West) et seq. See http://www.usdoj.gov/crt/ada/adahom1.htm.

[21] Va. Code 8.01-581.18(B)

[22] Auer v. Miller, 270 Va. 172, 613 S.E.2d 421 (2005) overruled by Oraee v. Breeding, 270 Va. 488, 621 S.E.2d 48 (2005)

[23] Oraee v. Breeding, 270 Va. 488 (2005)

favor. The 2006 General Assembly enacted compromise legislation that places the burden on a physician to affirmatively prove his immunity from liability.[24]

c. The Physician-Patient Relationship under Managed Care

American jurisprudence governing the physician-patient relationship has evolved over the past century. The past few decades has seen immense changes to the structure and delivery of health care in America. Physicians are now challenged in a number of ways that were inconceivable to a prior generation. For example, patients frequently change primary care providers based on what health care plan is purchased that year by an employer. The traditional continuity of care has disappeared.

Primary care physicians are under stress from managed care organizations to render more health care for less. For example, referrals to specialists are discouraged. This may lead to a patient being frustrated and feeling slighted as family physicians stretch beyond their expertise. Conversely, specialists often send patients back to primary care physicians for management of a condition or course of treatment initiated by the specialist. The tension has exposed primary care physicians to an unprecedented number of malpractice actions.

Under managed care programs, a family practitioner is often forced to close her practice to new patients of a particular health plan. An individual often chooses a primary care physician from a list in a health plan's directory. Unfortunately, the physician has no indication that the individual has done so. Both are troubled when the patient needs medical care and the physician is surprised at the request for her services. Virginia law gives no explicit guidance on this issue. However, the provider's contract may address the point. In looking at cases outside Virginia, an appellate court in Illinois ruled

---

[24]   HB 1110 (2006) deleted Va. Code 8.01-581.18(B) and enact 8.01-581.18:1

that a telephone call to a physician listed by a patient's HMO in an attempt to schedule an appointment did not give rise to a physician-patient relationship.[25]

A health insurer's decision is not a substitute for a physician's judgment. A physician must advise his patient as to the most prudent course. A health insurer is limited to saying for what it will pay and for what it will not. When a physician determines that a test or treatment is in the best interest of a patient and the health insurer says that it will not pay for it, then a physician should advise the patient of the situation, reasonable alternatives and the risks and benefits of the different options. The patient is the ultimate decision maker and is free to decide that he wants a test or treatment for which he will have to pay out of pocket. Documentation of the conversation is extremely important for risk management.

2. Hospital Practice / Emergency Department

The Emergency Department of a hospital has little, if any choice, in rendering emergency care to almost anyone that presents to the facility seeking help. The problem, of course, is defining *emergency care*. Most of this pressure exerted over the Emergency Department comes from the Emergency Medical Treatment and Active Labor Act (EMTALA)[26] and to a lesser extent from other legislative mandates, such as the Hill-Burton Act.[27]

a. The Emergency Medical Treatment and Active Labor Act

i) Background

EMTALA is an important piece of legislation that imposes an affirmative obligation on hospitals to provide medical care. The Act, which is also commonly known as the Anti-Dumping Act,

---

[25] Tsoukas v. Lapid, 315 Ill. App. 3d 372, 733 N.E.2d 823 (2000)
[26] EMTALA, 42 U.S.C.A. 1395dd et seq.
[27] Hill-Burton Act, 42 U.S.C.A. 291 et seq.

was a four-page portion of the immense Consolidated Omnibus Budget Reconciliation Act (COBRA) of 1985.[28] Congress perceived that "patient dumping" was a growing problem as hospitals faced increasing cost containment from the government and private payers.[29] EMTALA was amended in 1988 and 1989. In 1994, the Health Care Financing Administration (HCFA, now known as CMS) passed rules and regulations that further defined the obligations of hospitals. These and subsequent regulations continue to dramatically challenge the common-sense understanding of a health care provider's duty. Federal and state courts throughout America continue to apply their own interpretations to what EMTALA means. The simple intent behind the Act was to prevent the "dumping" of patients based solely on financial reasons. However, the result has been far more broad, tedious and devastating to hospitals. An additional Final Rule was issued by CMS on September 9, 2003 in an effort to clarify a hospital's responsibilities.[30]

ii) Basic Requirements of EMTALA

The foundation section of EMTALA requires that:

> [i]n the case of a hospital that has a hospital emergency department, if any individual (whether or not eligible for benefits under this title [42 U.S.C.A. § 1395 (West) et seq.]) comes to the emergency department and a request is made on the individual's behalf for examination or treatment for a medical condition, the hospital must provide for an appropriate medical screening examination within the capability of the hospital's emergency department, including ancillary

---

[28] 42 U.S.C.A. 1395dd et. seq. The legislation was signed into law by the President in 1986.

[29] Staab, "Is There A Private Cause of Action Under COBRA for Misdiagnosis?" J of Health & Hospital Law, Vol. 28, Jan-Feb 1995

[30] Medicare Program; Clarifying Policies Related to the Responsibilities of Medicare-Participating Hospitals in Treating Individuals With Emergency Medical Conditions, 68 Fed. Reg. 53222-01

services routinely available to the emergency department, to determine whether or not an emergency medical condition (within the meaning of subsection (e)(1)) exists.[31]

CMS, by regulation, has redefined the statute to read that:

[i]n the case of a hospital that has an emergency department, if any individual (whether or not eligible for Medicare benefits and regardless of ability to pay) *comes by him or herself or with another person to the emergency department* and a request is made on the individual's behalf for examination or treatment of a medical condition by *qualified medical personnel* (as determined by the hospital in its rules and regulations), the hospital must provide for an *appropriate medical screening examination* within the capability of the hospital's emergency department, to determine whether or not an *emergency medical condition* exists. The examinations must be conducted by individuals determined qualified by hospital by-laws or rules and regulations and who meet the requirements of §482.55 concerning emergency services personnel and direction.[32]

While these sections are fairly simple, the many complications of the statute come from the definitions and regulations promulgated by CMS and interpretation by the judiciary.

Regulations under EMTALA impose the following obligations on a hospital with a dedicated emergency department:[33]

---

[31] 42 U.S.C.A. 1395dd(a)
[32] (emphasis added) 42 C.F.R. 489.24
[33] CMS, State Operations Manual, Appendix V – Interpretive Guidelines – Responsibilities of Medicare Participating Hospitals in Emergency Cases (Rev. 60, 07-16-10)

- Adopt and enforce policies and procedures to comply with the requirements of 42 C.F.R. § 489.24;

- Post signs in the dedicated ED specifying the rights of individuals with emergency medical conditions and women in labor who come to the dedicated ED for health care services, and indicate on the signs whether the hospital participates in the Medicaid program;

- Maintain medical and other records related to individuals transferred to and from the hospital for a period of five years from the date of the transfer;

- Maintain a list of physicians who are on-call to provide further evaluation and/or treatment necessary to stabilize an individual with an emergency medical condition;

- Maintain a central log of individuals who come to the dedicated ED seeking treatment and indicate whether these individuals:
  - Refused treatment,
  - Were denied treatment,
  - Were treated, admitted, stabilized, and/or transferred or were discharged;

- Provide for an appropriate medical screening examination;

- Provide necessary stabilizing treatment for emergency medical conditions and labor within the hospital's capability and capacity;

- Provide an appropriate transfer of an unstabilized individual to another medical facility if:
  - The individual (or person acting on his or her behalf) after being informed of the risks and the hospital's obligations requests a transfer,
  - A physician has signed the certification that the benefits of the transfer of the patient to another facility outweigh the risks or

- ○ A qualified medical person (as determined by the hospital in its by-laws or rules and regulations) has signed the certification after a physician, in consultation with that qualified medical person, has made the determination that the benefits of the transfer outweigh the risks and the physician countersigns in a timely manner the certification. (This last criterion applies if the responsible physician is not physically present in the emergency department at the time the individual is transferred.
- ○ Provide treatment to minimize the risks of transfer;
- ○ Send all pertinent records to the receiving hospital;
- ○ Obtain the consent of the receiving hospital to accept the transfer,
- ○ Ensure that the transfer of an unstabilized individual is effected through qualified personnel and transportation equipment, including the use of medically appropriate life support measures;

- • Medical screening examination and/or stabilizing treatment is not to be delayed in order to inquire about payment status;
- • Accept appropriate transfer of individuals with an emergency medical condition if the hospital has specialized capabilities or facilities and has the capacity to treat those individuals; and
- • Not penalize or take adverse action against a physician or a qualified medical person because the physician or qualified medical person refuses to authorize the transfer of an individual with an emergency medical condition that has not been stabilized or against any hospital employee who reports a violation of these requirements.

A hospital may seek a waiver of EMTALA from its state agency when the hospital activates its disaster plan.[34]

---

[34] CMS Survey and Certification Letter, S&C-08-05

iii)   Key Terms in EMTALA

(A)   Coming to the Emergency Department

EMTALA imposes several requirements on hospitals before they can discharge or transfer a patient in compliance with the Act. An individual must first *come to the emergency department* to trigger the requirements of the Act.[35] Although this appears to imply that a person must actually physically appear in the emergency room, the regulations and case law have expanded the point of entry beyond the emergency room doors. CMS took the position that the Act applies to "all individuals who attempt to gain access to the hospital for an emergency." Under the regulations, *comes to the emergency department* is defined as when "the individual is on hospital property"[36] or in a hospital-owned ambulance.[37] EMTALA does not apply to a non-hospital ambulance when a hospital is on *diversionary status* unless the ambulance crew disregards the hospital's status and brings the patient anyway.[38] Outpatients who suffer an emergency medical problem after the start of the encounter are expressly exempt from the Act. The obligation to treat is triggered by 1) a specific request by an individual (or a request on his behalf) or 2) "inferred from what a prudent layperson observer would conclude from an individual's appearance or behavior."[39] CMS has stated that "the prudent layperson observer standard should

---

[35]   42 U.S.C.A. 1395dd(a)

[36]   HCFA considers "hospital property" to include not only the main campus but also departments that are operated by the hospital. 42 C.F.R. 416.35. Physician offices, rural health clinics, nursing homes, restaurants, shops or other non-medical facilities are excluded by the 2003 Final Rule. Medicare Program; Clarifying Policies Related to the Responsibilities of Medicare-Participating Hospitals in Treating Individuals With Emergency Medical Conditions, 68 FR 53222-01

[37]   42 C.F.R. 489.24(b)

[38]   Id. A federal district court has also held that EMTALA does not waive sovereign immunity of a federal healthcare facility, e.g. Portsmouth Naval Hospital. Hoffman v. United States, 593 F. Supp. 2d 873 (E.D. Va. 2009)

[39]   67 Fed Reg. 31403; 68 Fed Reg 53241

not be applied so broadly as to mandate EMTALA screenings for those individuals who are fully capable of making a verbal request for examination or for medical care, but elect not to do so."[40] On the other hand, CMS has stated that "parking"[41] patients violates EMTALA and Medicare *Conditions of Participation*.[42]

(B) Appropriate Medical Screening Exam

When an individual presents to the emergency department, the hospital must provide an *appropriate medical screening examination within the capability of the hospital's emergency department* to determine whether the patient is in *an emergency medical condition*.[43] Congress did not define what is meant by *appropriate medical screening examination*. The judges of the U. S. Court of Appeals, Sixth Circuit, called "appropriate" a "weasel word" when that court was called upon to define the phrase.[44] The Sixth Circuit "weaseled" its way out of defining the term by applying a disparate treatment test, i.e. was the patient treated differently than other patients? Likewise, the Fourth Circuit wrote:

> EMTALA requires a hospital to develop a screening procedure designed to identify such critical conditions that exist in symptomatic patients and to apply that screening procedure uniformly to all patients with similar complaints.[45]

According to CMS, the scope of a medical screening exam is to provide all necessary testing and on-call services within the capability of the

---

[40]   68 Fed Reg 53242
[41]   *Parking* occurs when hospital staff refuses to permit EMS staff to give report and transfer patients from ambulance stretchers to hospital beds.
[42]   CMS Center for Medicaid & State Operations / Survey & Certification Group, Guidance, 7/13/06
[43]   42 U.S.C.A. 1395dd(a).
[44]   Cleland v. Bronson Health Care Group., Inc., 917 F.2d 266, 271 (6th Cir. 1990)
[45]   Baber v. Hosp. Corp. of Am., 977 F.2d 872, 879 (4th Cir. 1992)

hospital to reach a diagnosis that excludes the presence of a legally-defined emergency medical condition. Triage is not sufficient.[46] The Fourth Circuit has stated that determination of *appropriate* is not some national standard of care but an individualized standard for each hospital.[47] The test, in personal injury actions, is one of uniformity as to all patients.[48] However, this is not met by uniformly poor care to all patients.[49] Improper motive is not a required element of proof.[50] Examination of a patient may not be delayed to inquire of the patient's method of payment or insurance status.[51] A hospital may follow reasonable registration procedures so long as the process does not delay screening or treatment.[52]

EMTALA does not require a hospital to expand its services, only that the hospital utilizes staff and facilities available. However, EMTALA requires the hospital to include its on-call physicians and its ancillary services as *available*. Modifications to the regulatory guidance indicate that a hospital must maintain "a level of on-call coverage that is within its capability."[53] Specialists are not required to be on call at all times.[54] An on-call physician may be permitted to schedule elective surgeries while on call and may have simultaneous call at more than one hospital if back-up coverage is arranged.[55] Coverage must be provided by a designated physician and not merely a group of physicians. The treating physician ultimately determines whether

---

[46] Scruggs v. Danville Regional Medical Center, 2008 U.S. Dist. LEXIS 6863 (WD Va. 2008)

[47] Baber v. Hosp. Corp. of Am., 977 F.2d 872, 879 (4th Cir. 1992)

[48] Baber, 977 F.2d at 881

[49] Matter of Baby K, 16 F.3d 590, 596 (4th Cir. 1994)

[50] Power v. Arlington Hosp. Ass'n, 42 F.3d 851, 857 (4th Cir. 1994); Roberts v. Galen of Virginia, Inc., 525 U.S. 249, 119 S. Ct. 685, 142 L. Ed. 2d 648 (1999).

[51] 42 C.F.R. 489.24(c)(3)

[52] 68 Fed. Reg. 53227

[53] 67 Fed. Reg. 31403

[54] 67 Fed. Reg. 31403; DHHS, CMS, Memo #S&C-02-34 "On-Call Requirements-EMTALA (6/13/02)

[55] 42 C.F.R. 489.24(j)

an on-call physician should come to the ED.[56] A hospital must have written policies and procedures to respond to situations in which a particular specialty is not available or the on-call physician cannot respond within a reasonable time period.[57] In October 2008, CMS proposed the use of voluntary community call plans, which would permit transfer to another facility where the specialty care was available.[58] Ideally, EMS would be aware of the community call plan and deliver patients to the appropriate facility. Virginia statutes require that at least one physician must be on call at all times, though not necessarily physically present on the premises, at each hospital that holds itself out as operating an emergency department.[59]

As an example, the Ninth Circuit of the U.S. Court of Appeals ruled that a rural California hospital did not violate EMTALA when it brought in a county crisis worker to evaluate a patient as opposed to conducting its own psychiatric evaluation.[60]

(C) Emergency Medical Condition

An *emergency medical condition*[61] is one that, without immediate treatment, could place the health of a patient in serious danger or cause significant impairment of bodily function or organ, or in the case of a pregnant woman, could cause harm to the woman or unborn child.[62] A woman experiencing contractions is presumed to be in true labor unless a physician, certified nurse midwife or other qualified medical person certifies that a woman is experiencing false labor.[63] If an *emergency medical condition* is determined to be present, the patient must be treated until *stabilized* or *transferred* in

---

[56] 42 C.F.R..24(j)(i); CMS Survey and Certification Letter S&C-07-23 (6/22/07)
[57] 42 C.F.R. 489.24(j)
[58] 42 C.F.R. 489.24(j)(2)(iii)
[59] Va. Code 32.1-127.B.2
[60] Baker v. Adventist Health, Inc., 260 F.3d 987 (9th Cir. 2001)
[61] 42 C.F.R. 489.24(b)
[62] 42 C.F.R. 489.24(b)
[63] 42 C.F.R. 489.24(b)

compliance with the Act. Lack of knowing that an *emergency medical condition* existed has been a successful defense in actions brought by patients.[64]

(D) Stabilization

Stabilization is judged from the perspective of professional standards, using the term *medical probability*, rather than standards established by each hospital. *Stabilization* means that no material deterioration is likely, within reasonable medical probability, to result from or occur during the transfer of the individual from a facility.[65] With respect to a woman in labor, *stabilization* is achieved when the woman has delivered her child and placenta. The language in the Act defining *stabilization* is vague, and the court decisions as to whether *stabilization* has occurred are decided on the facts of each case.

A hospital is deemed to have met the requirements of *stabilization* if the hospital offers an individual further medical examination and treatment to stabilize and informs the patient of the risks and benefits of such examination and treatment, but the individual refuses to consent to examination and treatment.[66] The hospital must take all reasonable steps to secure the individual's written informed consent to refuse such examination and treatment.

When a person is given an appropriate medical screening exam and is not diagnosed with an emergency condition, EMTALA obligations cease. If, however, a patient is determined to have an emergency medical condition, a hospital's EMTALA obligation does not end until that patient is stabilized or properly transferred. A federal court and the Virginia court have reached opposite conclusions as to the duration of EMTALA under this definition. The Supreme Court of Virginia ruled that EMTALA continued even after admission.[67]

---

[64] See James v. Sunrise Hosp., 86 F.3d 885 (9th Cir. 1996)
[65] 42 C.F.R. 489.24(b).
[66] 42 C.F.R. 489.24(c)(2)
[67] Smith v. Richmond Memorial Hospital, 243 Va. 445 (1992)

Four years later, the U.S. Court of Appeals, Fourth Circuit stated that once a patient is admitted, EMTALA disappears.[68] The federal court did not comment on the Supreme Court of Virginia's contrary conclusion. CMS subsequently adopted the federal court's position for an admitting hospital.[69]

(E) Transfer

Transfer is defined as any movement, including discharge, of an individual outside a hospital.[70] Transfer of a patient may occur after stabilization, or before if either the patient requests or a physician determines that the benefits outweigh the risks.[71] If a physician determines that at the time of transfer, the risks of transfer are outweighed by the reasonably anticipated benefits, the physician must document this certification and list specific individual risks and benefits, which must be supported by the record. In all cases, however, the transfer must be *appropriate.*

For an appropriate transfer, a transferring hospital must provide medical treatment that minimizes the risks to an individual's health, have written consent from the patient, transfer by appropriate medical vehicle with qualified personnel, and forward the medical records available at the time of transfer to the receiving hospital.[72] If an on-call physician refuses to treat or fails to appear within a reasonable time to provide necessary stabilizing treatment at the transferring hospital, this information must be documented in the medical records that are sent to a receiving facility. The receiving facility[73] must have available space and qualified personnel for the

---

[68]   Bryan v. Rectors & Visitors of Univ. of Virginia, 95 F.3d 349 (4th Cir. 1996); Baxter v. Holy Cross Hospital of Silver Spring, 155 F. 3d 557 (4th Cir. 1998), cert. den. 526 U.S. 1018; 119 S. Ct. 1253
[69]   68 Fed Reg 53245; also see 73 Fed Reg 48661
[70]   42 C.F.R. 489.24(b)
[71]   42 C.F.R. 489.24(d)
[72]   42 C.F.R. 489.24(d)(2)
[73]   A receiving hospital, whether it has an emergency room or not, is also under EMTALA regulations. 42 C.F.R. 489.24(f)

RODNEY K. ADAMS, ESQUIRE

treatment of the individual, and have agreed to accept transfer and to provide appropriate medical treatment. A receiving facility that has specialized capabilities (e.g., a burn unit, shock trauma unit, or neonatal intensive care unit) may not refuse to accept an appropriate transfer of an individual who requires such specialized capabilities if the specialty hospital has the capacity to treat the individual.[74] Similarly, a receiving hospital cannot refuse a transfer because it does not approve of the transportation mode to be employed by the transferring facility.[75]

The standard for stabilization and transfer is based on the actual knowledge of a hospital. If a hospital provides an appropriate examination that detects an emergency condition or if a patient's emergency condition is otherwise known to a hospital, the hospital is liable under the Act if it transfers or discharges the patient in an unstable medical condition. However, the lack of knowledge of the patient's emergency condition does not relieve the hospital of the duty to provide an appropriate medical screening exam. The motive behind a transfer is irrelevant and need not be established. Indigency is not an issue to be considered in order to state a claim under EMTALA.

A patient must be informed orally and in writing when she is placed under observation or in any other outpatient status at a hospital.[76] Additionally, the patient must be advised that the status may affect the patient's insurance coverage.

iv) Enforcement

Congress has created both administrative sanctions and a private cause of action. CMS and the Office of Inspector General, Department of Health and Human Services are responsible for administrative enforcement of EMTALA. Private enforcement against a hospital is

---

[74] 42 C.F.R. 489.24(e)
[75] CMS Survey & Certification Letter S&C-07-20 (4/27/07)
[76] Va. Code 32.1-137.03

by civil lawsuit in either federal or state court and should be separate and distinct from a state medical malpractice action.

(A) Administrative Procedures

A hospital's violation of EMTALA can result in revocation of Medicare certification and monetary penalties. Once a complaint is made, the CMS regional office directs the state survey agency to perform an initial investigation. The CMS regional office will then determine if a surprise facility-wide survey should be conducted. A survey of this kind, if conducted, would include a review of emergency department practices and procedures, a sampling of recent transfer records and interviews of personnel. If medical judgment or treatment is in question, a peer review organization will provide medical review.[77] The CMS regional office will then determine if a violation of EMTALA has occurred.

Providers are notified of violations through a preliminary notification letter. Sanctions can include fines or termination. Fines cannot be more than $50,000 for each negligent or knowing violation. Termination can be either on a 23-day fast track system or a 90-day track system depending on the severity of the violations. A 23-day fast track termination is warranted if CMS determines that the violation poses an immediate and serious threat to patient health and safety. A 90-day track termination occurs when termination is appropriate but there is not an immediate and serious threat to patient health and safety. A hospital's notification of violation allegations will be itemized and will solicit a response or a corrective action plan. If the corrective action plan is accepted by CMS, the termination process will be stopped.

(B) Whistle-Blower Obligation / Protection

Beginning in 1995, mandatory reporting requirements for hospitals

---

[77]   42 C.F.R. 489.24(g)

went into effect.[78] The obligation to "blow the whistle" is triggered when a hospital "has reason to believe it may have received an individual who has been transferred in an unstable emergency condition from another hospital in violation of the statute."[79] Possible violations of EMTALA must be reported by a receiving hospital within 72 hours of the possible violation to CMS or the state survey agency. CMS staff members have said that the agency treats the 72-hour rule as a benchmark, and requires only that the action be prompt.[80] The potential sanctions for failure to report range from monetary penalties to Medicare provider termination. A hospital in western New York has the dubious distinction of being the first hospital known to be cited for failing to report.[81]

A hospital employee or physician who refuses to approve a transfer or who reports a violation cannot be penalized or be the subject of adverse action by a hospital.[82]

(C)   Right to Sue under the Act

The Act provides a private cause of action for violations of the statute. Therefore, a patient who has suffered harm as a result of a hospital's violation has a civil cause of action against the hospital for personal injury. However, the Act is not intended to be a federal medical malpractice statute.[83] Patients have attempted to sue individual physicians under the Act. Courts have nearly uniformly rejected such civil suits, as well as those against physician groups or third-party payers.[84] The Virginia medical malpractice cap limits

---

[78]   Fed. Reg. Vol. 60, No. 189, pp. 50443-50448

[79]   42 C.F.R. 489.24(m)

[80]   "Latest Patient Transfer Regulations Raise Concerns," Hospitals & Health Networks, 10/20/94, p. 88

[81]   "Hospital Cited for Failing to Report Another Hospital's EMTALA Violation," Medical Malpractice Law & Strategy, Oct 1996, p. 1

[82]   42 C.F.R. 489.24(d)(3)

[83]   Brooks v. Maryland Gen. Hosp., Inc., 996 F.2d 708 (4th Cir. 1993)

[84]   Baber v. Hosp. Corp. of Am., 977 F.2d 872 (4th Cir. 1992)

recoverable damages under EMTALA.[85] State operated hospitals are granted immunity from EMTALA under the Eleventh Amendment.[86]

In addition, the Act provides the opportunity to any medical facility that suffers a financial loss as a result of a violation to recover damages from an offending hospital.[87] The statute provides for civil monetary penalties against both the hospital and the responsible physician for a violation.[88]

v) Prognosis for Hospitals Under EMTALA

Unfortunately, regulation and scrutiny of hospitals is ever increasing. Expansion of EMTALA responsibilities and investigative actions can only be predicted to expand as well. EMTALA will likely remain a powerful weapon for plaintiffs' attorneys to use in coercing settlement of medical malpractice actions. The best defense is to have comprehensive policies and procedures in place and constantly educate emergency personnel in compliance.

b. The Hill-Burton Act

The Hospital Survey and Construction Act,[89] widely known as the Hill-Burton Act, was passed by Congress in 1946. A 1975 amendment[90] requires health care facilities that received funds under Title XVI to provide free or reduced-charge medical services in perpetuity to eligible persons unable to pay. Many facilities have overlooked this obligation. However, the federal government has not.[91]

---

[85] Power v. Arlington Hosp. Ass'n, 42 F.3d 851 (4th Cir. 1994)
[86] Drew v. Univ. of Tennessee Reg. Medical Center Hospital, 2000 U.S. App. LEXIS 8936 (2000)
[87] 42 U.S.C.A. 1395dd(d)(2)(B).
[88] 42 U.S.C.A. 1395dd(d)(1).
[89] P. L. 79-725, codified at 42 U.S.C.A. 291
[90] Title XVI of the Public Health Service Act
[91] See Blumstein, "Court Action, Agency Reaction: The Hill-Burton Act as a Case Study," Iowa Law Review 69 (1984):1, 227

A facility that is under the Hill-Burton Act must annually provide a minimum dollar volume of uncompensated services that is the lesser of: 1) ten percent of the federal assistance it received, adjusted for inflation; or 2) three percent of its annual operating costs, minus Medicare or Medicaid reimbursement. Patients are eligible for free care if they have incomes less than the federal poverty level (Category A). The facility can elect to provide free or reduced-charge medical care for patients with income up to twice the poverty level (Category B). Nursing homes must make the same choice for patients with incomes up to three times the poverty level (Category C). Immigration status is not to be considered. A facility is required to post notices in the building and in a local newspaper of its compliance with the requirements of the Act.

3. Hospital Practice / Physician On-Call Obligations

EMTALA does not impose a requirement on physicians to participate in an on-call schedule for a hospital.[92] However, a hospital is obligated under Medicare[93] to maintain an on-call schedule. This is often erroneously interpreted as imposing a duty on a physician to be on-call to the emergency department. If a physician is on call, then he has an obligation to respond within a reasonable time period. The statute does not permit groups of physicians to be listed as on-call. An individual physician's name must be used. The medical staff does not have to provide 24/7 coverage if a limited number of physicians are available in a specialty. Conversely, a physician may be on call to more than one hospital, but each hospital is required to evaluate the situation to meet its obligations under EMTALA.[94] CMS uses a

---

[92]   DHHS, CMS guidance "On-call requirements - EMTALA," 2002, http://www.cms.hhs.gov/EMTALA/Downloads/sc0234.pdf

[93]   42 U.S.C.A. 1395cc(a)(1)(I) (West)

[94]   DHHS, CMS guidance "Simultaneously On-Call," 2002, http://www.cms.hhs.gov/EMTALA/Downloads/sc0235.pdf

reasonableness standard in evaluating whether adequate on-call coverage is available.

Most medical staff by-laws require that a physician participate in the call schedule for a hospital. The by-laws may not be so explicit as to set forth the time period in which a physician should respond to a page from the hospital or the time span in which a physician should see a patient about which the page was concerned. The speed with which a physician must respond to a request to provide care to a patient is determined by the standard of care in light of the situation. The better approach is for the physician to respond as quickly as necessary to avoid injury to a patient and avoid unnecessary suffering. This approach takes into account the problems with which each specialty deals. For example, a trauma surgeon would be expected to respond immediately to the emergency department. A family practitioner being advised of an admission for a chronic health problem may not need to see the patient for many hours. The treating physician ultimately determines whether an on-call physician should come to the ED.[95]

A physician has not *abandoned* a patient by not being available when another physician in his practice is available to attend the patient.[96]

A recurring issue is whether a physician can refuse to see a patient because the physician does not participate in the patient's health insurance plan. Many of the larger health plans have made arrangements for specialty coverage, and this issue is avoided. However, at times, the only specialist available is not a *participating provider*. In this situation, the specialist should provide the necessary care and fight the reimbursement battle later. Arguing over payment for services is much easier than defending a medical malpractice action or an EMTALA administrative sanction. The provider should

---

[95] 42 C.F.R..24(j)(i); CMS Survey and Certification Letter S&C-07-23 (6/22/07)
[96] Rosen v. Greifenberger, 257 Va. 373 (1999)

be clear with a patient at the inception of care or as soon as practical that the provider does not take the patient's insurance.

4. Termination of Health Care Services

a. Termination of Services by a Physician

The relationship between a physician and a patient is an *at will* relationship for the patient. For the physician, extricating himself can be more challenging. "After a physician has accepted employment in a case it is his duty to continue his services as long as they are necessary. He cannot voluntarily abandon his patient."[97] However, ultimately a physician has the right to withdraw from a patient's care. This is especially true where a patient fails to follow the physician's advice. Society, and therefore the court, looks less favorably on physicians who withdraw solely over money issues.

In terminating a patient relationship, a physician must always be mindful of allegations that the patient was *abandoned*. To avoid this, a physician should give a patient adequate time to obtain medical care from another physician and cooperate with the new physician in transferring the patient's care.[98] The Board of Medicine dictates that a physician "shall not terminate the relationship or make his services unavailable without documented notice to the patient that allows for a reasonable time to obtain the services of another practitioner."[99] *Documented notice* and *reasonable time* is not defined and must be evaluated on a case-by-case basis. The better course is to advise the patient verbally and in writing that the physician will not be providing services to the patient after a fixed date. The patient should immediately seek another physician. The patient's records will be transferred to a new provider of the

---

[97] Vann v. Harden, 187 Va. 555, 565 (1948) quoted in Rosen v. Greifenberger, 257 Va. 373, 380 (1999)

[98] Rosen v. Greifenberger, 257 Va. 373, 380 (1999) quoting Lyons v. Grether, 218 Va. 630, 634 (1977)

[99] 18 Va. Admin. Code 85-20-28.B.2

patient's choice. In the interim, the treating physician will continue to provide necessary medical care. The patient should go to the nearest Emergency Department if emergency medical problems develop. Providing reasons to the patient for the physician's desire to discharge the patient is usually not fruitful for either party. A patient's non-compliance should be documented whether or not the patient is being discharged. Similarly, a discharging physician would best be served in not providing a list of other potential physicians.

A physician-patient relationship that is created through an emergency department visit or hospitalization with an on-call physician terminates at the time of a patient's discharge unless the physician and patient affirmatively elect for the relationship to continue.[100] However, a physician still has the obligation to follow up on pending test results and other aspects of care as required by the standard of care.[101]

b. Discharge from a hospital

Before a patient is discharged from a hospital, the hospital must inform the patient (and others who may have been involved in decision-making or ongoing care) about his follow-up care, treatment, and services.[102] A patient (or his legal guardian) must be given the opportunity to designate an individual who will care for or assist the patient in his home following discharge.[103] The hospital must notify the designated individual of the patient's discharge; provide a copy of the patient's discharge plan; and offer a demonstration of specific follow-up care tasks that the designated individual will provide. Designation of an individual does not create any obligation on the individual to provide services to the patient. Failure to comply with these requirements does not create a private cause of action

---

[100] Va. Code 54.1-2962.2.A
[101] Va. Code 54.1-2962.2.B
[102] Va. Code 32.1-137.02
[103] Va. Code 32.1-137.03

against a hospital.[104] Additionally, a hospital is not liable for any injury caused by the designated individual.[105]

Before a maternity patient is discharged from a the care of a midwife or hospital, information must be provided to the mother and other family members present about postpartum blues and perinatal depression, shaken baby syndrome and safe sleep environments for infants.[106]

c. Eviction from a Facility

Virginia does not have any case law on the right of a facility versus the right of a patient when it comes to discharge decisions. Usually this is resolved when a physician feels it is appropriate for the patient to be discharged home or to a less-intensive care setting. A frequent challenge is when an incapacitated patient is ready for discharge from the hospital but does not have a nursing home placement or other appropriate destination.[107] Of recent vintage is pressure from a health insurer to limit the number of days for admission. A few statutes address minimum hospital stays for specific conditions, e.g. mastectomy[108] or hysterectomy.[109] However, this is a matter of the minimum coverage provided by a health insurance company. It does not directly address the health care provider's rights or responsibilities. A physician and hospital have only the *standard of care* to guide them as to what is medically appropriate.

A Virginia nursing home can discharge or transfer a patient (even internally) only, after consultation with the patient (or his decision maker) and the attending physician, except in an emergency:[110]

[104] Va. Code 32.1-137.03.F
[105] Va. Code 32.1-137.03.G
[106] Va. Code 32.1-134.01
[107] See Conard, "Granny Dumping: The Hospital's Duty of Care to Patients Who Have Nowhere to Go," Yale Law & Policy Review 10 (1992): 463
[108] Va. Code 38.2-3418.6
[109] Va. Code 38.2-3418.9
[110] Va. Code 32.1-138.1

1. If appropriate to meet that patient's documented medical needs;

2. If appropriate to safeguard that patient or one or more other patients from physical or emotional injury;

3. On account of nonpayment for his stay except as prohibited by Titles XVIII or XIX of the United States Social Security Act and the Virginia State Plan for Medical Assistance Services; or

4. 4. With the informed voluntary consent of the patient, or if incapable of providing consent, with the informed voluntary consent of the patient's authorized decision maker pursuant to § 54.1-2986 acting in the best interest of the patient, following reasonable advance written notice.

These state limitations on discharge of a nursing home patient mirror the federal Nursing Home Reform Law, also known as OBRA '87.[111] The reasons for the discharge must be documented in the resident's clinical record, and a written notice usually thirty days in advance must be given to the resident and a family member. The notice must contain:

- The reason for the discharge;
- The date of the discharge;
- The location to which the resident will be sent;
- Contact information for the State Long Term Care Ombudsman; and
- The right to appeal to DMAS

d. Patient Termination of Services

A patient retains the right to discontinue any or all of a health care provider's services at any time. This may be *against medical advice* (AMA), and should be so documented by the provider. If the patient

---

[111] 42 U.S.C.A. 1396r(c)(2) (West); 42 C.F.R. 483.12(a)

appears to be lacking competency in making this decision, then the health care provider should proceed to obtain surrogate consent under the provisions discussed below. However, the provider should be mindful of the fact that a patient is entitled to make poor, sometimes suicidal, decisions about his health care. The sole test is whether the patient has the capacity to make the decision.

e. Liability for Payment

In addition to being responsible to pay his own medical bills, some individuals may be surprised to learn that they are liable for the bills of others. For example, a parent is required to pay for necessary medical care provided to a child. An individual is liable for all emergency care furnished to his spouse by a physician or hospital, including all follow-up inpatient care provided during the initial admission to the hospital, while the spouses are living together.[112] Courts have narrowly interpreted this law and found, for example, that a surviving spouse was not liable for the care rendered in treating lung cancer over a number of months.[113]

Virginia has given health care providers a tool to stem the practice of a growing few that keep an insurance payment intended for a health care provider. A health care provider may sue a patient for 1) the amount of the payment, 2) the lesser of $250 or three times the amount of the payment and 3) any sanctions that may be imposed under Va. Code 8.01-271.1.[114] A health care provider must first bill the patient and wait until thirty days after the patient receives the insurance payment before filing a law suit.

[112] Va. Code 8.01-220.2
[113] Sentara Virginia Beach Gen. Hosp. v. LeBeau, 188 F. Supp. 2d 623 (E.D. Va. 2002)
[114] Va. Code 8.01-27.3

B. Patients with Limited English Proficiency

Health care providers that participate in Medicare or other government programs may not exclude patients who have limited English proficiency (LEP).[115] To do so is discrimination on the basis of national origin.[116] A provider must take reasonable steps to ensure that LEP patients have meaningful access to medical care. DHHS published a Revised LEP Guidance in September 2003.[117] The Joint Commission on Accreditation of Healthcare Organizations requires that a hospital provide assistance in a language understood by the patient.[118] Smaller organizations are expected to provide LEP assistance on a reasonable basis. The sanction for discrimination can be termination from federal financial programs.[119]

A health care provider must undertake an assessment balancing the following four factors:[120]

1. The number or proportion of LEP patients eligible to be served or likely to be encountered;

2. The frequency with which LEP individuals come into contact with the provider's service;

3. The nature and importance of the provider's service to people's lives; and

---

[115] 42 U.S.C.A. 2000d; 45 C.F.R. 80.3; also see The Rehabilitation Act, Section, which provides protection for the deaf. Loeffler v. Staten Island Univ. Hosp., 582 F.3d 268 (2d Cir. 2009)
[116] Lau v. Nichols, 414 U.S. 563, 568, 94 S. Ct. 786, 39 L. Ed. 2d 1 (1974)
[117] 68 Fed. Reg. 47311 (Sept. 30, 2003)
[118] Joint Commission Hospital Accreditation, "New and Revised Standards for Patient-Centered Communication," (2010)
[119] 45 C.F.R. 80.8
[120] 68 Fed. Reg. at 47314

4. The resources available to the recipient and costs

Provision of emergency care or surgery makes LEP assistance more important than for non-emergent care.[121] The level of language services should be based on the size of the provider and resources available. Sharing interpretative services among several providers, utilizing bilingual staff, using telephone interpreter conference services, and other cost-saving measures are encouraged. A provider must document his efforts to obtain the most cost-effective means of providing LEP assistance before deciding to limit the services due to a lack of resources.[122] A provider must also assess the quality and accuracy of the LEP services.[123] (How this is to be done is not well explained by the regulations.) Some allowance is made for referral of a patient to another provider that can provide greater access to an LEP patient. However, such a referral may be scrutinized for a discriminatory intent.[124] Utilization of a family member, especially a child, or a friend of the patient as a translator should be done carefully.[125]

Written translation of consent forms, intake forms, and other vital documents is an important component of complying with LEP Guidelines. DHHS advocates that written translations be available for any language group that composes 5% or 1,000 patients, whichever is less, of the population eligible to be served by the provider.[126] An alternative for smaller practices is to have a notice written in the primary language of the LEP group that its members have a right to free oral interpretation of written materials.

Even a practitioner who has no current LEP patients should have

---

[121]   68 Fed. Reg at 47315
[122]   68 Fed. Reg at 47315
[123]   68 Fed. Reg at 47316
[124]   68 Fed. Reg at 47315
[125]   68 Fed. Reg at 47317
[126]   68 Fed. Reg. at 47319

a plan in place in the event that such a patient does present.[127] A written LEP policy should include:[128]

- Identifying LEP individuals that need language assistance
- Providing information on methods through which language assistance will be facilitated
- Training of staff
- Providing notice to LEP patients; and
- Monitoring and updating the LEP plan

Signs should be posted in the reception area that explain free language assistance is available and how to obtain it.[129] Technical assistance and LEP resources are available from the Office of Civil Rights, which is charged with enforcing anti-discriminatory regulations.[130]

From a risk management perspective, a health care provider should avoid using family members as translators. The translating skill of the family member is usually unknown but often over estimated. The family member may embellish or minimize the significance of the statements by one party. On the other hand, the patient may be reticent to fully disclose pertinent information in the presence of a family member.

---

[127]   68 Fed. Reg. at 47314
[128]   68 Fed. Reg. at 47320-47321
[129]   68 Fed Reg. at 47320
[130]   See DHHS, Office of Civil Rights' web site for Limited English Proficiency: http://www.lep.gov

C. Consent to Treatment

Informed consent has become both extremely refined and misunderstood in American law. While almost every legal system recognizes an individual's right to autonomy, few take it to the extremes of the United States. The American assumption is that every patient will be told of the risks, benefits and alternatives for a given course of therapy. The patient is the one to control his own destiny. While practitioners often have a contrary experience with patients who are dealing with the stress of a medical problem, the law presumes a duty to give options to the patient.

1. The Concept of Informed Consent

Informed consent is a very recent development in the art of medicine.[131] Prior to the 20th Century, this doctrine was virtually unknown in Anglo-American law.[132] The American courts have strongly embraced the concept while the British courts have more reluctantly acknowledged its existence. Consent, under the traditional British rule, did not need even approach informed. The overriding theme was "What is in the patient's best interest?"[133]

The Supreme Court of Virginia has continued to follow the American trend of requiring more and more information to be conveyed to a patient prior to a therapy being undertaken. Today, *informed*

---

[131] For a more in-depth discussion as to the murky origin of *informed consent*, see Meisel and Kuczewski, "Legal and Ethical Myths About Informed Consent," <u>Arch. Intern Med.</u> 1996; 156:2521-2526

[132] The Supreme Court of Virginia appears to have first recognized the duty of a physician to advise of possible bad consequences in 1918. <u>Hunter v. Burroughs</u>, 123 Va. 113, 133-134 (1918) quoted in <u>Bly v. Rhoads</u>, 216 Va. 645, 647 (1976)

[133] For example, see <u>Hatcher v. Black</u>, The "Times", 2 July 1954

consent is a very strong force in consumer advocacy and medical malpractice litigation. Recently the Board of Medicine has enacted regulations requiring a physician to accurately inform a patient of his medical diagnoses, prognosis and prescribed treatment or care plan.[134] Deliberate false or misleading statements are prohibited. The patient must be informed of the risks, benefits and alternatives that would be disclosed by a reasonable practitioner.

Failing to obtain informed consent was traditionally considered a *battery* at civil law. That is, if the physician failed to obtain the patient's consent, then surgery was an unwanted touching.[135] Recognizing that a patient usually does consent to the physician touching him and that the real issue is how far that touching should go, the courts have moved the consent issue to a question of negligence. The distinction is important and still arises on occasion. For example, to prove *battery*, all that the patient must prove is that she did not consent to the touching.[136] Because *battery* is an intentional tort, the patient need not prove that the surgeon was negligent or that the patient was injured.[137] Expert testimony is not required.[138] In fact, a patient who had an excellent outcome can still win a battery case if she can prove that she did not consent to the touching. For example, a patient may sue in batter where she consented to surgery being performed by one surgeon but the surgery was actually performed by a second surgeon. Under negligence, a patient must prove what a reasonable surgeon would have disclosed, what a reasonable patient would have done if the risk had been disclosed, and the amount of damages flowing from

---

[134]   18 Va. Admin. Code 85-20-28.A

[135]   Pugsley v. Privette, 220 Va. 892, 899 (1980). This case is interesting in that the central issue was whether the patient actually withdrew her consent to surgery prior to the operation. The patient had specified that a particular surgeon be present for the surgery.

[136]   Washburn v. Klara, 263 Va. 586, 590 (2002)

[137]   Pugsley v. Privette, 220 Va. 892, 901 (1980)

[138]   Woodbury v. Courtney, 239 Va. 651 (1990)

the failure to disclose what a reasonable surgeon would have.[139] A good outcome may obviate any recovery in a negligence action.

In the hospital setting, federal[140] and state[141] laws now require that a patient be advised of his rights and responsibilities on admission. Similarly, a nursing home must inform a resident, and evidence it by the resident's written acknowledgment, of her rights and all rules and regulations governing resident conduct and responsibilities as well as many other factors.[142] All such policies must be printed in at least 12-point type and conspicuously posted. Similar notice requirements are required of a hospice by the Department of Health.[143] On request, a physician must inform a patient about 1) how to access information about the physician collected by the Board of Medicine and 2) that if the physician is not a participant in the patient's health plan, the patient may be subject to the doctor's full charge.[144]

Occasionally the concept of informed consent and the right to be free of unreasonable searches under the Fourth Amendment overlap. In the case of Ferguson v. City of Charleston,[145] the US Court of Appeals, Fourth Circuit reviewed the allegations of ten obstetrical patients whose urine was tested for cocaine, pursuant to a 1989 policy of the Medical University of South Carolina in coordination with law enforcement, without telling the patients that positive results would be reported to the police. The plaintiffs, all patients of the university's clinic, who tested positive were arrested and directed to drug rehab programs. The women claimed that the urine testing violated their Fourth Amendment protection from warrantless, unreasonable searches. The primary issue was whether the consent-

---

[139]   See Dessi v. United States, 489 F. Supp. 722, 728 (E.D. Va. 1980)
[140]   42 C.F.R. 482.13(a)(1) (also known as Medicare *Conditions of Participation*)
[141]   Va. Code 32.1-127.B.8
[142]   Va. Code 32.1-138
[143]   12 Va. Admin. Code 5-390-240
[144]   Va. Code 54.1-2910.01
[145]   Ferguson v. City of Charleston, S.C., 308 F.3d 380 (4th Cir. 2002)

to-treatment forms had adequately informed the patients of the ulterior law enforcement motives. The appellate court rejected the university's argument that the tests served primarily a medical purpose.

2. *Elements of Informed Consent*

The test of informed consent in Virginia is two-pronged.[146] First, what would a reasonable physician advise a patient regarding the risks, benefits and alternatives of a recommended therapy? Second, what would a reasonable patient do under the same circumstances?

a. Standard of Care: Reasonable Doctor

"What would a reasonable physician advise a patient regarding the risks, benefits and alternatives of a recommended procedure or treatment?" is the test for the standard of care. In other words, was the physician negligent by not advising of a risk that later materialized? Expert testimony is required to prove the standard of care.[147] The debate continues as to how much information should be disclosed. Court decisions offer no bright-line guidance. Obviously, this is frustrating to practitioners. Further aggravating is that medical treatment, in addition to surgical treatment, is becoming more closely scrutinized along the lines of informed consent

Virginia courts have recognized that "'it is the duty of a physician in the exercise of ordinary care to warn a patient of possible bad consequences of using a remedy,' but that failure to warn 'is not *per se* an act of negligence.'" [148] A physician:

> owes a duty to his patient to make reasonable disclosure of all significant facts under the

---

[146] Dessi v. United States, 489 F. Supp. 722 (E.D. Va. 1980)

[147] Moates v. Hyslop, 253 Va. 45, 48 (1997)

[148] Bly v. Rhoads, 216 Va. 645, 648 (1976) citing Hunter v. Burroughs, 123 Va. 113, 133-34 (1918); Tashman v. Gibbs, 263 Va. 65 (2002)

circumstances of the then situation. This duty is, however, limited to those disclosures which a reasonable medical practitioner would make under the same or similar circumstances, and the failure to disclose in all instances does not necessarily suggest a neglect of duty.[149]

To win a lack of informed consent allegation against a practitioner, a patient must show by expert testimony that "prevailing medical practice requires disclosure of certain information, that the information is material to an informed decision on treatment, and that disclosure would not pose an unreasonable threat of detriment to the patient's well-being or to his ability to make a rational decision."[150] The Supreme Court of Virginia, in reaching this decision, considered and rejected the *subjective standard*, which is based on what a patient might want to know.[151] As some courts have observed, using the subjective standard gives every patient with an unfavorable outcome the opportunity to contend that he would not have undergone the surgery if he had known of a potential risk that materialized. A physician does not need to communicate information that a patient already knows or of which any reasonably intelligent person should be aware.[152] In the case of a teaching hospital, a patient is entitled to know who will actually be performing a surgery even though the faculty surgeon can delegate certain portions of the surgery.[153]

One challenge of informed consent is the lack of a bright line for physicians. For example, a Pennsylvania physician had to defend on

[149] Bly v. Rhoads, 216 Va. 645, 648 citing Dietze v. King, 184 F. Supp. 944, 949 (E.D. Va. 1960)
[150] Bly v. Rhoads, 216 Va. 645, 651 (1976)
[151] Bly v. Rhoads, 216 Va. 645, 649-651 (1976) discussing Canterbury v. Spence, 464 F.2d 772, cert. denied, 409 U.S. 1064 (1972)
[152] Bly v. Rhoads, 216 Va. 645, 650 (1976)
[153] Va. Board of Medicine, "Guidelines Concerning The Ethical Practice of Surgeons & Surgery Interns & Residents," Guidance Document 85-15; also see CMS, Interpretive Guidelines 482.24(c)(2)(v)

the issue of whether he should have advised a patient of the FDA classification of safety for a particular medical device (pedicle bone screws). The Pennsylvania Supreme Court held that he did not.[154] This author recently defended a surgeon where plaintiff claimed the risk that materialized was 10% as opposed to the surgeon's contention that it was 5%. The jury returned a verdict in favor of the surgeon.

May a reasonable physician limit information or lie to the patient? While British courts have at times embraced this approach if it was in the best interest of the patient,[155] American courts have not followed suit. The closest that the Supreme Court of Virginia has come to this proposition is quoted above.

A growing debate is how much information a physician must disclose about herself. For example, must she tell a patient that this is the first time that she has performed the procedure? Must she tell a patient that this is the fortieth time that she is performing the procedure? Must the discussion of risks be reflective of the surgeon's actual experience or of the general population as published in peer-reviewed literature? Should a surgeon tell a patient about any medical or mental health conditions from which the surgeon suffers? For example, an Illinois appellate court held that a surgeon may have a duty to disclose his HIV-positive status to a patient prior to surgery.[156] Failure to do so gave rise to an action for negligent infliction of emotional distress but not battery or even failure to obtain informed consent as the patient did not contract AIDS. To date, the Supreme Court of Virginia has held that any of these points depend on the prevailing standard of care, which must be proven through expert testimony.[157]

---

[154] Southard v. Temple Univ. Hosp., 566 Pa. 335, 781 A.2d 101 (2001)

[155] Hatcher v. Black, 'The Times' 2 July 1954

[156] Doe v. Noe, 293 Ill. App. 3d 1099, 690 N.E.2d 1012 (1997), Va. Admin. Codeated sub nom. Doe v. Noe No. 1, 303 Ill. App. 3d 139, 707 N.E.2d 588 (1998)

[157] Tashman v. Gibbs, 263 Va. 65 (2002)

b. Proximate Cause: Reasonable Patient

"If informed of the risks, benefits and alternatives, what would a reasonable patient have done under the same circumstances?" is the test of proximate cause of the patient's injury. For example, if a reasonable patient would have undergone the procedure even if advised of a risk that later materialized, then the patient cannot recover.[158] Many jurisdictions require expert testimony as to what a *reasonable patient* would do.[159] Unfortunately, the Supreme Court of Virginia has not directly addressed the issue. Only a passing reference is made in a decision on a different issue that determination of what a reasonable patient would do may be a question for the jury.[160] At a minimum, a patient must state that she would have refused the surgery if properly advised of the facts.[161] The better course would be for the law to require expert testimony as to what a reasonable patient would do. This avoids speculation, sympathy, or second-guessing by the jury.

The spectrum of information that must be disclosed to a patient ranges from little, if any, in an acute, life-threatening condition to a great deal for elective, non-emergent surgery. For example, plastic surgeons performing cosmetic surgery are required to disclose much more than a trauma surgeon confronted with major bleeding. The key issue is what a reasonable patient would do if told of the foreseeable risks and benefits.

A prudent healthcare provider will practice the concept of *informed consent* almost without realizing it. The core of *informed consent* is speaking with one's patient about the condition suffered by the patient and what the provider recommends and listening to the patient's concerns. A good rapport with one's patient is the

---

[158] Dessi v. United States, 489 F. Supp. 722, 728 (E.D. Va. 1980); Cunningham v. United States, 683 F.2d 847, 849 (4th Cir. 1982)

[159] For example, see St. Gemme v. Tomlin, 118 Ill. App. 3d 766, 455 N.E.2d 294 (1983) and Pardy v. United States, 783 F.2d 710, 715 (7th Cir. 1986)

[160] Rizzo v. Schiller, 248 Va. 155 (1994)

[161] Tashman v. Gibbs, 263 Va. 65, 75 (2002)

best prevention of later retrospective criticism. Many lawsuits are avoided by speaking with a patient about what to expect after surgery or while on a therapy. A good outcome often does not equate to perfect health.

3. Types of Consent

Consent to medical procedures may be conveyed in three ways: express; implied in fact; or implied in law. The distinctions are important and are not well understood by practitioners of medicine or law.

a. Express Consent

Express consent is the direct oral or written agreement by a patient to the proposed medical procedure. This is the classic situation encountered in the surgical setting when a patient signs a written consent form after discussion with the surgeon.

b. Implied in Fact

Implied in fact consent is the nonverbal or indirect expression of a patient's desire. An example is where a person extends an arm for immunization. One trial court found that consent to delegating certain tasks to an assistant was implied by a patient's general consent for the assistant to participate in the surgery.[162] The line between the need for express consent versus implied in fact consent is fuzzy at best. Healthcare would grind to a halt if express consent was required for everything. Yet, consumers clamor for more involvement in decision making and many mistakes are avoided by staff verbalizing what they intend to do.

---

[162] Reed v. Austin, 21 Va. Cir. 222 (1990)

c. Implied in Law

Consent implied in law occurs when the law will presume that one has given consent because a patient is unable to consent, e.g. an unconscious patient brought to the emergency room. Consent may also be deemed to have been made in other situations as a matter of public policy, such as where a health care worker is exposed to blood products. The patient, by statute, is deemed to have consented to testing for HIV and other blood-borne pathogens when a health care provider is exposed to the patient's bodily fluids.[163]

4. Duty to Obtain Informed Consent: Physician v. Facility

A frequent debate erupts between physicians and facilities as to the role of each in "obtaining consent." The law does not have such confusion. The primary obligation to obtain a patient's consent falls on the physician. A doctor is presumed to have superior knowledge to other health care providers, such as nurses, about the procedure that is proposed. Therefore, the physician ordering the intervention is obligated to explain the risks, benefits and alternatives to a patient. Delegating the duty to a non-physician is at the surgeon's peril. While some organizations have very good patient educators, the responsibility remains on the physician to assure that a patient gives informed consent to the procedure.

The role of a hospital, or other facility, is strictly ministerial. A hospital employee, often a floor nurse, may witness that a patient consented to a procedure. As will be discussed below, informed consent requires more than the mere signing of a form by a patient. Some states, but not Virginia, have held that a hospital has a duty to assure that a patient has consented to the proposed procedure.[164] A hospital does not have the burden to explain the risks, benefits

---

[163]   Va. Code 32.1-45.1(A)

[164]   For example, see <u>Alexander v. Gonser</u>, 42 Wash. App. 234, 711 P.2d 347 (1985)

and alternatives. The Medicare *Conditions of Participation* state that a patient has a right "to make informed decisions regarding his or her care, including the right to be informed of his or her health status, to be involved in care planning and treatment, and to refuse treatment."[165] The federal regulation does not go any further to delineate who or how a hospital must assure that informed consent occurs. While the regulation covers the facility, not the physician, the preamble to the regulation when it was proposed stated that HCFA (now CMS) "expect[s] that the hospital will hold the responsible physician accountable for discussing all information regarding treatment, experimental approaches ... and possible outcomes of care to promote quality care delivery."[166] A hospital must provide information in a manner and form that can be understood by a patient, e.g. use of large print materials, interpreters, etc.[167]

The better practice, and as required by Virginia regulations, is for a hospital to assure that a patient has completed a written consent form prior to surgery or other procedure.[168] It would be improper for a hospital to get between a physician and a patient to try to verify the quality of that consent. At most, a hospital nurse should witness the patient signing a consent form and should bring any questions that a patient may have about the proposed procedure to the physician's attention. A nurse should not be put in a position, in lieu of the attending physician, where he must explain or describe the material risks, benefits, and alternatives to a particular procedure.

---

[165]   42 C.F.R. 482.13(b)(1); Interpretive Guidelines Tag A758
[166]   64 Fed. Reg. 36060, 36074
[167]   42 C.F.R. 482.13(a)(1) Interpretive Guidelines Tag A751
[168]   12 Va. Admin. Code 5-410-420.G.2 that covers hospital surgical suites requires that a patient's chart have "evidence of appropriate informed consent." Interestingly, regulations for outpatient surgical centers require a policy and procedure for "written informed consent of patient prior to the initiation of any procedures." 12 Va. Admin. Code 5-410-1170.A. Also see, CMS, Interpretive Guideline 482.24(c)(2)(v).

5. How Specific Must A Patient's Consent Be?

A recurring concern is exactly when and to what must a patient consent? For example, must a patient consent to each component of surgery? Does a patient need to consent to every pill, injection and IV fluid? Obviously, this is impractical. Unfortunately, no court has offered clear guidance. The general rule is that the more risky that an intervention is, the more the patient ought to be informed. The amount of disclosure is also heightened where the intervention is elective. Patients are rarely invited to choose techniques within a procedure.

A good example of informed consent evolving is with regard to blood transfusion. Due to the rising awareness of blood borne pathogens, society has become much more concerned about blood transfusion. Even though the risks are probably lower today than at any time in history, a physician must be on guard to discuss carefully the risks, benefits, and alternatives before starting a blood transfusion. The Joint Commission has mandated that a separate consent form must be signed in a hospital for the use of blood and blood products.

In Rizzo v. Schiller,[169] the Supreme Court of Virginia addressed the issue of whether a patient's signature on a hospital's general consent form precluded a claim for failure to obtain her informed consent to the use of obstetrical forceps during delivery. The patient contended that her obstetrician was negligent in the use of forceps during the delivery, that he failed to obtain her informed consent to use forceps, and that as a result, her son suffered from cerebral palsy and was permanently disabled. The patient had signed a general consent form upon her admission to the hospital wherein she authorized her obstetrician and other members of the medical staff at the hospital "to perform diagnostic or therapeutic medical and surgical procedures on and to administer anesthetics" to her. At the close of plaintiff's evidence, the trial court struck plaintiff's informed consent claim. The Supreme Court of Virginia reversed

---

[169] Rizzo v. Schiller, 248 Va. 155 (1994)

this decision, holding that the plaintiff presented sufficient expert testimony and evidence to let the jury decide her informed consent claim. As for the consent form, the Court stated:

> It is true that Ms. Rizzo signed a document that purportedly is a consent form. However, this form did not inform her of any specific procedures that Dr. Schiller intended to perform; nor did it inform her of foreseeable risks associated with any procedures or risks in failing to perform any procedures. As [plaintiff's expert] observed, the form is so general in nature that 'you could also justify amputating her foot.' **We hold that the duty imposed upon a physician to obtain a patient's informed consent requires more than simply securing the patient's signature on a generalized consent form, similar to the form present here. The law requires informed consent, not mere consent, and the failure to obtain informed consent is tantamount to no consent.**[170] (emphasis added).

Unfortunately, the Court gave practitioners little guidance beyond this general maxim. A physician may need the assistance of counsel or a professional risk manager to navigate these dangerous waters. In the obstetric setting, a good risk management practice would be to discuss various delivery techniques, such as the use of forceps and Cesarean section, with a patient prior to labor.

Apparently reacting to someone's unpleasant experience, the General Assembly enacted a statute prohibiting medical students performing pelvic examinations on anesthetized or unconscious female patients unless informed consent has been given.[171] Male patients do not enjoy such protection.

---

[170] Rizzo v. Schiller, 248 Va. 155, 159 (1994)
[171] Va. Code 54.1-2959

6. *Usefulness of the Written Consent Form*

The written consent form has taken on a being all its own, far removed from its original intent. At best, a written consent form is one way of having a patient acknowledge that she has received certain information from a physician regarding the risks, benefits and alternatives of a proposed therapy. Unfortunately, a patient will only rarely take the time to carefully review the form. It is often given to a patient shortly before the procedure along with several other long, dense documents.

The mere signature of a patient on a generic consent form gives little defense to a physician.[172] To be of value, a physician must be able to prove that she did have a detailed discussion with the patient as to the risks, benefits and alternatives of the proposed treatment; that the patient understood what was being discussed; and the patient freely agreed to undergo the treatment following the discussion. A written consent form is a useful tool in documenting the informed consent process, but is not conclusive as to any element of informed consent:

> [A] patient's consent form need not be viewed in a vacuum. Examining it in conjunction with the events prior to its completion, as well as the patient's understanding of what she was consenting to, does not transform the claim from battery to lack of informed consent. The surrounding circumstances are relevant to determine the scope of the patient's consent and ultimately whether the physician exceeded that scope.[173]

As discussed above,[174] a patient's signature on a generalized consent form does not offer much protection to a physician. The better

---

[172]   Rizzo v. Schiller 248 Va. 155 (1994)
[173]   Walters v. Leecost, M.D., 29 Va. Cir. 258 (1992)
[174]   Rizzo v. Schiller 248 Va. 155 (1994)

course is for a consent form to be as tailored as possible to the specific procedure and to a specific patient in easily understood prose. For example, one trial court wrote, "The issue of informed consent is one which is appropriate for expert testimony. The Court finds persuasive Plaintiff's evidence showing that the readability and understandability of consent forms is beyond the comprehension of most Americans."[175] To counter such a perspective, narratives, drawings, videotapes, or other educational material can supplement a written consent form. This will bolster a physician's contention as to exactly what risks, benefits and alternatives were discussed with a patient. It also furthers the true goal of having the patient understand and partner with the provider in improving the patient's health.

A consent document does not form a contract with a physician, and it does not usually represent a warranty or guarantee of a specific result.[176] Likewise, a *waiver of liability* in the healthcare setting is generally not enforceable in Virginia. The Supreme Court of Virginia has consistently held that an individual cannot waive another's liability for negligence that has not yet occurred.[177] This is considered to be against public policy. However, one should not confuse informed consent with a waiver. The former is a detailed discussion of the risks, benefits and alternatives with regard to a particular therapy. The patient is asked to agree to accept the known benefits, risks and alternatives. The latter is an effort to have a patient release a physician from liability for the physician's negligence before it occurs. Obviously, the patient is at a disadvantage since she does not know what negligence the doctor may commit or what injury the patient may suffer.

[175]   Roller v. Jane, 43 Va. Cir. 321 (1997)
[176]   Gray v. Burke, 32 Va. Cir. 407 (1994)
[177]   Hiett v. Lake Barcroft Comm. Ass'n, 244 Va. 191 (1992); Coles v. Jenkins, 34 F. Supp. 2d 381 (W.D. Va. 1998)

7. *Children*

The law generally presumes that a parent has the right to consent to medical treatment for his or her child who is under the age of eighteen.[178] Of note is the presumption that one parent and not necessarily both parents can consent to medical care for a child.[179] For example, even a non-custodial parent may consent to medical treatment.[180] Virginia statutes modify that presumption when parental custody of a child is modified, suspended or terminated by the Commonwealth.[181]

In a pediatric practice, obtaining informed consent from a parent can be difficult. Determining who is a parent as opposed to a step-parent, a neighbor, a nanny, or another caring individual who has no ability to give consent is an on-going challenge. A long-standing pediatrician/minor relationship does not negate the requirement to have a parent's consent. A "standing consent" is not likely to be considered valid. Having a parent sign a consent form for any intervention in the presence of a few witnesses would be ideal. Unfortunately, it rarely occurs. However, a parent's consent can be given verbally in person or by telephone. A parent can delegate the authority to consent for a child. This is preferably done in writing.

One trial court has held that under its equity jurisdiction, it had the power to declare the right of parents to consent to their daughter

---

[178] Va. Code 16.1-336. Informed consent in the research setting is guided by Va. Code 32.1-162.16 et seq.
[179] See Angeli v. Kluka, No 1D15-4 217 (Fla. Ct. App. 5/25/2016)(in an issue of first impression, the Florida Court of Appeal held that the consent of one parent is sufficient even if the other parent is known to object; action by non-consenting parent dismissed)
[180] See 1983-84 Op. Va. Atty. Gen. 219
[181] For example, a Fairfax Circuit Court judge awarded a mother sole authority over medical decisions for a child, including the right to assert the religious exemption to mandatory childhood immunizations in Va. Code 32.1-46(D)(1) despite the parents having joint custody of the child. Va. Code 20-124.3. Grzyb v. Grzyb, (Bellows, J.), CL2008-4659, 6/12/09, VLW 009-8-131

donating a kidney to their other daughter.[182] The facts of that case made the decision relatively easy. The girl wishing to donate the kidney was sixteen years old and had been considering the decision for over a year. The parents had initially tried to discourage her but were eventually persuaded by her sincerity and maturity. The family consulted their pastor, who endorsed the organ donation as morally and ethically sound. In contrast, another trial judge has ruled that he did not have the authority to withhold lifesaving medical care from a child.[183]

a. When A Parent Is Not Available

In an emergency situation (defined as a delay that may adversely affect a minor's recovery), a health care provider is granted immunity from liability for failing to obtain consent to medical or surgical treatment when no parent or authorized person is available.[184] However, a minor who is age fourteen or older (and physically able to consent) must consent to the emergency medical or surgical treatment.

When a parent cannot be located, a judge in the juvenile and domestic relations court has authority to consent to medical and surgical treatment.[185] The process for appointment of a standby guardian is set forth by statute and requires a court order.[186]

When a child is not in the custody of a parent, the person designated by statute to consent to medical or surgical treatment varies depending on the circumstances:[187]

1. The judge for a minor within the control of the judge's court;

---

[182] Hurdle v. Currier, 5 Va. Cir. 509 (1977)
[183] In Matter of Infant C, 37 Va. Cir. 351 (1995)
[184] Va. Code 54.1-2969.C
[185] Va. Code 54.1-2969.B
[186] Va. Code 16.1-349 et seq.
[187] Va. Code 54.1-2969.A

2. The local superintendent of public welfare or social services (or designee) for a minor who:

    a. is committed to the care and custody of the local board by the court;

    b. is taken into emergency protective custody for child abuse or neglect;[188] or

    c. is entrusted to the local board by the parent(s) or guardian[189] and consent by the parent(s) or guardian cannot be immediately obtained, and in the absence of such consent, a court order cannot be immediately obtained;

3. The director of the Department of Corrections or Director of the Department of Youth and Family Services (or designee) if the minor is sentenced or committed to custody of the department;

4. The principal executive officer of a state institution where the minor is a ward of the state institution;

5. The principal executive officer of any other institution or agency who has received custody of the minor separated from his or her parents or guardians; or

6. Any person standing in *loco parentis*, or a conservator or custodian for his ward or other charge under disability.

As one has probably gleaned from this list, when a child is removed from the custody of the parents, the authority to consent to medical treatment is usually transferred from the parents to the government agency or institution. However, there is one potential pitfall for the health care provider. Where a child is entrusted to a local agency without termination of parental rights, a health care provider needs to be concerned with who is consenting for the child for non-emergent medical or surgical care. If the parents retain

---

[188] Emergency custody is pursuant to Va. Code 63.2-1517
[189] Entrustment agreements are described in Va. Code 63.2-903 and 63.2-1817

the right to consent for medical and surgical care, then the agency does not have the authority to make health care decisions except as outlined above. The entrustment agreement or court order should be examined if the agency is not absolutely certain as to its authority to grant consent or the health care provider is not comfortable. Documentation of the agency's representation to a health care provider is extremely important for risk management.

When a surrogate consents to medical care for a child, she must make a reasonable effort to notify the minor's parent or guardian as soon as practicable.[190]

b. When a Child May Consent to Particular Treatment

The minority/majority age distinction as a basis for giving consent has been eroded in medical practice. In addition to the emergency treatment situation discussed above, statutory exceptions are discussed below.

A minor of any age is deemed to be an adult and capable of consenting to the following medical and mental health care: [191]

1. Medical or health services needed to determine the presence of or to treat venereal disease or any infectious or contagious disease that the State Board of Health requires to be reported;

2. Medical or health services required in case of birth control, pregnancy or family planning[192] except for the purpose of sexual sterilization;

3. Medical or health services needed in the case of outpatient care, treatment or rehabilitation for substance abuse; or

---

[190] Va. Code 54.1-2969.I
[191] Va. Code 54.1-2969.E
[192] The process for judicial authorization where a minor elects not to seek parental approval for an abortion is set forth in Va. Code 16.1-241.V

4. Medical or health services needed in the case of outpatient treatment or rehabilitation for mental illness or emotional disturbance.

A minor who is or was married is also deemed to be an adult for the purpose of giving consent to medical care.[193]

A pregnant minor can give consent for herself and her child to medical care related to the delivery of her child and for the duration of the related hospitalization.[194] After delivery, the under-age mother continues to be given the authority to give consent for medical care of her child. Interestingly, the young mother apparently loses the ability to consent to her own health care after discharge from the maternity ward.

At age sixteen, a minor can consent to donating blood.[195] Parental consent is still required if the youth receives any consideration for the donation and the collection agency is for-profit.

Parents may be liable for the cost of medical care even though they did not know of the care or even objected to the initiating event of treatment, such as an abortion that led to subsequent hospitalization for infection, if the medical care rendered is considered a *necessary*.[196]

c. Emancipated Minors

A minor in Virginia who has reached the age of sixteen may be emancipated through formal legal proceedings where a court finds:

1. The minor has entered into a valid marriage, whether or not the marriage has been terminated by dissolution; or

---

[193] Va. Code 54.1-2969.F
[194] Va. Code 54.1-2969.G
[195] Va. Code 54.1-2969.H
[196] Winchester Mem'l Hosp. v. Boyce, 10 Va. Cir. 541 (1984); Winchester Med. Ctr, Inc. v. Giffin, 9 Va. Cir. 260 (1987)

2. The minor is on active duty with any of the US armed forces; or

3. The minor willingly lives separate and apart from the parents or guardian, with the consent or acquiescence of the parents or guardian, and that the minor is or is capable of supporting himself and competently managing his own financial affairs.[197]

The formal requirement of a court order to become *emancipated* is often overlooked. While a child may be *de facto* emancipated in many instances, the law does not recognize it. Pregnancy or other adult attributes does not alone achieve *emancipation*. However, a minor who is or was married can consent to medical treatment.[198]

The emancipated minor is treated as an adult under Virginia law, and can consent to medical, dental or psychiatric care without the input of his parent or guardian.[199] Once emancipated, the parents are not liable for medical care or other bills incurred by the minor.

The Va. Attorney General described the general principle of emancipation in 1982, prior to enactment of the 1986 law set forth above that formalized the court-petition process:

> A minor continues to be subject to the care and direction of his or her parents until reaching the eighteenth birthday, or upon emancipation prior to that age. Emancipation occurs when there is a complete severance of the parent and child relationship so that the parents recognize no responsibility for the care and support of the child and the child does not rely on the parents for care or support. It is the "freeing of the child for all the period of its minority from the care, custody, control and service of its parents, conferring on the child

---

[197] Va. Code 16.1-331 and 16.1-333
[198] Va. Code 54.1-2969.F
[199] Va. Code 16.1-334

the right to its own earnings and terminating the parents' legal obligation to support it." (Emphasis added.) Brumfield v. Brumfield, 194 Va. 577, 580, 581, 74 S.E.2 d 170 (1953).

Emancipation does not arise merely because the child is living away from his or her parents, and the child also provides for his or her support. Nor does it arise when a child runs away from home, but the parents continue to recognize their parental responsibility to the child. With the exception of marriage, a minor is not emancipated until the parents clearly manifest that the child is completely free from their custody and control and the child is free to act independently of his or her parents' wishes, according to his or her own principles as if an adult. Buxton v. Bishop, 185 Va. 1, 37 S.E.2d 755 (1946).

A minor also becomes emancipated from his or her parents upon marriage. The fact that the marriage is voidable (as opposed to void) due to the lack of parental consent as may be required by law, does not change the result. Kirby v. Gilliam, 182 Va. 111, 28 S.E.2d 40 (1943); Lawson v. Brown, 349 F. Supp. 203 (W.D. Va. 1972).

Accordingly, except in the case of a valid or voidable marriage of a minor, a minor who claims emancipation must prove more than self-support. There must be proof that his or her parents do not provide, and will not provide during minority, for the care and support of the child (for example: food, shelter, clothing, medical expenses) and further that the parents recognize that the child is free to act independently of them as if the child were an adult, with no desire to supervise or control the future direction of their child.

A determination of emancipation must be made on a case-by-case basis. However, emancipation is never presumed, nor is parental consent to such a status lightly inferred. The student has the heavy burden of proving his or her claim through the presentation of credible facts to local school authorities. Emancipation must be "clearly proven" to the satisfaction of school authorities. Brumfield, supra. [200]

One must consider this Attorney General's Opinion in light of the current statute, but it is useful in understanding the reluctance of the law to presume that a minor is emancipated.

d. When Parents Refuse to Consent to Necessary Medical Care

The Department of Social Services may petition the Juvenile and Domestic Relations Court for consent for medical treatment over a parent's objection.[201] The task for the Court is to determine what is best for the child. Religious convictions of parents may conflict with the best interests of the child and must be considered by the Court.[202] The Supreme Court of the United States observed, "The right to practice religion freely does not include liberty to expose … the child … to ill health or death."[203] "Parents may be free to become martyrs themselves. But it does not follow that they are free … to make martyrs of their children before they have reached the age of full and legal discretion when they can make that choice for

---

[200] The Honorable Alson H. Smith, Jr., 1982-83 Va. Op. Atty. Gen. 416
[201] Va. Code 16.1-241.D and 54.1-2969
[202] Va. Code 16.1-228
[203] Prince v. Massachusetts, 321 U.S. 158, 166–167, 64 S. Ct. 438, 88 L. Ed. 645 (1944)

themselves."[204] For an example of making a decision in this difficult circumstance, a trial judge felt obligated, over the parents' religious objections, to authorize surgery for a two-year-old girl who would die if she did not receive cardiac surgery to repair a ventricular septal defect and severe mitral valve regurgitation.[205]

In the setting of a pregnant woman who refuses obstetrical intervention, the majority of courts are now favoring the rights of the mother over the unborn child.[206] However, this position is not universal and each case is determined on its particular facts.[207] An obstetrician may request a psychiatric consultation if it is indicated. A good risk management tool is to have the patient sign a written document or the medical chart acknowledging that she has been advised of the risk to herself and her child.

In response to a highly publicized case, the General Assembly redefined *a neglected child* to exclude a child age 14 or older who refuses medical care with a parent's agreement.[208] However, if a child's circumstances present "an imminent danger to the child's life or health to the extent that severe or irremediable injury would be likely," a physician, child-protective worker or police officer may take a child into custody for up to seventy-two hours while seeking an emergency removal order.[209]

[204] Prince v. Massachusetts, 321 U.S. 158, 170, 64 S. Ct. 438, 88 L. Ed. 645 (1944)
[205] Winchester Dep't of Soc. Servs. v. Roberts, 26 Va. Cir. 314 (1992) (appended to the case is a lengthy digest of decisions that impact this area)
[206] See In re A. C., 1990 D.C. App. LEXIS 90, 14-15 (1990)
[207] See Application of Jamaica Hosp., 128 Misc. 2d 1006, 491 N.Y.S.2d 898 (Sup. Ct. 1985) (court ordered medical treatment for previable fetus)
[208] Va. Code 63.2-100
[209] Va. Code 63.2-1517

8. Patients Lacking Capacity to Consent

The Health Care Decisions Act defines *incapable of making an informed decision* as:[210]

> The inability of an adult patient, because of mental illness, mental retardation, or any other mental or physical order that precludes communication or impairs judgment and that has been diagnosed and certified in writing by his physician with whom he has a bona fide physician-patient relationship and a second physician or licensed clinical psychologist after personal examination of such patient, to make an informed decision about providing, withholding or withdrawing a specific medical treatment or course of treatment because he is unable to understand the nature, extent or probable consequences of the proposed medical decision.

a. Judicial Decision-Making

Where a patient is incapable of making an informed decision on his own behalf or is incapable of communicating such a decision due to a physical or mental disorder, a judge may authorize the provision, withholding, or withdrawal of treatment if it is in the best interest of the patient and a person authorized under the Health Care Decisions Act is not reasonably available, is incapable of making an informed decision, or is unable or unwilling to make a decision.[211] (Where a legally authorized person is available to make the decision or the patient has provided an advance directive, the Health Care Decisions

---

[210] Va. Code 54.1-2982
[211] Va. Code 37.2-1101; see Cavuoto v. Buchanan County Dept. of Social Services, 44 Va. App. 326 (2004) (court erred in ordering medical exam when it failed to make finding that patient was incapable of making an informed decision regarding her health)

Act will apply.[212]) The patient is entitled to counsel and notice of the hearing.[213] The hearing may be conducted via electronic means.[214]

Prior to authorizing medical treatment, the court must find:

1. No legally authorized person is available to consent;
2. The patient lacks capacity to consent;
3. The patient is unlikely to regain the capacity to consent within the time required for deciding; and
4. The proposed treatment is in the best interest of the patient, taking into consideration the patient's religious beliefs or basic values unless such treatment is necessary to prevent death or a seriously irreversible condition.[215]

A judge may not authorize under this statute: [216]

1. Nontherapeutic sterilization, abortion, or psychosurgery;
2. Admission to mental retardation or psychiatric hospital;
3. Administration of antipsychotic medication for more than 180 days or electroconvulsive therapy (ECT) for more than 60 days; or
4. Restraint or transportation of a patient except in limited circumstances.

To order restraint or transportation of a patient, the court must find that the evidence is clear and convincing that restraint or transportation is necessary as part of an authorized treatment.[217] A physician or hospital providing, withholding, or withdrawing care under the authorization of the court is immune from liability based

---

[212] Va. Code 37.2-1108; See the Virginia Health Care Decisions Act, below.
[213] Va. Code 37.2-1101.C-D
[214] Va. Code 37.2-1109
[215] Va. Code 37.2-1101.G
[216] Va. Code 37.2-1102
[217] Va. Code 37.2-1102

on a lack of informed consent.[218] Likewise, a physician or hospital is granted immunity arising from following the patient's wishes if the court finds that the patient has capacity to consent.[219]

An order authorizing medical treatment may be appealed within ten days to the Court of Appeals.[220]

b. Appointment of Guardian

Where a patient is determined to lack competency to handle either her financial affairs or her well-being or both, a guardian can be appointed by the court.[221] A judge can tailor the terms of the appointment to the patient's need for protection.

c. Decision-Making in a State Facility

When a patient is a resident of a state mental health facility or is receiving case management from a community services board and is incapable of giving informed consent due to mental illness or mental retardation, the entity may consent on his behalf for treatment of physical injury or illness when: [222]

1. No guardian is available to give consent;

2. A reasonable effort has been made to advise a parent or other next of kin about the need for surgical, medical or dental treatment;

3. No reasonable objection is raised by or on behalf of the patient; and

4. Two physicians (or for dental care, two dentists or one dentist and one physician) state in writing that they have made a good faith effort to explain the necessary treatment

---

[218]   Va. Code 37.2-1106
[219]   Va. Code 37.2-1106
[220]   Va. Code 37.2-1105
[221]   Va. Code 64.2-2000 et seq.
[222]   Va. Code 54.1-2970

to the patient, and they have probable cause to believe that the patient is incapacitated and unable to consent and that delay in treatment might adversely affect recovery

d. Emergency Custody Order

A magistrate may issue an emergency custody order for an adult to be taken into custody and transported to a hospital emergency department for testing, observation or treatment if a physician believes that the adult is incapable of making an informed decision as a result of a physical injury or illness and that testing, observation and treatment are necessary to prevent imminent and irreversible harm.[223] The physician's opinion must be based on direct communication with the emergency personnel on the scene and after efforts to communicate directly with the adult.[224] Once reaching the emergency department, a physician must evaluate the patient to determine if a temporary detention order should be sought or not. The adult remains in custody until the evaluation is completed but not more than four hours.[225] An emergency custody order must be executed within four hours of its issuance.[226]

In the absence of a legally authorized person available to give consent, a magistrate must determine that an adult:[227]

1. Is incapable of making an informed decision regarding obtaining necessary treatment;

2. Has refused transport to obtain such necessary treatment;

3. Has indicated an intention to resist such transport; and

---

[223] Va. Code 37.2-1103
[224] Va. Code 37.2-1103.C
[225] Va. Code 37.2-1103.E
[226] Va. Code 37.2-1103.G
[227] Va. Code 37.2-1103.B

4. Is unlikely to become capable of making an informed decision regarding obtaining necessary treatment within the time required for such decision

e. Temporary Detention Order

A judge or a magistrate may authorize temporary detention of a patient by a hospital emergency department or other facility and authorize testing, observation, or treatment if: [228]

1. A licensed physician who has attempted to obtain consent advises the court that the patient is not capable of making an informed decision or is incapable of communicating such a decision;

2. The court finds that probable cause exists to believe that the patient is not capable of making an informed decision or is incapable of communicating such a decision; and

3. The medical standard of care calls for testing, observation or treatment of the disorder within the next 24 hours to prevent death, disability, or a serious irreversible condition.

Detention of a patient in a hospital emergency department meeting criteria may be ordered by a judge for up to 24 hours.[229] The detention may not be extended beyond twenty-four hours unless the order is part of previously ordered ongoing treatment. If the patient regains the capacity to consent, the physician must rely on the patient's decision.[230] This statute does not affect the authority to provide treatment in an emergency situation.[231]

---

[228] Va. Code 37.2-1104
[229] Va. Code 37.2-1104; if a judge is not available, a magistrate may authorize the temporary detention. The CSB must be notified of testing, observation or treatment is complete, and the CSB must conduct a TDO evaluation.
[230] Va. Code 37.2-1103.D and 37.2-1104
[231] Va. Code 37.2-1108

A temporary detention order may be appealed de novo to the Circuit Court. Any order of the Circuit Court may be appealed to the Court of Appeals within ten days.[232]

f. Treatment in Absence of Informed Consent

When a patient lacks the capacity to consent to medical care or unable to communicate his choice, one can ethically argue that treatment to prevent imminent and serious harm should be the preferred course of action. This may be the better course from a risk management perspective as well. One would rather defend a lack of consent claim than a wrongful death claim. Virginia law supports this position in regard to treatment of physical injury or illness for residents of state-operated mental health facilities and community service board consumers when no legally authorized decision maker is reasonably available; no reasonable objection is raised on behalf of the patient; and two physicians have stated in writing that they have made a good faith effort to communicate with the patient and that the patient is incapacitated and unable to consent due to mental illness or mental retardation and that delay of treatment might adversely affect recovery.[233] The statute does not apply beyond this limited situation.

9. The Right to Refuse Treatment

The fundamental corollary of a patient's right to consent to treatment is the right to refuse treatment. In its purest form, a patient should be able to refuse any treatment without an obligation to provide a justification to anyone. This is often described as a Constitutional right. However, society often takes the paternalistic view that a rational person will always choose treatment over no treatment. With that in mind, attempting to refuse treatment can be exasperating to one who does not choose the traditional role of

---

[232] Va. Code 37.2-1105
[233] Va. Code 54.1-2970

a patient being subservient to a professional's opinion. For example, one who elects to not receive oncology chemotherapy where the odds of success are high will often be labeled as depressed or irrational. He may be treated for this "depression" until consent is obtained. In contrast, refusal of treatment has become widely accepted in the circumstances surrounding the end of life. This is discussed in more detail in later sections.[234]

When a patient refuses treatment, a health care provider must be assured that the patient has been offered the opportunity to learn the risks, benefits and alternatives of the proposed therapy. However, a patient also enjoys the freedom of refusing to listen to any of the discussion. The health care provider should carefully document that the effort was made, as many patients have a selective recollection of such events when their health declines. Having the patient acknowledge in writing that he has been offered the therapy and declined is a very important risk management tool. A physician should consider whether he has a right or duty to advise government authorities about a patient who in refusing treatment may also put others in danger. This will be discussed in more detail in Chapter II. A physician may also want to consider requesting a psychiatric consultation if the physician has a concern about the patient's mental status or capacity to participate in the informed consent process. If important therapy is refused, a physician should document that:

1. The patient had capacity to participate in the informed consent process

2. The physician disclosed the risks, benefits and alternatives of the proposed therapy, including the risks and benefits of refusing the therapy

3. The patient verbalized an understanding of the information disclosed by the physician

4. The patient refused the proposed therapy

---

[234] See the Virginia Health Care Decisions Act, below

The right to refuse treatment must be balanced with the interests of society, such as preservation of life, protection of innocent third parties, safeguarding the integrity of the medical profession, and prevention of suicide. These competing interests have been discussed at length in court decisions addressing the refusal of medical treatment by Jehovah's Witnesses,[235] pregnant women[236] and "right to die" patients.[237]

A health care provider does not have an obligation to continue caring for a patient that refuses needed therapy. One has an ethical right to withdraw from such a situation. However, a health care provider must attempt to have another health care provider assume the care. Failing to do so may leave the health care provider open to allegations of abandonment.[238]

---

[235] See Raleigh Fitkin-Paul Morgan Mem'l Hosp. & Ann May Mem'l Found. in Town of Neptune v. Anderson, 42 N.J. 421, 201 A.2d 537 (1964); Jefferson v. Griffin Spalding Cty. Hosp. Auth., 247 Ga. 86, 274 S.E.2d 457 (1981)

[236] See Kolder, et al., "Court-Ordered Obstetrical Interventions," 316 New Eng. J. of Med. 1192-96 (1987)

[237] Cruzan by Cruzan v. Dir., Missouri Dep't of Health, 497 U.S. 261, 110 S. Ct. 2841, 111 L. Ed. 2d 224 (1990)

[238] See Section A.4: Termination of Health Care Services, above

D. Consent to Psychiatric Treatment

1. Determining Competency

An adult is presumed to be competent until proven otherwise. For example, with regard to having the capacity to make health care decision, every adult is presumed to have that capacity unless specifically determined otherwise.[239] An adult is *mentally incapacitated* and *mentally incompetent,* under the Virginia statute for appointment of a guardian or conservator, when found by a court to be: [240]

> incapable of receiving and evaluating information effectively or responding to people, events, or environments to such an extent that the individual lacks the capacity to (i) meet the essential requirements for his health, care, safety, or therapeutic needs without the assistance or protection of a guardian or (ii) manage property or financial affairs or provide for his support or for the support of his legal dependents without the assistance or protection of a conservator.

Unfortunately for a professional called upon to provide an expert opinion as to a patient's competency, no format is given as to how the expert reaches his conclusions. The professional should be guided by the practices and guidelines of his profession.[241] The Court ultimately makes the determination. Poor judgment alone does

---

[239] Va. Code 54.1-2983.2.A

[240] Va. Code 37.2-1000

[241] For a discussion of assessing mental capacity, see Appelbaum & Grisso, "Assessing Patients' Capacities to Consent to Treatment," 1988 New Eng J of Med 319:1635-8 and Annotation: Mental Competency of

not constitute sufficient evidence that a person is incompetent.[242] Admission to a mental health facility does not create a presumption of incapacity.[243] A professional should appreciate that the judge, or jury, will consider the bases for an expert's opinion in determining if a guardian or conservator is needed.[244] The finder of fact (a judge or a jury) must determine that the evidence is clear and convincing that a guardian or conservator is needed.[245]

A determination of *mental incompetency* is not the same as determining the need for involuntary psychiatric treatment. The process for authorizing involuntary assessment for the need for mental healthcare and involuntary treatment of adults is set forth by statute.[246]

2. Adults

a. Involuntary Treatment

i) Detention by a Police Officer

A police officer who has probable cause to believe that a person meets the criteria for an Emergency Custody Order (ECO), discussed below, may take the person into custody and transport him to an appropriate location to assess the need for hospitalization or treatment without prior authorization.[247] Such evaluation shall be conducted immediately.

This language tracks the language and includes essentially the same

---

Patient to Consent to Surgical Operation or Medical Treatment, 25 ALR 3d 1439
[242] Va. Code 37.2-1000
[243] Va. Code 37.2-825
[244] Va. Code 37.2-1007
[245] Va. Code 37.2-1007
[246] Va. Code 37.2-800 et seq.
[247] Va. Code 37.2-808.G

requirements as those set forth for a Temporary Detention Order. Under both statutes, a person may not be detained unless he is mentally ill. Refusal of medical treatment alone is insufficient to authorize an officer to take the person into custody. Detention by an officer under this section is limited to eight hours or less.[248]

ii)   Emergency Custody Orders

A magistrate shall issue an Emergency Custody Order (ECO) when probable cause exists that an individual:[249]

- Has a mental illness and there exists a substantial likelihood that, as a result of mental illness, the person will, in the near future,
  - (a) cause serious physical harm to himself or others as evidenced by recent behavior causing, attempting or threatening harm and other relevant information, if any, or
  - (b) suffer serious harm due to his lack of capacity to protect himself from harm or to provide for his basic human needs;
- Is in need of hospitalization or treatment; **and**
- Is unwilling to volunteer or incapable of volunteering for hospitalization or treatment

In determining whether probable cause exists, a magistrate may consider, in addition to the petition:[250]

- The recommendations of any treating or examining physician or psychologist;
- Any past actions of the person;

---

[248]   Va. Code 37.2-808.F
[249]   Va. Code 37.2-808
[250]   Va. Code 37.2-808.A

- Any past mental health treatment of the person;
- Any relevant hearsay evidence;
- Any available medical records;
- Any submitted affidavits, if the witness is not available and it so states in the affidavit; and
- Any other available information that the magistrate considers relevant to the determination

The magistrate should specify the primary law-enforcement agency and jurisdiction to execute the ECO and provide transportation to a medical facility.[251] (This should be the police serving the jurisdiction where the patient is in custody or, if not yet in custody, where the patient is currently located.[252] However, an officer is permitted to go beyond the jurisdiction that he serves.)[253] The General Assembly has added legislation allowing other designees to provide transportation.[254] An ECO must be executed within eight hours of its issuance.[255] The evaluation or treatment should be conducted immediately by an appropriately qualified person designated by the community service board (CSB).[256] The person must remain in custody until a temporary detention order is issued, until the person is released or until the ECO expires.[257] The custody time period cannot exceed eight hours unless good cause is found by the magistrate to exist for a four-hour extension to arrange placement in an alternative facility.[258]

A law-enforcement agency can transfer custody of a patient to an

[251] Va. Code 37.2-808.C
[252] Va. Code 37.2-808.D
[253] Va. Code 37.2-808.E
[254] Va. Code 16.1-345, 37.2-808.C and K, 37.2-810, 37.2-817.2 and 37.2-829. Immunity from negligence was added in 2015. See Va. Code 16.340.2.D
[255] Va. Code 37.2-808.N
[256] Va. Code 37.2-808.B
[257] Va. Code 37.2-808.K
[258] Va. Code 37.2-808.O

evaluating facility if: 1) the facility is licensed to provide the level of security necessary; 2) is actually capable of providing the level of security necessary; and 3) has entered into an agreement with the law-enforcement agency.[259]

iii) Temporary Detention Orders

The procedures and conditions for the short-term involuntary detention of an individual are set forth by statute.[260] This process is generally known as a Temporary Detention Order (TDO). Another term often heard is "Green Warrant." In general, the law is drafted to balance the flexibility needed to handle emergencies with an individual's right to be heard before he is involuntarily detained. Virginia law requires that a magistrate be available at all times for the TDO process.[261] Likewise, an on-line acute psychiatric bed registry exists for expediting placement of individuals under TDO.[262]

A magistrate is obligated to issue a TDO under limited circumstances and after certain procedural requirements have been met.[263] A TDO must be executed within twenty-four hours of its issuance.[264] The order should designate which law-enforcement agency will execute the TDO.[265] For a defendant awaiting trial, a TDO may designate that the defendant be moved to a suitable hospital or, if not available, remain in the jail until a hospital bed is available.[266]

---

[259] Va. Code 37.2-808.E
[260] Va. Code 37.2-809
[261] Va. Code 37.2-809.J
[262] Va. Code 37.2-308.1
[263] Va. Code 37.2-809
[264] Va. Code 37.2-809.I
[265] Va. Code 37.2-810.A
[266] Va. Code 37.2-811 and 19.2-169.6

A magistrate must find, usually based on an in-person evaluation by a Community Service Board (CSB),[267] that the individual:[268]

- Has a mental illness and there exists a substantial likelihood that, as a result of mental illness, the person will, in the near future
  - (a) cause serious physical harm to himself or others as evidenced by recent behavior causing, attempting or threatening harm and other relevant information, if any, or
  - (b) suffer serious harm due to his lack of capacity to protect himself from harm or to provide for his basic human needs;
- Is in need of hospitalization or treatment; **and**
- Is unwilling to volunteer or incapable of volunteering for hospitalization or treatment

Attention to each component of this test is extremely important. Information provided by the person initiating emergency custody and the recommendations of a treating or examining physician must also be considered.[269] The test requires a magistrate to find that a person is mentally ill before he may issue a TDO. Virginia law does not authorize involuntary detention based solely on physical injury or illness, or on a patient's refusal of needed medical care. For example, consider a hypothetical patient who is unwilling to accept treatment for an injury that threatens the loss of a finger. He may satisfy the requirement that he is "unwilling to volunteer for treatment." He may also satisfy the requirement that he is "in need of hospitalization" and may pose a "danger to self" because of his

---

[267] The CSB evaluation prerequisite is waived if such an evaluation has occurred with 72 hours or there is significant physical, psychological or medical risk associated with conducting such an evaluation. Va. Code 37.2-809.D
[268] Va. Code 37.2-809.B
[269] Va. Code 37.2-809.B

refusal to accept treatment. Nevertheless, if there is no evidence that he suffers a mental illness, he does not satisfy the requirements of a TDO. As such, the magistrate is not authorized to issue a TDO and the patient cannot be detained.

In determining whether probable cause exists for a TDO, a magistrate may consider, in addition to the petition:[270]

- The recommendations of any treating or examining physician or psychologist;
- Any past actions of the person;
- Any past mental health treatment of the person;
- Any relevant hearsay evidence;
- Any available medical records;
- Any submitted affidavits, if the witness is not available and it so states in the affidavit; and
- Any other available information that the magistrate considers relevant to the determination

In issuing a TDO, the magistrate should identify the facility where the individual will be detained as determined by the CSB.[271] A state facility cannot refuse a TDO patient but can find alternative placement for her.[272] The facility is authorized to provide emergency medical and psychiatric care within its capabilities when the facility determines that the services are in the best interest of the detainee.[273] The Commonwealth will pay for such services pursuant to DMAS guidelines after the facility seeks reimbursement from the detainee's insurance company.[274] The duration of a TDO may not exceed seventy-two hours prior to a hearing.[275] If the seventy-two

[270] Va. Code 37.2-809.C
[271] Va. Code 37.2-809.E and 37.2-809.1
[272] Va. Code 37.2-809.1
[273] Va. Code 37.2-809.F
[274] Va. Code 37.2-809.G
[275] Va. Code 37.2-809.H

hours expires on a weekend or legal holiday, the person may be detained to the next business day.

If the CSB evaluator recommends that a patient should not be subject to a TDO, the evaluator must 1) inform the person who sought emergency custody and the treating physician; 2) advise the person seeking emergency custody that CSB will facilitate communication with a magistrate if the person disagrees with the recommendation; and 3) arrange for the person seeking emergency custody appear before the magistrate.[276]

Fees for mental health professionals appearing as a witness or attorneys appointed to represent the patient are limited to $75 plus necessary expenses for involuntary admission hearings.[277]

Several Attorney General opinions have interpreted the role of the police and magistrate. Curiously, the Virginia Administrative Code has no regulations relating to the TDO process or the procedure for a CSB to follow. This leaves the logistics of how each county or city handles a request for a TDO very much in the local government's hands. Establishing working relationships with each Board will help smooth the process of these often-tense situations.

In situations where a patient presents to the Emergency Department of a hospital, the better course is to contact the CSB (or police) to take formal custody of the patient even though the patient may remain under the care of the hospital. The statute does not give any authority to a health care provider on his, her or its own volition to detain a psychiatric patient. However, a health care provider does have a *duty to warn* that may obligate the provider to take affirmative action.[278]

---

[276] Va. Code 37.2-809.L
[277] Va. Code 37.2-804
[278] Va. Code 54.1-2400.1. This is discussed below.

iv) Commitment for Involuntary Admission

An involuntary commitment hearing is conducted by a district court judge or special justice at a convenient facility or other place open to the public.[279] The petitioner must be given adequate notice of the place, date and time of the commitment hearing.[280] The healthcare provider must advise the patient's family or his agent of the proceedings.[281] If it appears from the evidence that the patient does not meet the criteria for involuntary commitment, a judge may release the patient on his personal recognizance or bond.[282]

Before commencing a hearing on involuntary admission, the judge must inform the patient that he has the right to apply for voluntary admission.[283] If the patient is "capable and willing," then the judge will require him to accept voluntary admission for a minimum period not to exceed seventy-two hours. After that, the patient must give at least forty-eight hours' notice to the hospital of his plan to leave the hospital.

If voluntary admission is not accepted, then the judge must inform the patient that he has a right to a commitment hearing and a right to counsel.[284] The judge must appoint an attorney to represent the patient unless the patient desires to employ one at his own expense. The patient has a right to testify and present evidence.[285] Likewise, the petitioner is encouraged, but is not required, to testify. A patient cannot be released solely due to the fact that the petitioner did not attend the hearing.[286] The hearing must be held after a sufficient time period to allow for completion of the required examination, preparation of the preadmission screening report and initiation

---

[279] Va. Code 37.2-820
[280] Va. Code 37.2-814.F
[281] Va. Code 37.2-804.2
[282] Va. Code 37.2-813
[283] Va. Code 37.2-814.B
[284] Va. Code 37.2-814.C
[285] Va. Code 37.2-814.F
[286] Va. Code 37.2-814.F

of mental health treatment to stabilize the person's psychiatric condition to avoid involuntary commitment.[287] If the patient is under a TDO, the hearing must be held within seventy-two hours from the execution of the TDO.

The judge must render his decision on the commitment petition after observing the person and receiving the reports of the examiner[288] and the CSB. If not opposed, the judge may base his opinion solely on this information.[289] The patient may be involuntarily committed to a facility designated by the CSB or the Commissioner for up to 180 days if the judge finds by clear and convincing evidence:[290]

- The person has mental illness and there exists a substantial likelihood that, as a result of mental illness, the person will, in the near future,
  - (a) cause serious physical harm to himself or others as evidenced by recent behavior causing, attempting or threatening harm and other relevant information, if any, or
  - (b) suffer serious harm due to his lack of capacity to protect himself from harm or to provide for his basic human needs; **and**
- Alternatives to involuntary inpatient treatment have been investigated and deemed unsuitable and there is no less restrictive alternative to involuntary inpatient treatment

The judge should consider:[291]

---

[287] Va. Code 37.2-814.A
[288] The examiner will usually be a licensed psychiatrist or psychologist. If not available, a licensed clinical social worker, professional counselor, psychiatric nurse practitioner or clinical nurse specialist that has been certified by the Department may conduct the examination. Va. Code 37.2-815
[289] Va. Code 37.2-817.A
[290] Va. Code 37.2-817.B
[291] Va. Code 37.2-817.C

- The recommendations of any treating or examining physician or psychologist;
- Any past actions of the person;
- Any past mental health treatment of the person;
- Any examiner's certification;
- Any available health records;
- The preadmission screening report; and
- Any other relevant evidence that may have been admitted

For a dangerous patient, the sheriff of the patient's resident jurisdiction[292] is obligated to transport the patient to a facility within six hours of a judge's commitment order.[293] A judge may order that any responsible person, including a representative of the facility where a patient was temporarily detained, transport the patient to the admitting facility.[294] A non-resident of the Commonwealth must, as soon as practicable, be "returned to his family or friends, if known, or the proper authorities of the state or country from which he came."[295] Patients who escape can be arrested with or without a warrant and returned to the facility.[296]

A course of outpatient treatment specifically recommended by the CSB may be ordered if a judge finds:[297]

---

[292] If located more than 100 miles from the jurisdiction in which the hearing is held, then the sheriff of the jurisdiction must provide transportation. Va. Code 37.2-829. A sheriff is generally not allowed to hold a patient in jail and never with other prisoners. Va. Code 37.2-831 and 37.2-832
[293] Va. Code 37.2-829
[294] Va. Code 37.2-829
[295] Va. Code 37.2-826
[296] Va. Code 37.2-833 through 37.2-835
[297] Va. Code 37.2-817.D

- Has mental illness and there exists a substantial likelihood that, as a result of mental illness, the person will, in the near future,
  - (a) cause serious physical harm to himself or others as evidenced by recent behavior causing, attempting or threatening harm and other relevant information, if any, or
  - (b) suffer serious harm due to his lack of capacity to protect himself from harm or to provide for his basic human needs;
- Less restrictive alternatives to involuntary inpatient treatment are deemed suitable;
- The person:
- Has agreed to abide by his treatment plan; and
- Has the ability to do so
- The ordered treatment will be delivered on an outpatient basis by the CSB or designated provider to the person

Mandatory outpatient treatment may include day treatment or night treatment in a hospital, outpatient involuntary treatment with anti-psychotic medication or other treatment modalities that meet the needs of the patient. [298] Mandatory outpatient treatment must not include the use of restraints or physical force of any kind in provision of anti-psychotic medication.

Failure to comply with involuntary outpatient treatment can be used as evidence at a subsequent commitment hearing. Converting involuntary outpatient treatment to an inpatient admission must be conducted in the prescribed manner for a commitment hearing.[299]

The presiding judge or special justice can authorize the treating physician to discharge the patient to mandatory outpatient

---

[298] Va. Code 37.2-817.E
[299] Va. Code 37.2-817.2

treatment under a specified discharge plan.[300] The motion may be brought by the treating physician, a family member, a personal representative or the CSB. The judge or special justice must find that the person has a history of lack of compliance with treatment for mental illness, that at least twice within the past thirty-six months has resulted in the person being subject to a temporary detention order, a voluntary admission, or an order for involuntary admission, that the person is in need of mandatory outpatient treatment following inpatient treatment in order to prevent a relapse or deterioration that would be likely to result in the person meeting the criteria for involuntary inpatient treatment; that the person is unlikely to voluntarily participate in outpatient treatment unless the court orders mandatory outpatient treatment following inpatient treatment, and the person is likely to benefit from mandatory outpatient treatment.[301]

An examination of the patient must be performed by an independent professional, preferably a psychiatrist or psychologist, in private.[302] The examination must include:[303]

1. A clinical assessment including a mental status examination; determination of current use of psychotropic and other medications; a medical and psychiatric history; a substance use abuse or dependency determination; and a determination of the likelihood that, as a result of mental illness, the person will, in the near future, suffer serious harm due to his lack of capacity to protect himself from harm or to provide for his basic human needs

2. A substance abuse screening, when indicated

3. A risk assessment that includes an evaluation of the likelihood that, as a result of mental illness, the person will, in the near future, cause serious physical harm to himself or

---

[300] Va. Code 37.2-805; 37.2-817.C
[301] Va. Code 37.2-805; 37.2-817.C
[302] Va. Code 37.2-815
[303] Va. Code 37.2-815.B

others as evidenced by recent behavior causing, attempting, or threatening harm and other relevant information, if any

4. An assessment of the person's capacity to consent to treatment, including his ability to maintain and communicate choice, understand relevant information, and comprehend the situation and its consequences

5. A review of the temporary detention facility's records for the person, including the treating physician's evaluation, any collateral information, reports of any laboratory or toxicology tests conducted, and all admission forms and nurses' notes

6. A discussion of treatment preferences expressed by the person or contained in a document provided by the person in support of recovery

7. An assessment of whether the person meets the criteria for an order authorizing discharge to mandatory outpatient treatment following a period of inpatient treatment

8. An assessment of alternatives to involuntary inpatient treatment; and

9. A recommendations for the placement, care and treatment of the person

The examiner must certify in writing prior to the commitment hearing as to whether, based on probable cause,

1. The patient has a mental illness and there is a substantial likelihood that, as a result of mental illness, the person will in the near future, (a) cause serious physical harm to himself or others as evidenced by recent behavior causing, attempting, or threatening harm and other relevant information, if any, or (b) suffer serious harm due to his lack of capacity to protect himself from harm or to provide for his basic human needs; and

2. The patient requires involuntary inpatient treatment

In lieu of the examiner appearing, the judge may accept a written certification of the examiner's findings if there is no objection to the acceptance of the written certification by the patient or his attorney. A judge cannot decide the case until the written report is presented.[304]

The CSB where the person resides or, if impractical, where the patient is located must submit a preadmission screening report within forty-eight hours (or the next business day) as to:[305]

1. The patient has a mental illness and there is a substantial likelihood that, as a result of mental illness, the person will in the near future, (a) cause serious physical harm to himself or others as evidenced by recent behavior causing, attempting, or threatening harm and other relevant information, if any, or (b) suffer serious harm due to his lack of capacity to protect himself from harm or to provide for his basic human needs;

2. Whether the person is in need of involuntary inpatient treatment;

3. Whether there is no less restrictive alternative to inpatient treatment; and

4. The recommendations for that person's placement, care and treatment

After the Virginia Tech tragedy, the General Assembly passed legislation that requires participation at the hearing by the examiner, treating physician at the facility, and the CSB in person or by two-way electronic communication.[306] Documented communication between CSBs is also now required.

The judge must confirm that prior to the commitment hearing the

---

[304]   Va. Code 37.2-815.C

[305]   Va. Code 37.2-816; the CSB report is not required for state inmates; also see Va. Code 37.2-505

[306]   Va. Code 37.2-817

patient has been informed in writing and by his attorney as to the involuntary admission process and the statutory protections.[307] At a minimum, the written explanation must describe the patient's rights to:

1. Be represented by an attorney appointed by the court or an attorney of the patient's choosing at his expense;

2. Present any defenses including an independent evaluation and expert testimony or the testimony of other witnesses;

3. Be present during the hearing and testify;

4. Appeal any order for involuntary admission to the circuit court; and

5. Have a jury trial on appeal

The attorney representing a patient, to the extent possible, must interview the patient, the petitioner, the examiner, the community service board staff, and any other material witnesses as well as actively defend the patient.[308]

Appeal of an involuntary commitment order must be filed within ten days from the date of the order, is given priority over all other matters, and is heard as soon as possible.[309] A circuit court judge, or a jury of seven, must hear the evidence and make a decision as to whether the criteria for involuntary admission exist at the time of the trial.[310] A judge has discretion to admit the psychological examination from the commitment hearing being appealed or to request a new one. An attorney appointed to represent the patient is entitled to a fee of $75 plus necessary expenses. Treatment necessary to protect

---

[307]   Va. Code 37.2-814.D

[308]   Va. Code 37.2-814.E

[309]   Va. Code 37.2-821

[310]   Va. Code 37.2-821; Under Va. Code 37.2-821(B), the judge must consider the patient's condition at the time of the hearing, not the date of the initial confinement. Paugh v. Henrico Area Mental Health and Developmental Services, 286 Va. 85 (2013)

the life, health or safety of the patient may be given while an appeal is pending unless prohibited by a court order.[311] A *writ of habeas corpus* to determine the legality of the patient's detention can be filed at any time.[312]

Within twenty-four hours of involuntary admission, a physician at the facility must examine the patient.[313] If the physician determines that insufficient cause exists for the involuntary admission, then the patient must be returned to the locality in which the petition was initiated or in which the patient resides. State facilities must review the appropriateness of inpatient admission at 30, 60 and 90 days after admission and then every six months.[314] A state facility[315] or other facility[316] may discharge a patient who does not meet involuntary commitment criteria after the CSB formulates a discharge plan.[317] A facility, a CSB, and providers may exchange information required to formulate a discharge treatment plan, with or without the patient's authorization.[318]

Unnecessarily placing a mentally disabled person in a state institution rather than a community home when a community home is available and appropriate may be a violation of the Americans with Disabilities Act.[319]

v)   Prisoners

A prisoner retains most of his civil rights, including the right to refuse

---

[311]   Va. Code 37.2-822
[312]   Va. Code 37.2-844
[313]   Va. Code 37.2-823
[314]   Va. Code 37.2-824
[315]   Va. Code 37.2-837
[316]   Va. Code 37.2-838
[317]   Va. Code 37.2-505.A.1
[318]   Va. Code 37.2-839
[319]   Olmstead v. L.C. ex rel. Zimring, 527 U.S. 581, 119 S. Ct. 2176, 144 L. Ed. 2d 540 (1999)

medical treatment.[320] However, this is limited if an inmate with a mental disorder presents a potential for disruption in a normal prison environment and for harm to himself and others if not treated.[321] The sheriff, or judge that has legal custody over an incarcerated juvenile, may consent to necessary surgical or medical treatment.[322] The process for temporary detention and involuntary admission for mental illness of a jail inmate is set forth by statute.[323] An inmate may not volunteer for admission or be subject to mandatory outpatient treatment.[324]

Where a prisoner is incapable of giving consent, the Director of the Department of Corrections may petition the circuit court of the county or city where the prisoner is located for an order authorizing treatment of the prisoner.[325] The court must find by clear and convincing evidence that the prisoner is incapable of giving consent and that the proposed treatment is in the best interest of the prisoner. The procedure for the Director and the court to follow is set forth in Va. Code 53.1-40.2.[326] Virginia's procedure provides more formal protection of the prisoner than mandated by the United States Supreme Court.[327]

The threshold is quite high when seeking judicial approval to administer psychotropic medications to a defendant in order to restore him to competency to stand trial. The government has the

---

[320] 1995 Va. AG LEXIS 8
[321] Washington v. Harper, 494 U.S. 210, 110 S. Ct. 1028, 108 L. Ed. 2d 178 (1990)
[322] 1996 Va. AG LEXIS 83 citing Va. Code 54.1-2969(A)(1) and (A)(5)
[323] Va. Code 19.2-169.6
[324] Va. Code 19.2-169.6.B
[325] Va. Code 53.1-40.1
[326] Also see Washington v. Silber, 805 F. Supp. 379 (W.D. Va. 1992), aff'd, 993 F.2d 1541 (4th Cir. 1993)
[327] Washington v. Harper, 494 U.S. 210, 110 S. Ct. 1028, 108 L. Ed. 2d 178 (1990)

burden to show that this is the least intrusive method available.[328] A judicial hearing is probably required as an administrative hearing may be inadequate.[329] "An overriding justification and a determination of medical appropriateness" is necessary.[330] The Government's interest in bringing a defendant to trial by restoring competency may outweigh the defendant's right to refuse psychotropic medication.[331]

b. Specific Therapies

A person voluntarily admitted, certified or even involuntarily admitted to a psychiatric hospital does not lose his legal rights solely by virtue of his admission.[332] A patient's advance directive should be given full effect to the extent that it does not conflict with emergency custody, temporary detention, involuntary admission and mandatory outpatient treatment orders.[333] Prior written informed consent must be obtained before a resident is subjected to hazardous treatment or irreversible surgical procedures.[334] The resident or his representative must be given adequate opportunity for further consultation at his own expense.[335] The rights of residents must be prominently posted in a psychiatric facility as well as a printed version given to each resident or his representative.[336]

A physician must determine and document the following criteria before initiating aversive conditioning techniques:

---

[328]   United States v. Sell, 282 F.3d 560 (8th Cir. 2002), vacated, 539 U.S. 166, 123 S. Ct. 2174, 156 L. Ed. 2d 197 (2003) ; Riggins v. Nevada, 504 U.S. 127, 112 S. Ct. 1810, 118 L. Ed. 2d 479 (1992)

[329]   United States v. Brandon, 158 F.3d 947 (6th Cir. 1998)

[330]   Kulas v. Valdez, 159 F.3d 453 (9th Cir. 1998)

[331]   Sell v. United States, 539 U.S. 166, 123 S. Ct. 2174, 156 L. Ed. 2d 197 (2003)

[332]   12 Va. Admin. Code 35-120-40.A

[333]   Va. Code 54.1-2983.C

[334]   12 Va. Admin. Code 35-120-40.F

[335]   12 Va. Admin. Code 35-120-40.F

[336]   12 Va. Admin. Code 35-120-70

1. Other forms of conditioning have been tried and found to be unsuccessful;

2. The behaviors to be modified are injurious to the individual or others;

3. Immediate control of the behavior is considered essential;

4. More appropriate behaviors are concurrently reinforced; and

5. Frequency, time, and limitations of treatment.

If a patient has been deemed by the CSB and the state facility physician to be in need of "treatment, training, or habilitation in a state facility," a state facility must admit that person.[337] The criteria and procedure for admission of a person suffering mental retardation are also set forth by statute.[338] In state-operated facilities, a resident's informed consent must be obtained for "any proposed treatment that involves the use of noxious stimuli or presents significant risk to the resident."[339] A resident's authorized representative can give informed consent if a resident lacks sufficient capacity to make an informed decision regarding the risks and benefits of the proposed treatment, or disclosure to the resident of material information concerning the proposed treatment would seriously damage the patient's condition.[340] In this situation, the determination by the head of the treatment team and a physician not involved in the treatment must be documented and explained in the resident's chart and reviewed as the resident's condition changes.[341] If the resident objects to the proposed treatment to which his representative has consented, an appeal process is set forth in the state regulations.[342] Consent is not required when "a psychiatrist or the senior physician on duty determines upon personal examination that the resident is likely to cause serious harm to himself or another or to suffer

---

[337] Va. Code 37.2-805

[338] Va. Code 37.2-806

[339] 12 Va. Admin. Code 35-110-80.A

[340] 12 Va. Admin. Code 35-110-80.B.1

[341] 12 Va. Admin. Code 35-110-80.B.1

[342] 12 Va. Admin. Code 35-110-80.B.2

serious deterioration unless the proposed treatment is immediately initiated, administered or undertaken."[343] No surgical procedure should be performed on a resident until an independent reviewer determines that consent has been obtained.[344]

A person who is civilly committed may be given psychotropic medications against his will if approved by an administrative hearing.[345]

Electro-convulsive therapy (ECT) may be authorized by a court for an incompetent patient only if the evidence, including the testimony of a psychiatrist, is clear and convincing that all other reasonable forms of treatment have been considered and that ECT is the most effective for the person.[346] The appropriateness of continuing antipsychotic drugs must be reviewed every thirty days.[347] ECT or antipsychotic medication, even if authorized by the court, can only be administered over the patient's objection if he is subject to an order of involuntary commitment, including outpatient involuntary commitment.[348]

ECT cannot be administered to any resident of a state facility unless the Local Human Rights Committee (LHRC) has determined:

1. Valid informed consent has been obtained; and

2. A qualified psychiatrist not involved in the resident's treatment has concurred with the judgment of the treating psychiatrist that the treatment is indicated.[349]

---

[343]   12 Va. Admin. Code 35-110-80.C

[344]   12 Va. Admin. Code 35-110-80.D.1. The exception is where a court authorizes the procedure under Va. Code 37.1-134.2

[345]   Jurasek v. Utah State Hosp., 158 F.3d 506 (10th Cir. 1998) (interpreting Utah law)

[346]   Va. Code 37.2-1102

[347]   Va. Code 37.2-1101.H

[348]   Va. Code 37.2-1102

[349]   12 Va. Admin. Code 35-110-80.D.2

Likewise, behavior modification therapy involving any intrusive aversive therapy cannot be initiated in a state facility until the LHRC has determined that informed consent has been obtained and the facility has proved that the risks of the treatment do not outweigh the behavior sought to be modified.[350] Psychosurgery is prohibited.[351]

3. Use of Restraints

CMS has issued final regulations with comments on the use of restraints in a facility.[352] To say the least, restraints are discouraged. See discussion below under Section H. Security in the Facility.

4. Minors

a. Outpatient Care

A minor,[353] apparently regardless of age, may consent to outpatient treatment or rehabilitation for mental illness or emotional disturbance.[354] The question of whether a parent would be responsible for payment of such services would be determined by whether a court deemed the services to be necessary.

b. Inpatient Care

i) Where Minor Consents

For inpatient psychiatric care, one must comply with *The Psychiatric Treatment of Minors Act*.[355] A child under 14 years of age can be

[350]   12 Va. Admin. Code 35-110-80.D.3
[351]   12 Va. Admin. Code 35-110-80.D.4
[352]   Medicare and Medicaid Programs; Hospital Conditions of Participation: Patients' Rights, 71 Fed. Reg. 71378, 71428, 71 Fed. Reg. 71378-01, 71428; 42 C.F.R. Part 482
[353]   Defined as "a person less than eighteen years of age." Va. Code 16.1-336
[354]   Va. Code 54.1-2969
[355]   Va. Code 16.1-335 et seq.

admitted to a willing facility solely with the consent[356] of a parent.[357] A child over age 14 may be admitted with the joint consent of the minor and a parent.[358]

The admission of a minor must be approved by a qualified evaluator[359] who has evaluated the minor within twenty-four hours of admission. The evaluator must make the following written findings: [360]

1. The minor appears to have a mental illness serious enough to warrant inpatient treatment and is reasonably likely to benefit from the treatment;

2. The minor has been provided with a clinically appropriate explanation of the nature and purpose of the treatment;

3. If the minor is fourteen or older, that he has been provided with an explanation of his rights under this Act as they would apply if he were to object to admission, and that he has consented to admission; and

---

[356] Defined as "the voluntary, express, and informed agreement to treatment in a mental health facility." Va. Code 16.1-336

[357] Defined as "(i) a biological or adoptive parent who has legal custody of the minor including either parent if custody is shared under a joint decree or agreement, (ii) a biological or adoptive parent with whom the minor regularly resides, (iii) a person judicially appointed as a legal guardian of the minor, or (iv) a person who exercises the rights and responsibilities of legal custody by delegation from a biological or adoptive parent, upon provisional adoption or otherwise by operation of law. The director of the local department of social services, or his designee, may stand as the minor's parent when the minor is in the legal custody of the local department of social services." Va. Code 16.1-336

[358] Va. Code 16.1-338.A

[359] Defined as "a licensed psychiatrist or psychologist who is skilled in the diagnosis and treatment of mental illness in minors." Where such a professional is not available, a mental health professional licensed by the Board of Health Professions or employed by a community services board may conduct the evaluation. Va. Code 16.1-336

[360] Va. Code 16.1-338.B

4. All available modalities of treatment less restrictive than inpatient treatment have been considered and no less restrictive alternative is available that would offer comparable benefits to the minor.

If the admission is to a state hospital, the community service board (CSB) serving the area where the minor lives must provide the evaluation and ensure that the necessary written findings have been made before approving the admission. The written findings should be provided to the consenting parent and the parent should have the opportunity to discuss them with the evaluator.[361]

Within ten days of admission, an individualized treatment plan must be prepared by the provider responsible for the minor's treatment and be explained to the consenting parent and the minor.[362] The minor and the consenting parent should be involved in the development of the treatment plan to the "maximum feasible extent." A copy of the treatment plan must be provided to the consenting parent and the minor. The treatment plan must include:

1. A preliminary plan for placement and aftercare upon completion of the inpatient treatment; and

2. Specific behavioral and emotional goals against which the success of treatment may be measured.

If the consenting parent or the minor, if fourteen or older, revokes the previously given consent to admission, the minor must be discharged within forty-eight hours to the custody of the parent unless steps are taken for involuntary admission.[363] Admission for more than ninety days is prohibited unless the hospital personnel make the same written findings as listed above.[364]

---

[361] Va. Code 16.1-338.B
[362] Va. Code 16.1-338.C
[363] Va. Code 16.1-338.D
[364] Va. Code 16.1-338.E

If a minor turns age fourteen while admitted for involuntary treatment, the facility must advise the minor and the consenting parent within ten days orally and in writing that continued treatment requires the minor's consent.[365]

ii) Where Minor Objects or Unable to Consent

A minor age fourteen or older may be admitted over his objection to a willing facility for up to 120 hours on the application of his parent.[366] Likewise, a minor incapable of making an informed decision[367] may be admitted to a willing facility.[368] A qualified evaluator who is appointed by the CSB, who will not be involved in the minor's treatment, and who has no significant financial interest in the minor's hospitalization must examine the minor within twenty-four hours of admission. The evaluator must prepare a written report and immediately submit it to the juvenile and domestic relations court where the facility is located as to the following conclusions: [369]

1. Because of mental illness, the minor (i) presents a serious danger to himself or others to the extent that severe or irremediable injury is likely to result, as evidenced by recent acts or threats or (ii) is experiencing a serious deterioration of his ability to care for himself in a developmentally age-appropriate manner, as evidenced by delusionary thinking or by a significant impairment of functioning in hydration, nutrition, self-protection, or self-control;

2. The minor is in need of inpatient treatment for a mental illness and is reasonably likely to benefit from the proposed treatment; and

3. Inpatient treatment is the least restrictive alternative that meets the minor's needs.

---

365 Va. Code 16.1-338.F
366 Va. Code 16.1-339.A
367 Va. Code 16.1-336 defines "incapable of making an informed decision,"
368 Va. Code 16.1-339.A,
369 Va. Code 16.1-339.B

When a minor over age 14 is unwillingly admitted, the facility must file a petition for judicial approval no sooner than twenty-four hours and no later than 120 hours after admission.[370] A copy of the petition must be delivered to the minor's consenting parent. The judge will then appoint a guardian *ad litem* for the minor. Based on the views of the minor, the consenting parent, the evaluator, and the attending psychiatrist, as well as the recommendations of the guardian *ad litem*, the court should order that:[371]

1. If the minor does not meet the criteria for admission, the facility shall release the minor into the custody of the consenting parent; or

2. If the minor meets the criteria for admission, continued hospitalization of the minor for up to 90 days shall be authorized based on the parent's consent. Just as for the voluntary admission, a plan of treatment must be prepared within 10 days and include the input of the minor and the consenting parent; or

3. If the available information is insufficient to make a determination, a commitment hearing shall be scheduled. The minor may be detained in the hospital for up to 96 additional hours pending the commitment hearing.

If the parent consenting to the admission revokes his consent at any time, the minor must be released within forty-eight hours[372] to the parent's custody unless involuntary commitment is ordered.[373] If the minor withdraws his objection to the admission, he may be retained in the hospital as described above.[374]

A healthcare provider must make a reasonable effort to contact a

---

[370] Va. Code 16.1-339.C
[371] Va. Code 16.1-339.C
[372] If the 48 hour time period expires on a weekend or holiday, the period is extended to the next day that court will be in session.
[373] Va. Code 16.1-339.E
[374] Va. Code 16.1-339.D

parent and provide relevant information about the minor, including his location and general condition unless the provider knows that 1) the parent is prohibited by a court order from contacting the minor; or 2) information has already been provided to the parent.[375]

iii) Emergency Custody

A minor may be taken into emergency custody and admitted for inpatient treatment based upon the petition of the minor's treating physician or parent, or any responsible adult if the parent is unable or unwilling to file a petition based on probable cause to believe that because of mental illness, the minor present a serious danger to himself or others"

> to the extent that severe or irreversible injury is likely to result, as evidenced by recent acts or threats or is experiencing a serious deterioration of his ability to care for himself in a developmentally age-appropriate manner, as evidenced by delusionary thinking or by a significant impairment of functioning in hydration, nutrition, self-protection, or self-control; and (ii) the minor is in need of compulsory treatment for a mental illness and is reasonably likely to benefit from the proposed treatment."[376]

The minor must remain in custody until a temporary detention order is issued, until released, or until the emergency custody order expires.[377] An emergency custody order is valid for up to eight hours from the time of execution. However, a magistrate may grant an extension for a second period not to exceed four hours if the child is detained in a state facility and efforts are being made to identify an alternative facility.[378]

---

[375] Va. Code 16.1-337.B
[376] Va. Code 16.1-340.A
[377] Va. Code 16.1-370.K
[378] Va. Code 16.1-340.M

iv) Involuntary Temporary Detention

A magistrate may also issue a temporary detention order based on a petition from the same persons and upon the same grounds as that for an emergency custody order.[379] A magistrate may issue a temporary detention order without an emergency custody order proceeding.[380] The duration of temporary detention cannot exceed 96 hours prior to a hearing. If the ninety-six hour period expires on a Saturday, Sunday, or legal holiday, the minor may be detained until the close of business on the next day that is not a Saturday, Sunday, or legal holiday.[381]

v) Involuntary Commitment

A petition for involuntary commitment of a minor may be filed in the juvenile and domestic relations court by a parent or, if the parent is not available or unwilling to file a petition, by any responsible adult.[382] The petition must include the name and address of the petitioner and the minor; set forth in specific terms why the petitioner believes the minor meets the criteria for involuntary commitment; and be made under oath. Where the minor is admitted over his objection but with the parent's consent, the petition filed by the facility will be sufficient assuming that it contains the requisite elements.

When a petition for involuntary commitment is filed, a hearing must be scheduled within no less than twenty-four hours and no more than ninety-six hours from the time that the petition is filed.[383] If the outer limit occurs on a weekend or a holiday, the hearing must be conducted on the next business day not later than ninety-six hours after the petition is filed. A copy of the petition and the notice of

---

[379] Va. Code 16.1-340.1.A
[380] Va. Code 16.1-340.1.C
[381] Va. Code 16.1-340.1.G
[382] Va. Code 16.1-341.A
[383] Va. Code 16.1-341.B

hearing must be served immediately on the minor and the minor's parents[384] if they are not the petitioners.[385]

The CSB serving the area where the minor is located will arrange for an evaluation, if one has not already been performed, by a qualified evaluator who is not and will not be treating the minor and has no significant financial interest in the facility to which the minor would be committed.[386] The petitioner, all public agencies, and all providers or programs who have or who are treating the minor are obligated to cooperate with the evaluator. They also are obligated to promptly deliver, on request and without charge, all records of treatment or education of the minor. At least twenty-four hours before the hearing, the evaluator must submit his written report, which includes his opinion of whether the minor meets the criteria for involuntary commitment. The evaluator is also obligated to attend the hearing as a witness.

If the minor does not have an attorney, the court must appoint a lawyer for him not less than twenty-four hours before the hearing.[387] Counsel may request a continuance of the hearing once for not more than ninety-six hours if good cause is shown. As soon as possible, the minor's attorney must interview the minor; the minor's parent, if available; the petitioner; the qualified evaluator; and all other material witnesses.[388] She is also obligated to examine all relevant diagnostic and other reports. During the hearing, the minor's attorney must obtain independent experts when possible, cross-examine adverse witnesses, present witnesses on behalf of the minor, articulate the wishes of the minor, and otherwise fully represent the minor in the proceeding. A guardian ad litem must

---

[384]   Of interest is that this is the first part of the procedure that appears to require that both parents participate.
[385]   Va. Code 16.1-341.B
[386]   Va. Code 16.1-342
[387]   Va. Code 16.1-341.B
[388]   Va. Code 16.1-343

also be appointed for the child.[389] Counsel will be paid not more than $100 for these efforts.[390]

An involuntary commitment hearing must be conducted under the rules of evidence and similar to a trial.[391] The hearing is to be closed to the public unless the minor and the petitioner request that it be open. The minor or the petitioner has the right of appeal to the circuit court for a *de novo* hearing.

At the commencement of the hearing, the court must inform the minor of his/her right to be voluntarily admitted for inpatient treatment and provide the minor an opportunity for voluntary admission with the consent of the parent(s). In determining whether a minor is capable of consenting to voluntary admission, the court may consider evidence regarding the minor's past compliance or noncompliance with treatment.[392]

The order to involuntarily commit a minor must be supported by clear and convincing evidence that:

1. Because of mental illness, the minor (i) presents a serious danger to himself or others to the extent that severe or irremediable injury is likely to result, as evidenced by recent acts or threats or (ii) is experiencing a serious deterioration of his ability to care for himself in a developmentally age-appropriate manner, as evidenced by delusionary thinking or by a significant impairment of functioning in hydration, nutrition, self-protection, or self-control;

2. The minor is in need of compulsory treatment for a mental illness and is reasonably likely to benefit from the proposed treatment; and

---

[389] Va. Code 16.1-341.B
[390] Va. Code 16.1-343
[391] Va. Code 16.1-344
[392] Va. Code 16.1-344.B

3. If inpatient treatment is ordered, such treatment is the least restrictive alternative that meets the minor's needs. If the court finds that inpatient treatment is not the least restrictive treatment, the court may order the minor to participate in outpatient or other clinically appropriate treatment.[393]

If the parent or parents with whom the minor resides are not willing to approve the proposed commitment, the court will order inpatient treatment only if it finds, in addition to the above criteria, that such treatment is necessary to protect the minor's life, health, or normal development, and that issuance of a removal order or protective order is appropriate.[394] The court may also order outpatient treatment if less restrictive alternatives are appropriate and available.[395]

For the best interests of the minor, the court may enter an order directing either or both of the minor's parents to comply with reasonable conditions relating to the minor's treatment.[396]

Within ten days of commitment, an individualized treatment plan must be developed as described above.[397] The minor must be discharged when he no longer meets the commitment criteria as determined by the hospital staff.[398] A detailed pre-discharge plan must be formulated.[399]

---

[393] Va. Code 16.1-345
[394] Va. Code 16.1-345. Removal or protective orders are described at Va. Code 16.1-252 or 16.1-253.
[395] Va. Code 16.1-345.2
[396] Va. Code 16.1-345
[397] Va. Code 16.1-346.A
[398] Va. Code 16.1-346.B. Of interest is that no independent evaluation is routinely required.
[399] Va. Code 16.1-346.1

E. Human Experimentation

Research involving human subjects conducted in Virginia is regulated by state[400] and/or federal[401] regulations.[402] The definition of human research is very broad. Virginia law defines *human research* as:

> [A]ny systematic investigation, including research development, testing and evaluation, utilizing human subjects, that is designed to develop or contribute to generalized knowledge.[403]

Likewise, federal regulations, in an oblique way of defining human research, define *human subject* as:

> [A] living individual about whom an investigator (whether professional or student) conducting research obtains (1) data through intervention or interaction with the individual, or (2) identifiable private information. 'Intervention' includes both physical procedures by which data are gathered (for example, venipuncture) and manipulations of the subject or the subject's environment that are performed for research purposes. 'Interaction' includes communication or interpersonal contact between investigator and subject. 'Private

---

[400] Va. Code 32.1-162.16 et seq.

[401] 45 C.F.R., Part 46; FDA research is regulated by 21 C.F.R., Parts 50 and 56. An extensive bibliography on the ethical issues of human experimentation can be found at http://www.nlm.nih.gov/pubs/cbm/ hum_exp.html#10.

[402] For a detailed discussion of human research regulation, see Rozovsky & Adams, Clinical Trials and Human Research: A Practical Guide to Regulatory Compliance, Jossey-Bass, 2003

[403] Va. Code 32.1-162.16

information' includes information about behavior that occurs in a context in which an individual can reasonably expect that no observation or recording is taking place, and information which has been provided for specific purposes by an individual and which the individual can reasonably expect will not be made public (for example, a medical record). Private information must be individually identifiable (i.e., the identity of the subject is or may readily be ascertained by the investigator or associated with the information) in order for obtaining the information to constitute research involving human subjects.[404]

This definition from the regulations of the Department of Health & Human Services (HHS) has been summarized in the following question: *"Is there an intervention or an interaction with a living person that would not be occurring or would be occurring in some other fashion but for this research?"*[405]

1. The Common Rule

The regulations promulgated by HHS applying to human research[406] are often referred to as "The Common Rule" because they have been adopted by most other federal departments and agencies that fund research. The Common Rule, which was undergoing major revision in 2016, does not apply to research conducted without federal funds or at institutions that do not receive federal funds. Guidance on what constitutes research under the Common Rule can be found at a number of federal government agency web sites.[407]

---

[404]   45 C.F.R. 46.102(f)

[405]   Office of Human Research Protection, DHHS, http://www.hhs.gov/ohrp/humansubjects/guidance/decisioncharts.htm

[406]   45 C.F.R., Part 46

[407]   For example, helpful charts can be found at http://www.hhs.gov/ohrp/humansubjects/guidance/decisioncharts.htm

Research that is exempted from The Common Rule includes:

1. Educational testing and educational research;

2. Survey or interview techniques where the human subject remains anonymous;

3. Public observation where the human subject remains anonymous;

4. The collection or study of existing data, documents, records, pathological specimens, or diagnostic specimens, "if these sources are publicly available or if the information is recorded so that the human subjects remain anonymous; and

5. Research and demonstration projects of the Social Security program.[408]

The federal government agency overseeing a program retains final authority to determine whether a particular activity is covered by these regulations.[409] It also has the authority to waive applicability of the regulations to specific research activities or classes of research activity.[410] The Office for Human Research Protection has a toll-free telephone number for research activity questions.[411]

Additional protections are provided for groups considered to be vulnerable, such as pregnant women;[412] prisoners;[413] and children.[414]

2. *The Virginia Human Research Statute*

The Virginia statute applies to all human research conducted in the

[408] 45 C.F.R. 101(b)
[409] 45 C.F.R. 101(c)
[410] 45 C.F.R. 101(e)
[411] OHRP toll-free telephone number 866/447-4777
[412] 45 C.F.R., Part 46, Subpart B
[413] 45 C.F.R., Part 46, Subpart C
[414] 45 C.F.R., Part 46, Subpart D

Commonwealth, without regard to funding source.[415] *Human research* is defined as "any systematic investigation, including research development, testing and evaluation, utilizing human subjects, that is designed to develop or contribute to generalized knowledge."[416] The only exceptions are those specifically enumerated[417] or where the research is subject to federal regulation.[418] The key features of the statute are the functions of the human research review committee and the obtaining of informed consent.

The several specified exemptions to the state statute rarely pertain to the clinical research setting. However, they include:

1. Specified activities of the Virginia Department of Health;

2. Learning outcomes assessments in the educational setting;

3. Survey or interview procedures where the responses are anonymous;

4. Surveys or interviews of elected or appointed public officials or candidates for public office;

5. Solely the observation of public behavior where participants remain anonymous; or

6. "Research involving the collection or study of existing data, documents, records, pathological specimens, or diagnostic specimens, if these sources are publicly available or if the information is recorded by the investigator in a manner so that subjects cannot be identified, directly or through identifiers linked to the subjects."[419]

The coverage of the Act is muddied by a modification of the definition

---

[415] Va. Code 32.1-162.18

[416] Va. Code 32.1-162.16

[417] Va. Code 32.1-162.17

[418] Va. Code 32.1-162.20. State agencies may also opt out of the statute by promulgating their own regulations that incorporate the federal policies and regulations.

[419] Va. Code 32.1-162.17.

section that added, "Human research shall not be deemed to include research exempt from federal research regulation pursuant to 45 CFR 46.101(b)."[420] The 101(b) exemptions are listed above.

The crux of these exemptions is to require application of the state statute except in the instance where the human subject is not put at any risk from participating in the research and cannot be identified.

Enforcement of the state statute is only obliquely described as by injunction or other enforcement actions available.[421]

a. Human Research Review Committee

Each institution or agency that conducts or authorizes human research in Virginia must establish a human research review committee (HRRC)[422] to review and approve research.[423] The definition of who is included in this requirement is much broader than solely hospitals or large health care organizations. The definition includes all legal entities, including individuals.[424] Every person conducting or proposing to conduct human research must affiliate with a research review committee.[425]

The composition of the HRRC is not explicitly stated or even suggested beyond forbidding the researcher or administrative supervisor of the research to be on the committee. The only admonition is that it "should be composed of representatives of varied backgrounds to ensure the competent, complete, and professional review of human research activities ..."[426] A minimum or maximum size of the

---

[420] Va. Code 32.1-162.16

[421] Va. Code 32.1-162.20

[422] Federal regulations refer to this committee as an Institutional Review Board (IRB)

[423] Va. Code 32.1-162.19.A

[424] Va. Code 32.1-162.16

[425] Va. Code 32.1-162.19.D

[426] Va. Code 32.1-162.19.A

committee is also not delineated. The members of a research review committee may be immune from civil liability.[427]

An HRRC must review and approve all proposed human research before it is started. The committee must consider: [428]

1. The adequacy of the description of the potential benefits and risks involved and the adequacy of the methodology of the research;

2. If the research is nontherapeutic, whether it presents more than a minimal risk to the human subjects;

3. Whether the rights and welfare of the human subjects involved are adequately protected;

4. Whether the risks to the human subjects are outweighed by the potential benefits to them;

5. Whether the informed consent is to be obtained by methods that are adequate and appropriate and whether the written consent form is adequate and appropriate in both content and language for the particular research;

6. Whether the persons proposing to conduct the particular human research are appropriately competent and qualified; and

7. Whether the criteria for selection of subjects are equitable.

An HRRC also must require periodic reports from each existing project to ensure that the project is being carried out in conformity with the proposal as approved.[429] Unfortunately, no further guidance is available as to what is sufficient to meet the *periodic* requirement.

An expedited review may be done, pursuant to an HRRC's policies, if

---

[427]   Va. Code 8.01-44.1
[428]   Va. Code 32.1-162.19.B
[429]   Va. Code 32.1-162.19.B

a project involves no more than minimal risk to the human subjects and:

1. Another research review committee has reviewed and approved the project; or

2. The review involves only minor changes in previously approved research and the changes occur during the approved project period.[430]

The activities of an HRRC have rarely been considered by a trial court. In one of the few judicial opinions on the topic, the failure of a facility's review committee to consider the ramifications of the inter-institutional transfer of cryo-preserved human pre-zygotes did not vitiate the contract between the parties nor did it usurp the court's jurisdiction to settle contractual disputes between the parties.[431]

An HRRC must publish a list of its approved projects and results on a website.[432]

b. Informed Consent

Written and witnessed informed consent[433] must be obtained from:

1. Any person who is the subject of *human research*, as defined in the statute,[434]

2. If incompetent at the time consent is required, from the person's authorized representative;[435] or

---

[430] Va. Code 32.1-162.19.C

[431] York v. Jones, 717 F. Supp. 421 (E.D. Va. 1989) interpreting former Virginia statute on human research

[432] Va. Code 32.1-162.19.E

[433] Va. Code 32.1-162.18.A. Written informed consent is also explicitly required for psychiatric in-patients. 12 Va. Admin. Code 35-120-40.D

[434] Va. Code 32.1-162.16

[435] Va. Code 32.1-162.16 lists the priorities of individuals who may consent as a legally authorized representative

3. If a minor otherwise capable of rendering informed consent, from both the minor and his authorized representative.

Informed consent is defined as:

> the knowing and voluntary agreement, without undue inducement or any element of force, fraud, deceit, duress, or other form of constraint or coercion, of a person who is capable of exercising free power of choice."

The written consent form must include:[436]

1. A "reasonable and comprehensible" explanation of the proposed procedures and protocols to be followed and their purposes;

2. A description of any attendant discomfort;

3. A description of reasonably expected risks and benefits;

4. A disclosure of advantageous alternative procedures or therapies;

5. An instruction that the person may withdraw consent and discontinue participation at any time;

6. An explanation of the costs or compensation involved; and

7. An offer to answer any inquiries about the procedures or protocols.

The written consent form must not include any language suggesting that the subject "waives or appears to waive any of his legal rights, including any release of any individual, institution, or agency or any agents thereof from liability for negligence."[437] Where a prospective research participant is incapacitated, his representative is not allowed to consent to nontherapeutic research 1) if the representative knows,

---

[436] Va. Code 32.1-162.16.
[437] Va. Code 32.1-162.18.A

or reasonably should know, that the research protocol is contrary to the religious beliefs or basic values of the prospective subject or 2) unless the HRRC has determined that it will present no more than a minor increase over minimal risk to the incompetent individual.[438] An investigator has an obligation to obtain the prospective consent of a research participant or his surrogate decision maker. In addition, an investigator must assure that a prospective participant has sufficient opportunity to consider his decision and the possibility of coercion or undue influence is minimized.[439]

An HRRC may alter or waive the requirement to obtain written informed consent if it finds and documents that:

1. The research involves no more than minimal risk to the subjects;

2. The omission, alteration or waiver will not adversely affect the rights and welfare of the subjects;

3. The research could not practicably be performed without the omission, alteration or waiver; and

4. After participation, the subjects are to be provided with additional pertinent information, whenever appropriate.[440]

An HRRC may also waive the requirement of written informed consent where the only record linking the human subject and the research would be the consent document and the principal risk would be potential harm resulting from a breach of confidentiality. However, a written statement explaining the research may be required to be provided to each subject, and he should be asked whether he wants documentation linking him to the research. The subject's wishes will govern.[441]

---

[438]   Va. Code 32.1-162.18.B
[439]   Va. Code 32.1-162.18.C
[440]   Va. Code 32.1-162.18.D
[441]   Va. Code 32.1-162.18.E

3. Health Insurance Coverage for Clinical Trials

Virginia law requires that a health insurance company provide coverage for patient costs incurred during participation in clinical trials for treatment studies of cancer.[442] *Patient costs* do not include expenses associated with managing or conducting the clinical trial or the cost of the investigational drug or device.[443] Such costs are routinely borne by the sponsor of the study. The National Cancer Institute, Food & Drug Administration, Veteran's Administration, or one of their affiliates must approve the clinical trial.[444] In other studies, the health insurer pays for the usual and customary treatment while the study sponsor pays for the additional services required to accomplish the study.

---

[442] Va. Code 38.2-3418.8.A
[443] Va. Code 38.2-3418.8.C
[444] Va. Code 38.2-3418.8.E

F. Family / Reproductive Issues

1. Sterilization

Written consent must be obtained prior to performing a permanent sterilization procedure.[445] A "full, reasonable and comprehensible medical explanation as to the meaning and consequences of such an operation" by the surgeon is required. Alternative methods of contraception must also be explained. The Virginia statute also has a thirty-day "cooling off" period for anyone who is not a natural or adoptive parent. The consent of a spouse is not required. However, the better practice is to try to include a husband and wife in this important decision. This helps reduce potential misunderstandings by either spouse as to the expected outcome of the procedure.

Similarly, sterilization of one under age eighteen[446] or mentally incompetent[447] is limited. For mentally impaired minors between the age of fourteen and eighteen, a court may approve permanent sterilization where the evidence is clear and convincing that a child will never mentally develop to the point of being able to make his own informed judgment.[448] The procedure must occur more than thirty days after entry of the court's order. A similar mechanism is available for mentally incompetent adults.[449] The court must report all such authorizations to the State Registrar of Vital Records.[450]

---

[445] Va. Code 54.1-2974
[446] See Va. Code 54.1-2969 and 54.1-2986.C
[447] See Va. Code 37.2-1102 as well as the Virginia Health Care Decisions Act, below
[448] Va. Code 54.1-2975
[449] Va. Code 54.1-2976
[450] Va. Code 54.1-2978

2. Assisted Conception

a. Disclosure to Patient

Prior to a physician commencing infertility therapy, a patient must execute a disclosure form that includes at least the following information:

1. The rates of success for the particular procedure at the clinic or hospital;

2. The testing protocol for assuring that donor material is free of known HIV infection;

3. The total number of live births;

4. The total number of live births as a percentage of completed retrieval cycles;

5. The rates for clinical pregnancy and delivery per completed retrieval cycle bracketed by age groups consisting of women under age 30, 30 to 34, 35 to 39, and 40 and older.

Any donor gametes used in artificial insemination, in vitro fertilization or other techniques must be screened for HIV status.[451]

b. Parent / Child Designation

i) Assisted Conception

Where a child is born to a married couple due to assisted conception, Virginia law presumes that the husband and the wife are the parents of the child. Donors of sperm or ova have no parental rights or duties for such a child.[452]

---

[451]   Va. Code 32.1-45.3

[452]   Va. Code 32.1-257.D; Va. Code 20-158; However, a father and mother who executed a sworn "Acknowledgment of Paternity," a pre-birth custody and visitation agreement and had his name placed on the birth certificate is not barred from petitioning for a determination of parentage pursuant to Va. Code 20-49.1(B)(2). Breit v. Mason, 59 Va.

With modern techniques, conception can occur after one spouse is deceased or the couple has divorced. Virginia law addresses these scenarios. Where a spouse dies within ten months prior to the birth, the law states that the husband and the wife are the parents of the child.[453] On the other hand, a person is not the parent where he or she dies prior to conception unless implantation occurs before notice of the death can reasonably be communicated to the physician performing the procedure or the person consents to be a parent in writing. A child born more than ten months after the death of a parent is not recognized as an heir.[454]

Any child conceived using a husband's sperm, with his consent, to inseminate a wife's ovum is the child of the husband and wife even if either of them has filed for divorce or annulment in the ten months prior to the birth.[455] Where the husband and wife are parties to a divorce or annulment action, the person is not deemed to be the parent of an artificially conceived child unless implantation occurs before notice of the filing can reasonably be communicated to the physician performing the procedure or the person consents in writing to be a parent, either before or after implantation.

Looking at court decisions in other states, the Massachusetts Supreme Judicial Court has held that a consent form signed by a husband giving frozen pre-embryos to wife was invalid due to a change in circumstances (the couple were in divorce proceedings) and public policy against enforcement.[456] The husband's interest in avoiding procreation outweighed the wife's interest in having additional children. The Court was "dubious at best that [the consent form] represents the intent of the husband and the wife regarding disposition of the pre-embryos in the case of a dispute between

App. 322, 718 S.E.2d 482 (2011), aff'd sub nom. L.F. v. Breit, 285 Va. 163, 736 S.E.2d 711 (2013)

[453] Va. Code 20-158.B

[454] Va. Code 20-164; also see Va. Code 64.1-8.1 (afterborn heirs)

[455] Va. Code 20-158.C

[456] A.Z. v. B.Z., 431 Mass. 150, 725 N.E.2d 1051 (2000)

them" and that, in any event, the circumstances indicated that the form should not be enforced.

The New Jersey Appellate Court has reached a similar result by concluding that a contract whereby a husband and wife would relinquish ownership of their cryo-preserved embryos to the in vitro fertilization program if their marriage was dissolved was unenforceable.[457]

ii) Surrogacy Arrangements

Surrogacy arrangements raise all sorts of curious situations. Acting as a surrogacy broker is prohibited.[458] This does not include the role of an attorney in advising a surrogate or the intended parents as part of entering into a surrogacy contract.[459] Virginia law expressly recognizes that surrogacy contracts are permissible.[460] The procedure for petitioning a court for approval of a surrogacy contract is set forth by statute.[461] The court is to consider the appropriateness of such a contract prior to conception. Either party may terminate a surrogacy contract prior to conception.[462] The surrogate may also terminate the agreement up to 180 days after the last assisted conception procedure.[463] Where court approval of a surrogacy contract has not been obtained prior to conception, the court has the authority to reform the agreement to comply with the statute.[464] The intended parents are generally responsible for payment of medical care and ancillary services, unless the surrogate

---

[457] J.B. v. M.B., 331 N.J. Super. 223, 751 A.2d 613 (App. Div. 2000), aff'd as modified, 170 N.J. 9, 783 A.2d 707 (2001)
[458] Va. Code 20-165.A. Violation of the statute is a Class 1 misdemeanor. In addition, the surrogate and intended parents can split an award of three times the fee due to the broker. Va. Code 20-165.B
[459] Va. Code 20-165.C
[460] Va. Code 20-159
[461] Va. Code 20-160
[462] Va. Code 20-161.A
[463] Va. Code 20-161.B
[464] Va. Code 20-162

terminates the contract.[465] The surrogate is solely responsible for the clinical management of the pregnancy.[466] A child born within 300 days of assisted conception procedures is presumed to have resulted from the assisted conception.[467]

Virginia law deems the intended parents to be the parents after approval of a surrogacy contract by the court.[468] If the court vacates the surrogacy contract, the surrogate is deemed to be the mother of the resulting child and her husband is the father. The intended parents may only obtain parental rights through adoption.

Where a court does not approve a surrogacy contract, the parentage is determined by the following rules in Virginia:

1. The gestational mother is the child's mother unless the intended mother is a genetic parent, in which case the intended mother is the mother.

2. If either of the intended parents is a genetic parent, the intended father is the child's father. However, if (i) the surrogate is married, (ii) her husband is a party to the surrogacy contract, and (iii) the surrogate exercises her right to retain custody and parental rights to the resulting child, then the surrogate and her husband are the parents.

3. If neither of the intended parents is a genetic parent, the surrogate woman is the mother and her husband is the father if he is a party to the contract. The intended parents may only obtain parental rights through adoption.

4. After signing and filing of the surrogate consent and report form in conformance with the statute, the intended parents are the parents of the child. The surrogate and her husband, if any, are not the parents of the child.[469]

---

[465] Va. Code 20-162

[466] Va. Code 20-163.A

[467] Va. Code 20-163.D

[468] Va. Code 20-158.D

[469] Va. Code 20-158.E

Birth certificates may be amended to reflect the intended parents.[470]

3. Abortion

a. In General

Virginia law starts with the broad statement that intending to destroy an unborn child is a criminal act.[471] Likewise, the Board of Medicine considers procuring, performing, aiding or abetting a criminal abortion to be unprofessional conduct.[472] The law then goes on to describe a number of exceptions. Abortion is legal in Virginia during the first trimester[473] of pregnancy if performed by a licensed physician.[474] During the second trimester, abortion is permitted if performed by a licensed physician in a licensed hospital.[475] Abortion is legal after the second trimester only if it is performed in an attempt to protect against significant danger to the medical or mental health of the woman.[476] This must be certified by the physician and two consulting physicians "and so entered in the hospital record of the woman."[477] If an abortion is performed after the second trimester, the physician must attempt to sustain the life of the product of such abortion if there is any "clearly visible" evidence of viability.[478]

---

[470]   Va. Code 20-49.1(A) and 20-49.4; see Davenport v. Little-Bowser, 269 Va. 546 (2005)

[471]   Va. Code 18.2-71

[472]   Va. Code 54.1-2914.A

[473]   "Trimester" is not defined by in the Virginia statutes. See Roe v. Wade, 410 U.S. 113

[474]   Va. Code 18.2-72. Outpatient abortion clinics are deemed to be a category of outpatient hospital. 12 Va. Admin. Code 5-410-10

[475]   Va. Code 18.2-73. See Simopoulos v. Com., 221 Va. 1059, 277 S.E.2d 194 (1981), aff'd sub nom. Simopoulos v. Virginia, 462 U.S. 506, 103 S. Ct. 2532, 76 L. Ed. 2d 755 (1983)

[476]   Va. Code 18.2-74

[477]   Va. Code 18.2-74(b)

[478]   Va. Code 18.2-74(c)

A physician may perform an abortion at any time in order to save a woman's life.[479]

When an abortion is to be performed in an outpatient surgical hospital,[480] the physician performing the procedure is responsible for diagnosing pregnancy.[481] An outpatient surgical hospital must offer each patient appropriate counseling and instruction in the abortion procedure and in birth control methods.[482]

b. Informed Consent

A physician must obtain the *informed written consent* of the pregnant woman before performing an abortion.[483] The statute is very detailed in the information that must be given to a woman.[484] In 2012, the General Assembly added the controversial provision of requiring an ultrasound to be performed and made available to the woman.[485] Consent of the husband or putative father of the fetus is not required.[486] In the event that the woman is incapacitated, the performing physician must obtain the written consent of a parent, guardian or other person standing in *loco parentis*. A court is not allowed to authorize a nontherapeutic abortion for an incompetent patient.[487] Likewise, a judge is prohibited from authorizing a nontherapeutic abortion for an incompetent prisoner.[488]

---

[479] Va. Code 18.2-74.1

[480] Abortion clinics are deemed to be outpatient hospitals. 12 Va. Admin. Code 5-410-10

[481] 12 Va. Admin. Code 5-410-1270.D

[482] 12 Va. Admin. Code 5-410-1270.E

[483] Va. Code 18.2-76

[484] Va. Code 18.2-76.D

[485] Va. Code 18.2-76.B & C, as amended by HB462 (2012)

[486] Planned Parenthood of Cent. Missouri v. Danforth, 428 U.S. 52, 74, 96 S. Ct. 2831, 49 L. Ed. 2d 788 (1976)

[487] Va. Code 37.2-110.2

[488] Va. Code 53.1-40.1

c. Conscientious Objector

Neither a physician nor a hospital is required to perform abortions.[489] If a physician or hospital refuses to perform abortions for moral, ethical, personal or religious reasons, the refusal cannot form the basis of any claim for damages on account of such refusal. The statute is interesting in that it also covers *persons* in addition to hospitals and physicians who may elect not to participate in abortions. Presumably this is intended to cover nurses and other allied health employees. A "conscientious objector" cannot be the subject of disciplinary actions or refused employment solely on the basis of his objection to participating in abortions.[490]

d. Partial Birth Abortion

The 1998 version of the Virginia partial birth abortion statute[491] is unconstitutional and cannot be enforced by the Commonwealth. The Virginia Attorney General attempted to distinguish between partial birth abortion and the dilation and extraction procedure (D & E), interpreting Va. Code 18.74.2.[492] The Attorney General stated that D & E is distinguishable from a partial birth abortion. In a D & E, the fetus is terminated and dismembered in the uterus. In partial birth abortion, the fetus is substantially delivered before being terminated. Not accepting this argument, the U. S. District Court struck down the partial birth abortion statute as being too vague. [493] This decision was upheld by the U. S. Court of Appeals, Fourth Circuit,[494] and indirectly by the U. S. Supreme Court reviewing a

---

[489] Va. Code 18.2-75
[490] Va. Code 18.2-75
[491] Va. Code 18.2-74.2
[492] 1998 Op. Va. Att'y Gen. DL-7
[493] Richmond Med. Ctr. for Women v. Gilmore, 55 F. Supp. 2d 441 (E.D. Va. 1999), aff'd, 224 F.3d 337 (4th Cir. 2000)
[494] Richmond Med. Ctr. for Women v. Gilmore, 144 F.3d 326 (4th Cir. 1998); stay lifted 219 F.3d 376 (4th Cir. 2000)

similar Nebraska statute.[495] The General Assembly annually attempts to enact another version.

e. Minors

Virginia law requires *notice* to an *authorized person* or a judicial authorization before a minor receives an abortion.[496] *Authorized person* is defined as a parent, guardian or custodian of a minor or a person standing *in loco parentis*.[497] Examples of the latter include a grandparent or adult sibling with whom the minor regularly resides and who has care and control of the minor. No notice or judicial authorization is required where a minor is emancipated.[498] Laws requiring parental or spousal consent in all instances, as Virginia once had, were found to be unconstitutional.[499] *Notice* can be achieved in any of the following ways:

1. The physician or his agent has given actual notice of his intention to perform such abortion to an authorized person, either in person or by telephone, at least twenty-four hours prior to the performance of the abortion; or

2. The physician or his agent, after a reasonable effort to notify an authorized person, has mailed notice to an authorized person by certified mail, addressed to such person at his

[495] Stenberg v. Carhart, 530 U.S. 914, 120 S. Ct. 2597, 147 L. Ed. 2d 743 (2000)
[496] Va. Code 16.1-241.V. For a discussion of the law prior to the amendment adding Va. Code 54.1-2969.I, see Winchester Mem'l Hosp. v. Boyce, 10 Va. Cir. 541 (1984)
[497] Va. Code 16.1-241.V
[498] Va. Code 16.1-241.V. Emancipation for the purposes of this statute are defined as having been validly married; on active duty in US armed forces; willingly living separate and apart from her parents or guardian, with their acquiescence; or having received an order of emancipation under Va. Code 16.1-331.
[499] Planned Parenthood of Cent. Missouri v. Danforth, 428 U.S. 52, 74, 96 S. Ct. 2831, 49 L. Ed. 2d 788 (1976) discussed in The Honorable Aubrey M. Davis, Jr., 1978-79 Va. Op. Atty. Gen. 3; Bellotti v. Baird, 443 U.S. 622, 99 S. Ct. 3035, 61 L. Ed. 2d 797 (1979)

usual place of abode, with return receipt requested, at least seventy-two hours prior to the performance of the abortion; or

3. At least one authorized person is present with the minor seeking the abortion; or

4. The minor has delivered to the physician a written statement signed by an authorized person and witnessed by a competent adult that the authorized person knows of the minor's intent to have an abortion.[500]

A physician may perform an abortion on a minor without notice or judicial authorization if he makes a good faith judgment and documents in the patient's medical record that:

1. The minor declares that she is abused or neglected and the attending physician has reason to suspect that the minor may be an abused or neglected child[501] and reports the suspected abuse or neglect[502]; or

2. In the attending physician's good faith medical judgment, (i) the abortion is medically necessary immediately to avert the minor's death or (ii) there is insufficient time to provide the required notice or judicial authorization because a delay would create a serious risk of substantial impairment of a major bodily function or substantial physical injury.[503]

The procedure for obtaining authorization from a Juvenile and Domestic Relations District Court is set forth by statute.[504] A minor may elect to pursue this route in lieu of notifying her parent or guardian. She may participate in the proceedings. No filing fee is charged, and the Court must advise her that counsel can be

---

[500] Va. Code 16.1-241.V
[501] As defined in Va. Code 63.1-248.2
[502] In accordance with Va. Code 63.1-248.3
[503] Va. Code 16.1-241.V
[504] Va. Code 16.1-241.V

appointed for her. The judge may authorize the abortion if the judge finds that:

1. The minor is mature and capable of giving informed consent to the proposed abortion; or
2. If the minor is found not to be mature, the performance of an abortion upon the minor without notice to an authorized person would be in the minor's best interest.

The hearing of a minor's petition for an abortion is given precedence over other pending matters and in no event should be delayed more than four days after the petition is filed. If the court does not authorize the abortion, a minor has the right to be heard by the Circuit Court in an expedited appeal not more than five days after the appeal is filed. An order authorizing the abortion without notification cannot be appealed. If the court does not proceed with the minor's request in a timely manner, the court is required to immediately provide the minor with such an authorization.

f. Public Funding of Abortion

In general, Medicaid will not pay for elective abortion. However, the legislature has mandated that the Department of Medical Assistance fund abortions for pregnant women who otherwise qualify for Medicaid where a pregnancy occurs as a result of rape or incest and the crime is reported to the police or public health agency.[505] Medicaid is also mandated to pay for abortions of qualified women where a physician certifies in writing, "after appropriate tests have been performed, that he believes the fetus will be born with a gross and totally incapacitating physical deformity or with a gross and totally incapacitating mental deficiency."[506]

---

[505] Va. Code 32.1-92.1
[506] Va. Code 32.1-92.2; 12 Va. Admin. Code 30-140-350

g. Security Issues

One means of attempting to control anti-abortion activists is by injunction. A court may grant a temporary or permanent injunction to prohibit unlawful interference with the clinic and harassment of its patrons. However, an activist must either be a party to the injunction or have actual notice of the injunction.[507] If enforcement of such an injunction is by criminal contempt proceeding, the defendant is entitled to a trial by jury.[508] An attempt by activists to avoid conviction for trespassing at an abortion clinic under the defense of necessity has been rejected.[509] The Court of Appeals based its decision on the finding that "reasonable, noncriminal means were available to achieve the defendants' purposes."[510]

h. Advertising of Abortion Services

The Virginia law[511] prohibiting the publication, lecture, advertisement, or by the sale or circulation of any publication, or through the use of a referral agency for profit, or in any other manner, encourage or promote the performing of an abortion or the inducing of a miscarriage was struck down by the Supreme Court of the United States.[512] The statute unconstitutionally infringed on a physician's First Amendment rights.

4. Tort Liability Related to Reproduction

For a case discussing the negligence of a physician in testing for birth defects and therefore preventing the informed decision of a couple about aborting or continuing a pregnancy, see Naccash

---

[507] Powell v. Ward, 15 Va. App. 553 (1993)
[508] Powell v. Ward, 15 Va. App. 553 (1993)
[509] Buckley v. City of Falls Church, 7 Va. App. 32 (1988)
[510] Buckley v. City of Falls Church, 7 Va. App. 32, 34 (1988)
[511] Va. Code 18.2-76.1
[512] Bigelow v. Com., 214 Va. 341, 200 S.E.2d 680 (1973), rev'd sub nom. Bigelow v. Virginia, 421 U.S. 809, 95 S. Ct. 2222, 44 L. Ed. 2d 600 (1975)

v. Burger.[513] The father's blood sample was mislabeled, and the couple was incorrectly advised that the fetus did not suffer from Tay-Sachs disease. The parents were entitled to recover damages for expenses incurred in caring for the afflicted child and emotional distress. Virginia does not recognize a cause of action by the child for "wrongful life."[514] Further, Virginia does not allow recovery by the parents for the cost of rearing a reasonably healthy child.[515]

A physician may be liable to a woman when an abortion fails and a child is born.[516] However, damages in a *wrongful pregnancy* case exclude the cost of raising a reasonably healthy child.[517] The damages potentially recoverable include medical expenses, pain and suffering, lost wages for a reasonable period resulting from the negligently performed abortion, continuing pregnancy, and ensuing childbirth. The mother is also allowed to seek recovery of damages for emotional distress proximately caused by the physical injury.

5. *Establishing Paternity*

Virginia law sets forth the procedure for genetic testing where paternity is disputed.[518] Establishing that no breaks in the chain of custody from the time of collecting a sample to completion of definitive testing occurred is important.[519] However, an affidavit as to the test results may be sufficient proof on which a court can base a finding of paternity.[520] Evidence is permissible as to the putative father's access to the mother during the probable period

---

[513] Naccash v. Burger, 223 Va. 406 (1982). This cause of action is known as "wrongful birth."

[514] Miller v. Johnson, 231 Va. 177 (1986) discussed in Glascock v. Laserna, 30 Va. Cir. 366 (1993)

[515] Miller v. Johnson, 231 Va. 177, 186-87 (1986)

[516] Miller v. Johnson, 231 Va. 177 (1986)

[517] Miller v. Johnson, 231 Va. 177 (1986)

[518] Va. Code 20-49.3

[519] Buckland v. Commonwealth, 229 Va. 290, 296 (1985)

[520] Va. Code 20-49.3.C

of conception.[521] Likewise, evidence as to the mother's sexual activity is properly limited to a reasonable period of conception.[522] The standard of proof required to establish paternity is "clear and convincing evidence."[523]

Hospitals are obligated to give "unwed parents the opportunity to legally establish the paternity of a child" prior to the child's discharge from the hospital.[524] This takes the form of providing information to the couple about how to voluntarily acknowledge paternity and the implications of doing so. The Department of Social Services is to pay a hospital for each acknowledgement signed by both parents under oath.

[521] Va. Code 20-49.4
[522] Buckland v. Commonwealth, 229 Va. 290, 296 (1985)
[523] Va. Code 20-94.4
[524] Va. Code 20-49.9

G. Prescription of Medications

1. In General

A controlled substance may only be dispensed by a pharmacy based on a prescription by a physician, podiatrist, dentist, nurse practitioner, physician assistant or TPA-certified optometrist.[525] A prescription must be based on a valid practitioner-patient relationship and for a valid medicinal or therapeutic purpose. Otherwise, the prescriber is subject to criminal penalties.[526] Writing a prescription for a fictitious patient can be prosecuted as a felony.[527] A pharmacist knowingly filling an invalid prescription is also subject to criminal penalties.[528]

A bona fide practitioner-patient relationship for prescribing is defined as including:[529]

- Obtaining a medical or drug history
- Providing information to the patient about the benefits and risks of the drug being prescribed

---

[525] Va. Code 54.1-3303.A; the schedules of controlled substances begin at Va. Code 54.1-3444

[526] Va. Code 54.1-3303.A citing Va. Code 18.2-248; an exception is the prescribing of antibiotics and antivirals for those in close contact with a diagnosed contagious patient of the practitioner. See Va. Code 54.1-3303

[527] Va. Code 18.2-258.1; Pancoast v. Commonwealth, 2 Va. App. 28 (1986)

[528] Va. Code 54.1-3303.B citing Va. Code 18.2-248

[529] Va. Code 54.1-3303.A

- Perform or have performed an appropriate examination of the patient, usually by the prescriber; and

- Initiate additional interventions and follow-up care, if necessary, especially if a prescribed drug may have serious side effects.

A pharmacist may fill a prescription of an out-of-state licensed physician, podiatrist or dentist.[530] On the other hand, out-of-state pharmacies shipping Schedule II through VI prescriptions into Virginia must register with the Board of Pharmacy and comply with the state's pharmacy laws and regulations.[531] A non-resident pharmacy can be registered with the Virginia Board only if it is licensed as a pharmacy in a jurisdiction that can lawfully deliver drugs within the United States.[532]

Prior to filling a prescription, a pharmacist may obtain a fingerprint from a customer as proof of the customer's identification, provided the pharmacist complies with the requirement that the fingerprint be retained for no more than twenty-one days.[533] A pharmacist may provide the fingerprint of any customer suspected of prescription fraud to law-enforcement officials.[534] Beginning in 2010, a pharmacist must obtain proof of identify from anyone seeking to fill a Schedule II prescription before dispensing, must make a copy of it and keep it for at least one year unless the patient is known to the pharmacist.[535] One enjoys immunity from civil damages for reporting in good faith that one suspects that a patient has obtained or attempted to obtain controlled substances by fraud or deceit to the police.[536] Similarly,

---

[530]   Va. Code 54.1-3303.C. However the statute does not list nurse practitioners, physician assistants, or optometrists among "practitioners." It also does not recognize non-U.S. licensed practitioners.
[531]   Va. Code 54.1-3434.1.
[532]   Va. Code 54.1-3434.1
[533]   Va. Code 59.1-478
[534]   2002 Op.Atty.Gen., January 11, 2002
[535]   Va. Code 54.1-3420.1
[536]   Va. Code 54.1-3408.2

a wholesale distributor that ceases distribution of controlled drugs to a dispenser because of suspicious orders of controlled substance must notify the Board within five days.[537] The wholesale distributor is immune from civil liability for giving the notice.

Some courts of other states have ruled that a pharmacist can be held liable for filling prescriptions in a dangerous amount of narcotic drugs, even though the prescriptions were written by a physician.[538] The Supreme Court of Virginia has not considered the issue yet. Additionally, the US Drug Enforcement Administration has begun cracking down on wholesale distributors who fill suspicious orders for narcotics from pharmacy customers.[539]

The Supreme Court of the United States has affirmed that a pharmacist has a free speech right to advertise his ability to mix specific drug compounds.[540] Pharmacists are authorized to compound under certain circumstances.[541] *Compounding* does not include mixing, diluting or reconstituting a manufacturer's product when performed by a physician for administration to his patient.[542]

In 2008, the General Assembly directed the Board of Pharmacy to establish a Prescription Drug Donation Program that would accept previously dispensed prescriptions for redistribution to the indigent.[543] Filling a prescription with a biosimilar product is permitted unless specifically not prohibited by the prescriber.[544]

---

[537] Va. Code 54.1-3435.B and 54.1-3435.01.D
[538] For example, see <u>Powers v. Thobani</u>, (Fla. Ct. App. June 1, 2005)
[539] See "Cardinal Agrees to Shipping Ban Over Oxycodone Orders," Law360, 15 May 2012
[540] <u>Thompson v. W. States Med. Ctr.</u>, 535 U.S. 357, 122 S. Ct. 1497, 152 L. Ed. 2d 563 (2002)
[541] Va. Code 54.1-3410.2
[542] Va. Code 54.1-3401
[543] Va. Code 54.1-3411.1.B
[544] Va. Code 54.1-3408.04

a. Prescription versus Administration

A prescribing health care professional may delegate the actual administration of a medication to others who have been trained to do so.[545] This not only includes nurses and other licensed health care providers, but may also include, for example, a school official who has been trained to give insulin to a diabetic student. Staff at assisted living, mental health, or other licensed facilities may also give medications within Board of Pharmacy guidelines after completing a training program approved by the Board of Nursing.[546] Collaborative practice agreements to have a pharmacist more actively involved in patient care are governed by state statutes[547] and regulation.[548]

Police officers and firefighters who have completed training may possess and administer opioid antagonists for overdose reversal.[549]

b. The Form of a Prescription

Though substantially replaced by electronic prescribing, the form of a prescription is quite specific under Virginia law.[550] A prescription must be written with ink, individually typed or printed and contain:

- The name, address & telephone number of the prescriber
- The prescriber's DEA number, if prescription is for other than Schedule VI substance
- The first and last name of the patient
- The address of the patient (may be placed by the dispenser or recorded in an electronic dispensing record)
- The date of issue

---

[545] Va. Code 54.1-3408; Medical assistant explicitly was added by HB 2037 (2007)
[546] Va. Code 54.1-3408.J
[547] Va. Code 54.1-3300 et seq.
[548] 18 Va. Admin. Code 110-40-10 through 70
[549] Va. Code 54.1-3408.X
[550] Va. Code 54.1-3408.01

- The prescriber's signature on the day of issue; and
- Only one prescription

A nurse or other agent may prepare a prescription document for the prescriber.[551] A prescription by a medical intern or resident must bear an identification number assigned by the hospital.[552] The prescriber's information must be either preprinted, electronically printed, typewritten, rubber stamped, or printed by hand on the prescription blank. The form must also indicate if it is a "brand medically necessary."[553] This may be handwritten or pre-printed as a check box or other option on a prescription form. Prescriptions for federal healthcare plan patients (Medicaid, Medicare, FAMIS, etc.) must be on tamper-resistant prescription pads.[554]

A prescription may be transmitted to a pharmacy electronically in lieu of a telephone call.[555] An e-prescription should contain all of the prescribing information listed above.[556] The pharmacy has an obligation to maintain a paper copy of either the subsequently received prescription form or the electronic message.[557] Prescription orders for Schedule III through VI drugs and prescription refills may be transmitted by facsimile device.[558] Prescription orders for Schedule II drugs may only be faxed for information purposes and may not serve as the original written prescription, except for nursing home, home infusion and hospice patients.[559] Anyone receiving a Schedule II drug from a pharmacist must present an ID if he or she is not known to the pharmacist.[560] An ID may be requested by a

---

[551] Va. Code 54.1-3408.01.A
[552] 18 Va. Admin. Code 110-20-510
[553] Va. Code 54.1-3408.03
[554] CMS implementation of Deficit Reduction Act of 2005
[555] Va. Code 54.1-3408.02 and 18 Va. Admin. Code 110-20-285.A
[556] 18 Va. Admin. Code 110-20-285.B
[557] 18 Va. Admin. Code 110-20-285.C
[558] 18 Va. Admin. Code 110-20-280.A and D
[559] 18 Va. Admin. Code 110-20-280.B
[560] Va. Code 54.1-3420.1

pharmacist for other prescriptions. The pharmacist must keep a copy of a requested ID for one month.

2. Management of Chronic Pain

Virginia has created a *safe harbor* for physicians to prescribe an *excess dosage* of drugs when administered "in good faith for recognized medicinal or therapeutic purposes."[561] However, the Board of Medicine still has the authority to determine if the prescription is for a recognized, accepted therapeutic purpose regardless of the good faith by the prescribing physician.[562] To comply with the Virginia Intractable Pain Act, a physician must certify the medical necessity of the excess dose in the patient's medical record.[563] The Board of Medicine has endorsed *Guidelines for the Use of Opioids in the Management of Chronic, Noncancer Pain,*[564] which was created by the Medical Society of Virginia in 1997 as well as the *Model Policy for the Use of Controlled Substances for the Treatment of Pain* from the Federation of State Medical Boards.[565] The guidelines recommend close monitoring of patients and careful documentation. The physician must carefully and frequently document the necessity of the prescription, including the consideration of alternative treatment, such as surgery or TENS units, and lower doses. The importance of documentation cannot be over emphasized in using narcotics for chronic pain management. A physician would be prudent to become conversant with the CDC *Guidelines for Prescribing Opioids for Chronic Pain, United States 2016.*[566]

---

[561] Virginia Intractable Pain Act, Va. Code 54.1-3408.1

[562] Hurwitz v. Bd. of Med., 46 Va. Cir. 119 (1998) citing Va. Code 54.1-2914 et seq.

[563] Va. Code 54.1-2971.01.

[564] Va. Board of Medicine, "Guidelines for the Use of Opioids in the Management of Chronic, Noncancer Pain," Guidance Document 85-14

[565] http://www.dhp.state.va.us/medicine/guidelines/85-24.doc

[566] Dowell D, Haegerich TM, Chou R, *Guidelines for Prescribing Opioids for Chronic Pain – United States, 2016.* MMWR Recomm.Rep. ePub: 15 March 2016

A hospice caring for a patient at home at the time of death must notify every pharmacy dispensing Schedule II drugs for the patient within 48 hours of the patient's death.[567]

Virginia has a Prescription Monitoring Program that is accessible by any prescriber or pharmacist.[568] Where treatment is anticipated to include prescribing benzodiazepine or an opiate for more than 90 days, a prescriber must query the Program at the outset of treatment.[569] A physician must notify a patient that he intends to query the database. This can be done as a direct conversation with written consent or by posting a sign prominently in the reception area. A prescriber may delegate authority to access the Prescription Monitoring Program to other healthcare providers in the same facility and under the direct supervision of the prescriber.[570] Information within the Prescription Monitoring Program cannot be disclosed or be compelled to be produced in a civil proceeding.[571] Likewise, such information is not admissible in a civil proceeding.

Virginia law theoretically allows the dispensing of marijuana, or its active ingredient THC, for the treatment of cancer or glaucoma.[572] Cannabidiol oil or THC-A oil may be possessed by a patient and dispensed for intractable epilepsy when properly certified by a physician.[573] However, the US Drug Enforcement Agency and the Justice Department have stated that they will prosecute the practice. This would appear to be supported by the Supreme Court of the United States.[574] The defense of *medical necessity* was rejected

---

[567] Va. Code 32.1-162.5:1

[568] Va. Code 54.1-2520 et seq. 18 Va. Admin. Code 76-20-10 et seq.

[569] Va. Code 54.1-2522.1.B

[570] Va. Code 54.1-2523.B.2

[571] Va. Code 54.1-2523.A

[572] Va. Code 18.2-251.1

[573] Va. Code 54.1-3408.3 and 18.2-250.1.C

[574] Gonzales v. Raich, 545 U.S. 1, 125 S. Ct. 2195, 162 L. Ed. 2d 1 (2005)

in a similar case.[575] Despite this, many states now permit use of marijuana for medical purposes.

3. Prescription of Medication for Self or Immediate Family

The Board of Medicine frowns on a physician treating herself or immediate family members. In 2005, the Board of Medicine adopted regulations on this topic.[576] In essence, a physician should not prescribe a controlled substance for herself or a family member, other than Schedule VI, unless it is an emergency situation or where no other qualified practitioner is available or for a single course of medication for an acute illness. A similar approach should be taken in dealing with employees of a physician or at a hospital. A physician must maintain a proper patient record substantiating a bona fide physician-patient relationship.

The Board of Medicine guidelines for treatment of self or immediate family,[577] which predate the Board's regulations, are:

Documentation

The presence of a medical record is an essential part of a valid practitioner-patient relationship. The medical record must contain the following:

1. An appropriate history and physical examination (if pain is present and controlled substances prescribed, the

---

[575] United States v. Oakland Cannabis Buyers' Coop., 190 F.3d 1109, 1111, 1114 (9th Cir. 1999), rev'd sub nom. United States v. Oakland Cannabis Buyers' Co-op., 532 U.S. 483, 121 S. Ct. 1711, 149 L. Ed. 2d 722 (2001)
[576] 18 Va. Admin. Code 85-20-25
[577] Va. Board of Medicine, "Self-Treatment and Treatment of Family," Guidance Document 85-8, reprinted in "Board Briefs" #60, Summer 2000

assessment of pain, substance abuse history, and co-existing diseases or conditions should be recorded);

2. Diagnostic tests when indicated;

3. A working diagnosis;

4. A treatment plan; and

5. Documentation by date of all prescriptions written to include name of medication, strength, dosage, quantity and number of refills. The prescription should be in the format required by law.

Self-Prescribing

1. A physician cannot have a bona fide doctor-patient relationship[578] with herself;

2. Only in an emergency should a physician prescribe for herself schedule VI drugs; and

3. Prescribing of schedule II, III, IV, or V drugs to herself is prohibited.

Immediate Family

1. Treatment of immediate family members should be reserved only for minor illnesses or emergency situations;

2. Appropriate consultation should be obtained for the management of major or extended periods of illness;

3. No schedule II, III, or IV controlled substances should be dispensed or prescribed except in emergency situations; and

4. Records should be maintained of all written prescriptions or administration of any drugs.

In this author's experience, most physicians who are facing the Board's scrutiny on allegations related to prescribing practices

---

[578]   Defined in Va. Code 54.1-3408; see Va. Code 54.1-3303

have failed to maintain a proper medical chart, giving the Board an additional opportunity to mete out disciplinary action.

4. Weight-loss Medications

A physician prescribing controlled substances of Schedules III through VI to treat obesity must do the following:[579]

1. Perform and document an appropriate history and physical examination at the time of initiating the medication and review indicated lab work, including thyroid function;

2. Review the results of an EKG performed and interpreted within ninety days of initial prescribing if the drug could adversely affect cardiac function;

3. Prescribe and record a diet and exercise program for the patient;

4. See the patient within the first thirty days of prescribing, at which time blood pressure, pulse and other appropriate tests to monitor for adverse drug effects must be recorded;

5. Direct follow-up care, including the intervals for patient visits and determination of whether the medication is effective and has no significant adverse effects

5. Office-based Anesthesia

The administration of moderate sedation/conscious sedation, deep sedation, general anesthesia, or regional anesthesia consisting of conductive block is regulated by the Board of Medicine.[580] A physician or podiatrist must:[581]

---

[579] 18 Va. Admin. Code 85-20-90
[580] 18 Va. Admin. Code 85-20-310 et seq.
[581] 18 Va. Admin. Code 85-20-320.B

1. Perform a preanesthetic evaluation and examination (or ensure that it has been performed);

2. Develop the anesthesia plan (or ensure that it has been developed);

3. Ensure that the anesthesia plan has been discussed (presumably with the patient) and informed consent obtained;

4. Ensure assessment and monitoring of the patient through the pre, peri and post-procedure phases, addressing the physical, functional, physiological and cognitive status;

5. Ensure provision of indicated post anesthesia care; and

6. Remain physically present or immediately available, as appropriate, to manage complications and emergencies until discharge criteria have been met.

A physician that utilizes office-based anesthesia must ensure that all medical personnel are appropriately trained, qualified and supervised; are sufficient in number to provide adequate care; and current in basic CPR training.[582] The supervising physician must maintain current certification in advanced resuscitation techniques and have completed four hours of CME in topics related to anesthesia each biennium.[583] Deep sedation, general anesthesia or major conductive block can only be administered by an anesthesiologist or CRNA.[584] Moderate sedation/conscious sedation may be administered by the operating physician, assisted by a licensed nurse, physician assistant, intern or resident.[585]

A long list of written protocols must be developed as part of organizing an office-based anesthesia program.[586] Likewise, informed consent must be evidenced by a written document signed by the patient before the procedure.[587] Any incident of patient death

---

[582] 18 Va. Admin. Code 85-20-330.A
[583] 18 Va. Admin. Code 85-20-330.C
[584] 18 Va. Admin. Code 85-20-330.B.1
[585] 18 Va. Admin. Code 85-20-330.B.2
[586] 18 Va. Admin. Code 85-20-340, 360, 370, 380
[587] 18 Va. Admin. Code 85-20-350

within seventy-two hours of surgery or of a patient being admitted to a hospital for more than twenty-four hours must be reported to the Board within thirty days.[588]

6. "Right to Try": Access to Investigational Drugs

In 2015, the General Assembly expanded the ability of terminally-ill patients to have access to investigational drugs, biologics and devices.[589] (The state statute does not address limitations on manufacturers under FDA regulations.) A patient is eligible for expanded access if:

- He has a terminal condition certified by his treating physician and a second independent physician;

- He has considered all other FDA-approved treatment options, and his treating physician has determined that no reasonable opportunity exists for the patient to participate in a clinical trial for his terminal condition;

- The potential benefit is greater than the potential risk;

- The treating physician has recommended the investigational drug, biologic or device to treat the patient's terminal condition; and

- He has given written informed consent as specified in the statute

A physician, manufacturer and others in the distribution chain enjoy immunity for any adverse event as a result of the patient gaining access to an investigational drug, biologic or devise under this statutory scheme.[590]

---

[588] 18 Va. Admin. Code 85-20-390
[589] Va. Code 54.1-3442.1 et seq.
[590] Va. Code 54.1-3442.4

H. Security in the Facility

The Supreme Court of Virginia has held that a hospital owes a duty of reasonable care to its patients for their safety as their mental and physical condition, if known, requires.[591] Federal regulations proclaim that a patient has a right to *personal privacy*, to receive care in a *safe setting*, and to be free of abuse or harassment.[592] Further, a facility is obliged to promote a safe workplace for its employees.[593] These seemingly simple responsibilities are extremely difficult to carry out in practice as a facility attempts to balance the rights of a patient, other patients, visitors, and employees.

1. Restraint of Patients

Federal regulations mandate that "a patient has a right to be free from restraints of any form that are imposed for coercion, discipline, convenience, or retaliation by staff – including drugs that are used as restraints."[594] A restraint is defined as:

> [a]ny manual method or physical or mechanical device that restricts freedom of movement or normal access to one's body, material, or equipment, attached or adjacent to the patient's body that he or she cannot easily remove. Holding a patient in a manner that restricts his/her movement constitutes restraint for that patient.[595]

---

[591] Danville Community Hospital v. Thompson, 186 Va. 746, 757 (1947)

[592] 42 C.F.R. 482.13(c)

[593] OSHA 3148: "Guidelines for Preventing Workplace Violence for Health Care and Social Service Workers". This is advisory only.

[594] 42 C.F.R. 482.13(e) and (f); Interpretive Guidelines Tag A769

[595] 42 C.F.R. 482.13(e) and (f); Interpretive Guidelines Tag A769 and Tag A770

A physician or licensed independent practitioner must conduct a face-to-face evaluation of the patient within one hour of restraint and seclusion intervention used for behavior management.[596] If the patient's treating physician did not order the restraint, he or she must be consulted as soon as possible.[597] Restraints (but not seclusion) can be used for purposes of providing acute medical or surgical care only if necessary to improve the patient's well-being and less restrictive interventions would be ineffective.[598] The use of standing or PRN orders is now forbidden.[599] "The rationale that the patient should be restrained because he/she 'might' fall is an inadequate basis for using a restraint."[600] A hospital must terminate the order at the earliest possible time.[601] "A voluntary mechanical support used to achieve proper body position, balance, or alignment so as to allow greater freedom of mobility than would be possible without the use of such a mechanical support is not considered a restraint."[602] A lay person might think of this as a bed rail or other common safety device.

If the restraint or seclusion is for behavior management, a hospital may use it only in emergency situations, when it is necessary to ensure a patient's physical safety, and in the least restrictive means possible.[603] CMS limits the time-length of a restraint order by the patient's age: four hours for an adult; two hours for children ages 9 through 17; and one hour for children under the age of 9.[604] The order may only be renewed in accordance with these limits for up to a total of twenty-four hours.[605] After the original order expires, a physician or other licensed independent practitioner must see

---

[596] 42 C.F.R. 482.13(e) and (f)
[597] 42 C.F.R. 482.13(e)(3)(ii)(B); Interpretive Guidelines Tag A773
[598] 42 C.F.R. 482.13(e)(1); Interpretive Guidelines Tag A770
[599] 42 C.F.R. 482.13(e)(3)(ii)(A); Interpretive Guidelines Tag A772
[600] 42 C.F.R. 482.13(e) and (f); Interpretive Guidelines Tag A769
[601] 42 C.F.R. 482.13(e)(3)(B)(vi); Interpretive Guidelines Tag A777
[602] 42 C.F.R. 482.13(3) and (f); Interpretive Guidelines Tag A769
[603] 42 C.F.R. 482.13(f)(1); Interpretive Guidelines Tag A780
[604] 42 C.F.R. 482.13(f)(ii)(D); Interpretive Guidelines Tag 787
[605] 42 C.F.R. 482.13(f)(ii)(D)(i); Interpretive Guidelines Tag 788

and assess the patient before issuing a new order.[606] Restraint and seclusion may not be used simultaneously unless the patient is continually monitored face-to-face by an assigned staff member,[607] or is continually monitored by staff in close proximity to the patient using both video and audio equipment.[608]

Federal guidance for use of restraints in nursing homes has been long standing but still challenging.[609] This includes the controversy of whether a side rail is a restraint or an enabling device.[610]

A resident of a Virginia psychiatric facility must be treated under the least restrictive conditions consistent with his treatment needs. Restraining or secluding a patient is prohibited unless "it is evident that a patient might harm himself or others and in which less restrictive means of restraint are not feasible."[611]

Injuries or deaths related to the use of restraints must be reported to the FDA within ten days.[612]

2. Search & Seizure

The right or duty of a facility to search a patient's personal

---

[606]   42 C.F.R. 482.13(f)(ii)(D)(ii); Interpretive Guidelines Tag 787

[607]   42 C.F.R. 482.13(f)(4); Interpretive Guidelines Tag A794

[608]   42 C.F.R. 482.13(f)(4)(ii); Interpretive Guidelines Tag A795

[609]   See 42 U.S.C.A. 1395i-3 and 1396r; 42 C.F.R. 483.10 and .13(a); 42 C.F.R. 483.20(d) and 483.10(b); HCFA Interpretive Guidelines, State Operations, Manual 274, Appendix P; HCFA Guidance to Surveyors - Long Term Care Facilities (Transmittal 274, June 1995); 42 C.F.R. Part 488l FDA regulation: 21 C.F.R. 880.6760(a); "Potential Hazards With Restraint Devices" (July 15, 1992); complaint files re: restraints: 21 C.F.R. 880.6760(b) and 880.6140(b); DHHS, Office of the Inspector General, *Minimizing Restraint Use in Nursing Homes*, 1992

[610]   Side Rails Interim Policy, HCFA 2-10-97 Memorandum; Side rails: FDA Safety Alert (August 23, 1995)

[611]   12 Va. Admin. Code 35-120-40.H

[612]   Safe Medical Devices Act of 1990, eff. 11/28/91

belongings may depend on whether the facility is public or private and the patient's reasonable expectation of privacy. No Virginia court decisions have been found on this topic. Several analogous situations decided by other courts are discussed below.

One jurisdiction held that where a hospital's searches of patient lockers were done for contraband or sanitary reasons alone, no fault lay with the hospital.[613] Moreover, one jurisdiction has held that Congress did not intend drug rehabilitation programs to become "sanctuaries for drug abusers who violate the law while enrolled in the program."[614] The court found that the doctor-patient confidentiality standard "must yield to the practical necessity to permit protection from, and prompt reporting of, criminal acts," and to that end reasonable searches were appropriate.[615]

In reviewing searches by public school officials, the U.S. Supreme Court has written that school officials do not have to strictly adhere to the probable cause standard ordinarily used by police.[616] The legality of searching students depends on the reasonableness under all the circumstances of the search. Reasonableness is determined by balancing the student's privacy interests against the special need of the school to maintain a safe educational environment. Reasonable suspicion is usually adequate. Likewise, random drug testing of student athletes has been upheld using the reasonableness standard.[617] Strip searches of students require a higher standard of suspicion.[618]

---

[613]   Falter v. Veterans Admin., 632 F. Supp. 196 (D.N.J. 1986)
[614]   United States v. Johnston, 810 F.2d 841, 843 (8th Cir. 1987)
[615]   United States v. Johnston, 810 F.2d 841, 843 (8th Cir. 1987)
[616]   New Jersey v. T.L.O., 469 U.S. 325, 105 S. Ct. 733, 83 L. Ed. 2d 720 (1985)
[617]   Vernonia School Dist. 47J v. Acton, 515 U.S. 66 (1995); Miller ex rel. Miller v. Wilkes, 172 F.3d 574 (8th Cir. 1999), Va. Admin. Codeated (June 15, 1999); However, see Trinidad Sch. Dist. No. 1 v. Lopez By & Through Lopez, 963 P.2d 1095 (Colo. 1998)
[618]   See Kennedy v. Dexter Consol. Sch., 1998-NMCA-051, 124 N.M. 764, 955 P.2d 693, aff'd in part, rev'd in part sub nom. Kennedy v. Dexter Consol.

In reviewing actions by police in the hospital setting, the Virginia Court of Appeals held that the police did not violate a patient's Fourth Amendment rights when they entered a hospital emergency ward where the patient was being treated after a traffic accident. The patient was not in a private room and there was "no specific rental of a hospital room." The door to his treatment room was open when the police arrived. Medical staff and family were freely entering and leaving the room. Therefore, the police acted appropriately in giving the patient his Miranda rights, questioning him about the disappearance of a girl, seizing his clothing and personal effects, and taking PERK samples.[619] Similarly, the Supreme Court of Virginia denied suppression of a bullet delivered to the police after the emergency medicine physician removed it from the defendant patient's body.[620]

One federal appeals court has held that contraband discovered after a nurse searched the clothes of an emergency room patient was not obtained in violation of the Fourth Amendment.[621] Similarly, where drugs were removed from a patient's rectum pursuant to a valid search warrant, one court has held that "[t]here is nothing in the Bill of Rights which makes body cavities a legally protected sanctuary for carrying narcotics. It is not per se violative of the Constitution [for a trained medical doctor] to remove [contraband] from body cavities."[622]

Conversely, a hospital may face allegations that it has a duty to search residents. Where a psychiatric patient was stripped and searched prior to entry to a hospital and who later died from an overdose while admitted, the U.S. Court of Appeals, Eighth Circuit,

---

Sch., 2000-NMSC-025, 129 N.M. 436, 10 P.3d 115; Konop for Konop v. Nw. Sch. Dist., 1998 DSD 27, 26 F. Supp. 2d 1189 (D.S.D. 1998)

[619] Matthews v. Commonwealth, 30 Va. App. 412 (1999), relying on Craft v. Commonwealth, 221 Va. 258 (1980).

[620] Craft v. Commonwealth, 221 Va. 258 (1980).

[621] United States v. Winbush, 428 F.2d 357 (6th Cir. 1970)

[622] State v. Fowler, 89 N.C. App. 10, 365 S.E.2d 301 (1988)(quoting Breithaupt v. Abram, 352 U.S. 432, 77 S. Ct. 408, 1 L. Ed. 2d 448 (1957)

held that the patient's entry into the hospital with contraband was not tantamount to a breach of the hospital's duty to diligently search and seize any contraband from him. The hospital merely owed its patients the specific duty of exercising reasonable care to safeguard and protect them from self-injury as their known mental condition required. It was sufficient that the hospital's standard of care reflect that of reasonable anticipation of the probability of self-inflicted harm.[623]

a. When Contraband Is Inadvertently Discovered

Using the hypothetical of drug paraphernalia being discovered inadvertently while a hospital room was being cleaned, what should the hospital do with the contraband? In short, the drug paraphernalia should be secured and not returned to the patient. He clearly did not have the items for any therapeutic purpose. Virginia law requires that:

> [e]ach person, association or corporation which has lawfully obtained possession of any of the controlled paraphernalia mentioned in § 54.1-3467 shall exercise reasonable care in the storage, usage and disposition of such devices or substances to ensure that they are not diverted for reuse for any purposes other than those for which they were lawfully obtained. Any person who permits or causes, directly or indirectly, such controlled paraphernalia to be used for any other purpose than that for which it was lawfully obtained shall be guilty of a Class 1 misdemeanor.[624]

This places the burden on the hospital to make sure that syringes and other observed drug paraphernalia are not used for illegal purposes. Moving on, one needs to consider how to dispose of the items.

---

[623] Stuppy v. United States, 560 F.2d 573 (8th Cir. 1977)
[624] Va. Code 54.1-3469

b. Obligations of Facility When Contraband Is Discovered

Where the expressed desire of a hospital is to turn drug paraphernalia over to the police in order to protect the safety of a patient, other patients and the staff; the legal issue is whether this would be a breach of patient confidentiality. Historically Virginia did not recognize a common law right of confidentiality for patient/ physician information, especially in the criminal investigation setting.[625] However, the Virginia Patient Health Records Privacy Act[626] provides that:

> A. There is hereby recognized a patient's right of privacy in the content of a patient's medical record. Patient records are the property of the provider maintaining them, and, except when permitted by this section or by another provision of state or federal law, no provider, or other person working in a health care setting, may disclose the records of a patient.

Record is defined as:

> any written, printed or electronically recorded material maintained by a provider in the course of providing health services to a patient concerning the patient and the services provided. "Record" also includes the substance of any communication made by a patient to a provider in confidence during or in connection with the provision of health services to a patient or information otherwise acquired by the provider about a patient in confidence and in connection with the provision of health services to the patient.

A narrow reading of this statutory language leads to the conclusion

---

[625] Gibson v. Commonwealth, 216 Va. 412 (1975)
[626] Va. Code 32.1-127.1:03

that inadvertently discovered drug paraphernalia is not within the definition of *medical record*. The items are not part of any therapeutic regime nor were they brought to the staff's attention in confidence by the patient. Therefore, it would not be a breach of patient confidentiality to turn the paraphernalia over to the police. However, a broad reading of this statute would lead to the opposite conclusion that this would be a breach of patient confidentiality. Therefore, caution should be used in relaying any information obtained from the patient to the police.

3. *Monitoring of Patients or Visitors*

The Medicare *Conditions of Participation* are interpreted by the federal authorities as entitling a patient to privacy during personal hygiene activities (e.g. toileting, bathing, dressing), during medical/ nursing treatments, and when requested as appropriate.[627] For example, a patient should not be videotaped during an examination without his explicit consent.[628] An exception is noted to allow for continuous monitoring in situations when immediate and serious risk of harm to self or others exists.[629]

The Medicare *Conditions of Participation* state that a patient has the right to receive care in a safe setting.[630] This is interpreted as requiring the hospital to provide protection for the patient's emotional health and safety as well as physical safety. Respect, dignity and comfort are components of an emotionally safe environment.[631] The federal government has announced that it will evaluate a hospital's compliance with this regulation by reviewing policies and procedures on what the facility does to curtail unwanted visitors or contraband materials.[632] "The intent of the requirement is to prohibit all forms

---

[627] 42 C.F.R. 482.13(b)(4); Interpretive Guidelines Tag A763
[628] 42 C.F.R. 482.13(b)(4); Interpretive Guidelines Tag A763
[629] 42 C.F.R. 482.13(b)(4); Interpretive Guidelines Tag A763
[630] 42 C.F.R. 482.13(c)(2)
[631] Interpretive Guidelines Tag A764
[632] Interpretive Guidelines Tag A764

of abuse, neglect (as a form of abuse) and harassment whether by staff, other patients or visitors."[633] No court has yet tried to reconcile these potentially conflicting mandates of the Medicare *Conditions of Participation*.

Virginia nursing homes and assisted living facilities must register with the Sex Offender Registry to receive notification and to ascertain if a potential patient is an offender.[634] A facility must give notice of the registry to its residents.[635]

4. *Regulating Patient Conduct*

Virginia hospitals have an obligation to exercise ordinary care and prudence to render its premises reasonably safe to business invitees, such as patients and visitors.[636] A hospital may also have an obligation to protect a patient from other patients if a *special relationship* is found to exist between the hospital and the patient.[637] What is not explained by court decisions in cases brought by injured visitors or patients is how far a hospital can go in regulating a patient's conduct. For example, can a hospital prohibit a patient from smoking in her room?[638] How far can a facility go to enforce this prohibition? With little guidance from courts or regulators, the hospital must balance the personal rights of a patient with protecting the safety and well-being of others. Does the Americans with Disabilities Act[639] and Rehabilitation Act of 1973[640] prohibit discrimination against a disruptive patient if his conduct is due to mental illness? What is

---

[633] Interpretive Guidelines Tag A765

[634] Va. Code 32.1-127.B.13 and 14

[635] Va. Code 63.2-1732.G and H

[636] Roanoke Hospital Association v. Hayes, 204 Va. 703 (1963)

[637] Delk v. Columbia/HCA Healthcare Corp., 259 Va. 125 (2000)

[638] The disastrous consequence of a patient ignoring safety precautions for smoking resulted has been multiple deaths and injuries of other patients in hospital fires.

[639] 42 U.S.C.A. 12182(a) (West)

[640] 29 U.S.C.A. 794 (West); see 45 C.F.R. 84.4(a)

reasonable accommodation? OBRA of 1987 prohibits involuntary transfer or discharge of a patient unless there is a showing that the patient's needs cannot be met or safety of others is endangered.[641]

A continuing challenge in long-term care is the concept of "aging in place" wherein a resident may demand that an assisted living facility acquiesce in his demand to stay in the facility even though his health has deteriorated to the state of requiring an intensive level of nursing assistance.[642]

5. Regulating Visitor Conduct

A hospital must have a policy allowing an adult patient to receive visitors that the patient desires.[643] The 2011 Medicare Conditions of Participation[644] and the standards of the Joint Commission require that a hospital explain to all patients their right to choose who may visit them during an inpatient stay. A resident in a psychiatric facility has the right to receive or refuse visitors, unless a physician certifies in a written order that it would be detrimental to the resident.[645] In contrast, Virginia regulations also state that a psychiatric resident has the right to safe housing.[646] It is frighteningly all too frequent that a visitor may be abusing the patient.

The better practice is to assure patient safety with as little intrusion as possible. If the patient is competent, she has the right to decide whom she will or will not welcome as visitors. If the patient is incompetent, the hospital has a heightened responsibility to protect

---

[641] 42 U.S.C.A. 1395:-3(c)(2)(A)(i); 42 C.F.R. 483.12(a)(2)(i); 42 C.F.R. 483.12(a)(2)(iii)

[642] For example, see HB 3207 (2007)

[643] Va. Code 32.1-127.B.15

[644] Medicare and Medicaid Programs: Changes to the Hospital and Critical Access Hospital Conditions of Participation To Ensure Visitation Rights for All Patients, 75 FR 70831-01; codified at 42 C.F.R. 482 and 485

[645] 12 Va. Admin. Code 35-120-40.C.5

[646] 12 Va. Admin. Code 35-120-40.C.11

her. Unfortunately, a bill in the 2012 General Assembly granting a guardian the authority to restrict visitation of an incapacitated person failed.[647] However, this is included within the 2011 Medicare *Conditions of Participation*, which also require that a hospital adopt written policies and procedures concerning a patient's visitation rights, including any clinically reasonable and necessary restrictions or limitations on visitations.

Localities are authorized to establish a procedure by ordinance permitting a property owner to give local police the authority to enforce trespass violations on the owner's property.[648] This, for example, would give a hospital an additional basis to use local police on its premises to maintain order. Assault of an emergency medical provider is a misdemeanor in Virginia.[649]

6. *Laboratory Testing without Patient's Consent*

The U.S. Supreme Court reversed the U.S. Court of Appeals, Fourth Circuit, and held that a South Carolina university hospital drug-testing policy intended to encourage pregnant women who tested positive for cocaine to obtain substance abuse counseling did violate the patients' civil rights under the Fourth Amendment.[650] The court held that this was a warrantless search and that disclosure of the test results to law enforcement officials violated the patients' constitutional right to privacy.[651] Under the drug testing policy, all maternity patients were tested when one or more of the following events occurred:

- Separation of the placenta from the uterine wall;

---

[647] SB9 (2012) proposed amendment of Va. Code 37.2-1020
[648] Va. Code 15.2-1717.1 enacted by HB 1862 (1999)
[649] Va. Code 18.2-57.E
[650] Ferguson v. Charleston, S.C., 532 U.S. 67 (2001); consideration on remand at 308 F.3d 380 (4th Cir. 2002)
[651] For a similar result, see Birchfield v. North Dakota, __ US __ (2016) (warrant required to draw blood for DUI prosecution)

- Intrauterine fetal death;

- No prenatal care;

- Later prenatal care;

- Incomplete prenatal care;

- Preterm labor without an obvious cause;

- A history of cocaine use;

- Unexplained birth defects; or

- Intrauterine growth retardation without an obvious cause.

When a patient tested positive, she was arrested for distributing cocaine to a minor. The policy was later amended so that a patient could choose between being arrested and receiving drug rehabilitation. Those arrested could avoid prosecution by completing a drug rehabilitation program. The appellate court held, which was later reversed, that the searches were reasonable as *special needs searches*. The method chosen (urine tests) to address this special need beyond law enforcement goals effectively advanced the public interests. The intrusion suffered by the women was minimal. No means of accomplishing this goal were demonstrated by the patients that would have had less of a disparate racial impact. Any privacy interest possessed by the patients in their medical records was outweighed by a compelling governmental interest, especially in light of the limited disclosure. The U. S. Supreme Court did not agree.

In a similar vein, Virginia hospitals are required to develop and implement a protocol requiring written discharge plans for "identified, substance-abusing, postpartum women and their infants."[652] The discharge plan must be discussed with the woman. Appropriate referrals for the mother and infant must be made. The father is to be involved to the extent possible. The hospital

---

[652]   Va. Code 32.1-127.B.6

is also obligated to notify, subject to federal law restrictions,[653] the community services board where the woman resides. The community service board is required to implement and manage the discharge plan.

Testing for many metabolic and congenital diseases is required by Virginia statute. One federal district court has ruled that state-mandated testing of newborns does not violate the First, Fourth or Fourteenth Amendments of the U.S. Constitution.[654]

7. Liability for Criminal Acts of Others

A medical facility does not guarantee the safety of patients or visitors.[655] However, like landlords, a facility must exercise reasonable diligence in hiring employees.[656] For example, a medical facility has a duty to screen potential employees for criminal records.[657] Failing to do so, a facility may be liable for criminal acts of its employee.[658]

Facilities and professionals often have the added burden of protecting patients who are in their custody as well as protecting others (e.g. other patients, visitors, and other third parties) from patients who are in their custody. The parameters of this in Virginia are somewhat unclear in light of the Supreme Court's opinion in a failure-to-warn case that rejected the Tarasoff v. Regents of the University of California ruling[659] and the subsequent effort by the

---

[653] Va. Code 32.1-127.B.6 does not identify to which federal law it is referring. Considerable debate could arise as to whether this breach of confidentiality is allowed under federal law.

[654] Spiering v. Heineman, 448 F. Supp. 2d 1129 (D. Neb. 2006)

[655] Burns v. Johnson, 250 Va. 41 (1995); Gulf Reston, Inc. v. Rogers, 215 Va. 155 (1974)

[656] J. v. Victory Tabernacle Baptist Church, 236 Va. 206 (1988)

[657] Hospital: 42 C.F.R. 482.13(c)(3) and Va. Code 32.1-126.02; Nursing homes: Va. Code 32.1-126.01; Home care organizations: Va. Code 32.1-162.9:1; Adult care residences: Va. Code 63.1-173.2

[658] J. v. Victory Tabernacle Baptist Church, 236 Va. 206 (1988)

[659] Nasser v. Parker, 249 Va. 172 (1995)

General Assembly to reverse the Court's opinion.[660] Recently, the Supreme Court of Virginia held that a psychiatric hospital may be liable for the alleged failure to protect a patient from sexual abuse by another patient.[661] The court found that a *special relationship* existed between the patient and the psychiatric hospital because the staff knew of her long history of psychiatric problems related to sexual abuse and that she needed constant supervision. A nurse allegedly documented the presence of a male patient in her room but failed to take any further action. The case highlights the challenge of protecting a patient versus respecting a patient's rights, as mandated by Joint Commission and the Medicare *Conditions of Participation*.

In contrast, one Circuit Court judge has commented that a landlord is not to act as a policeman.[662] Generally a landlord has no liability to a tenant for criminal actions of a third party.[663] Even knowledge of the neighborhood being a high crime area does not create an obligation to protect tenants.[664] The Supreme Court of Virginia found that an assisted living facility operator did not owe a duty to its residents to protect them from the criminal acts of outsiders.[665] However, one should be cautious as society continues to become generally older and assisted living facilities increasingly advertise their high level of service and security. Under the proper circumstances, a court is likely to find a facility liable for failing to protect a resident from the acts of others or even the resident's own frailty.

---

[660] Va. Code 54.1-2400.1

[661] Delk v. Columbia/HCA Health care Corp., 259 Va. 125 (2000)

[662] Frazier v. Strobel, 58 Va. Cir. 456 (2002) citing Yuzefovsky v. St. John's Wood Apartments, 261 Va. 97 (2001)

[663] Gulf Reston v. Rogers, 215 Va. 155 (1974); Klingbeil Management Group Co. v. Vito, 233 Va. 445 (1987)

[664] Dupree v. Buckman Gardens, 25 Va. Cir. 172 (1991)

[665] Holles v. Sunrise Terrace, Inc., 257 Va. 131 (1999); also see Emerson v. Adult Community Total Services, 842 F. Supp. 152 (ED Pa. 1994)

8. *Quarantine and Isolation*

As the second edition of this book went to press in 2006, fears of an influenza pandemic were at the forefront of public health issues. Virginia has a comprehensive, but largely untested, statutory scheme in place.[666] The Board of Health has authority to promulgate regulations and orders to meet any actual or potential emergency.[667] The Health Commissioner can require quarantine, isolation, decontamination or treatment to control the spread of disease.[668]

Similar to the process for a temporary detention order, the Commissioner can issue an emergency order for a person to be taken immediately into custody and placed in the least restrictive facility when the person has an air-borne communicable disease of public health significance and is or has been unwilling to comply with a prescribed treatment.[669] The Commissioner can petition the general district court to issue an order for isolation of up to 120 days.[670] More stringent isolation steps may be invoked if simple detention in a facility is insufficient to protect the public.[671] The Commissioner must petition the circuit court to review and confirm an isolation order.[672] Appeal of an order of isolation must be held within 48 hours or the subsequent business day.[673] A circuit court's ruling may be appealed directly to the Supreme Court of Virginia on an expedited basis.[674]

The Commissioner may declare a quarantine of a person or persons or an affected area after he finds that the quarantine is necessary to contain a communicable disease of public threat.[675] The quarantine

---

[666] Va. Code 17.1-503.C and 32.1-42 et seq.
[667] Va. Code 32.1-42
[668] Va. Code 32.1-43 et seq.
[669] Va. Code 32.1-48.02
[670] Va. Code 32.1-48.03 and 48.04
[671] Va. Code 32.1-48.11 et seq.
[672] Va. Code 32.1-48.12
[673] Va. Code 32.1-48.13
[674] Va. Code 32.1-48.13.H
[675] Va. Code 32.1-48.08

must be the least restrictive possible. To quarantine an area, the Governor must also declare a state of emergency for the affected area.[676] An order of quarantine must be reviewed and confirmed by the circuit court of the affected area.[677] An appeal of a quarantine order must be heard by the circuit court within forty-eight hours or on the subsequent business day thereafter, but the person appealing has the burden of proof.[678] The final order of the circuit court is appealable directly to the Supreme Court of Virginia on an expedited basis.[679]

Failure to comply with an order of quarantine or isolation is a Class 1 misdemeanor and may prompt civil penalties.[680] In addition, the Commissioner may order immediate detention by law enforcement agencies.[681] Under a declared state of emergency, the Commissioner can commandeer public or private property to implement quarantine or isolation, with compensation to the owner.[682]

---

[676]   Va. Code 32.1-48.09.B

[677]   Va. Code 32.1-48.09.D

[678]   Va. Code 32.1-48.10

[679]   Va. Code 32.1-48.11.H

[680]   Va. Code 32.1-48.14

[681]   Va. Code 32.1-48.14.B and C

[682]   Va. Code 32.1-48.17

I. Decision-Making for the Incompetent Patient

In the wake of judicial decisions, such as <u>Quinlan</u>[683] and <u>Cruzan</u>,[684] about surrogate decision-making for patients at the end of life, federal and state legislatures have enacted laws to provide a road map in such situations.

1. Patient Self-Determination Act

The Patient Self-Determination Act[685] creates duties for several entities. The most onerous burden, however, is placed on health care institutions. Hospitals and other facilities must now make information available to all patients that describes the state law regarding a patient's right to refuse medical treatment, including the withdrawal of food and water. A patient must also be informed of the institution's own policies and procedures in carrying out such patient directives. A facility must inquire of every patient whether he has an advance directive. Of more recent genesis is the Medicare *Conditions of Participation* requiring that a hospital advise a patient of his rights, including the right to refuse treatment.[686] It is important to note that the law does not require a facility to acquiesce in a patient's demand for the withdrawal of life support.

A sometimes more complicated mandate was placed on each state by the Patient Self-Determination Act to set forth a description of what the state's law is regarding a patient's right to refuse medical

---

[683] <u>In re Quinlan</u>, 348 A.2d 801 (NJ Super Ct. 1975) *modified and remanded* 355 A.2d 647, *cert. denied*, 429 US 992 (1976)

[684] <u>Cruzan v. Director, Missouri Dept. of Health</u>, 760 SW.2d 408, *aff'd* 497 US 261 (1990)

[685] Patient Self-Determination Act, 42 USC 1395i-3, 1395l, 1395cc, 1395bbb

[686] 42 C.F.R. 482.13(b)(3)

treatment. Virginia has now collected most of its statutory guidance in the Health Care Decisions Act.

2. *Virginia Health Care Decisions Act*

Virginia law on advance directives, formerly called "living wills," and decision-making for an incapacitated patient is now contained in the Health Care Decisions Act.[687] It pulls together and clarifies much of the law in Virginia on decision-making in medical situations. The legislation extensively revised the former Natural Death Act and incorporates much of the repealed Surrogate Decision-Maker Act.

The Health Care Decisions Act brings into one location the concepts of a living will, durable power of attorney, and surrogate decision-making. However, the best part of the Act is that it does not use any of these terms. The terminology change is very helpful to medicine and law practitioners working with patients and their families. Often the lay public misunderstands the catchy phrases, such as "living will". The confusion experienced by the public can be illustrated by a talk this author gave several years ago to a group of senior citizens. After giving a very concise and clear presentation, the author believed, it was obvious that many of the audience members were unable to distinguish between a living will and a living trust. Two older ladies were overheard walking out the door loudly debating whether real estate should be put in a living will! Avoiding the legal jargon all together is a giant step forward. Thankfully in Virginia, "living will" is now referred to as an advance directive, a term which brings with it a much more easily understood concept.

---

[687]   Va. Code 54.1-2981, et seq.

a. Procedure for Making an Advance Directive

i) Written Advance Directive

A competent[688] adult may, at any time, make a written advance directive to address any health care decisions in the future if the patient is unable to give informed consent.[689] A written advance directive may also appoint an agent to make health care decisions for the patient under the circumstances stated in the advance directive if the patient should be determined to be incapable of making an informed decision. A written advance directive must be signed by the patient in the presence of two subscribing witnesses. The witnesses may be anyone over the age of 18, including a spouse or blood relative.[690] In addition, a hospital must document in a patient's medical record whether or not the patient has executed an advance directive.[691]

A written advance directive may, but need not, be in the form set forth in the statute.[692] When the patient is determined to be incapable of making an informed decision, the advance directive may, if specified:

1. Specify the healthcare that the patient does or does not authorize;

2. Appoint an agent to make health care decisions for the patient;

3. Specify an anatomical gift of all or parts of the patient's body after death;[693]

---

[688] An adult is presumed to be capable of making an informed decision. Va. Code 54.1-2983.2

[689] Va. Code 54.1-2983

[690] Va. Code 54.1-2982

[691] 42 C.F.R. 482.13(b)(3); Interpretive Guidelines Tag A761

[692] Va. Code 54.1-2984. A model form is available at www.vsb.org/site/public/healthcare-decisions-day

[693] Va. Code 32.1-289

4. Authorize an agent to authorize participation in a clinical research study[694]

If a portion of an advance directive is determined to be invalid or illegal, the remaining provisions are not affected.[695] If an advance directive conflicts with the statutory provisions for emergency custody, temporary detention, involuntary admission or mandatory outpatient treatment, the statutory provisions trump the advance directive.

Prior to providing, continuing, withholding or withdrawing health care pursuant to an advance directive, or as soon as reasonably practical, the attending physician must certify in writing that the patient is incapable of decision-making. In addition, the attending physician must obtain written certification from a physician or licensed clinical psychologist then and every 180 days.[696] The second opinion should be from a physician or licensed clinical psychologist not involved in the patient's care. At any time, a single attending physician can determine that a patient has regained the ability to make decisions, and the physician should document his determination.[697]

If the patient appoints an agent in an advance directive, that agent has the authority to make health care decisions for the declarant as specified in the advance directive if the declarant is determined to be incapable of making an informed decision. The agent has decision-making priority over any other individuals and is empowered to take whatever lawful actions are required to carry out the patient's advance directives.[698] This includes granting releases of liability to medical providers, releasing medical records, and making

[694] Va. Code 54.1-2983.1
[695] Va. Code 54.1-2983
[696] Va. Code 54.1-2983.2.B
[697] Va. Code 54.1-2983.2.D
[698] Va. Code 54.1-2983

decisions regarding who may visit the patient.[699] An agent may also be authorized to approve the declarant's participation in clinical research.[700] Based on a letter from a physician, a spouse or other next-of-kin may access the safe-deposit box of an incapacitated patient to look for an advance directive.[701]

In 2008, the General Assembly authorized creation of the Advance Health Care Directive Registry to which one can post an advance directive to avoid the challenge of getting the document to the location of the patient.[702]

ii) Oral Advance Directive

A competent adult who has been diagnosed by his attending physician as being in a terminal condition may make an oral advance directive to authorize the providing, withholding or withdrawing of life prolonging procedures or to appoint an agent to make health care decisions for the patient under the circumstances stated in the advance directive if the patient should be determined to be incapable of making an informed decision.[703] An oral advance directive must be made in the presence of the attending physician and two witnesses.

iii) Notification of Physician

The patient has the responsibility to provide notification to an attending physician[704] that an advance directive has been made.[705]

---

[699] Va. Code 54.1-2984. The power to restrict visitation of the patient must be expressly granted in the advance directive.
[700] Va. Code 54.1-2983.1
[701] Va. Code 6.1-332.1 and 54.1-2989.1
[702] Va. Code 54.1-2983 and 2994
[703] Va. Code 54.1-2983
[704] Attending physician is defined as the primary physician who has responsibility for the treatment and care of the patient.
[705] Va. Code 54.1-2983. If an advance directive has been submitted to the Advance Health Care Directive Registry, the declarant is responsible for providing the physician or agent with the necessary information to

In the event the declarant is comatose, incapacitated or otherwise mentally or physically incapable of communication, any other person may notify the physician of the existence of an advance directive. An attending physician who is so notified must promptly make the advance directive or a copy of the advance directive, if written, or the fact of the advance directive, if oral, a part of the declarant's medical records.

b. Revocation of an Advance Directive

An advance directive may be revoked at any time by a declarant that is capable of understanding the nature and consequences of his actions (an interesting change in language from determining decision-making capacity).[706] An advance directive can be revoked by a signed, dated writing; by physical destruction or cancellation of the document; or by an oral statement intending to revoke it. An advance directive can be partially revoked in the same manner with the remainder remaining in effect. Any such revocation or modification is effective when communicated to that attending physician. If an advance directive has been submitted to the Advance Health Care Directive Registry, any revocation or modification must be notarized before being submitted to the Department of Health.[707]

c. Procedure in the Absence of an Advance Directive

Where an attending physician of an adult patient has determined after personal examination that the patient is incapable of making an informed decision about providing, withholding or withdrawing a specific medical treatment or course of treatment and the adult has not made an advance directive or the patient's advance directive does not indicate his wishes with respect to the specific course of

---

access the registry. Va. Code 54.1-2983, amended by HB 805 (2008). The Advance Health Care Directive Registry was created by Va. Code 54.1-2994 via HB 805 (2008).

[706] Va. Code 54.1-2985
[707] Va. Code 54.1-2985.B

treatment at issue and does not appoint an agent to make health care decisions upon his becoming incapable of making an informed decision, the attending physician may provide to, or withhold or withdraw from such patient medical or surgical treatment, including, but not limited to, life-prolonging procedures, upon the authorization of any of the following persons, in the specified order of priority, if the physician is not aware of any available, willing and capable person in a higher class:[708]

1. A guardian for the patient. (Such appointment is not required in order that a treatment decision can be made. An agent appointed in an advance directive also stands in the first position); or

2. The patient's spouse except where a divorce action has been filed and the divorce is not final;[709] or

3. An adult child of the patient; or

4. A parent of the patient; or

5. An adult brother or sister of the patient;

6. Any other relative of the patient in the descending order of blood relationship;

7. Except when withholding or withdrawing a life-prolonging procedure is at issue, any adult who i) has exhibited special care and concern for the patient, and ii) is familiar with the patient's religious beliefs and basic values and any preferences previously expressed by the patient.[710] Next

---

[708] Va. Code 54.1-2986.A

[709] The "except . . ." portion of this phrase was added by SB 1174ER (1999).

[710] Va. Code 54.1-2986.A was amended to add this "special friend" class in 2008. The adult must not be an employee of any health care providers currently involved in care. Appointment must be approved by a patient care consulting committee, or in its absence, two physicians not involved in the patient's care or employed by those who are. The determination of meeting the criteria for appointment must be documented in the chart.

in order would be a majority of a facility's patient care consulting committee and then two disinterested physicians.

If two or more of the people listed in the same class with equal decision-making priority inform the attending physician that they disagree as to a particular treatment decision, the attending physician may rely on the authorization of a majority of the reasonably available members of that class.[711] The statute does not provide a "tie-breaker" mechanism.

Any person authorized to consent to the providing, withholding or withdrawing of treatment must:[712]

1. Prior to giving consent, make a good faith effort to ascertain the risks and benefits of the alternatives to the treatment and the religious beliefs and basic values of the patient receiving treatment, and to inform the patient, to the extent possible, of the proposed treatment and the fact that someone else is authorized to make a decision regarding that treatment; and

2. Base his decision on the patient's religious beliefs and basic values and any preferences previously expressed by the patient regarding such treatment to the extent they are known, and if unknown or unclear, on the patient's best interests.

The Health Care Decisions Act does not authorize providing, continuing, withholding or withdrawing of treatment if the provider of the treatment knows that the patient protests such an action.[713] Specifically, no person is permitted to authorize treatment that such person knows, or upon reasonable inquiry ought to know, is contrary to the religious beliefs or basic values of the patient unable to make a decision, whether expressed orally or in writing. A provision added in 2009 states that an agent appointed under an advance directive or a statutory agent loses his decision-making

---

[711] Va. Code 54.1-2986.A
[712] Va. Code 54.1-2986.1B
[713] Va. Code 54.1-2986.2.A

power if the patient protests unless the patient's advance directive explicitly authorizes the agent's authority even over the patient's protest.[714] The absence of an advance directive by an adult patient does not give rise to any presumption as to his intent to consent to or refuse any health care procedures.[715]

Non-therapeutic sterilization, abortion, psychosurgery, or admission to a mental retardation facility or psychiatric hospital[716] cannot be authorized by a surrogate under the Health Care Decisions Act.[717] However, the provisions of the Health Care Decisions Act, if otherwise applicable, may be employed to authorize a specific treatment, or a course of treatment, for a person who has been lawfully admitted to a mental retardation facility or psychiatric hospital.

d. Certification of Incapacity

Prior to withdrawing or withholding treatment, and prior to, or as reasonably practical thereafter, the initiation of treatment, the attending physician must certify in writing that the patient is incapable of making an informed decision regarding the treatment and obtain written certification from a licensed physician or clinical psychologist that corroborates that opinion.[718] The second physician or clinical psychologist must make her determination based on a personal examination of the patient. The second physician or licensed clinical psychologist must not be otherwise currently involved in the treatment of the person assessed. A second opinion is not required if the patient is unconscious or profoundly impaired due to trauma, stroke or other acute physiological condition.[719] If a patient is determined to be incapable of giving informed consent, the patient, as well as his agent or other decision maker, must

---

[714]   Va. Code 54.1-2986.2.E
[715]   Va. Code 54.1-2983.3.A
[716]   As defined in Va. Code 37.1-1
[717]   Va. Code 54.1-2986.C
[718]   Va. Code 54.1-2983.2.B
[719]   Va. Code 54.1-2983.2.B

be notified.[720] No less frequently than every one hundred eighty days while treatment continues, the patient's incapacity must be recertified. A single physician, at any time, may determine that a patient has regained the capability of making an informed decision.[721] The cost of the assessment is to be considered for all purposes a cost of the patient's treatment.[722]

e. Procedure in Event of Patient Protest

As a general rule, a physician should not act on a request for health care services that is protested by the patient.[723] A decision by the patient's agent may trump an incapable patient's protest where:[724]

1. The advance directive explicitly authorizes the patient's agent to make the decision at issue, even over the patient's later protest, and the patient's physician or clinical psychologist stated in writing at the time that the advance directive was made that the patient was capable of making an informed decision and understood the consequences;

2. The decision does not involve withholding or withdrawing life support; and

3. The attending physician documents that the health care to be provided, continued, withheld or withdrawn to be medically appropriate

Where the action has not been explicitly authorized over the patient's protest, the agent's decision may trump an incapable patient's protest if:

---

[720] Va. Code 54.1-2983.2.C
[721] Va. Code 54.1-2983.2.D
[722] This does not address the question of whether this is part of the hospital bill or physician bill.
[723] Va. Code 54.1-2986.2
[724] Va. Code 54.1-2986.2.B

1. The decision does not involve withholding or withdrawing life support;

2. The decision does not involve i) admission to a mental health facility or ii) mental health treatment or care;

3. The decision is based, to the extent known, on the patient's religious beliefs and basic values and any preferences previously expressed by the patient or, if unknown, is in the patient's best interests

4. The attending physician has documented that the health care is medically appropriate; and

5. The facility's patient care consulting committee (or if none, two non-treating physicians) has affirmed and documented the health care is ethically acceptable.

If a patient protests the authority of a named agent or a person authorized to make health care decisions, the protested individual will have no authority to make decisions unless the advance directive explicitly grants such authority even over later protest. If the protested individual loses his authority to make decisions, that authority goes to the next class of decision makers.[725]

f. Judicial Review

Anyone can petition the Circuit Court to challenge a surrogate health care decision. The appropriate Circuit Court is located where the patient is residing or is located. A court may enjoin the providing, withholding or withdrawal of treatment if the judge finds by a preponderance of the evidence that the action is not lawfully authorized by the Health Care Decisions Act or other state or federal law.[726]

The U. S. Court of Appeals, Second Circuit, has held that an advance directive cannot be overridden by a court to force involuntary

---

[725] Va. Code 54.1-2986.2.E
[726] Va. Code 54.1-2986.E

medication of the insane in a nonemergent situation.[727] This would discriminate on the basis of disability by singling out a particular group of mentally disabled individuals for adverse treatment not applied to any other group.

g. Physician Who Refuses to Comply

An attending physician[728] who refuses to comply with the advance directive of a qualified patient or treatment decision of a person designated to make the decision must make a reasonable effort to transfer the care of the patient to another physician.[729] This is required even if the attending physician believes that the treatment requested is medically or ethically inappropriate.

h. Durable Do Not Resuscitate Order

Virginia legislation creating the Durable Do Not Resuscitate (DDNR) Order[730] was intended to avoid the common problem of facilities, emergency medical personnel and other health care providers being under the impression that they could not honor a Do Not Resuscitate Order (DNR) issued elsewhere. The Office of Emergency Medical Services issued revised regulations in August 2011 that simplified and clarified the process.[731]

i) Creation of DDNR Order

A physician may issue a DDNR Order for his patient.[732] The physician and patient must have a bona fide physician-patient relationship. The patient must consent, after being advised of the alternatives

---

[727] Hargrave v. Vermont, 340 F.3d 27 (2nd Cir. 2003)
[728] *Attending physician* is defined as the primary physician who has responsibility for the treatment and care of the patient.
[729] Va. Code 54.1-2987
[730] Va. Code 54.1-2987.1
[731] 12 Va. Admin. Code 5-66
[732] Va. Code 54.1-2987.1.A

available.[733] If the patient is a minor or is otherwise incapable of making an informed decision regarding consent for such an order, the person authorized to consent on the patient's behalf must agree. The DDNR Order may be written for a patient regardless of his health condition. The prerequisite that the patient be suffering a terminal condition or for whom a DNR Order has been issued, including religious objections to resuscitation, has been eliminated from the statute. In drafting a DDNR Order, the physician has the responsibility to:

1. Explain the circumstances under which qualified health care personnel may follow a Durable DNR Order.

2. Explain how to and who may revoke the Durable DNR Order.

3. Document the patient's full legal name.

4. Document the execution date of the Durable DNR Order.

5. Obtain the signature of the patient or the person authorized to consent on the patient's behalf on all three forms: the patient's copy, medical record copy, and the copy used for obtaining Alternate DNR jewelry.

6. Make sure that the issuing physician's name is clearly printed and the form is signed.

7. Record the contact telephone number for the issuing physician.

8. Issue the original Durable DNR Order Form, and the patient and Alternate DNR jewelry copies to the patient and maintain the medical record copy in the patient's medical file.

The Department of Health has relaxed its former strict requirement that only an official form could be used for a DDNR. However, the Department still encourages use of the preprinted form.[734] The official form is distinctive in color and appearance. The authorized

---

[733]   12 Va. Admin. Code 5-66-70

[734]   Forms are available from the Dept. of Health. A request for forms may be faxed to 804/371-3543. Additional information is available at

DDNR form is also available for download from the Office of Emergency Medical Services web site.[735] Even a photocopy[736] of a DDNR or approved Alternate DDNR jewelry[737] can now be honored by a healthcare provider if an original DDNR Order form cannot be readily located. A DDNR cannot be ordered verbally by a physician.[738]

A DDNR does not entirely replace the traditional DNR order. A physician is still at liberty to write a traditional DNR order in appropriate circumstances:

> This section shall not prevent, prohibit or limit a physician from issuing a written order, other than a Durable Do Not Resuscitate Order, not to resuscitate a patient in the event of a cardiac or respiratory arrest in accordance with accepted medical practice.[739]

The regulations recognize that a DNR order also can be given verbally by a physician who is physically present.[740] Note should be taken that the regulations do not require this physician to be the attending or primary physician of the patient.

Valid DNR orders or Emergency Medical Services DNR orders issued before July 1, 1999, pursuant to the then-current statute, remain valid and are to be followed.[741]

DNR bracelets are no longer being issued by the Department of

---

http://www.vdh.state.va.us/OEMS/DDNR/. The Durable DNR Forms Distribution assistant may be contacted at 804/371-3500.
[735]   Office of EMS web site: http://www.vdh.state.va.us/OEMS/DDNR/
[736]   12 Va. Admin. Code 5-66-40.5
[737]   12 Va. Admin. Code 5-66-50
[738]   Office of Attorney General, Opinion 12-071, 2013 WL 3270092
[739]   Va. Code 54.1-2987.1.F; 12 Va. Admin. Code 5-66-60
[740]   12 Va. Admin. Code 5-66-60.C; Also see Office of Attorney General, Opinion 12-071, 2013 WL 3270092, in which the Attorney General opines that a DNR order can only be given by a physician that is physically present, not over the telephone.
[741]   Va. Code 54.1-2987.1.G

Health. Provisions are made in the regulations for the Department of Health to approve a vendor to supply necklaces or bracelets to individuals, or their decision-makers, who have a DDNR Order. An original DDNR Order Form must be provided to the authorized jewelry vendor.[742]

The revised regulations permit a healthcare provider to follow a DDNR Order in a facility if it is an order entered in a patient's chart and regardless of whether it has the patient's signature.[743] Likewise, this "Other DDNR Order" can be honored while a patient is in transit.

ii)   Revocation of a DDNR Order

A DDNR Order is presumed to remain in effect until it is revoked.[744] If a patient expresses the desire to be resuscitated to the health care provider, then the DDNR Order is revoked and must not be followed.[745] When a competent patient makes a DDNR, only the patient may revoke it.[746] A new order may be subsequently issued if the patient or his surrogate consents.

iii)   Response by Health Care Providers to a DDNR Order

Emergency medical services personnel and licensed health care practitioners in any facility, program or organization can follow a valid DDNR Order.[747] This is an important improvement from prior practice that mandated a DNR Order be written in each facility and often was not available to EMS personnel. The exception that hospital personnel can only follow a DDNR Order drafted before admission for twenty-four hours after admission has been deleted from the statute.

---

[742]   12 Va. Admin. Code 5-66-50

[743]   12 Va. Admin. Code 5-66-60.B

[744]   Va. Code 54.1-2987.1.C

[745]   Va. Code 54.1-2987.1.B

[746]   Va. Code 54.1-2987.1.B; 12 Va. Admin. Code 5-66-80.E

[747]   Va. Code 54.1-2987.1.D

In approaching a patient with a DDNR, a healthcare provider must:[748]

1. Determine the presence of a Durable DNR Order, approved Alternate Durable DNR jewelry, or Other DNR Order.

2. If the patient is within a qualified health care facility or in transit between qualified health care facilities, any qualified health care personnel may honor an Other DNR Order as set forth in 12VAC5-66-60.

3. Determine that the Durable DNR form or Alternate DNR jewelry is not altered.

4. Verify, through driver's license or other identification with photograph and signature or by positive identification by a family member or other person who knows the patient, that the patient in question is the one for whom the Durable DNR Order, Alternate DNR jewelry, or Other DNR Order was issued.

5. If the Durable DNR Order, Alternate DNR jewelry, or Other DNR Order is intact, unaltered, and verified as issued for the patient, qualified health care personnel may consider it valid.

Execution of a DDNR Order does not authorize the withholding of other medical interventions, such as intravenous fluids, oxygen or other therapies deemed necessary to provide comfort care or to alleviate pain.[749] A DDNR Order authorizes only the withholding of cardiopulmonary resuscitation.[750] That is defined as including:

• Cardiac compression

• Endotracheal intubation and other advanced airway management

• Artificial ventilation

• Defibrillation and related procedures

[748] 12 Va. Admin. Code 5-66-80.B
[749] Va. Code 54.1-2987.1.D
[750] Va. Code 54.1-2982; 54.1-2987.1.D

Emergency service technicians are guided by the following protocol in the face of a DDNR Order: [751]

1. If a misunderstanding with family members or others present at the scene occurs or if there are any concerns about following the DDNR Order, the patient's physician or EMS medical control should be contacted for guidance; and

2. If any question exists about the validity of the DDNR Order, resuscitation should be administered until the validity of the DDNR Order is established.

When following a DDNR Order, a health care provider must document in the patient's record: [752]

1. Use standard patient care reporting documents (i.e. patient chart, pre-hospital patient care report).

2. Describe assessment of patient's cardiac or respiratory arrest status.

3. Document which identification (Durable DNR Order, Alternate Durable DNR jewelry, or Other DNR Order or alternate form of identification) was used to confirm Durable DNR status and that it was intact, not altered, not canceled or not officially revoked.

4. Record the name of the patient's physician who issued the Durable DNR Order, or Other DNR Order.

5. If the patient is being transported, keep the Durable DNR Order, Alternate Durable DNR jewelry, or Other DNR Order with the patient.

In summary, the DDNR Order statute and regulations provide a mechanism for carrying out a patient's wishes not to be resuscitated from cardiac or respiratory arrest. However, a practitioner must be

---

[751] 12 Va. Admin. Code 5-66-80.G
[752] 12 Va. Admin. Code 5-66-80.F

conscious of the specific protocols that are required in adhering to the patient's wishes.

i.   Immunity from Liability

A health care facility, physician or anyone acting under a physician's direction is not subject to criminal or civil liability as a result of issuing a DDNR or withholding or withdrawing life-prolonging procedures under the provisions of the Health Care Decisions Act.[753] Nor will one be considered to have engaged in unprofessional conduct.[754] Likewise, a person authorizing withholding or withdrawal of treatment pursuant to the Act is not subject to criminal or civil liability, or the cost of treatment.[755] One is presumed to enjoy such immunity unless it is shown by a preponderance of the evidence that the person did not act in good faith.[756] An advance directive or DDNR is presumed to have been made, consented to or issued voluntarily and in good faith.[757] Distribution of or assisting in the completion of advance directive or DDNR forms is not considered to be the unauthorized practice of law.[758]

On the opposite side, any person can petition the circuit court to enjoin any provision, continuation, withholding or withdrawal health care action that is not lawfully authorized by the Health Care Decisions Act or by other state or federal law.[759]

j.   Willful Destruction or Concealment of Advance Directive

The willful concealment, cancellation, defacement, obliteration or

---

[753]   Va. Code 54.1-2988
[754]   Va. Code 54.1-2988
[755]   Va. Code 54.1-2988
[756]   Va. Code 54.1-2988
[757]   Va. Code 54.1-2988
[758]   Va. Code 54.1-2988
[759]   Va. Code 54.1-2985.1

damaging of an advance directive or DDNR without the patient's consent and thereby causing life-prolonging procedures to be utilized in contravention of the previously expressed intent of the patient is a Class 6 felony.[760] Similarly, deception as to the revocation of an advance directive or DDNR thereby causing life-prolonging procedures to be withheld or withdrawn and death being hastened is a Class 2 felony.

k. Futile Medical Care Not Required

The Health Care Decisions Act specifically states "Nothing in this article shall be construed to require a physician to prescribe or render medical treatment to a patient that the physician determines to be medically or ethically inappropriate."[761] However, a physician must make a reasonable effort to transfer the care of the patient to another physician if the treating physician's determination is contrary to the patient's advance directive, a DDNR, or his surrogate decision-maker's request.[762] The physician must provide the patient ... "a reasonable time of not less than fourteen days to affect such transfer. During this period, the physician shall continue to provide any life-sustaining care to the patient which is reasonably available to such physician, as requested by the patient ..."[763] Disputed health care does not have to be provided if it would deprive another patient of such care.[764]

l. Active Euthanasia / Assisted Suicide

"Mercy killing" or active euthanasia is not condoned, authorized or approved by the Health Care Decisions Act.[765] A licensed health care provider who assists or attempts to assist a suicide will be

---

760 Va. Code 54.1-2989
761 Va. Code 54.1-2990.A
762 Va. Code 54.1-2990.A
763 Va. Code 54.1-2990.A
764 Va. Code 54.1-2990.C
765 Va. Code 54.1-2990.D

deemed to have engaged in unprofessional conduct.[766] *Suicide* is defined as "the act or instance of taking one's own life voluntarily and intentionally."[767] *Assisting* is defined as:

1. Providing the physical means by which another person commits or attempts to commit suicide; or

2. Participating in a physical act by which another person commits or attempts to commit suicide[768]

If a health care provider does either of these actions, he can be liable for compensatory and punitive damages in a civil action by a spouse, parent, child or sibling of a person who commits or attempts to commit suicide.[769] A person reasonably expected to assist or attempt to assist a suicide can be enjoined.[770] Statutes of other states prohibiting assisted suicide, such as this one in Virginia, have been upheld by the U.S. Supreme Court.[771] However, the federal government is prohibited from interfering with a physician's prescription that may result in a terminal patient's suicide.[772] Similarly, Virginia does not prohibit prescription or administration of medications that relieve pain or discomfort but that may hasten or increase the risk of death as an unintended consequence.[773]

m. Manner of Death

The withholding or withdrawal of life-prolonging procedures in

---

[766] Va. Code 8.01-622.1.D

[767] Va. Code 8.01-622.1.F

[768] Va. Code 8.01-622.1.A

[769] Va. Code 8.01-622.1.C. The statute is silent as to what compensatory damages can be recovered. One may assume that these would be the same as those set forth in Virginia's wrongful death statute.

[770] Va. Code 8.01-622.1.B

[771] Washington v. Glucksberg, 117 S.Ct. 2258 (1997) (upholding Washington law prohibiting assisted suicide); Va. Admin. Codeco v. Quill, 117 S. Ct. 2293 (1997) (upholding a New York statute prohibiting assisted suicide).

[772] Gonzales v. Oregan, 126 S. Ct. 904; 163 L. Ed. 2d 748 (2006)

[773] Va. Code 8.01-622.1.E

accordance with the provisions of the Health Care Decisions Act, which might be described as passive euthanasia, does not constitute suicide for any purpose.[774] This, however, does not answer related questions such as: Is one guilty of murder (as opposed to assault) if a crime victim decides to forgo life-saving medical therapy, e.g. blood transfusion? Is a negligent party liable for wrongful death (as opposed to personal injury) if a patient refuses further medical treatment (e.g. renal dialysis) that will ultimately lead to the patient's death?

Insurance decisions cannot be based on nor affected by whether or not one has executed an advance directive or a DDNR.[775] Similarly, health care cannot be preconditioned on whether or not an advance directive or DDNR has been executed by a patient.[776]

n. Preservation of Prior Declarations & Reciprocity

The Health Care Decisions Act explicitly recognizes the validity of declarations, regardless of the name used in its title, made under prior Virginia law or under the law of another state. Such declarations will be construed in accordance with Virginia law.[777]

3. Prescription of Excessive Doses of Pain Medication

Virginia law specifically allows a physician to prescribe a dosage of analgesia in excess of the routine dosage for a patient with intractable pain, if the physician certifies the medical necessity in the patient's record.[778] If prescribing, dispensing or administering such a dose is done in good faith for accepted medicinal or therapeutic purposes, a practitioner will not be in violation of the Virginia licensure act.

---

[774]   Va. Code 54.1-2991
[775]   Va. Code 54.1-2991
[776]   Va. Code 54.1-2991
[777]   Va. Code 54.1-2992 and Va. Code 54.1-2993
[778]   Va. Code 54.1-3408.1

A physician must carefully monitor the patient and exhaustively document.

Administering large doses of a narcotic to reduce pain may hasten a patient's death. While hastening a patient's death is not condoned, the management of pain is not only reasonable but expected of a clinician. Thus, the *rule of double effect* has been adopted and is applied to situations in which it is impossible to avoid all harmful effects of an action. The doctrine dates back to Roman Catholic theology of the Middle Ages.[779] However, as discussed above, Virginia law prohibits a clinician from active euthanasia.

---

[779] For a detailed discussion, see Quill, Dresser, & Brock, "The Rule of Double Effect –A Critique of Its Role in End-of-Life Decision-making," 337 New Eng J of Med 1768-1171 (1997) as well as the subsequent Letters to the Editor, 338 New Eng J of Med 1389 -1390 (1998)

J.   Death

1. Defining Death

Virginia law deems one to be medically and legally dead if:

1. The absence of spontaneous cardiac and respiratory functions are believed by physician to be irreversible; or

2. The absence of brain stem reflexes, spontaneous brain functions and spontaneous respiratory functions are believed to be irreversible. A specialist in neurology, neurosurgery, electroencephalography or critical care medicine must determine *brain death*.[780] The determination must be recorded in the patient's record.[781]

A registered nurse or a physician assistant may pronounce death if the following criteria exist:[782]

1. The nurse is employed by a home health agency,[783] hospital, nursing home, a hospice,[784] a continuing care retirement community, or the Department of Corrections;

2. The nurse is directly involved in the care of the patient;

3. The patient's death has occurred;

4. The patient is under the care of a physician when his death occurs;

5. The patient's death has been anticipated;

---

[780]   Va. Code 54.1-2972.A
[781]   Va. Code 54.1-2972.C
[782]   Va. Code 54.1-2972.B
[783]   As defined in Va. Code 32.1-162.7
[784]   As defined in Va. Code 32.1-162.1

6. The physician is unable to be present within a reasonable period of time to determine death; and

7. There is a valid Do Not Resuscitate Order[785] for the patient who has died.

The nurse is explicitly prohibited from determining the cause of death. This remains the responsibility of the attending physician.[786]

2. Reporting Death

a. Death Certificate

A death certificate must be filed with the local registrar within three days of death and prior to final disposition or removal of the body from the Commonwealth.[787] Filing of the death certificate is the responsibility of the funeral director or person who first assumes custody of the dead body.[788] Unless investigation by the medical examiner is required, the physician attending the patient for the illness or condition resulting in death or the physician pronouncing death must complete and sign the death certificate within twenty-four hours of the death.[789] If the attending physician is not available, then her associate, her nurse practitioner or physician assistant,[790] the chief medical officer of the facility, or the autopsy pathologist may complete and sign the certificate if the substitute physician has

---

[785] As defined in Va. Code 54.1-2987.1
[786] Va. Code 54.1-2972.B
[787] Va. Code 32.1-263.A
[788] Va. Code 32.1-263.B
[789] Va. Code 32.1-263.C; If the cause of death cannot be determined within 24 hours, then an extended period is allowed. Va. Code 32.1-263.E. Also see 12 Va. Admin. Code 5-550-360 which mirrors the statutory duty. HB1802 (2015) added that willful failure, refusal or neglect to complete and sign a death certificate is a Class 1 misdemeanor. Va. Code 32.1-263.C and Va. Code 54.1-2973.1
[790] Added by SB 1117 (2011) amending Va. Code 32.1-263.C and 54.1-2972. However, the authority of a nurse practitioner or physician assistant to determine the cause of death remains limited. Va. Code 54.1-2972.B

access to the medical history and death is due to natural causes. If investigation by the medical examiner is required, then the medical examiner will complete the death certificate.[791] If the medical examiner declines the case, then the physician last providing care shall sign the death certificate.[792]

In litigation, a death certificate is not admissible into evidence at a trial as to the opinions stated therein, i.e. the cause of death.[793] Likewise, the opinions contained in an autopsy report are not admissible.[794] However, the Medical Examiner's records, including autopsy report and investigation statements are admissible without the ME testifying.[795] Whether this violates the right to cross examination has not been tested.

When the date of death is unknown, it must be determined by approximation based on all of the available information, including when the immediate family last saw the deceased alive if he died in his home.[796]

b. Fetal Death Report

A fetal death report must be filed for each fetal death, including abortion, that occurs in Virginia with the local registrar within three days after delivery or abortion.[797] The report must be filed by whoever is first in the following list:

1. The funeral director or person who first assumes custody of a dead fetus;

---

[791] Va. Code 32.1-263.D
[792] Va. Code 32.1-263.D
[793] Bailey, Adm'x v. Hunter, Inc., 207 Va. 123 (1966)
[794] Va. Code 19.2-188.B and 32.1-272(b); Hopkins v. Commonwealth, 230 Va. 280
[795] Va. Code 8.01-390.2
[796] Va. Code 32.1-263
[797] Va. Code 32.1-264.A

2. The hospital representative who first assumes custody of the fetus;

3. The physician or other person in attendance at or after the delivery or abortion.[798]

The medical certification portion of a fetal death report must be completed and signed within twenty-four hours after delivery or abortion by the physician in attendance except when investigation or inquiry by the medical examiner is required.[799] A physician or facility attending a woman who has delivered a dead fetus must:

1. Maintain a copy of the fetal death report for one year; and

2. Must furnish the woman with a copy of the report, if she makes a written request.[800]

3. *Investigating Cause of Death*

a. Medical Examiner

A Medical Examiner[801] is expressly authorized to investigate the cause and manner of the death of any person:

> from trauma, injury, violence, poisoning, accident, suicide or homicide, or suddenly when in apparent good health, or when unattended by a physician, or in jail, prison, other correctional institution or police custody, or suddenly as an apparent result of fire, or

---

[798] Va. Code 32.1-264.B

[799] Va. Code 32.1-264.C

[800] Va. Code 32.1-264.F

[801] A physician, a physician assistant or a nurse practitioner may be appointed as a Medical Examiner. A physician assistant must be under the continuos supervision of a physician. A nurse practitioner must practice in collaboration with a physician. Va. Code 32.1-282

in any suspicious, unusual or unnatural manner or Sudden Infant Death Syndrome.[802]

Physicians and hospitals have the duty to notify the medical examiner of such deaths.[803] The better practice, however, is to report all deaths that are of concern, placing the decision on the Medical Examiner to decline to investigate. (The Medical Examiner maintains a log of all reported deaths and whether investigation was undertaken or declined.) This avoids later criticism by investigating agencies, family members or others.

Where a fetal death occurs without the mother receiving medical attention, "or when inquiry or investigation by the medical examiner is required," the medical examiner is obliged to investigate the cause of death.[804]

b. Deaths Associated with Restraints or Seclusion

A hospital must report to the Center for Medicare and Medicaid Services (CMS) any death that occurs while a patient is restrained or in seclusion, or where it is reasonable to assume that a patient's death is a result of restraint or seclusion.[805] The Food and Drug Administration (FDA) also must be advised within ten days.[806]

c. Consent to Autopsy

An autopsy may be authorized "for the purpose of determining the cause of death of the decedent, for the advancement of medical or dental education and research, or for the general advancement of medical or dental science" by any of the following persons, in order of priority:[807]

---

[802]   Va. Code 32.1-283.A
[803]   Va. Code 32.1-283.A
[804]   Va. Code 32.1-264.D
[805]   42 C.F.R. 482.13(f)(7); Interpretive Guidelines Tag A799
[806]   Safe Medical Devices Act of 1990
[807]   Va. Code 54.1-2973

1. Any person designated to make arrangements for the disposition of the decedent's remains upon his death;[808]

2. The spouse;

3. An adult son or daughter;

4. Either parent;

5. An adult brother or sister;

6. A guardian of the person of the decedent at the time of his death; or

7. Any other person authorized or under legal obligation to dispose of the body.

This authority is allowed if:

1. No person in a higher class exists or no person in a higher class is available at the time authorization or consent is given;

2. There is no actual notice of contrary indications by the decedent, and

3. There is no actual notice of opposition by a member of the same or a prior class.

An autopsy may be authorized before or after death. A surgeon or physician performing an autopsy pursuant to this authorization will not be liable for civil or criminal damages. However, an autopsy cannot be performed where official inquiry is required until the body has been released by the Medical Examiner.[809]

4. The Dead Body

a. Ownership of the Body

Virginia follows the common law in holding that human remains

---

[808] See Va. Code 54.1-2825
[809] Va. Code 54.1-2973

are not owned by the next of kin or anyone else.[810] This concept of res nullius[811] is eroding as courts across the country review the ownership question in civil rights cases. For example, the U.S. Court of Appeals, Ninth Circuit has held that parents had an ownership interest in the bodies of their children thus triggering a civil rights claim when the medical examiner removed the corneas without the permission of the parents.[812] Likewise, the U.S. Court of Appeals, Sixth Circuit, held that constitutionally protected property rights exist in the human body, and the next of kin have standing to bring a civil rights action against a county that was responsible for removing tissue from the deceased.[813]

Based on historic common law, defiling a body can lead to being liable to the family for monetary damages[814] and prosecution under criminal law.[815] Similarly, buying or selling human bodies is prohibited in Virginia, unless approved by the Commissioner of Health.[816]

If no next of kin, an agent named in an advance directive or a

---

[810] E.g. In re Estate of Moyor, 577 P.2d 108, 110 (Utah 1978); Hearon v. Chicago, 510 N.E.2d 1192, 1195 (Ill. App. 1987); State v. Powell, 497 So.2d 1188, 1191 (Fla. 1986), cert. denied 481 US 1059 (1987) also see 72 Michigan L Rev 1242-43 and 21 ALR 2d 472, 485 for a discussion of the res nullius concept.

[811] For a historic discussion, see 3 Edward Coke, Institutes of the Laws of England 203 (1644). For a more current discussion, see Boulier, "Sperm, Spleens, and other Valuables: The Need to Recognize Property Rights in Human Body Parts," 23 Hofstra L Rev 693 (1995)

[812] Newman v. Sathyavaglswaran, 287 F.3d 786 (9th Cir, 2002)

[813] Whaley v. County of Tuscola, 58 F.3d 1111 (6th Cir. 1995), cert .denied 116 S.Ct 476 (1995)

[814] Sanford v. Ware, 191 Va. 43 (1950); Siver v. Rockingham Memorial Hospital, 48 F. Supp. 2d 608 (WD Va. 1999); also see Risal v. SCI Virginia Funeral Services, Inc., (J. Maxfield, Fairfax Cir. Ct., 11/19/2010), VLW 010-8-225. A claim for conversion was rejected by a Circuit Court. Opinion letter of J. Fulton, Norfolk Circuit Court, 10/31/14, Anderson v. LifeNet, relying on McHenry v. Adams, 248 Va. 238, 241 (1994)

[815] Va. Code 18.2-126

[816] Va. Code 32.1-303

guardian, any adult who is able to provide positive identification of the decedent and is willing to pay the funeral costs may authorize make arrangements for disposition of a body.[817] Likewise, a public guardian or conservator has the authority to make arrangements for the funeral and disposition of remains if the public guardian or conservator is not aware of any person that has otherwise been designated.[818]

Where a body is unclaimed, is required to be buried at public expense, or has been lawfully donated for scientific study, the Commissioner of Health must be notified. The Commissioner is permitted to remove such a body, without fee or reward, to be used for the advancement of health science.[819] The Commissioner is then obligated to distribute available bodies in the following priority:

1. Virginia medical schools;

2. Virginia colleges and schools authorized to teach health sciences;

3. Such physicians and surgeons as the Commissioner may designate; and

4. Colleges and schools outside the Commonwealth that teach health science.[820]

The recipient (an individual or institution) must post bond before receiving a body insuring that the cadaver will be used solely for scientific education and training.[821] The recipient is also obligated to pay all expenses related to delivery of the body.[822] After the body has been used for instruction, it must be decently interred or cremated by the institution or individual. If the decedent or the family have

---

[817]   Va. Code 54.1-2807.02

[818]   Va. Code 2.2-713 and 37.2-1020

[819]   Va. Code 32.1-298

[820]   Va. Code 32.1-299.A

[821]   Va. Code 32.1-299.B

[822]   Va. Code 32.1-299.C

requested in writing, the cremated remains must be returned to the family.[823]

At the other end of the spectrum of life, frozen human embryos have been held to lack standing to challenge federal regulations.[824]

b. Storage, Transportation and Disposition

A facility storing a cadaver must maintain it at refrigeration of 40° F or less. The expense for doing so is the responsibility of the person claiming the body or the local city or county.[825]

A private individual may transport the remains of a deceased family member either by preference or in observation of religious beliefs and customs.[826] However, anyone in the business of such transportation must be licensed. A transit permit must be obtained from the local health department prior to moving a body out of state.[827]

---

[823]   Va. Code 32.1-301
[824]   Doe v. Obama, 631 F.3d 157 (4th Cir. 2011)
[825]   Va. Code 32.1-309.5
[826]   Va. Code 54.1-2819
[827]   Va. Code 32.1-265

K. Organ Transplantation

1. Organ Donation

a. Post-Humous Donation

Any adult, minor old enough to apply for a driver's license, parent for a minor that is not old enough to apply for a driver's license, or an agent of a patient may consent to the donation of any anatomical tissue to be collected at the time of death.[828] Likewise, refusal or restrictions on gifts may be made. Organ donation may be made by a written declaration, by joining a donor registry, via designation on one's driving license, in a will, or in an advance directive.[829] During a terminal illness or injury, a donor may express his intent by any form of communication addressed to at least two adults.[830] The concurrence of the surviving relatives is not needed.[831] Donating or refusing to donate a specific organ is not to be construed to bar donation of other tissue by the next of kin.[832] Likewise, donation of an organ is inferred to include one's consent to any testing necessary to determine suitability of the donation.[833]

A Virginia driver's license can denote a driver's willingness to be an organ donor.[834] Such designation is sufficient authority to remove, following death, the driver's organs or tissues without further authority from the donor, his family or estate.[835] A police officer,

---

[828] Va. Code 32.1-291.4
[829] Va. Code 32.1-291.5
[830] Va. Code 32.1-291.5.A.3
[831] Va. Code 32.1-291.8
[832] Va. Code 32.1-291.8
[833] Va. Code 32.1-291.14
[834] Va. Code 46.2-342.D
[835] Va. Code 46.2-342.F

fireman, paramedic or other emergency rescuer, and hospital staff are permitted to make a reasonable search for a donor card.[836] A procurement organization may conduct an administrative search of the patient's Department of Motor Vehicle file to determine if the patient has authorized or refused organ donation.[837] An organ donor registry was established by statute.[838]

As in the Health Care Decisions Act, relatives in the following priority can authorize donation of organs at the time of death: [839]

1. An agent appointed by the decedent
2. The guardian;
3. The spouse;
4. Adult children;
5. Parents;
6. Adult siblings;
7. Adult grandchildren
8. Grandparents
9. An adult who exhibited special care and concern for the decedent; and
10. Any other person having the authority to dispose of the decedent's body

An anatomical gift authorized by one of the above individuals must be documented by either 1) a document signed by the authorized person; or 2) a recorded message that is electronically recorded or is contemporaneously reduced to writing and signed by the

---

[836] Va. Code 32.1-291.12.A
[837] Va. Code 32.1-291.14.A
[838] Va. Code 32.1-292.2. The Virginia Transplant Council was established by Va. Code 32.1-297.1.
[839] Va. Code 32.1-291.9

recipient.[840] Appropriate steps may be taken by a facility to preserve the viability of organs while awaiting the decision of the family.[841]

The practitioner needs to be on guard that an unrevoked refusal by the patient to donate cannot be overridden by the next of kin. Likewise, an agent appointed by the decedent in an advance directive has higher standing than even a spouse.[842] A donation by one of the above family members can be revoked by a same or higher priority relative if the organ harvesting team is notified of the revocation before starting the procedure.[843]

A physician attending the patient at death or certifying the time of death is not allowed to participate in the procedures for removal or transplantation of the donated tissue.[844] The recipient of an organ donation must remove the organ without unnecessary mutilation of the body.[845] Once harvesting is completed, the remainder of the body returns to the custody of the next-of-kin.

A health care provider harvesting organs in compliance with the state statute is immune from civil or criminal liability.[846] Health care providers who may receive donated organs are set forth by statute.[847] Where broad terms are used to indicate a willingness to donate organs, priority will be given to therapeutic use.[848]

b. Obligation to Inquire

An acute care hospital must notify an organ procurement

---

[840]   Va. Code 32.1-291.10
[841]   Va. Code 32.1-291.14.C
[842]   Va. Code 32.1-291.9
[843]   Va. Code 32.1-291.10.C
[844]   Va. Code 32.1-291.14.I
[845]   Va. Code 32.1-291.14.H
[846]   Va. Code 32.1-291.18; Fuss v. LifeNet, 61 Va. Cir. 422 (2003)
[847]   Va. Code 32.1-291.11
[848]   Va. Code 32.1-291.11.F

organization every time someone dies in the facility.[849] A Virginia hospital must establish "a routine contact protocol which ensures that the families of suitable organ and tissue donors are offered the opportunity ... to consider organ, tissue and eye donation."[850] Once consent has been obtained, the Medical Examiner may provide such tissue to appropriate recipient health care providers assuming that it will not interfere with the investigation, autopsy or facial appearance of the deceased.[851] If consent cannot be obtained from the next of kin, the organs must be replaced. The Medical Examiner has immunity from civil or criminal liability if this law is observed.

2. Sale of Organs

Virginia law prohibits the sale of human body parts.[852] However, hair, ova, blood, and other self-replicating body tissues and fluids are exempted. Reimbursement of expenses associated with the removal and preservation of a body part for medical and scientific purposes is allowed. The sale of organs is also prohibited by federal statute.

With regard to product liability litigation, no warranty is implied by the law for blood, organs, or other tissue except where a pathogen is detectable using established medical and technical procedures.[853]

The donation or sale of blood, organs, or other tissue knowing that

---

[849] 63 Fed. Reg. 33856. This regulation is drafted as a condition of Medicare participation, eff. 8/21/98.

[850] Va. Code 32.1-127 and 32.1-292; An agreement with a procurement organization is required by Va. Code 32.1-291.15; See Bushlow v. INOVA Health System Hospitals, 40 Va. Cir. 121 (1996) (statute bars action by family for hospital staff asking family about organ donation); Interestingly, the duty of others to seek consent from the next of kin was repealed in 2008. Va. Code 32.1-283, amended by HB 216 and 278 (2008)

[851] Va. Code 32.1-291.22 and 32.1-291.23

[852] Va. Code 32.1-291.16. Sale of body parts is a Class 4 felony.

[853] Va. Code 32.1-297

the donor is, or was, infected with HIV is a criminal offense unless the material is being collected solely for scientific research.[854]

3. Living Donors

Virginia has very little law, either by statute or court decision, on the transplantation of organs from live donors. Only one trial court decision has been found discussing kidney donation from a minor to her sister.[855] The judge had little difficulty approving the kidney transplantation. Every available precaution had been taken with this teenage donor to assure that she was not being pressured to give up her kidney. In the absence of legal precedent, the health care provider would be well advised to strongly counsel the donor as to the risks of the procedure.[856] Although challenging, every effort should be made to avoid pressuring the potential donor to consent to the gift. Where a minor is involved, the court should be petitioned for approval. Courts of other states have entertained several unusual fact situations. For example, the Illinois Supreme Court held that a minor could not be forced to undergo tissue typing for his half-brother.[857]

4. Product Development from Human Tissue

No Virginia court decision has been found regarding the use of a patient's tissue for product development. The landmark case in this area, the "Mo cell" case, comes from California.[858] During treatment of John Moore at the University of California, physicians discovered that Mr. Moore had an extremely rare and valuable cell

---

[854] Va. Code 32.1-289.2

[855] Hurdle v. Currier, 5 Va. Cir. 509 (1977)

[856] For a more detailed discussion, see R. Adams, "Organ Donors & Informed Consent: A Difficult Minuet," 8 Journal of Legal Medicine 555 (1987)

[857] Curran v. Bosze, 141Ill. 2d 473 (1990)

[858] Moore v. Regents of the University of California, 51 Cal.3d 120, 271 Cal. Rptr. 146, 793 P.2d 479 (1990); cert. den. 499 U.S. 936 (1991)

type in his spleen. When his spleen was removed, the researchers secretly took cells from it and developed the "Mo cell" with huge economic potential. Mr. Moore sued for conversion (theft), lack of informed consent, breach of fiduciary duty, fraud, and negligent misrepresentation. The California Supreme Court held that a cause of action could be brought for the physician's breach of his obligation to disclose but not for conversion. The patented cell line derived from the harvested cells, wrote the Court, is factually and legally distinct from Mr. Moore's cells. Further, the Court reasoned, selling of human body parts is prohibited by statute. Thus, Mr. Moore was not entitled to any royalties from the sale of commercial products based on his cells.

L. Incident Management

Every health care provider, especially facility administrators, should take a few moments to anticipate what steps should be taken to handle an untoward event. For example, if a patient unexpectedly dies in the facility, who should be notified? What actions should be taken if one resident attacks another? In general, a list of names, addresses and telephone numbers, including cell phones and after-hours numbers, should be developed for the following:

- Decision maker (e.g. administrator, president of group, or chairman of department);
- Risk manager;
- Responsible physician;
- Health care attorney;
- State and federal agencies that must be notified;
- Public relations representative of the organization; and
- Insurance company claims manager and / or risk manager

The key issues to anticipate are:

- Immediate health care for patient(s) involved;
- Communication with the following groups:
  - Patients and families;
  - Other health care providers;
  - Owners; shareholders; or investors;
  - The general public and media; and
- Interaction with state and federal government agencies that license or regulate the health care provider(s).

With these thoughts in mind, a health care provider should become familiar with the federal and state regulations as well as Joint Commission guidance that affect his practice, especially in a facility setting. Good communication with state and federal agencies before a crisis will go a long way toward diffusing the often tense confrontations when government agents arrive after an event. Early involvement of experienced health care counsel will also help reduce the aftershocks of a difficult situation.

Joint Commission and other health care organizations have strongly pushed for immediate full disclosure of unexpected events to a patient and family.[859] The task is more daunting than a lay person might believe. Collecting accurate information must be a priority but is not easy with health care providers constantly coming and going from a facility. The true cause of an adverse event may be hotly debated. Most health care providers are not comfortable discussing a bad outcome, particularly if it reflects badly on the provider's performance. Helpful guides are available to assist the clinician.[860]

Documentation by a health care provider is often critical in defending against scrutiny by government agencies and plaintiff's attorneys. A provider should **not** write the following in the chart:

- "Called Risk Management"
- "Called attorney"
- "Filed incident report with hospital administration"
- "Called malpractice carrier"
- Disciplinary actions against an employee
- Speculation as to cause of incident or casting blame

A health care provider should carefully consider the most prudent way in which to make a late entry. It should be done in a manner that minimizes the conjecture that the entry was intended to be self-serving.

---

[859] Joint Commission, Standard RI.1.2.2

[860] See ASHRM, "Disclosure of Unanticipated Events: The Next Step in Better Communication with Patients," http://www.ashrm.org/ashrm/resources/files/Disclosure.Pt1.pdf

II. Management of Medical Information

A. Content of Medical Records

The minimum content of medical records is a very contentious topic. Medicare has emphasized objective criteria of evaluation and management (E & M).[861] While this has been resisted by physician organizations, the standards for medical record departments in hospitals are delineated by Department of Health regulation.[862] The Virginia Board of Medicine has recently adopted regulations requiring a physician to maintain timely, accurate, legible and complete patient records.[863] These adjectives are not defined, but the basic goal of medical records remains the same: documenting adequate information for continuity of care. Unfortunately, the amount of documentation expected continues to increase.

The Office of Inspector General (OIG) for the US Department of Health and Human Services has stated that "timely, accurate and complete documentation is critical to nearly every aspect of a physician practice" and "one of the most important physician practice compliance issues is the appropriate documentation of diagnosis and treatment."[864] At a minimum, OIG contends that a physician chart should: [865]

    a. Be complete and legible

    b. State for each encounter:

---

[861] See "HCFA Unveils Long-Awaited Evaluation, Management Draft Documentation Guidelines," 9 BNA Health Law Reporter, p. 1009 (6/29/00).

[862] 12 Va. Admin. Code 5-410-370. Also see 12 Va. Admin. Code 5-410-1260 regarding outpatient hospital records.

[863] 18 Va. Admin. Code 85-20-26

[864] Compliance Program Guidance for Individual and Small Group Physician Practices, Office of Inspector General (September 2000)

[865] Compliance Program Guidance for Individual and Small Group Physician Practices

      i.   The reason

     ii.   Relevant history

    iii. Exam findings

    iv. Prior test results

     v.   Assessment

    vi. Clinical impression or diagnosis

   vii. Plan of care

  viii. Date

    ix. Identity of provider, and

c. Identify:

      i.   Health risk factors

     ii.   Progress

    iii. Response

    iv. Changes in treatment, and

     v.   Any revisions to the diagnosis

As an example of documentation requirements, the content of a medical record for an outpatient surgical center[866] must "contain sufficient information to satisfy the diagnosis or need for medical or surgical service"[867] and include the following: [868]

- Patient identification;
- Admitting information, including patient history and physical examination;
- Signed consent;
- Confirmation of pregnancy, if applicable;

---

[866] Outpatient hospital is defined in 12 Va. Admin. Code 5-410-10, and explicitly includes abortion clinics.

[867] 12 Va. Admin. Code 5-410-1260.A

[868] 12 Va. Admin. Code 5-410-1260.A

- Physician orders;
- Laboratory tests, pathology reports, and radiology reports;
- Anesthesia record;
- Operative record;
- Surgical medication and medical treatments;
- Recovery room notes;
- Physician and nursing progress notes;
- Condition at time of discharge;
- Patient instructions, preoperative and postoperative; and
- Names of referral physicians or agencies

Intentionally falsifying a patient record is a Class 1 misdemeanor.[869] Prior to enactment of the healthcare-specific statute, a licensed practical nurse was convicted of forgery for making entries in a nursing home patient's chart for services that she did not perform.[870]

---

[869]   Va. Code 18.2-260.1
[870]   Beshah v. Commonwealth, 60 Va. App. 161 (2012)

B. Confidentiality

Confidentiality of medical information has been a major tenet of health care for many years. However, Virginia law did not demand this as recently as a few years ago.[871] Not until 1997 did the Supreme Court of Virginia first recognize a personal right of confidentiality for the patient:

> In our jurisprudence, **a health care provider owes a duty of reasonable care to the patient. Included within that duty is the health care provider's obligation to preserve the confidentiality of information about the patient which was communicated to the health care provider or discovered by the health care provider during the course of treatment.** Indeed, confidentiality is an integral aspect of the relationship between a health care provider and a patient and, often, to give the health care provider the necessary information to provide proper treatment, the patient must reveal the most intimate aspects of his or her life to the health care provider during the course of treatment.
>
> We hold that **in the absence of a statutory command to the contrary, or absent a serious danger to the patient or others, a health care provider owes a duty to the patient not to disclose information gained from the patient without the patient's authorization,**

---

[871] See <u>Pierce v. Caday</u>, 244 Va. 285 (1992) and <u>Gibson v. Commonwealth</u>, 216 Va. 412 (1975). The Psychotheraptist-Patient Privilege was only recently recognized by the US Supreme Court in federal common law. <u>Jaffee v. Redmond</u>, 51 F.3d 1346 (7th Cir. 1995), <u>aff'd</u>, 518 U.S. 1, 116 S. Ct. 1923, 135 L. Ed. 2d 337 (1996)

and that **violation of this duty gives rise to an action in tort.**[872] (emphasis added).

The Patient Health Records Privacy Act (PHRPA)[873] and other statutes have created considerable protection for health care data confidentiality. Conversely, this new legislation has created potential liability for the imprudent health care provider.[874]

The basic rule, under current Virginia statutes, is that a health care provider must maintain the confidentiality of medical records.[875] This is an obligation to protect a patient's privacy from all others, including even health care professionals who are not caring for the patient. Multiple exceptions exist to the rule, but a health care provider must be careful to assure that he has complied with state and federal statutes and regulations.

For example, Virginia regulations afford the resident of a psychiatric facility "protection against the unnecessary disclosure of his identity and of personal information contained in his records ..."[876] Likewise, a mother's right to confidentiality is not waived because she files a medical malpractice action on behalf of her infant child.[877] However, a physician who is a potential defendant in a medical malpractice action by his patient can discuss the patient's medical record with his attorney.[878]

Virginia law defines *record* as "any written, printed or electronically

---

[872] Curtis v. Fairfax Hospital, 254 Va. 437 (1997)
[873] Va. Code 32.1-127.1:03.
[874] S.R. v. Inova Healthcare Servs., 49 Va. Cir. 119 (1999) (violation of Virginia computer invasion of privacy act when nurse accessed hospital database to learn about co-worker's psychiatric admission.)
[875] Va. Code 32.1-127.1:03.A. See 18 Va. Admin. Code 85-20-26 and 85-20-27 for Board of Medicine regulations. See 42 C.F.R. 482.24(b)(3) for Medicare regulation of hospitals.
[876] 12 Va. Admin. Code 35-120-40.J
[877] Curtis v. Fairfax Hospital, 254Va. 437 (1997)
[878] Archambault v. Roller, 254 Va. 210 (1997)

recorded material maintained by a provider in the course of providing health services to a patient concerning the patient and the services provided," including "the substance of any communication made by a patient to a provider in confidence during or in connection with the provision of health services to a patient or information otherwise acquired by the provider about a patient in confidence and in connection with the provision of health services to a patient."[879] Strictly applying this definition, it appears that even a patient's reason for visit or chief complaint recorded on a sign-in log maintained by a physician's office constitutes a patient's medical record, which a patient would expect to remain private and confidential. However, a rule of reason has been adopted.

1. The Health Insurance Portability and Accountability Act

Information that relates to an individual's health, medical treatment, or payment for health care may be protected by the Health Insurance Portability and Accountability Act of 1996 (HIPAA). The act did not change the fundamental tenet that a patient's medical information should be kept confidential. Its primary impact is to require written documentation of policies, procedures, and compliance.[880] HIPAA was amended by the Health Information Technology for Economic and Clinical Health Act (HITECH) enacted by Congress in 2009.[881]

HITECH seeks to toughen enforcement of HIPAA by increasing

---

[879] Va. Code 32.1-127.1:03.B.

[880] HITECH requires the Office of Civil Rights to perform periodic audits to assure compliance with the Privacy Rule and the Security Rule. 42 U.S.C.A. 13411; See Wagner, "Early Results from New HIPAA Audit Pilot Reveal Emphasis on Policy Documentation and Business Associate Agreements," ABA Health eSource, May 2012

[881] Title XIII of the American Recovery and Reinvestment Act (ARRA) of 2009

civil penalties and permitting state attorneys general to bring civil actions in federal court on behalf of state residents.[882]

a. The Privacy Rule

The regulations generated by the Department of Health and Human Services (HHS) are known as "Standards for Privacy of Individually Identifiable Health Information," or simply as the "Privacy Rule,"[883] and became effective for most providers on April 14, 2003. The Office of Civil Rights (OCR) within HHS is empowered to enforce the regulations.

A *covered entity* that is subject to the provisions of HIPAA includes:

- A health care provider that conducts certain *electronic transactions*,[884]
- A health care clearinghouse, or
- A health plan:
  - An employee health benefit plan
  - with 50 or more participants **or**
  - is administered by a TPA
  - Employer as plan sponsor

---

[882] ARRA at 13410(d), (e)(1) and (a)(2)
[883] 45 C.F.R. 160 and 164, Subparts A and E. The regulations exceed 600 pages in their final (Aug 2002) form. The best summary of these regulations found by this author is contained in "The Confidentiality of Alcohol and Drug Abuse Patient Records Regulation and the HIPAA Privacy Rule: Implications for Alcohol and Substance Abuse Programs," US Dept of Health & Human Services, Substance Abuse and Mental health Services Administration, Center for Substance Abuse Treatment, www.samhsa.gov, June 2004. Much of the discussion here on HIPAA was extracted from that document.
[884] *Electronic form* does not include transmission via telefax or telephone.

Electronic transactions include:[885]

- Submission of claims to health plans;
- Coordination of benefits with health plans;
- Inquiries to health plans regarding eligibility, coverage or benefits or status of health care claims;
- Transmission of enrollment and other information related to payment to health plans; and
- Referral certification and authorization

HIPAA requires that a patient be given a notice of the provider's privacy practices as well as the patient's rights under the Privacy Rule.[886] The written notice must be given to the patient as well as prominently posted where it is reasonably expected that a patient would be able to read it.[887] Any provider that maintains a web site must also prominently post its notice on the site and make it available for download from the site.[888] A provider must make a good faith effort to obtain the patient's acknowledgement of receiving the notice on the date of the first service provided. If acknowledgment is not obtained, the provider must document its efforts and the reason it was not able to obtain the acknowledgment.[889]

A patient is given additional rights under HIPAA, including the right to request restrictions on uses and disclosure of protected health information (PHI); the right to review and amend PHI; and the right to receive an accounting of disclosures of PHI.[890]

A patient must be allowed to request that a provider restrict uses or disclosures of PHI in treatment, payment or health care operations.[891]

---

[885]   45 C.F.R. 160.103
[886]   45 C.F.R. 164.520(b)
[887]   45 C.F.R. 164.520(c)(2); 164.530(i)(4)(i)(C)
[888]   45 C.F.R. 164.520(c)(3)
[889]   45 C.F.R. 164.520(c)(2)(ii)
[890]   45 C.F.R. 164.522, 164.524, 164.526, 164.528
[891]   45 C.F.R. 164.522

A provider is not required to agree to a requested restriction, but if he does, then he may not violate the agreed restriction. The provider may terminate the agreement to a restriction, effective after the patient has been informed.[892]

In addition, a patient has the right to request that communication of PHI be done in a specific fashion.[893] For example, a patient may ask that communications be only to his office phone number and not his home number. HIPAA requires that the provider accommodate reasonable requests.

A *covered entity* is also obligated to:

- Designate
    - a privacy officer who is responsible for the development and implementation of privacy policies and procedures; and
    - a contact person responsible for receiving complaints and able to provide further information[894]
- Train all employees on privacy policies and procedures. New employees must be trained within a reasonable period after starting employment. Employees must also receive supplemental training as material changes occur in privacy policies and procedures. All training must be documented and records retained for six years after the training.[895]
- Establish a process for patients to make complaints about the provider's privacy policies and procedures or the provider's compliance with its procedures or the requirements of the HIPAA regulations.[896] This process must be documented in writing and provided to a patient on request.

---

[892]   45 C.F.R. 164.522(a)
[893]   45 C.F.R. 164.522(b)(1)(i)
[894]   45 C.F.R. 164.530(a)
[895]   45 C.F.R. 164.530(b)
[896]   45 C.F.R. 164.530(d)

- Assure appropriate administrative, technical, and physical safeguards to protect the confidentiality of PHI.[897] The Privacy Rule applies to all PHI, whether in paper, oral or electronic format. The Security Rule applies only to electronic media.

- Limit access to PHI among employees to the level consistent with their function and need to know. To achieve this, the provider must have policies and procedures that identify staff members or classes of staff members who need access to PHI, the categories of PHI to which they need access, and any conditions appropriate to such access.[898]

- Ensure that disclosure of PHI is limited to the minimum necessary by creating policies and procedures to accomplish this goal.[899]

- Establish and apply appropriate sanctions against employees who fail to comply with the privacy policies and procedures.[900]

- Mitigate, to the extent practical, any harmful effect known to the provider from the use or disclosure of PHI in violation of the privacy policies and procedures.[901]

- Avoid retaliation against any one who participates in a complaint, investigation or hearing on possible violations of the privacy policies and procedures.[902]

- Not require patients to waive their rights under HIPAA as a condition of treatment, payment, enrollment in a health plan, or eligibility for benefits.[903]

---

[897] 45 C.F.R. 164.530(c); Security is addressed in more detail at "Security Standards for the Protection of Electronic Protected Health Information," 45 C.F.R. Part 160 and Part 164, known as the "Security Rule" and must be implemented by April 20, 2005

[898] 45 C.F.R. 164.514(d)(2)

[899] 45 C.F.R. 164.502(b) and 514(d)(3) for routine and recurring disclosures; 45 C.F.R. 164.514(d)(3)(ii) and 514(d)(4) for other disclosures

[900] 45 C.F.R. 164.530(e)

[901] 45 C.F.R. 164.530(f)

[902] 45 C.F.R. 164.530(g)

[903] 45 C.F.R. 164.530(h)

- Implement policies and procedures to comply with HIPAA, and maintain copies of them for six years from when created or last effective, whichever is later.[904]

The final Privacy Rule and OCR interpretations have reduced the initial concerns that provision of health care would be impaired by the stringent general mandates of the initial regulations. For example, OCR has clarified that a hospital can inform visitors or callers about a patient's location in the facility and general condition, unless the patient expresses a preference to the contrary.[905]

The first criminal conviction under HIPAA is believed to have been under a plea agreement in Seattle, Washington.[906] A recent decision of a federal appeals court has clarified that anyone who "knowingly and in violation of this part" obtains individually identifiable health information without a valid reason is guilty of a misdemeanor.[907] One does not need to know that his or her action is illegal. Similarly, HIPAA provides that a Covered Entity may terminate a service contract for breach of a business associate agreement.[908]

The Genetic Information Nondiscrimination Act (GINA)[909] brings genetic information within the definition of *protected health information* under HIPAA. An employer must treat any such information obtained from an employee as confidential under the Americans with Disabilities Act. Questions about family medical history and direct genetic testing are not permitted to be used as a basis for employment decision.

---

[904] 45 C.F.R. 164.530(i) and (j)
[905] OCR, Answer ID 483, updated 11/4/03 citing 45 C.F.R. 164.510(a)
[906] U.S. v. Gibson, No. CR04-0374 RSM (WD WA, 2004)
[907] U.S. v. Zhou, 678 F.3d 1110 (9th Cir. 2012)
[908] See Managed Care Solutions, Inc. v. Community Health Sys., Inc., No. 10-60170 (S.D. Fla. June 20, 2013)
[909] 42 U.S.C.A. 300gg et seq

b. The Security Rule

The Security Rule[910] requires the following elements in protecting electronic personal health information (EPHI):

- Administrative Safeguards: assignment of security responsibilities to an individual; security training of employees;[911]

- Physical Safeguards: the mechanisms required to protect electronic systems, equipment and data contained therein from threats, environmental hazards and unauthorized access;[912]

- Technical Safeguards: the automated processes used to protect data and control access to data, including the use of authentication controls (passwords), encryption, etc.[913]

- Organizational Requirements: delineation of who has access to what EPHI;[914]

- Policies & Procedures / Documentation: drafting and revision of written policies and procedures for security of EPHI[915]

In complying with the Security Rule, a provider should consider:[916]

- Risk analysis: What current circumstances leave the provider open to unauthorized access and disclosure of EPHI?

---

[910] "Security Standards for the Protection of Electronic Protected Health Information," 45 C.F.R. Part 160 and Part 164, known as the "Security Rule," was effective on April 20, 2005. Under HITECH, a business associate must comply directly with the Security Rule

[911] 45 C.F.R. 164.308

[912] 45 C.F.R. 164.310

[913] 45 C.F.R. 164.312

[914] 45 C.F.R. 164.314

[915] 45 C.F.R. 164.316

[916] 45 C.F.R. 164.306(b)

- Security analysis: What security measures are already in place or could reasonably be put into place?

- Financial analysis: How much will implementation cost?

The Security Rule is intended to be flexible and scalable to meet the unique situation of any organization over time. To this end, the regulations do not have specific technical criteria.

2. *Health Information Technology for Economic and Clinical Health Act*

The Health Information Technology for Economic and Clinical Health Act (HITECH) amendments to HIPAA not only increased penalties and expanded the enforcement authority of states attorney generals; it applied enhanced privacy and security requirements to Business Associates (BA). On July 14, 2010, HHS published proposed regulations implementing the HITECH changes to HIPAA and seeking comment from the public on several key provisions.[917] If finalized, these regulations would "expand individuals' rights to access their information and to restrict certain types of disclosures of protected health information to health plans, require business associates of HIPAA-covered entities to be under most of the same rules as covered entities; set new limitations on the use and disclosure of protected health information for marketing and fundraising; and prohibit the sale of protected health information without patient authorization."[918]

---

[917]   See Modifications to the HIPAA Privacy, Security, and Enforcement Rules Under the Health Information Technology for Economic and Clinical Health Act, 75 FR 40868-01, *et seq.*

[918]   "HHS Strengthens Health Information Privacy and Security through New Rules," HHS Press Office News Release (July 8, 2010)

C. Access by Patient

1. The General Rule

A competent adult patient, or legally authorized representative, has a right to obtain copies of his or her medical record.[919] The health care provider must provide these copies to the patient, or legally authorized representative, within fifteen days of receiving a proper written request.[920] Federal regulations provide: [921]

> The hospital must not frustrate the legitimate efforts of individuals to gain access to their own medical records and must actively seek to meet these requests as quickly as its record keeping system permits.

The obligation of a health care provider to communicate openly with a patient about his health and the treatment continues to become more conspicuous. For example, the Joint Commission mandates that patients, and when appropriate their families, be advised of *unanticipated outcomes*.[922] Interestingly, the standard does not require that an explanation of why the actual outcome was significantly different from the anticipated outcome. Certainly, disclosure of the *unanticipated outcome* does not equate to an admission of liability.[923] This is analogous to the ethical obligation of

---

[919]   Va. Code 8.01-413. Also see Va. Code 37.1-84.1 regarding patient access to psychiatric records.

[920]   Va. Code 32.1-127.1:03.E and Va. Code 8.01-413.B While HIPAA, 45 C.F.R. 164.524(b), allows 30 days (or 60 days if the records are maintained off site), the more restrictive statute will apply

[921]   42 C.F.R. 482.13(d)(2); Interpretive Guidelines Tag A768

[922]   Joint Commission Standard RI.1.2.2 (effective 7/1/01)

[923]   Joint Commission Intent of Standard RI.1.2.2

physicians, as stated by the American Medical Association's Council on Ethical and Judicial Affairs.[924]

a. Definition of *patient*

A *patient* is any person who has received care from a health care professional, "including but not limited to examination, diagnosis, evaluation, treatment, pharmaceuticals, aftercare, habilitation, or rehabilitation, and mental health therapy of any kind."[925]

Anyone acting on behalf of a patient, such as the custodial parent of a minor child, the guardian of an incompetent individual, or one authorized by a power of attorney or advance directive, may review the records of a patient.[926] Any time medical information is requested by a patient's representative, the health care provider must assure that the representative is adequately identified and proof of the representative relationship be provided. For example, this may consist of a verified copy of the letters of guardianship. A copy of this verification should be kept with the medical record.

b. Patient Request and Documentation

HIPAA lists the following elements that must be included in an authorization to release medical records:[927]

1. A specific and meaningful description of the information to be disclosed;

2. The name or class of persons authorized to make the requested use or disclosure;

3. The name or class of persons to whom the covered entity may make the requested use or disclosure;

---

[924] AMA Council on Ethical & Judicial Affairs, Opinion E-8.12
[925] Va. Code 32.1-127.1:03.B.
[926] Va. Code 32.1-127.1:03.D.
[927] 45 C.F.R. 164.508(C)(1)

4. A description of each purpose of the requested use or disclosure ("at the request of the individual," is sufficient)

5. An expiration date or expiration event ("end of research study," "none" or similar language is sufficient);

6. Signature of the individual and date (if signed by personal representative, a description of the representative's authority)

In addition, HIPAA requires an authorization to include statements notifying the patient 1) he has a right to revoke the authorization in writing and any exceptions to that right; and 2) whether treatment, payment, enrollment or eligibility for benefits will be conditioned on signing an authorization.[928] The authorization must be written in plain language and a copy given to the patient.[929] These requirements presumably do not prohibit a patient from drafting her own authorization.

In contrast, Virginia law provides that requests for copies of medical records need only:[930]

1. Be in writing, dated and signed by the requester;

2. Identify the nature of the information requested; and

3. Include evidence of the authority of the requester to receive such copies and identification of the person to whom the information is to be disclosed.

HIPAA mandates that a written form be used when the patient is authorizing release of information to a third party. HIPAA does not require a written authorization before permitting a patient to see his own records. However, it does permit a provider to require that

---

[928] 45 C.F.R. 164.508(C)(2)

[929] 45 C.F.R. 164.508(C)(3) and (4)

[930] Va. Code 32.1-127.1:03.E. Also see 12 Va. Admin. Code 5-410-370.F.2 for hospitals

such requests be in writing.[931] A written authorization form is set forth in the Virginia statute,[932] but a provider or patient is free to draft his own document. A photocopy, facsimile, or other copy of the original document signed by the patient must be accepted by a provider.[933]

Patients often request far more information than they really want. Quoting the appropriate fee per page for providing the copies may help fine-tune a patient's request.

HITECH provides an additional right for patients. A covered entity that uses an electronic medical record must, on request, provide an electronic copy to the patient or, if requested, electronically transmit the data to the patient or his designee.[934] A covered entity is limited to charging for its labor costs in complying with the request.

A physician can inform a laboratory, if requested by a patient, to send test results directly to the patient.[935]

For a deceased or incompetent patient, medical records can be released to the following individuals in the listed priority where the health care provider is not aware of a higher class:[936]

1. Personal representative of deceased;
2. Legal guardian of an incompetent;
3. Spouse;
4. Adult son or daughter;
5. Either parent;
6. Adult brother or sister; or

---

[931] 45 C.F.R. 164.524(b)(1)
[932] Va. Code 32.1-127.1:03.G.
[933] Va. Code 32.1-127.1:03.E and 8.01-413.B
[934] ARRA at 13405(e)(1)
[935] Va. Code 54.1-2409.4
[936] Va. Code 8.01-413.B and Va. Code 32.1-127.1:03.D.23

7. Any other relative in descending order of relationship.

c. Ownership of the Original Chart

After years of debate and public misperception, the General Assembly has clearly set forth that the original medical record documents of a patient are the property of the health care provider.[937] If a health care provider is employed by another health care provider, then the original chart is the property of the employer.[938] The original is not to be removed from the possession of the health care provider except as required by subpoena or court order.[939] A patient is entitled to obtain only a copy of her medical records.

d. Records to Which A Patient Does Not Have Access

A patient does not have a right to access all information that may refer to him. For example, HIPAA sets forth that a patient does not have a right of access to:[940]

- Psychotherapy notes
- Information compiled in reasonable anticipation of or for use in a civil, criminal, or administrative action or proceeding; and
- Information that may be subject to or exempt from certain Clinical Laboratory Improvement Amendment (CLIA) provisions

Both federal regulations and state statutes distinguish *psychotherapy notes* from other medical records and prohibit disclosure of *psychotherapy notes* to anyone, including the patient, except in limited circumstances. *Psychotherapy notes* are strictly defined under HIPAA

---

[937] Va. Code 32.1-127.1:03.A and Va. Code 54.1-2403.3
[938] Va. Code 54.1-2403.3
[939] Va. Code 32.1-127.1:03.A citing Va. Code 8.01-413.C. Also see 12 Va. Admin. Code 5-410-370.F.3 for hospitals
[940] 45 C.F.R. 164.524(a)(1)

and Virginia law[941] as "notes recorded (in any medium) by a health care provider who is a mental health professional documenting or analyzing the contents of conversation during a private counseling session or a group, joint, or family counseling session and that are separated from the rest of the individual's medical record."[942] To qualify as *psychotherapy notes*, they are never shared with another provider or anyone else and do not include:

- Medication prescriptions and monitoring;
- Counseling session start and stop times;
- The modalities and frequencies of treatment furnished;
- Results of clinical tests; or
- Any summary of:
  - Diagnosis;
  - Functional status
  - Treatment plan
  - Symptoms
  - Prognosis; or
  - Progress to date

The mental health care provider must be careful to observe these criteria in order to protect *psychotherapy notes*. For example, *psychotherapy notes* cannot be interspersed with other records for a patient. Conversely, a provider must have a complete chart that can be used to document care for a patient with at least the enumerated items above.

HIPAA permits a clinical research program to deny a patient access to his treatment records for as long as the research is in progress, provided that the patient was advised that his right of access would

---

[941]   Va. Code 32.1-127.1:03.B
[942]   45 C.F.R. 164.501

be reinstated at the end of the protocol.[943] If a researcher intends to proceed in this fashion, the limitation will need to be included in the research protocol and the patient consent form submitted to the Institutional Review Board for approval.[944]

2. *Therapeutic Privilege*

From time to time, a treating physician or psychologist may determine that full disclosure of the information contained in a patient's record would be detrimental to the patient. Virginia law allows a patient's treating physician or psychologist to assert a *therapeutic privilege* under limited circumstances, and withhold information contained in a patient's medical record from the patient where the practitioner reasonably believes that there is a likelihood that release of records to the patient will endanger the life or physical safety of the patient or another individual, or that a reference to another person in the medical record might cause substantial harm if the records are released.[945] HIPAA's therapeutic privilege provision also includes protection of a third party.[946]

Instead of providing the potentially injurious record to the patient, the practitioner should make *"a part of the patient's record* a written statement that in his opinion the furnishing to or review by the patient of such records would be injurious to the patient's health or well-being."[947] The patient must be advised that a copy of the record will be made available to a like-qualified practitioner[948] for

---

[943] 45 C.F.R. 164.524(a)(2)(iii)

[944] See Rozovsky & Adams, Clinical Trials and Human Research: A Practical Guide to Regulatory Compliance, Jossey-Bass Publishers (2003)

[945] HB 877 (2004) amending Va. Code 8.01-413, 32.1-127.1:03.F, 37.1-230 and 38.2-608

[946] 45 C.F.R. 164.524(a)(3)

[947] Va. Code 32.1-127.1:03.F and Va. Code 8.01-413.B. Also see Va. Code 37.1-84.1

[948] This is defined as "whose licensure, training and experience relative to the patient's condition is at least equivalent to that of the physician or

review and copying. A statement of the record custodian should accompany copies of such restricted records "that the patient's attending physician or clinical psychologist determined that the patient's review of his record would be injurious to the patient's health or well-being."[949]

HIPAA articulates a different process where records are withheld under therapeutic privilege. Instead of limiting therapeutic privilege to only physicians and psychologists, HIPAA extends the privilege to any licensed healthcare provider. The patient has a right to have the denial reviewed by a licensed professional who is designated by the provider as a reviewing official and who did not participate in the original decision to deny access.[950] The provider must also give a timely denial in plain language explaining:[951]

- The basis for the denial;
- If applicable, a statement of the patient's right to a review of the decision and the process for requesting a review; and
- A description of how the patient can complain to the program or to the Secretary of HHS, including the name or title and telephone number of the contact person designated by the provider to receive complaints.

Where the denial of access to the record is related to litigation, copies of the medical record must be provided to the patient's attorney when a patient requests that the records be forwarded to the attorney. The health care provider should request a document signed by the patient confirming the attorney's authority to make the request.[952] The better practice is for the physician to also discuss the situation with the attorney.

---

clinical psychologist upon whose opinion the denial is based." Va. Code 32.1-127.1:03.F
[949] Va. Code 32.1-127:03.F
[950] 45 C.F.R. 164.524(a)(4)
[951] 45 C.F.R. 164.524(d)(1) and (3)(i)
[952] Va. Code 8.01-413.B

3. *Minor Patients*

A person is generally considered a minor until he or she reaches the age of 18.[953] Health care providers can release information contained in the medical records of a minor when authorized by the minor's biological or adoptive parent(s) who has legal custody of the minor, or a judicially appointed legal guardian.[954]

a. Divorced or Separated Parents

Any parent, regardless of whether he or she has custody of a child, is entitled to inspect academic and medical records of a minor child.[955] A court may limit this access for good cause shown.[956] In 2005, the Virginia legislature added *therapeutic privilege* for the minor's treating physician or clinical psychologist to limit access to his records by a parent.[957] To invoke the *therapeutic privilege*, a physician or psychologist must comply with the process described above.[958] The point is that a parent may not prohibit an estranged parent from reviewing the medical records of their child. This can be a challenging situation for the medical information manager.

In a custody proceeding, the court should enter an order granting the guardian ad litem of a minor access to the child's medical records.[959] When the court orders paternity testing, confidentiality as to the results is waived.[960]

---

[953] Va. Code 1-13.42
[954] Va. Code 32.1-127.1:03.D.1; 16.1-266(G)
[955] Va. Code 20-124.6
[956] Va. Code 20-124.6
[957] Va. Code 20-124.6.B as amended by HB 2516 (2005); Va. Code 20-124.3:1 was repealed by SB 330 (2008). It provided that a licensed mental health care provider can not be compelled to testify in a custody or visitation matter for or against a parent unless the parent gives advance written sent.
[958] See Va. Code 32.1-127.1:03.F
[959] Va. Code 32.1-127.1:03.D.11 and D.13; Va. Code 16.1-266(G)
[960] Va. Code 20-49.7

b. Emancipated Minor

A minor in Virginia who has reached the age of sixteen may be *emancipated* through formal legal proceedings where a court finds:

1. The minor has entered into a valid marriage, whether or not the marriage has been terminated by dissolution; or

2. The minor is on active duty with any of the United States armed forces; or

3. The minor willingly lives separate and apart from the parents or guardian, with the consent or acquiescence of the parents or guardian, and that the minor is (or is capable of) supporting himself and competently managing his own financial affairs.[961]

The formal requirement of a court order to become *emancipated* is often overlooked. While a child may be *de facto* emancipated in many instances, the law does not recognize it. Pregnancy or other adult attributes do not alone achieve *emancipation*. However, a minor who is or was married can consent to medical treatment without the formal process of *emancipation*.[962]

The *emancipated minor* is treated as an adult under Virginia law, and can consent to medical, dental or psychiatric care without the input of his parents or guardian.[963] Therefore, the emancipated minor should be treated as an adult with respect to the release of the information contained in his medical record. An emancipated minor is entitled to a copy of his own medical record under the same circumstances as an adult would be. The medical record should not be released to the emancipated minor's parents without the consent of the emancipated minor.

---

[961] Va. Code 16.1-331 and 16.1-333
[962] Va. Code 54.1-2969.F
[963] Va. Code 16.1-334

c. Mature Minor

Several state laws allow that once a minor reaches a certain age, for example, age fourteen or sixteen, the minor is capable of making his or her own decisions. Along this line, some Virginia statutes allow a minor to consent to his own medical treatment in particular situations. For example, minors age fourteen or older may not be admitted to a mental health facility for inpatient treatment unless the facility procures the consent of *both* the parent(s) and the minor.[964] When a minor age 14 or older joins in the application for admission, he has a right of access to his medical records.[965] Concurrent authorization of both the parent and the minor is required to disclose the information to third-parties.[966] A minor age 14 or older, when a parent is not available, can consent to emergency medical treatment if delay may adversely affect the child's recovery.[967]

Other examples of when a minor is deemed to be an adult and capable of consenting to medical care, as well as for accessing or authorizing the release of confidential information, include medical or health services: [968]

1. Needed to determine the presence of or to treat venereal disease or any infectious or contagious disease that the State Board of Health requires to be reported;

2. Required in the case of birth control, pregnancy or family planning except for the purpose of sexual sterilization;

3. Needed in the case of outpatient care, treatment or rehabilitation for substance abuse;[969]

4. Needed in the case of outpatient treatment or rehabilitation for mental illness or emotional disturbance

[964] Va. Code 16.1-338.A
[965] Va. Code 16.1-338.G
[966] Va. Code 16.1-338
[967] Va. Code 54.1-2969.C and D
[968] Va. Code 54.1-2969.E
[969] Substance abuse programs are defined in Va. Code 37.1-203

In 2005, the General Assembly attempted to clarify the vagary as to whether parents of children consenting to the above health care services could access a child's records. It legislated that parents do have a right to nondiagnostic drug test results from non-treatment settings and the child's other medical records unless the physician or psychologist determines that access would be "reasonably likely to cause substantial harm to the minor or another person."[970] If so, then the process for *therapeutic privilege* described above must be followed.

4. Health Information in an Educational Institution

Health information is often maintained in education records. In general, access to educational records is controlled by the Family Educational Rights and Privacy Act (FERPA) in those institutions that receive funds under any program administered by the US Department of Education.[971] Private and religious schools at the elementary and secondary level do not usually receive such federal funds. Public school systems generally fall within FERPA.

Generally, HIPAA does not apply in the elementary or secondary school setting because the school is not a HIPAA-covered entity or the school does not have protected health information. Most schools maintain health information, such as immunization history or school clinic records, only in education records under FERPA.

Under FERPA, parents have a right to review health information maintained by a school as education records. The records may not be shared with third parties without written parental authorization except under specified exceptions. The most commonly used exceptions are:

---

[970]   Va. Code 54.1-2969.K
[971]   20 U.S.C.A. 1232g; 34 C.F.R. Part 99

- Disclosure to teachers and other educators for legitimate educational purposes in accordance with school policy;[972] or

- Disclosure to appropriate parties in connection with an emergency when disclosure is necessary to protect the health or safety of the student or other individuals[973]

In a post-secondary educational institution, treatment records of a student generally fall under FERPA as educational records. An important distinction between FERPA and HIPAA is that FERPA permits an institution to prohibit access by the student to his treatment records. However, the records must be made available to a physician or appropriate professional of the student's choice.[974] The determination of whether medical records fall under FERPA or HIPAA can be tricky and advice from counsel is recommended.[975]

For a discussion of whether a public school educator must release academic information on a student to law enforcement, see Attorney General's Opinion, 3 May 2013. The Attorney General concluded that an educator may release such information only if an articulable and significant threat to the health or safety of a student or other individuals exists.[976] In the absence of a warrant or subpoena, an educator is not required to release such information.

5. Adoption Issues

Where an adoption is finalized on or after July 1, 1994, Virginia

---

[972] 34 C.F.R. 99.31(a)(1)

[973] 34 C.F.R. 99.31(a)(10) and 99.36

[974] 20 U.S.C.A. 1232g(a)(4)(B)(iv); 34 C.F.R. 99.3

[975] For additional guidance, see US Dept. of Health and Human Services and US Dept. of Education, "Joint Guidance on the Application of the Family Educational Rights and Privacy Act (FERPA) and the Health Insurance Portability and Accountability Act of 1996 (HIPAA) to Student Health Records," November 2008

[976] The Attorney General believed that FERPA, 34 C.F.R. 99(c), was consistent with Va. Code 22.1-287.

statutes set forth a mechanism for parties to an adoption to obtain information and identify the other parties to the adoption.[977] The statutes do not explain how the court is to proceed in adoptions before this date. The law is silent as to any obligation of a health care provider that is unique to the adoption situation.

6. Fees for Providing Copies of Records to Patients

When a patient, or someone on the patient's behalf, requests copies of health care records, Virginia law allows the health care provider to charge *a reasonable cost-based fee* to the patient to cover the labor in making the copies, supplies, and postage.[978] Formerly, the same fee schedule could be used for responding to a patient's request as for responding to a subpoena. The General Assembly in its 2005 legislation muddied the waters by using *reasonable cost-based fee* and expressly avoiding the maximum-fee schedule set forth in Va. Code 8.01-413.B, which still says that the same fee schedule could apply to a patient's request for records as for responding to a subpoena.[979]

In 2016, the federal Office of Civil Rights reiterated that the Privacy Rule of HIPAA limits a provider to billing for only:

1) Clerical labor for copying PHI into the format requested;

2) Supplies for creating the requested paper copy or electronic media, e.g. CD or USB drive if electronic version requested on portable media; and

3) Postage when the patient requests that the records be mailed.

---

[977]   Va. Code 63.2-1246 and 1247

[978]   Va. Code 32.1-127.1:03.J. This is consistent with 42 C.F.R. 482.13(d)(2); Interpretive Guidelines Tag A768

[979]   Va. Code 8.01-413.B

OCR was very clear that "The fee may not include costs associated with verification, documentation, searching for and retrieving the PHI ... or other costs not listed above <u>even if such costs are authorized by State law</u>." [emphasis in original]. A practice is permitted to develop a fee schedule based on average labor costs to fulfill standard types of record requests. Without explanation, OCR has stated that a flat fee not exceeding $6.50, inclusive of labor, supplies, and any applicable postage, is reasonable for providing electronic copies of PHI maintained electronically. Per page fees are prohibited unless the records are being produced on paper. The fees from an outside service can't simply be passed through to the patient.

To make it even more complicated, a provider should provide an estimate of the fee when a patient requests the records. OCR says that a provider ought to be able to provide a breakdown of the total fee charged when OCR asks a provider for it. No fee can be imposed where a patient uses an EMR web portal and downloads her own records. Access to records can't be withheld due to an unpaid bill. No fee can be charged if a patient just wants to look at her records, even if she wants to take pictures of them on her smartphone.

Thus, it would appear that each provider has to undertake an analysis of what the cost of labor and supplies are for responding to a patient's request for records. This is a very unfortunate over-reach of regulations by the federal government.

The fee for supplying records to a third-party payor may be limited by contract. No statute addresses whether a fee is appropriate in supplying records to another health care provider for the benefit of a patient. Traditional practice has been to not charge a fee when another provider requests information.

7. Fee Statements for Health Care Services

A health care professional must provide an itemized bill if requested by a patient at no cost up to three times every twelve months to either the patient or his attorney.[980]

8. *Copying the Driver's License of a Patient*

A belief that it is illegal to photocopy a Virginia driver's license has long circulated among medical information managers. The source of this urban legend appears to stem from a misinterpretation of a statute. Va. Code 46.2-346 states that it is illegal to photocopy a driver's license *with the intent to commit an illegal act.* Thus, the traditional ritual of photocopying a driver's license as part of patient registration does not appear to be an illegal act.

9. *Amendment or Correction by the Patient*

Analogous to the obligations of credit reporting agencies, health care providers, under HIPAA regulations, must allow a patient to request amendments or corrections to his records.[981] The provider must act on the request for amendment or correction within sixty days. The provider can extend the response period by thirty days if within the sixty days, the provider advises the patient of why an additional thirty days will be needed.

If the provider agrees with the patient's request to amend or correct the provider's record, then the provider must:[982]

- Inform the patient of the decision in a timely manner;
- Make the appropriate amendment by identifying the records in the designated record set that are affected by the

---

980   Va. Code 54.1-2404; 8.01-413
981   45 C.F.R. 164.526
982   45 C.F.R. 164.526(c)

amendment and appending or otherwise providing a link to the location of the amendment; and

- If the patient agrees, make reasonable efforts to notify and provide the amendment to persons identified by the patient as having received the patient's PHI and need the amendment; and others, including business associates, that the provider knows has received the PHI and that may have relied, or could foreseeably rely, on the incorrect information to the detriment of the patient.

A provider can deny a patient's request to amend information if the provider determines that:

- The provider did not create the information, unless the patient provides a reasonable basis to believe that the originator of the PHI is no longer available;
- The information is accurate and complete; or
- The information that is the subject of the request is not part of a designated record set or would not otherwise be available for inspection by the patient.

If the provider denies the patient's request to amend information, then the provider must give a timely written denial in plain language to the patient that contains:[983]

- The basis for the denial;
- Notice that the patient has a right to file a written statement of disagreement with the denial and how the patient can go about doing this;
- Notice that, if the patient does not submit a statement of disagreement, the patient can request that the provider include the patient's request for amendment and its denial

---

[983] 45 C.F.R. 164.526(d)(1)

with any future disclosures of PHI that is the subject of the requested amendment; and

- A description of how the patient can complain about the provider's actions to the organization or to the Secretary of HHS, including the procedure for filing a complaint and the title or name and telephone number of the provider's contact person for receiving complaints.

The provider can prepare a written rebuttal to a patient's statement of disagreement. The provider must provide a copy of the rebuttal to the patient.[984] Documentation must be maintained for six years from when it was created or last effective, whichever is later.[985]

10. Tips for Complying with OCR Initiative on Patient Access

In early 2016, The Office of Civil Rights (OCR) within the US Dept. of Health and Human Services announced a renewed interest (and an enforcement priority) in assuring that patients have access to their medical records. In other words, OCR will be looking to assure that a healthcare provider "does not create a barrier to or unreasonably delay the individual from obtaining access to her PHI [Personal Health Information]."

Here are some tips on being in compliance:

Requests for Access: A healthcare provider may require that a request by a patient for access to her records be in writing on a form that the provider has created. However, a provider must accept faxed or scanned copies of the signed form. Additionally, a healthcare provider may accept requests using an electronic means (e.g. e-mail or web portal). A healthcare provider can (and should) take reasonable steps to verify that the individual requesting the

---

[984] 45 C.F.R. 164.526(d)(3), (4), and (5)
[985] 45 C.F.R. 164.526(f)

records is actually the provider's patient or a proper personal representative. For example, the authorization form can ask for basic information about the requester. However, a provider can't require the patient to appear in person in the provider's office to sign the form. Likewise, the provider can't limit conveyance of the access form to snail mail if that would be an unreasonable delay. Nor can a provider require all requests to go through the provider's web portal. Of note, a provider can ask a patient why she is asking for her records. The patient isn't obligated to tell the provider, and the provider can't refuse to produce her records if she refuses. Still, it may be worth asking in order to defuse an adversarial situation.

Form, Format and Manner of Access: A patient has a right to receive her PHI in a form and format that she requests, if readily producible. If not, then in a readable hard copy form or other form and format to which the provider and the patient agree. Regardless of whether the provider is using an EMR or old fashioned paper records, the patient can request a copy of her records in paper. Conversely, a provider will be required to produce electronic copies of paper records if they are readily producible, e.g. scanning the paper records. Last but not least, a provider must deliver the records in the manner requested by the patient, which may include a convenient time and place to pick up the records or inspect them. If the patient wants an electronic version, arrangements must be made for delivery, which may be by e-mail, web portal or storage device. A provider can't require the patient to appear in the office to pick up the records if she wants them mailed or e-mailed.

Fees for Providing Records: One should forget all of the fee schedules and rules of thumb that have been previously discussed! OCR is adamant that the Privacy Rule limits a provider to billing for only 1) clerical labor for copying PHI into the format requested; 2) supplies for creating the requested paper copy or electronic media, e.g. CD or USB drive if electronic version requested on portable media; and 3) postage when the patient requests that the records be mailed. "The fee may not include costs associated with verification, documentation, searching for and retrieving the PHI ... or other costs not listed above <u>even if such costs are authorized by State law.</u>" [emphasis in original]. A practice is permitted to develop a fee schedule based on average labor costs to fulfill standard types of record requests. Without explanation, OCR has stated that a flat fee not exceeding $6.50, inclusive of labor, supplies, and any applicable postage, is reasonable for providing electronic copies of PHI maintained electronically. Per page fees are prohibited unless the records are being produced on paper. The fees from an outside service can't simply be passed through to the patient. To make it even more complicated, a provider should provide an estimate of the fee when a patient requests the records. OCR says that a provider ought to be able to provide a breakdown of the total fee charged when OCR asks a provider for it. No fee can be imposed where a patient uses an EMR web portal and downloads her own records. Access to records can't be withheld due to an unpaid bill. No fee can be charged if a patient just wants to look at her records, even if she wants to take pictures of them on her smartphone.

Denying Access to Records: A provider likely will not be able to refuse to produce records to a patient unless: 1) the provider maintain psychotherapy notes separate and apart from the patient chart; 2) the information was obtained by someone other than the healthcare provider, e.g. a family member, under a promise of confidentiality, and providing access would be reasonably likely to reveal the source of the information; or 3) a provider has a reasonable basis to believe that disclosure of records to a patient will result in endangering the life or physical safety of the patient or someone else or likely cause substantial harm to another person referenced in the records. OCR has little sympathy for concerns over psychological or emotional injury. If the provider refuses to produce the records under the therapeutic privilege, then the provider must document the reasoning in the chart and advise the patient of the process by which she can have the records reviewed by another healthcare provider who will decide whether the records should be released.

This review can be done by someone of the patient's choice or by someone paid for by the healthcare provider.

Correcting Records: A patient has a right to request that a provider correct the records in a manner similar to a consumer's right to correct a credit report. A provider should think carefully about whether or not to make the changes. Emotion should not overshadow good clinical judgment. If a provider feels that the patient's request should be declined, then she has a right to put her explanation in the provider's chart.

D. Access by Other Health Care Providers

1. In General

In modern health care, many professionals other than a physician may need access to a patient's chart. Medical information may be disclosed to other health care providers without the patient's authorization where it is necessary for diagnosis and proper treatment of the patient.[986] The health care provider who is releasing the information has the burden of assuring that the recipient health care provider has a valid reason for wanting access to the patient information. Curiosity is not a sufficient reason.

Pursuant to federal Health Insurance Portability and Accountability Act (HIPAA)[987] and the Virginia Patient Health Records Privacy Act,[988] a healthcare provider is permitted to use and disclose PHI without an individual's authorization for *treatment, payment and healthcare operations*.[989] Generally, no distinction is made between records of medical care and records of behavioral health care.

Treatment is the provision, coordination, or management of health care and related services for an individual by one or more healthcare providers, including consultation between providers regarding a patient and referral of a patient by one provider to another.[990]

The ability to share information among healthcare providers,

---

[986] Va. Code 32.1-127.1:03.7
[987] Regulations promulgated by HIPAA and subsequent Health Information Technology for Economic and Clinical Health Act (HITECH) for the "Privacy Rule" are set forth in 45 C.F.R. 160 and 164
[988] Va. Code 32.1-127.1:03
[989] 45 C.F.R. 164.506(c)
[990] 45 C.F.R. 164.501

which includes mental healthcare providers, is not limited to those practicing in the same office or within the same discipline.

A patient must be allowed to request that a provider restrict uses or disclosures of PHI in treatment, payment or health care operations.[991] A provider is not required to agree to a requested restriction, but if he does, then he may not violate the agreed restriction. The provider may terminate the agreement to a restriction, effective after the patient has been informed.[992]

Psychotherapy notes[993] pose a unique issue for sharing information between providers. Usually an express authorization by a patient is required before the originator of the psychotherapy notes may share them with others.[994] Additionally, a patient may request that the provider restrict the sharing of PHI with a particular provider or person.[995] A provider is not obligated to agree to the restriction. In the absence of an express restriction, the presumption is that providers are expected to communicate in the best interests of the patient to provide collaborative care. A provider must make

---

[991] 45 C.F.R. 164.522

[992] 45 C.F.R. 164.522(a)

[993] *Psychotherapy notes* have a specific and quite limited definition in HIPAA and Virginia law. Va. Code 32.1-127.1:03.B provides: "Psychotherapy notes" means comments, recorded in any medium by a health care provider who is a mental health professional, documenting or analyzing the contents of conversation during a private counseling session with an individual or a group, joint, or family counseling session that are separated from the rest of the individual's health record. "Psychotherapy notes" shall not include annotations relating to medication and prescription monitoring, counseling session start and stop times, treatment modalities and frequencies, clinical test results, or any summary of any symptoms, diagnosis, prognosis, functional status, treatment plan, or the individual's progress to date. Also see 45 C.F.R. 164.501

[994] 45 C.F.R. 164.508(a)(2)

[995] 45 C.F.R. 164.522(a)

reasonable efforts to use, disclose and request only the minimum amount of PHI needed to accomplish the intended purpose.[996]

The Joint Commission on Accreditation of Health Care Organizations (Joint Commission)[997] allows hospital staff access to medical records for the purpose of treatment, quality assurance, utilization review, education and research. Virginia law supports these goals. However, the facility has an obligation to assure that its staff is obtaining patient information for one of these defined purposes.

As an example of a frequent situation arising in health care, a hospital employee who alleged that fellow employees invaded her privacy by accessing a hospital computer database to learn about her admittance to a psychiatric unit in another hospital was permitted to sue for *computer invasion of privacy* under a Virginia statute.[998]

2. *Subsequent Health Care Providers*

The ever-growing situation of patients changing health care providers has sharply increased the transference of medical information between health care practices. Often this is routine, but occasionally the patient or practice manager generates friction. The American Medical Association (AMA) has taken the position that a physician cannot ethically refuse to promptly provide records to another treating physician on request.[999] Unpaid bills are not a basis upon which records may be withheld. The AMA and Virginia statutes are silent as to whether charging a fee to the patient or physician is appropriate when medical records are provided to another health care provider. The Board of Medicine simply states that the records

---

[996] 45 C.F.R. 164.502(b) and 164.514(d)

[997] Accreditation Manual for Hospitals, MR. 1. 12 Va. Admin. Code 5-410-230 adopts the Joint Commission standards as compulsory regulations for patient rights and responsibility.

[998] S.R. v. Inova Healthcare Servs., 49 Va. Cir. 119 (1999) VLW 099-8-191; See Pierce v. Caday, 244 Va. 285 (1992)

[999] AMA Opinion 7.01

should be provided in a timely manner.[1000] Efforts to do so often generate considerable animosity between providers. These disputes occasionally end up in litigation related to practitioners parting ways.[1001]

3. Peer Review and Utilization Review

Virginia law[1002] provides that communications originating in or provided to a peer review entity is privileged and cannot be disclosed to third parties unless a circuit court judge finds good cause arising from extraordinary circumstances. However, the privilege was more narrowly defined in 2011 to protect analysis, findings, conclusions, recommendations and the deliberative process as well as the proceedings, minutes, records and reports. Factual information known to a healthcare provider and oral communication to a QA or peer review committee within twenty four hours of the event are not privileged.[1003]

The Virginia peer review privilege[1004] has been expanded to expressly address the situation of a medical group policing its physicians. In addition, the federal Health Care Quality Improvement Act of 1986 (HCQIA)[1005] supports the conclusion that physician practice peer review is privileged and protected from discovery in medical malpractice actions. The Medical Society of Virginia (MSV) has adopted Quality Assurance and Peer Review Guidelines.[1006] HCQIA

[1000] 18 Va. Admin. Code 85-20-26

[1001] See Peyton v. Countryside Orthopaedics, PC, 1999 WL 600422 (Loudoun County Cir. Ct. 1999) wherein the judge ordered that a departing partner pay 10¢ per page for copies of patient charts and $5.00 as a handling fee per chart. Other judges may reach different conclusions.

[1002] Va. Code 8.01-581.17

[1003] Va. Code 8.01-581.17 amended by HB 2373 (2011)

[1004] Va. Code 8.01-581.16 and 17

[1005] 42 U.S.C.A. 11111 et seq.

[1006] The Medical Society of Virginia's Quality Assurance and Peer Review Guidelines are available on MSV's web site: http://www.msv.org/i4a/pages/index.cfm?pageid=6059

includes a group medical practice within the Act's definition of a *health care entity* that "provides health care services and that follows a formal peer review process for the purpose of furthering quality health care ..." Thus, if a physician practice complies with the formal peer review process set forth in HCQIA,[1007] the more detailed criteria set forth in the Joint Commission guidelines, [1008] or the American College of Radiology or MSV's model; the practice's peer review should be protected from discovery under Virginia's peer review statute.

A physician practice must be very careful in performing peer review to insure that the review falls within the statutory protections for immunity of the participants and confidentiality of the information. A group medical practice's peer review activity, in order to be protected, must meet the formal and rigorous peer review process. For example, formal committee meetings must be held, due process must be accorded the physician, and corrective actions must be reported to the National Practitioner Data Bank. Many medical groups are going to find it much easier to participate in a hospital's peer review process than to undertake their own.

The Supreme Court of Virginia has not dealt with whether medical group practice peer review is fully protected within Va. Code 8.01-581.17. In the Court's only decision on the peer review privilege,[1009] the Court was very protective of the privilege and concluded that even the physician who was the subject of a hospital medical staff's peer review could not waive the confidentiality of the committee's work. Unfortunately, we will not have the definitive interpretation of how physician practices can conduct privileged peer review until the Supreme Court makes that determination.

Peer review and utilization review discussions, reports and

[1007] 42 U.S.C.A. 11112
[1008] Joint Commission Standards are contained in its Comprehensive Accreditation Manual for Hospitals
[1009] HCA Health Services of Virginia, Inc. v. Levin, 260 Va. 215 (2000)

documents are confidential, and are not subject to discovery in civil litigation except in extraordinary circumstances.[1010] Unfortunately, many Circuit Court judges have yet to find a situation in a medical malpractice case that is not "extraordinary." A physician who is the subject of the peer review cannot waive the confidentiality of peer review.[1011] Hospitals must report initiation of peer review to the Board of Medicine. [1012]

In a similar fashion, efforts to improve patient safety are cloaked with confidentiality under the federal Patient Safety and Quality Improvement Act of 2005.[1013] Likewise, the General Assembly extended the peer-review confidentiality statute to include patient safety activities.[1014] Additionally, reports generated for self-assessment of compliance with Joint Commission requirements or standards are not discoverable in civil or administrative proceedings.[1015]

Record reviews can be conducted of inpatient hospital deaths, in conformance with federal law, to promote identification of all potential organ, eye and tissue donors.[1016] This is not considered to be a breach of confidentiality.

[1010] Va. Code 8.01-581.17; U.S. Dept. of Defense institutions are guided by 10 U.S.C.A. 1102. As to utilization review, see Va. Code 38.2-613 and 37.1-228

[1011] HCA Health Services of Virginia v. Levin, 260 Va. 215 (2000). This decision is in contrast to Virmani v. Novant Health, Inc., 259 F.3d 284 (4th Cir. 2001) (the federal appeals court held that a physician pursuing a discrimination claim after termination of his hospital privileges was entitled to see the peer review material under federal law as opposed to North Carolina law).

[1012] Va. Code 54.1-2906

[1013] Patient Safety And Quality Improvement Act of 2005, PL 109–41, July 29, 2005, 119 Stat 424

[1014] Va. Code 8.01-581.17

[1015] Va. Code 8.01-581.17.I

[1016] Va. Code 32.1-127.1:03.D.24

4. Emergency Services

Emergency medical service records should be transported with the patient since those records are often necessary for the proper treatment of a patient when he reaches the receiving institution. The federal Emergency Medical Treatment and Active Labor Act[1017] mandates the transfer of records when patients are transferred from an emergency department to another facility.

If an attending physician believes that a patient suffering from a communicable disease poses a risk to ambulance personnel or subsequent patients transported in the same ambulance, the transferring facility[1018] (including correctional facilities) must tell the leader of the ambulance crew about the patient's general condition and appropriate precautions to prevent the spread of disease. These diseases include: [1019]

- Tuberculosis
- Measles
- Meningococcal infections
- Mumps
- Chicken pox
- Haemophilus Influenza type b
- Human immunodeficiency virus (HIV)
- Hepatitis B
- Hepatitis Non-A, Non-B (now known as Hepatitis C)

A physician or other health care professional may disclose to an emergency medical care attendant, technician, or another physician the medical or hospital records of a patient to whom the attendant,

---

[1017] EMTALA, 42 U.S.C.A. 1395dd et seq. Interpretive regulations can be found at 42 C.F.R. 489 et seq.
[1018] As defined by Va. Code 32.1-116.3
[1019] Va. 32.1-116.3

technician or other physician is providing, or has provided, emergency medical care for the purpose of promoting the medical education of the specific person who provided the care.[1020] The attendant, technician or other physician is prohibited from further disclosure of this information. Hospitals are also required to submit abstracts of records to the Virginia Statewide Trauma Registry and to regional emergency medical services councils.[1021]

5. *Morticians*

Hospitals, nursing homes, and correctional facilities must advise morticians if a person was known to suffer from any of the following diseases prior to death:[1022]

- Creutzfeldt-Jakob disease
- HIV
- Hepatitis B
- Hepatitis Non-A, Non-B
- Rabies
- Infectious Syphilis

A health care provider failing to identify a patient suffering from one of these diseases is granted immunity. In other words, a provider knowing that a patient was suffering from a listed disease is obligated to convey the information. However, a provider is not required to test a patient antemortem or postmortem solely for the purpose of this statute. A mortician must keep information received regarding infectious disease confidential.[1023] He may not refuse to accept a body because of information he or she receives as to infectious disease.[1024]

[1020] Va. Code 32.1-116.1:1
[1021] Va. Code 32.1-116.1
[1022] Va. Code 32.1-37.1; 12 Va. Admin. Code5-90-90.F
[1023] Va. Code 54.1-2807.1
[1024] Va. Code 54.1-2807.1

E. Access by Third-Parties

Medical information managers have a challenging task of distinguishing those individuals who should have access to patient information from those who should not have access. These are often emotionally charged situations, and a manager is well advised to have planned in advance for these encounters. The following are some common examples:

1. *State & Federal Government*

A health care provider should not allow a government agency to have access to confidential patient information absent specific statutory authority or unless acting pursuant to a valid legal process, such as a subpoena, a search warrant or a court order. However, there are a multitude of statutes and regulations in Virginia that allow government agencies to have access to information. For example, certain information contained in a medical record must be made available to government agencies pursuant to various reporting requirements without the patient's consent. The Virginia Board of Health is the primary agency that requires the reporting of confidential medical information. Although a health care provider should know which agencies are entitled to medical record information, it is the burden of the agency to prove it is entitled to access. If there is any question, the health care facility administrator should be contacted. The administrator, in turn, may choose to contact the facility's attorney for verification. The following is an overview of some situations where government agencies have the right of access to patient information. It is not all-inclusive.

a. Independent Inspection Rights of Governmental Agencies Without Subpoenas

Virginia and federal statutes provide that a variety of governmental agencies have the authority to inspect and secure medical records which otherwise would be protected by the physician-patient privilege. These agencies often have the express power to inspect and secure records, with or without a subpoena. In many cases, the authority to inspect the records is coupled with a requirement that the health care provider report certain information to the agency. For example, the Department of Health has a right to inspect medical records without prior notice during investigation, research or study of diseases or deaths of public health importance.[1025] Likewise, the Department of Health Professions has the power "to request and obtain patient records, business records, papers, and physical or other evidence in the course of any investigation or to issue subpoenas requiring the production of such evidence."[1026]

b. Medicare / Medicaid

Audit concerns in Medicare and Medicaid range from innocent billing errors, assignment of the patient to an incorrect diagnostic related group (DRG), inappropriate admissions, to intentional fraud and abuse. Accordingly, utilization review for Medicare and Medicaid patients is created by federal statute.[1027] Peer review organizations (PROs) have the responsibility to monitor the appropriateness and quality of care under the Medicare program. This requires access to medical records. Access by a PRO does not require specific consent by a patient. There are extensive provisions in the federal regulations relating to PRO access to data and the extent to which the data must

---

[1025] Va. Code 32.1-40
[1026] Va. Code 54.1-2506
[1027] 42 U.S.C.A. 1395 et seq. and 42 C.F.R. 462.101 et seq.

be kept confidential.[1028] Virginia statutes require that data collected during utilization review be kept strictly confidential as well.[1029]

A health care provider should have a policy outlining the procedures that the PRO, as well as other utilization review personnel, should follow. Often the problems in these areas center not around the legal rights of access to the records, but the logistical problems involved, such as where the records are to be reviewed, the timeliness of the review, and identification of utilization review personnel.

More overt methods of investigation by federal agents are discussed later in this chapter.

2. *Insurance Companies / Managed Care*

a. Health Insurance Claims

When a patient requests that a provider submit the bills for professional services to a third-party payor under a contract of insurance, the patient is deemed to have consented to permitting the third-party payor or its agents to review the pertinent medical records.[1030] Care should be taken by the health care provider to release only the pertinent portion of the medical record to support the fee statement, unless the patient has consented to more. The *minimum necessary* edict of HIPAA applies to this situation.

b. Managed Care Audits

Many managed care companies audit provider charts. This is done for a variety of reasons. For example, the HMO may be looking at the indications for utilization of specialists or confirming data to support a particular diagnosis. Regardless, the managed care company has

---

[1028]   42 C.F.R. Part 476; Va. Code 38.2-613
[1029]   Va. Code 38.2-613. Also see, Va. Code 37.1-228
[1030]   Va. Code 32.1-127.1:03.D.16 and 17

no right to review patient information unrelated to its insureds.[1031] In fact, the medical information manager has an obligation to protect such information. HIPAA mandates the *minimum necessary* standard even for managed care audits.[1032]

c. Life Insurance Applications

Most life insurance companies are very careful to obtain the consent of a person seeking a life insurance policy for access to medical information. However, the medical information manager should confirm that this consent has been obtained. The insurance company is not allowed to go beyond the parameters of the consent from the patient.

If one disagrees with personal information maintained by an insurance company, an agent or an insurance-support organization, the individual has rights similar to the situation of a dispute over information contained in a credit report.[1033]

3. *Employers*

Frequently employers will contact an emergency department or physician's office to inquire about the well-being of an employee. Aggressive employers are known to bring an employee to a facility to perform drug testing without the patient's consent. Aside from the worker's compensation setting, an employer enjoys no right of access to an employee's medical information. This is a growing concern, as more and more companies take management of health care insurance claims in-house. An employee's prescription history alone may have a significant effect on how the employee is

---

[1031] Managed care companies almost universally have an agreement with their insureds to allow access to a provider's charts. However, this should not be presumed if there is any doubt.

[1032] See 45 C.F.R. 164.506(c)(4); 164.514(d)(3)(ii) & (d)(4) as well as Va. Code 32.1-127.1:03.D.16 & 17 and 37.1-227

[1033] Va. Code 38.2-609

perceived by fellow workers. Several federal courts[1034] have held that unauthorized disclosure of medical information by an employer is a violation of the Americans with Disabilities Act.[1035]

4. Researchers

Virginia law provides that health data can be accessed by a researcher, including pharmaceutical companies, without a patient's consent if patient identifier information has been deleted or encoded.[1036] If the data is not de-identified, then the organization must comply with the regulations for research, discussed in Chapter I above.

5. Family & Friends

No matter how well meaning, spouses, adult children or other relatives have no general right to a patient's medical information without the patient's consent. Where the patient is unable to make health care decisions, the protocol under the Health Care Decisions Act discussed previously should be utilized.[1037] A family member or personal representative can be informed of a patient being subject to an involuntary admission if the patient does not object or is not capable of decision making.[1038] Recent guidance from the Office of Civil Rights states that HIPAA allows a healthcare provider to discuss a patient's health information with a family, friends or others "if the patient agrees or, when given the opportunity, does not object."[1039]

[1034] Cossette v. Minnesota Power & Light, 188 F.3d 964 (8th Cir. 1999); Fredenburg v. Conra Costa County Dept of Health Services, 172 F.3d 1176, 1182 (9th Cir. 1999); Griffin v. Steeltek, Inc., 160 F.3d 591, 594 (10th Cir. 1998)
[1035] 42 U.S.C.A. 12112(d)(3)(1994)
[1036] Va. Code 32.1-127.1:03.A
[1037] Va. Code 32.1-127.1:03; 45 C.F.R. 164.502(a)(2)(i) and (g)
[1038] Va. Code 37.2-804.2 and Va. Code 32.1-127.1:03.D.34
[1039] 45 C.F.R. 64.510(b)(2); also see HHS, Office of Civil Rights, "A Health Care Provider's Guide to the HIPAA Privacy Rule: Communicating with a Patient's Family, Friends, or Others Involved in the Patient's Care"

Additionally, a provider can disclose relevant information to a family member that is involved in a patient's care when the patient is not present or unable to consent if 1) the provider believes it is in the patient's best interest; 2) the patient has not otherwise objected to such disclosures; and 3) the disclosure is limited to that which is relevant to the third person's involvement in the patient's care.[1040] To reduce risk for the healthcare provider, a provider would be well served to document the situation of the disclosure or have the patient sign an authorization for release of information.

A facility may maintain a directory of patients who are resident. The directory may contain the following information unless the patient has objected to such disclosure:[1041]

- The patient's name
- The patient's location in the facility
- The patient's condition described in general terms that does not communicate specific information of about the patient's diagnosis, e.g. good, fair, critical, etc.

6. *News Media*

Dealing with reporters seeking a story can be very challenging to the medical information manager and others in a health care facility. A patient's privacy must be respected at all times. Before any statement is made to the media that would identify a particular patient, the patient's consent should be obtained. Photographs or recordings of any kind should be forbidden in patient care areas. The staff should all be cautioned about the need for patient confidentiality, especially for celebrity patients. Just as with any patient's chart, a celebrity's chart should be maintained in a secure fashion. Even the fact that a patient has been admitted or discharged should not be publicly disclosed without the patient's consent. Federal regulations

[1040] 45 C.F.R. 64.510(b)(3)
[1041] 45 C.F.R. 164.510(a)

specifically require this strict confidentiality of patients who are in a substance abuse rehabilitation program.[1042] State regulations protect the identity of those admitted to psychiatric facilities.[1043]

7. Accounting of Disclosures

HIPAA creates an obligation on the provider to keep a log of disclosures of PHI. A patient has a right to request an accounting for six years prior to his request.[1044] The provider's response must be made within sixty days.[1045] The period can be extended an additional thirty days if the provider gives a written statement to the patient as to the reasons for the delay. One accounting during a twelve-month period must be provided without charge. A provider can charge a reasonable, cost-based fee for subsequent requests within the twelve months. If a fee will be charged, the patient must be advised in advance and given the opportunity to withdraw or modify his request. An accounting must be in writing and include:[1046]

- The date of each disclosure;
- The name and address of the person or entity who received the information;
- A brief description of the information disclosed; and
- A brief statement of the purpose of the disclosure that reasonably informs the patient of the basis for the disclosure. In the alternative, a copy of a written request for disclosure can be provided.

A provider does not have to provide an accounting of disclosures that were made:[1047]

[1042] 42 C.F.R., Part 2
[1043] 12 Va. Admin. Code 35-120-40.J
[1044] 45 C.F.R. 164.528(a)
[1045] 45 C.F.R.164.528(c)
[1046] 45 C.F.R. 164.528(b)(2)
[1047] 45 C.F.R. 164.528(a)(1)

- For treatment, payment, and health care operations,[1048] including where the provider is a party to the litigation.[1049] This exemption does not apply to electronic health records.[1050]

- To the patient[1051]

- Incident to a use or disclosure that was otherwise permitted[1052]

- Pursuant to the patient's written authorization[1053]

- For the facility's directory or to persons involved in the patient's care[1054]

- For national security or intelligence purposes[1055]

- To correctional facilities or police having custody of a patient[1056]

- As part of a limited data set[1057]; or

- Before April 14, 2003

This leaves only a few situations in which release of a medical record would require an accounting, such as disclosures to health oversight agencies; to researchers that include patient-identifying information; to public health authorities; in response to court-orders; in reporting patient crimes on program premises or against program personnel; and/or in reporting abuse or neglect.[1058] Accounting for recurrent

---

[1048] 45 C.F.R. 164.506
[1049] See OCR, Answer ID 710, updated 1/24/05
[1050] ARRA at 13405(c). The log must be kept for 3 years instead of the usual 6 years.
[1051] 45 C.F.R. 164.502
[1052] 45 C.F.R. 164.502
[1053] 45 C.F.R. 164.508
[1054] 45 C.F.R. 164.510
[1055] 45 C.F.R. 164.512(k)(2)
[1056] 45 C.F.R. 164.512(k)(5)
[1057] 45 C.F.R. 164.514(e)
[1058] 45 C.F.R. 164.512

disclosures and for research is covered by special regulations that do not require annotation in each medical record.[1059]

HIPAA requires that procedures be established for the entire process of logging disclosures and responding to patient requests for accountings. On an individual patient basis, the provider must document and retain for six years:[1060]

- The information that the provider was required to provide to the patient;

- The written accounting provided to the patient; and

- The titles of the persons or offices responsible for receiving and processing requests for accountings

8. Notification of a Breach

A covered entity must notify a patient of an unauthorized acquisition, access, use or disclosure of unsecured PHI which compromises the security or privacy of such information that poses a significant risk of financial, reputational, or other harm to the affected individual.[1061]

This notification requirement also extends to where a *breach* is reasonably believed to have occurred. For example, the Office of Civil Rights has stated that a ransomware attack to a covered entity's electronic medical record system is presumed to be a *breach* because it was an unauthorized disclosure.[1062] Business associates

---

[1059] 45 C.F.R. 164.528(b)(3) and (b)(4)

[1060] 45 C.F.R. 164.428(d)

[1061] Interim Breach Notification Regulation, effective 23 Sept 2009; *Breach* is defined in 45 C.F.R. 164.402; A Virginia entity will also want to be aware of Va. Code 18.2-152.5 (computer invasion criminal statute), Va. Code 18.2-152.12 (computer trespass civil remedy) and Va. Code 18.2-186.6 (breach of personal information notification)

[1062] See "Fact Sheet: Ransomware and HIPAA," Office of Civil Rights, http://www.hhs.gov/sites/default/files/RansomwareFactSheet.pdf, accessed

must notify covered entities of any *breach*.[1063] Business associates are not required to notify affected patients. Written notification of a *breach* must occur without unreasonable delay and in no case more than sixty days after discovery or after a covered entity should have been known.[1064] If more than five hundred patients in a state are involved, a covered entity must give notice of the *breach* to prominent media outlets in the state.[1065] Notice to a patient must include:[1066]

- A description of the facts surrounding the breach
- The type of PHI involved
- What a patient should do to protect himself/herself
- What the provider is doing to investigate, mitigate and protect against future breaches
- Contact information for a patient to ask questions or obtain more information

A covered entity must notify HHS of any *breach*.[1067] An incident does not rise to the level of a *breach* if:[1068]

- Unsecured PHI is not involved;
- No violation of the Privacy Rule occurred;
- No risk of harm to the patient occurred; or
- An exception applies[1069]

If an incident does not rise to the definition of a *breach*, the covered

---

7/20/2016, interpreting 45 C.F.R. 164.103 and 164.402 and Section 13402 of HITECH.

[1063] ARRA at 13402(b)
[1064] ARRA at 13402(d)(1) and (e)
[1065] ARRA at 13402(e)
[1066] 45 C.F.R. 164.404; ARRA at 13402(f)
[1067] ARRA at 13402(3)
[1068] 45 C.F.R. 164.402(2)
[1069] See 45 C.F.R.164.402(1)

entity must document in the form of a risk assessment how it determined that the incident was not a *breach*.[1070] If more than five hundred patients are involved, HHS must be notified immediately. If fewer than five hundred patients, a log may be produced to HHS annually.

[1070] 45 C.F.R. 164.414 and 164.530(j)(iv)

F. Obligation to Report to Government Agencies

1. *Abuse or Neglect*

a. Child Abuse

In Virginia all licensed health care providers, including physicians, nurses, hospital residents or interns, social workers, mental health professionals, EMS personnel and others, who suspect that a child has been abused or neglected "shall report the matter immediately" to the local Department of Social Services where the child resides or where the abuse or neglect is believed to have occurred.[1071] Alternatively, the report may be made to the Child Abuse & Neglect Hotline (800/552-7096).[1072]

In a hospital or other facility, suspected abuse situations should be reported to the administrator, or an individual designated to receive such reports. The administrator must advise the employee when the report has been made to the appropriate government agency.[1073] Where the suspected abuser is an employee of the facility, reports should be made directly to the Department of Social Services, Child Protective Services or police. The person making the report "shall disclose all information which is the basis for his suspicion of abuse or neglect of the child." The reporting health care provider also has an obligation, if requested, to provide all documents (presumably medical records) supporting the allegation.[1074] The physician-patient

---

[1071] Va. Code 63.2-1509.A; 45 C.F.R. 164.512(b)(1)(ii); failure to report within 24 hours of the first suspicion can result in a fine. Va. Code 63.2-1509.D
[1072] Va. Code 63.2-1509.A
[1073] Va. Code 63.2-1509.A
[1074] Va. Code 63.2-1509.A

and husband-wife privileges are expressly voided by statute.[1075] A health care provider reporting suspected abuse is protected from liability, unless he acted in bad faith or with malicious intent.[1076]

The child abuse reporting statute also requires a healthcare provider to report newborn children demonstrating evidence of *in utero* drug exposure in the following circumstances:

1. The child's blood or urine indicates the presence of a controlled substance not prescribed for the mother.

2. The child is found to be dependent on a controlled substance that was not prescribed for the mother and the child has demonstrated withdrawal symptoms.

3. The child within six weeks of birth has an illness, disease or condition that, to a reasonable degree of medical certainty, is attributable to *in utero* exposure to a controlled substance that was not prescribed for the mother.

4. The child suffers fetal alcohol syndrome.[1077]

These reports by an attending physician of a newborn must be made immediately, no later than twenty-four hours, of the medical finding. Failure to report exposes a provider to a fine of up to $500 for the first offense and up to $1,000 for subsequent offenses.[1078] A physician making the report is immune from civil or criminal prosecution if the report is made in good faith.[1079]

A hospital must maintain and follow protocols for written discharge plans for identified substance-abusing postpartum women and their infants.[1080] A hospital must immediately refer the mother to the local Community Services Board where the mother resides to implement

[1075] Va. Code 63.2-1519
[1076] Va. Code 63.2-1509.C; Va. Code 63.2-1512
[1077] Va. Code 63.2-1509.B
[1078] Va. Code 63.2-1509.D
[1079] Va. Code 63.2-1509.C; Va. Code 63.2-1512
[1080] Va. Code 32.1-127

a discharge plan. Identification of a substance-abusing postpartum woman is the responsibility of a physician, not the hospital.

Any physician who diagnoses a venereal disease in a child twelve years old or younger must report this to the Department of Health, unless the physician believes that the infection was acquired congenitally or by a means other than sexual abuse.[1081] More problematic is the situation where a minor is found to be pregnant. Should a physician presume that abuse or neglect exists? The Department of Social Services has recommended to one health care system that a provider should err on the side of reporting to the Department in that situation.

A challenging question is whether a report must be made of alleged child abuse that occurred in the distant past and the alleged victim is now over age eighteen. The statutes refer to a "child," which by definition would be someone under age eighteen, and would suggest that reporting of an event occurring long ago is not necessary. However, several practitioners have reported that local departments have taken the view that even events occurring in the distant past must be reported to them.

A child's medical records may be provided to the investigating agency, if requested.[1082] Photographs and x-rays of suspected child abuse victims may be taken without the consent of the parent or other person responsible for the child as part of the medical evaluation.[1083] These photographs and x-rays may be introduced into evidence in any subsequent proceeding.

A judge may order psychological, psychiatric, and physical examinations of a child alleged to be abused or neglected and of the parents, guardians, caretakers or siblings of the child.[1084] The

[1081] Va. Code 32.1-36.B
[1082] Va. Code 32.1-127.1:03.D.6
[1083] Va. Code 63.2-1520
[1084] Va. Code 63.2-1524

results of such testing and other documentation should be kept confidential by the health care professional, unless directed by the Court to do otherwise.

b. Adult Abuse

The Virginia statute requiring health care providers to report adult abuse, neglect or exploitation[1085] parallels the child abuse statute. Reports must be made to Adult Protective Services at 888/832-3858.[1086] Immunity is provided for those who act in good faith. Adult protective services must be provided to a person over age 60, or a person over age 18 who is incapacitated,[1087] and who is found to be abused, neglected or exploited. Health care providers must cooperate with investigators and provide records.[1088] A judge may order adult protective services (APS) on an emergency basis when the court finds that an adult is incapacitated, an emergency exists, the adult lacks the capacity to consent to APS, and the proposed order is substantially supported by the findings of the local department or there are other compelling reasons for ordering the services.[1089]

2. The Quandary of "Drug Seekers"

At common law in Virginia, there was no physician-patient privilege in criminal matters and probably not in general.[1090] The statute that addresses a treating physician's testimony in civil cases states that its confidentiality requirement does not "apply to information communicated to any such practitioner in an effort unlawfully to procure a narcotic drug, or unlawfully procure the administration

---

[1085] Va. Code 63.2-1606; 45 C.F.R. 164.512(c)
[1086] Additional information is available at http://www.dss.state.va.us/family/aps_mandated.html
[1087] Va. Code 63.2-1603
[1088] Va. Code 63.2-1606.B
[1089] Va. Code 63.2-1609
[1090] Pierce v. Caday, 244 Va. 285 (1992) citing Gibson v. Commonwealth, 216 Va. 412 (1975)

of any such drug."[1091] This gave health lawyers the bravado to state that a physician was at liberty to call the police or anyone else to report drug seekers.

In 1997, the Supreme Court of Virginia finally recognized a privacy interest by a patient in her medical records.[1092] The General Assembly also passed the Patient Health Records Privacy Act (PHRPA)[1093]. Unfortunately, PHRPA is silent as to drug seeking. The closest it comes is to allow exceptions to the general confidentiality rule:

1. Where necessary in connection with the care of the patient;

2. As required or authorized by law for ... public safety, and suspected child or adult abuse.[1094]

This does not give much guidance to the health care provider. The better course is for a physician to communicate with other health care providers, including pharmacies, who are caring for the patient, about drug seeking behavior. However, caution should be exercised in calling the police unless the patient appears threatening in some manner. If that is the case, then the physician is protected (and probably obligated) in such communication with the police.[1095] One can also argue that seeking drugs for non-therapeutic purposes does not give rise to a physician-patient relationship.

A General Assembly statutory amendment in 2010 gives some clarity to the quandary. One enjoys immunity from civil damages for reporting to the police in good faith that one suspects that a patient has obtained or attempted to obtain controlled substances by fraud or deceit.[1096]

[1091] Va. Code 8.01-399
[1092] Curtis v. Fairfax Hospital, 492 S. E. 642 (1997)
[1093] Va. Code 32.1-127.1:03
[1094] Va. Code 32.1-127.1:03.D.6 & 7
[1095] See Va. Code 54.1-2400.1
[1096] Va. Code 54.1-3408.2

3. Disease Registry

a. Virginia Government Agencies

Virginia statutes require physicians, hospitals, and other providers to report many health conditions for epidemiological and other purposes. Various statutes protect the confidentiality of information reported to the Department of Health.[1097] Examples of the many state registries are:

1. Blindness: The diagnosis of blindness must be immediately reported to the Board for the Visually Handicapped.[1098] Information in the registry is confidential.[1099]

2. Cancer: Abstracts of patient records regarding malignant tumors and cancer, including possible exposure to Agent Orange or other defoliants used in the Vietnam War, must be made available to the Commissioner of Health.[1100] All physicians must report cases of cancer to the Virginia Cancer Registry in those instances that a usual instate reporting source (e.g. a hospital, clinic or independent pathology laboratory) has not reported.[1101] Basal and squamous cell carcinoma of the skin is not included in this reporting requirement.[1102]

3. Handicaps: A physician **may** advise state agencies of a handicapped child or adult, if the physician believes the

---

[1097] Va. Code 32.1-64.2; Va. Code 32.1-67.1; Va. Code 32.1-71.4; Va. Code 32.1-116.2

[1098] Va. Code 63.1-71

[1099] Va. Code 63.1-71.1

[1100] Va. Code 32.1-70.A; 12 Va. Admin. Code 5-90-170

[1101] Va. Code 32.1-70.A

[1102] Va. Code 32.1-70.A. For further information, see Board Briefs, Va. Board of Medicine, Newsletter #55, Fall 1998.

patient would benefit from agency programs.[1103] A brain and spinal cord injury registry was created in 2007.[1104]

4. Infant Screening: Newborn screening for many conditions and reporting of many abnormalities is mandatory.[1105] Congenital anomalies diagnosed in children under age two must be reported by every hospital.[1106] These records must be kept confidential.[1107]

5. Infectious Diseases: Certain diseases must be reported to the Department of Health by any physician or laboratory director who diagnoses or "reasonably suspects" that a patient has any disease on the Department's list. [1108] Most of these are infectious diseases. A physician must report to the local health department the identity of any patient who tests positive for exposure to human immunodeficiency virus (HIV).[1109] Added by the General Assembly in 2002, diseases that may be caused by an agent or substance that has the potential for use as a weapon must be reported.[1110] Beginning on July 1, 2008, Virginia hospitals will be required to report nosocomial infections to the Centers for Disease Control and the Virginia Board of Health.[1111]

6. Trauma: Prehospital trauma care must be reported by EMS providers to the Emergency Medical Services Registry. Hospitals must report trauma care to the Virginia Statewide Trauma Registry. Both registries are within the Emergency Medical Services Patient Care Information System.[1112] Trauma

---

[1103] Va. Code 54.1-2968
[1104] Va. Code 51.5-11
[1105] Va. Code 32.1-64.1 (hearing impairment); Va. Code 32.1-65 (phenylketonuria and other inborn errors of metabolism)
[1106] Va. Code 32.1-69.1
[1107] Va. Code 32.1-64.2; Va. Code 32.1-67.1
[1108] Va. Code 32.1-36.A; 12Va. Admin. Code5-90-90
[1109] Va. Code 32.1-36.C; 12Va. Admin. Code5-90-90
[1110] Va. Code 32.1-35 et seq.
[1111] Va. Code 32.1-35.1
[1112] Va. Code 32.1-116.1

Registry information will be used by the Virginia Department of Rehabilitative Services to develop programs and services for citizens suffering brain injury.[1113]

7. Vital Statistics: Birth or death must be reported to the State Registrar by health care facilities.[1114] Confidentiality is mandated by statute.[1115] A record of an abortion and proper information for the issuance of a fetal death certificate must be furnished to the Division of Vital Records, Department of Health within ten days of the abortion.[1116] A fetal death report must be provided to the local registrar within three days.[1117] In the case of an induced abortion, the form does not identify the patient by name.[1118]

A healthcare provider may share immunization information with other providers, state, district and local health departments, and the Virginia Immunization Information System without parental consent.[1119]

The following notice must be given to any patient receiving a test for Lyme disease:[1120]

ACCORDING TO THE CENTERS FOR DISEASE CONTROL AND PREVENTION, AS OF 2011 LYME DISEASE IS THE SIXTH FASTEST GROWING DISEASE IN THE UNITED STATES.

YOUR HEALTH CARE PROVIDER HAS ORDERED A LABORATORY TEST FOR THE PRESENCE OF LYME DISEASE FOR YOU. CURRENT LABORATORY TESTING

[1113] Va. Code 32.1-116.1.D
[1114] Va. Code 32.1-249 et seq.
[1115] Va. Code 32.1-271
[1116] 12 Va. Admin. Code 5-410-1260
[1117] Va. Code 32.1-264.A
[1118] Va. Code 32.1-264.B
[1119] Va. Code 32.1-46
[1120] Va. Code 54.1-2963.2

FOR LYME DISEASE CAN BE PROBLEMATIC AND STANDARD LABORATORY TESTS OFTEN RESULT IN FALSE NEGATIVE AND FALSE POSITIVE RESULTS, AND IF DONE TOO EARLY, YOU MAY NOT HAVE PRODUCED ENOUGH ANTIBODIES TO BE CONSIDERED POSITIVE BECAUSE YOUR IMMUNE RESPONSE REQUIRES TIME TO DEVELOP ANTIBODIES. IF YOU ARE TESTED FOR LYME DISEASE, AND THE RESULTS ARE NEGATIVE, THIS DOES NOT NECESSARILY MEAN YOU DO NOT HAVE LYME DISEASE. IF YOU CONTINUE TO EXPERIENCE SYMPTOMS, YOU SHOULD CONTACT YOUR HEALTH CARE PROVIDER AND INQUIRE ABOUT THE APPROPRIATENESS OF RETESTING OR ADDITIONAL TREATMENT."

b. Federal Agencies

Federal government agencies require reports for certain incidents. For example, the following events must be reported:

1. Defective Medical Devices: Health care facilities and manufacturers must report any serious injuries or deaths to which a medical device may have caused or contributed to the Food & Drug Administration within ten days.[1121]

2. Misadministration of Radioactive Material: All incidents of radioactive material being administered in a fashion not considered appropriate must be reported to the Nuclear Regulatory Commission.[1122]

3. Occupational Exposure to Bloodborne Pathogens: Employers[1123] must maintain records of employee exposure

---

[1121] 21 U.S.C.A. 360i; See "Medical Device Reporting for User Facilities," at http://ww.fda.gov

[1122] 10 C.F.R. 35.33

[1123] 29 C.F.R. 1910.1030, et seq.

to[1124] and training in handling[1125] blood contaminated with pathogens such as hepatitis or human immunodeficiency virus. Employee medical records created pursuant to this statute must be maintained for the duration of employment plus 30 years.[1126] These records must be kept confidential but made available for inspection and copying by OSHA or the employee.[1127]

4. Behavior or Condition of Health Care Professionals

a. Impaired Health Care Provider

Every Virginia hospital or other licensed facility must report treatment or knowledge of a licensed health care provider suffering substance abuse, psychiatric illness, or other professional impairment to the Department of Health Professions.[1128] The report must be made within thirty days with the exception that commitment or admission of a professional must be reported within five days. In addition, a licensed health care professional is required to report to the Department of Health Professions that he is treating a health care professional for a mental, emotional, or personality disorder if the condition is a danger to the patient or others.[1129] (Treatment of drug addiction or alcoholism also must be reported unless the impaired health care provider is receiving treatment within a program qualified under the federal Alcohol & Substance Abuse Rehabilitation Regulations.)[1130] The reporting professional is granted immunity unless the professional is acting in bad faith

---

[1124] 29 C.F.R. 1910.1030(h)(1)

[1125] 29 C.F.R. 1910.1030(h)(2)

[1126] 29 C.F.R. 1910.1030(h)(1)(iv)

[1127] 29 C.F.R. 1910.1030(h)(3)

[1128] Va. Code 54.1-2400.6; a more detailed discussion is below in Chapter V: Licensure

[1129] Va. Code 54.1-2400.7. This is endorsed by the American Medical Association in AMA Opinions 9.03 and 9.11

[1130] Va. Code 54.1-2906 and Va. Code 54.1-2907

or with malicious intent. Immunity for reporting unprofessional conduct or competency issues was expanded in 2005 to include anyone, including those who voluntarily report such problems.[1131]

b. Improper Conduct of Mental Health Care Providers

A mental health care provider must advise a patient of the patient's right to file a complaint with the Department of Health Professions (DHP) when the provider learns of evidence indicating a "reasonable probability" that another mental health care provider is or may be guilty of violating standards of conduct set forth by statute or regulation.[1132] Failure to do so can result in a civil penalty not to exceed $100.[1133] The patient must be provided with DHP's toll-free complaint hotline number for consumer complaints and written information from DHP explaining how to file a report.[1134] The mental health care provider must also document in her chart what the alleged misconduct was, the category of licensure or certification and approximate dates of treatment, if known, of the mental health care provider who will be subject of the report, and the actions taken by the provider to advise the patient of his rights.[1135] The mental health care provider is given immunity from civil or criminal liability if these actions are taken in good faith.[1136]

5. *Medical Examiner*

The Medical Examiner is expressly authorized to investigate the cause and manner of the death of any person:

> from trauma, injury, violence, poisoning, accident, suicide or homicide, or suddenly when in apparent

---

[1131] Va. Code 54.1-2400.8
[1132] Va. Code 54.1-2400.4.A
[1133] Va. Code 54.1-2400.4.D
[1134] Va. Code 54.1-2400.4.B
[1135] Va. Code 54.1-2400.4.B
[1136] Va. Code 54.1-2400.4.C

good health, or when unattended by a physician, or in jail, prison, other correctional institution or police custody, or suddenly as an apparent result of fire, or in any suspicious, unusual or unnatural manner.[1137]

Physicians and hospitals have the duty to notify the Medical Examiner of such a death.[1138] The better practice is to report all deaths that are of concern, permitting the Medical Examiner to decline to investigate. This avoids later criticism by investigating agencies or family members. Confidential information gathered by the Medical Examiner remains confidential.[1139] However, the Medical Examiner must release a copy of the autopsy report to the attending physician and the decedent's personal representative or executor upon request.[1140]

A fetal death report must be filed for each fetal death, including abortion, which occurs in Virginia.[1141] Where a fetal death occurs without the mother receiving medical attention, "or when inquiry or investigation by the Medical Examiner is required," the Medical Examiner is obliged to investigate the cause of death.[1142] A physician or facility attending a woman who has delivered a dead fetus must maintain a copy of the fetal death report for one year, and must furnish the woman with a copy of the report, if she makes a written request.[1143]

A hospital must report to the Center for Medicare and Medicaid Services any death that occurs while a patient is restrained or in seclusion, or where it is reasonable to assume that a patient's death is a result of restraint or seclusion.[1144]

[1137] Va. Code 32.1-283
[1138] Va. Code 32.1-283.A; 45 C.F.R. 164.512(f)(4) and (g)(1)
[1139] Va. Code 32.1-283.4
[1140] Va. Code 32.1-283.C
[1141] Va. Code 32.1-264.A
[1142] Va. Code 32.1-264.D
[1143] Va. Code 32.1-264.F
[1144] 42 C.F.R. 482.13(f)(7); Interpretive Guidelines Tag A799

6. *Transportation Safety*

a. Air Craft Pilots

A physician may report the existence, or probable existence, of a mental or physical impairment in any person licensed to operate an aircraft to the Federal Aviation Administration (or other interested government agency), where the physician believes this condition reasonably could affect an individual's ability to safely operate the aircraft.[1145] Any physician also may testify in an administrative hearing or other procedure regarding the issuance, renewal, revocation or suspension of an aircraft pilot license. The physician is granted immunity, regardless of whether the person is, or has been, a patient of such physician, except where the report was made with malice.[1146]

This statute is voluntary. The law does not require a physician to divulge such information about a pilot. Curiously, immunity is granted only to physicians. Other health care professionals who may become privy to a pilot's mental or physical impairment are not protected. However, one might argue that a provider has "a duty to warn," as discussed below.

b. Automobile Drivers

A physician may report the existence, or probable existence, of a mental or physical disability or infirmity of any person licensed to operate a motor vehicle to the Division of Motor Vehicles (DMV). This report does not violate the physician-patient privilege unless the physician acted with bad faith or malicious intent.[1147] A physician is not required to report any such impairment to DMV. Curiously, immunity is not extended to other health care providers who may become aware of a driver's impairment. The Medical Review Request

---

[1145] Va. Code 54.1-2966.1
[1146] Va. Code 54.1-2966.1
[1147] Va. Code 54.1-2966.1

form is posted on DMV's website.[1148] DMV will not reveal that a health care provider was the source of the concern prompting a driver evaluation.[1149] A driver is obligated to report any impairment, even if temporary, in his driving ability to DMV. The process that DMV uses in evaluating a driver who suffers from an impairment to determine if a driver's license should be issued or restricted is posted on DMV's website.[1150]

When a patient is impaired, a health care provider should also consider whether he has a *duty to warn*, as is discussed below. A provider should err on the side of protecting the public when a patient may present a danger on the road. For example, the police should be notified when an intoxicated patient leaves the ER and drives away. The more difficult ethical situation is that confronting the physician caring for an aging patient.

7. *Violent Crime*

Any physician or other *person* who renders medical aid or treatment to a patient for any wound which that treater knows, or has reason to believe, is a wound inflicted by a weapon, and was not self-inflicted, must report the injury to the local police as soon as practicable.[1151] The report should include the wounded person's name and address, if known. Failure to comply with this statute is a Class 3 misdemeanor. Immunity from any civil liability is granted to anyone filing a report or participating in a judicial proceeding, unless the health care provider acted in bad faith or with malicious intent.[1152]

[1148] http://www.dmv.virginia.gov/webdoc/pdf/med3.pdf
[1149] Va. Code 46.2-322
[1150] http://www.dmv.virginia.gov/webdoc/citizen/medical/spec_restrict.asp
[1151] Va. Code 54.1-2967, citing weapons listed in Va. Code 18.2-308; 45 C.F.R. 164.512(f)(1)(i)
[1152] Va. Code 54.1-2967

8. *Involuntary Commitment Proceedings*

Attempting to address perceived problems after the Virginia Tech tragedy, the 2008 General Assembly passed legislation that requires a health care provider, on request, to disclose any information about a minor that is needed by a magistrate, juvenile intake officer, the court, the minor's attorney, the minor's guardian ad litem, an evaluator, a CSB performing an evaluation, preadmission screening or monitoring, or a police officer.[1153] The same obligation was enacted for health care providers in regard to adults[1154] or criminal defendants being evaluated.[1155]

[1153] Va. Code 16.1-337.B and 32.1-127.1:03.C.13

[1154] Va. Code 37.2-804.2

[1155] Va. Code 19.2-169.6

G. Duty to Warn

The duty of a health care provider to warn an identifiable victim of threatened harm by a patient has become clearly defined in Virginia.

1. The Historical Context

Tarasoff v. the Regents of the University of California[1156] was the first well-publicized case to hold that a mental health provider had a duty to warn a foreseeable victim of violence. The California Supreme Court decided that a psychiatrist had a duty to warn a patient's former girlfriend when the patient stated that he was going to kill the woman. The doctor was concerned enough about the threat to have the patient temporarily detained while the psychiatrist sought advice from the university attorney. The doctor was told that the patient could not be detained and that the woman could not be warned as this would be a breach of confidentiality, which was the prevailing ethics position of the time. The former girlfriend was murdered by the patient. The California Supreme Court announced the law going forward would be that a psychiatrist in this situation had a duty to warn an identifiable victim. Though only applicable to California, the decision has been widely quoted and followed by courts in other states. Many, including several circuit court judges, assumed that it was the law of Virginia.

2. The Virginia Judicial Decisions

Citing the Tarasoff decision, several Virginia circuit court judges concluded that mental health care providers owed a duty to protect foreseeable victims of violence by patients where a therapist-patient

---

[1156] Tarasoff v. Regents of the University of California, 17 Cal. 3d 425, 551 P.2d 334 (1976)

relationship exists. For example, the Hon. F. Bruce Bach in the Circuit Court of Fairfax County held that such a duty existed. However, plaintiff was required to allege that the therapist was aware of specific threats against the foreseeable victim. Judge Bach did not believe that a hospital would have such a duty to protect because it "cannot engage in a doctor-patient relationship which would give rise to a duty to protect third persons from foreseeable harm."[1157] Further, the therapist had no duty to warn if the foreseeable victim was already aware of the threat.[1158]

The law as understood by most practitioners was thrown out by the Supreme Court of Virginia's decision in Nasser v. Parker.[1159] The court refused to adopt the reasoning of Tarasoff. A doctor-patient relationship is not sufficient to trigger a duty to protect foreseeable victims because it was not the standard set forth in the Restatement (First) of Torts, §§315(a) and 319. The Restatement required "taking charge" of a violent individual before a duty was created to warn foreseeable victims. Even admission of a patient to a facility does not meet the definition of "taking charge." Before the ink was dry on the Nasser decision, the Virginia General Assembly created a duty to warn.

3. *The Virginia Statutory Duty*

Effective July 1, 1995, a Virginia health care provider[1160] must take steps to protect a foreseeable victim of violence by the health care

---

[1157] Keophumihae v. Brewer, 6 Va. Cir. 80, 85 (1985)
[1158] Keophumihae v. Brewer, 6 Va. Cir. 80, 92 (1985)
[1159] Nasser v. Parker, 249 Va. 172 (1995)
[1160] *Mental health service provider* as used in the statute is defined broadly to cover almost every licensed health care professional and does not limit its definition by requiring that the health care provider be engaged in rendering mental health care services at the time. Curiously, nurse practitioners and physician assistants are not included in the list of providers. This is in contrast to physicians, registered nurses and licensed practical nurses being listed.

provider's client when the provider reasonably believes that his client has the intent and ability to carry out the threat immediately or imminently to cause serious bodily injury or death.[1161] This can be accomplished by: [1162]

1. Seeking involuntary admission of the patient,[1163]

2. Making reasonable efforts to warn the potential victims (or parents of a minor),

3. Making reasonable efforts to notify the police having jurisdiction over the location of the client or the potential victims,

4. Attempting to prevent physical violence by the client until police can be summoned and takes custody of the client, or

5. Rendering therapy or counseling in the session with the client until the provider reasonably believes that the client no longer has the intent or ability to carry out the threat

A health care provider is not granted any right to detain a patient, but is given immunity from liability for breaching confidentiality, for failing to predict dangerous behavior in the absence of an explicit threat, and for not taking any steps other than those enumerated.[1164]

Along the same line, health care providers have an obligation to report certain situations to the appropriate government agency. The following are several examples frequently encountered by health care professionals:

• Child abuse[1165]

[1161] Va. Code 54.1-2400.1; 45 C.F.R. 164.512(j)(1)(i)

[1162] Va. Code 54.1-2400.1.C

[1163] Involuntary admission for psychiatric care would be pursuant to Va. Code 16.1-335 or 37.2-800

[1164] Va. Code 54.1-2400.1.D; 45 C.F.R. 164.512(j)(1)(i)

[1165] Va. Code 63.2-1512

- Adult abuse[1166]
- Violent injury[1167]
- Impaired health care provider[1168]

If a provider believes in good faith that communication with law enforcement, family or others is necessary to prevent or lessen the serious and imminent threat of harm to a patient under care, then the provider is permitted to do so.[1169] Disclosure is permitted to "law enforcement, family members of the patient, or any other persons who may reasonably be able to prevent or lessen the risk of harm."[1170] For example, a counselor may be concerned that a student is at risk for attempting suicide. If the student misses a check-in with the counselor, quickly determining the location and well being of the student may be best accomplished by campus security. As described previously, the minimum amount of PHI should be disclosed to accomplish the task at hand.

Where danger to a patient is not imminent, a provider is permitted to communicate with a patient's family and/or others involved in the patient's care to be on watch for concerning behaviors or ensure compliance with medication regimens where the patient does not object to the disclosure.[1171] For example, this may arise where a friend or relative is brought to an appointment by the patient, and the patient does not object to the provider speaking to the third party during the course of the visit. A more common scenario is

---

[1166] Va. Code 63.2-1606
[1167] Va. Code 54.1-2967
[1168] Va. Code 54.1-2907
[1169] 45 C.F.R. 164.512(j); also see Office of Civil Rights, "HIPAA Privacy Rule and Sharing Information Related to Mental Health," 20 Feb 2014, p. 8-9, citing Office of Civil Rights, "Message to Our Nation's Health Care Providers," 15 Jan 2013
[1170] Office of Civil Rights, "Message to Our Nation's Health Care Providers," 15 Jan 2013
[1171] 45 C.F.R. 164.510(b)(2)

where a provider may ask a patient if he objects to the provider having a friend or relative check in on the patient over the weekend.

Looking at the situation from the opposite end, family members, friends, and others are not prohibited from providing information about a patient to a provider. Nothing in HIPAA or state statutes should cause a health care provider to avoid receiving and acting on information provided by third parties.[1172]

When in doubt as to whether sensitive information should or should not be divulged to someone other than a patient, an experienced health care attorney should be consulted.

[1172] See Office of Civil Rights, "HIPAA Privacy Rule and Sharing Information Related to Mental Health," 20 Feb 2014, p. 8

H. Alcohol & Substance Abuse Rehabilitation

Congress recognized that absolute confidentiality is an indispensable prerequisite to successful alcohol and substance abuse treatment and prevention. Without guarantees of confidentiality, many individuals with alcohol or substance dependence would be reluctant to participate in treatment programs. The Comprehensive Alcohol Abuse and Alcoholism Prevention, Treatment, and Rehabilitation Act of 1970[1173], and the Drug Abuse, Prevention, Treatment, and Rehabilitation Act of 1972[1174], were drafted with these considerations in mind. Together with the implementing regulations, 42 C.F.R. Part 2, federal law provides a regulatory scheme designed to ensure that the medical records of patients receiving treatment for drug and alcohol abuse are managed with extreme confidentially.

The federal statute expressly authorized the Secretary of Health and Human Services to promulgate regulations to effectuate the

---

[1173] 42 U.S.C.A. 290dd-3(a) prohibits disclosure of medical records containing:

[T]he identity, diagnosis, prognosis, or treatment of any patient which are maintained in connection with the performance of any program or activity related to alcoholism or alcohol abuse education, training, treatment, rehabilitation, or research which is conducted, regulated, or directly or indirectly assisted by any department or agency of the United States.

42 U.S.C.A. 290dd-3(a)

[1174] 42 U.S.C.A. 290ee(a) prohibits disclosure of medical records containing:

[T]he identity, diagnosis, prognosis, or treatment of any patient which are maintained in connection with the performance of any drug abuse prevention function conducted, regulated, or directly or indirectly assisted by any department or agency of the United States.

42 U.S.C.A. 290ee-3(a)

purposes of this statute. The Alcohol, Drug Abuse and Mental Health Administration, now known as the Substance Abuse and Mental Health Services Administration, Center for Substance Abuse Treatment, promulgated final regulations that place strict safeguards on the privacy of alcohol and substance abuse records in most settings, effective August 10, 1987.

The regulations set out in great detail the manner in which substance abuse rehabilitation and related medical records must be handled, and impose penalties in the event that confidentiality is breached. HIPAA[1175] supplements but does not replace 42 C.F.R. Part 2. The most restrictive of the two code sections will apply. Generally, this means that 42 C.F.R. Part 2 will continue to guide the handling of confidential information in substance abuse rehabilitation programs.

1. What Facilities Are Covered

The regulations impose restrictions on the disclosure and use of alcohol and drug abuse patient records which are maintained in connection with the performance of any federally-assisted alcohol and drug program. These regulations cover any federally-assisted program that provides or holds itself out as providing alcohol or drug abuse diagnosis, treatment or referral for treatment.[1176] A facility which provides general medical care is not viewed as a qualified program unless it has either (1) an identified substance abuse unit or (2) personnel who are identified as providers of diagnosis, treatment or a referral for treatment and whose primary function is the provision of those alcohol or drug abuse services.[1177]

Facilities that provide blood alcohol tests for the sole purpose

---

[1175] 42 C.F.R. Part 162
[1176] Residential methadone treatment facilities in Virginia must comply with these federal regulations on confidentiality regardless of funding source. Rules and Regulations for the Licensure of Residential Facilities, 7.38
[1177] 42 C.F.R. 2.11

of providing evidence to law enforcement authorities regarding a person's intoxication do not fall under the current regulations. An open question is whether medical centers who have qualified treatment programs may provide substance abuse testing for employers and law enforcement agencies.

2. Exceptions

These regulations do not apply to information on alcohol and drug abuse patients maintained in connection with the Veterans Administration's provision of medical care or services; to exchanges within the armed forces or between the armed forces and the Veterans Administration; to reporting under state law of incidences of suspected child abuse and neglect to appropriate state or local authorities; to communications with an entity having direct administrative control over the program; to communications between a program and a qualified service organization; or to disclosures to law enforcement officers concerning a patient's commission of or threat to commit a crime at the program or against personnel at the program.

3. Notice to Patients of the Federal Confidentiality Requirements

At the time of admission, or as soon thereafter as a patient is capable of rational communication, the program must tell the patient that his medical records are protected by federal law and regulations and give the patient a written summary of the federal law and regulations.[1178] The summary must include:

1. A general description of the limited circumstances under which a program may acknowledge that an individual is present at the facility or disclose outside the program information identifying a patient as a drug or alcohol abuser;

[1178]   42 C.F.R. 2.22

2. A statement that violation of the federal law and regulations by a program is a crime and that suspected violations may be reported to appropriate authorities;

3. A statement that information related to a patient's commission of a crime on the premises of the program or against personnel of the program is not protected;

4. A statement that reports of suspected child abuse and neglect made under state law to appropriate state or local authorities is not protected;

5. A citation to the federal law and regulations.

HIPAA additionally requires that a patient be given a notice of the program's privacy practices as well as the patient's rights.[1179] These requirements can be combined into a single notice. A program may devise its own statement, or use the statement contained in the regulations.[1180]

4. What Information is Covered

The restriction contained in 42 C.F.R. Part 2 applies to any information, whether or not recorded, which would identify a patient as a drug or alcohol abuser. The primary reason for seeking treatment at the program need not be drug or alcohol related for the records to be protected. However, a diagnosis of drug or alcohol abuse that is entirely unrelated to the reason the individual is seeking medical treatment is probably not protected, even if limited treatment is provided to the patient for drug or alcohol abuse.

Recently, the Center for Substance Abuse Treatment of HHS has articulated guidance that appears to loosen the strict interpretation of not identifying anyone that may be enrolled or sought enrollment in a program. "Part 2 permits a substance abuse treatment program to disclose information about a patient if the disclosure does not

[1179] 45 C.F.R. 164.520
[1180] See 42 C.F.R. 2.22(d)

identify the patient as an alcohol or drug abuser or as someone who has applied for or received substance abuse assessment or treatment services."[1181] This is a more practical approach to the situation where a program is part of a larger entity such as a health care system.

As a general rule, disclosure of any information related to a patient is prohibited, even the fact that the person is currently a patient, has been a patient in the past, or has sought evaluation or treatment. The response to requests for this information should be simply that the release of this information is protected by the federal statutes. No further explanation is required. Also, "the restrictions on disclosure of information apply whether the holder of the information believes that the person seeking the information already has it, has other means of obtaining it, is a law enforcement or other official, has obtained a subpoena, or asserts any other justification for a disclosure or use not permitted by these regulations."[1182] Any disclosure permitted under a regulation must be limited to that information which is necessary to carry out the purpose of the disclosure.

There are several exceptions to the prohibition on disclosure of patient information, which are described below.

5. Disclosure of Information With the Patient's Consent

Sections 290dd-3(b)(1) and 290ee-3(b)(1) provide that disclosure may be authorized in accordance with the prior written consent of

---

[1181] "The Confidentiality of Alcohol and Drug Abuse Patient Records Regulation and the HIPAA Privacy Rule: Implications for Alcohol and Substance Abuse Programs," US Dept of Health & Human Services, Substance Abuse and Mental health Services Administration, Center for Substance Abuse Treatment, www.samhsa.gov, June 2004, p. 10, citing 42 C.F.R. 2.11 and 2.12(a).

[1182] 42 C.F.R. 2.13

the patient. (HIPAA uses the term *authorization* in lieu of *consent*.) The regulations outline the procedure for such disclosure.[1183] The release of information with the patient's consent must include the following:

1. The specific name or general designation of the program or person permitted to make the disclosure;

2. The name or title of the individual or the name of the organization to which the disclosure is to be made;

3. The name of the patient;

4. The purpose of the disclosure;

5. How much and what kind of information is to be disclosed;

6. The signature of the patient and when required for a patient who is a minor, the signature of the person authorized to give consent or when required for a patient who is incompetent or deceased, the signature of a person authorized to sign in lieu of the patient;

7. The date on which the consent is signed;

8. A statement that the consent is subject to revocation at any time except to the extent that the program or person which is to make the disclosure has already acted in reliance on it. Acting in reliance includes the provision of treatment services and reliance on a valid consent to disclose information to a third party payor; and

9. The date, event or condition upon which the consent will expire if not revoked before. This date, event or condition must insure that the consent will last no longer than reasonably necessary to serve the purpose for which it is given.

The regulations include a sample consent form that complies with the regulations above.[1184] HIPAA additionally requires that a copy of

---

[1183] 42 C.F.R. Part 2, Subpart C
[1184] See 42 C.F.R. 2.31

the signed form be given to the patient[1185] and the program must keep a copy of each signed form for six years from its expiration date.[1186] The rehab regulations permit oral revocation of the patient's consent to release of records.[1187] In contrast, HIPAA requires written revocation.[1188] Therefore, a program should continue to honor oral revocations but request written documentation in follow up.

Each disclosure made with a patient's written authorization must be accompanied by the following written statement:

This information has been disclosed to you from records protected by federal confidentiality rules. (42 C.F.R. Part 2). The federal rules prohibit you from making any further disclosure of this information unless further consent of the person to whom it pertains or as otherwise permitted by 42 C.F.R. Part 2. A general authorization for the release of medical or other information is NOT sufficient for this purpose. The federal rules restrict any use of the information to criminally investigate or prosecute any alcohol or drug abuse patient.[1189]

A provider must exercise judgment to limit disclosures to that information necessary to carry out the purpose of the disclosure. HIPAA specifies that only the minimum necessary amount of information be disclosed.

Health care providers may disclose patient records to a central registry or to a detoxification or maintenance treatment program within 200 miles to prevent a patient from enrolling in multiple programs. The patient must be in treatment and the disclosure must be made with the patient's written authorization and when the patient's treatment is started, changed or interrupted. Disclosure is limited to patient identifying information, the nature of the treatment, the

---

[1185] 45 C.F.R. 164.508(c)(4)
[1186] 45 C.F.R. 164.508(b)(6)
[1187] 42 C.F.R. 2.31(a)(8)
[1188] 45 C.F.R. 164.508(b)(5)
[1189] 42 C.F.R. Part 2, 2.32

relevant dates, and disclosure must be for the purpose of preventing multiple enrollments.

Patient records may also be disclosed to those in the criminal justice system that have made participation in the program a condition of the disposition of the criminal proceeding, parole, or other release from custody. The patient must sign an authorization form releasing this information. The disclosure is limited to those individuals who need to monitor the patient, and redisclosure is prohibited.

The regulations do not prohibit a patient from reviewing his own records.[1190] However, the regulations do not compel disclosure, leaving decisions concerning patient access to the individual program. In contrast, HIPAA mandates that a patient can review his records and request changes to inaccurate entries.

6. *Disclosure of Information Without Patient's Consent*

Disclosure of information without a patient's authorization is permitted in the following circumstances.[1191]

1. To medical personnel to the extent necessary to meet a bona fide medical emergency.

2. To qualified personnel for the purpose of conducting scientific research, management audits, financial audits, or program evaluation, but such personnel may not identify, directly or indirectly, any individual patient in any report of such research, audit, or evaluation, or otherwise disclose patient identities in any manner.

3. If authorized by an appropriate court order of a court of competent jurisdiction granted after application showing good cause therefore. In assessing good cause, the court

---

[1190]   42 C.F.R. 2.23
[1191]   Sections 290dd(b)(2) and 290ee-3(b)(2)

shall weigh the public interest and the need for disclosure against the injury to the patient, and to the physician-patient relationship, and to the treatment services. Upon the granting of such order, the court, in determining the extent to which any disclosure of all or any part of any record is necessary, shall impose appropriate safeguards against unauthorized exposure.

The regulations clarify the statute and define the permissible disclosure of information without the patient's written authorization.[1192]

1. Medical Emergencies. (a) Patient identifying information may be disclosed to medical personnel who have a need for information about a patient for the purpose of treating a condition that poses an immediate threat to the health of any individual and that requires immediate medical intervention.[1193] (b) Information may be disclosed to medical personnel of the Food and Drug Enforcement Administration (FDA) who have reason to believe that the health of any individual may be threatened by an error in the manufacturing, labeling or sale of a product under FDA jurisdiction and the information will be used for the exclusive purpose of notifying patients and their physicians of potential dangers.[1194]

If a disclosure is made under this provision, the program must document the disclosure in the patient's record setting forth the following: (a) the name of the medical personnel to whom the disclosure was made and their affiliation with any health care facility, (b) the name of the individual making the disclosure, (c) the date

---

[1192] 42 C.F.R. Part 2, Subpart D
[1193] 42 C.F.R. 2.51(a)
[1194] 42 C.F.R. 2.51(b)

and time of the disclosure and (d) the nature of the emergency (or if error, that the report was to the FDA).[1195]

2. Scientific Research. Patient identifying information may be disclosed for the purpose of conducting scientific research if the program director makes a determination that the recipient of the patient identifying information (a) is qualified to conduct the research, (b) has a research protocol under which the patient identifying information will be maintained in accordance with security requirements and will not be redisclosed, (c) has provided a satisfactory written statement that a group of three or more individuals who are independent of the research project have reviewed the protocol and have determined that it protects the information according to the regulations, and the risks of disclosing patient identifying information are outweighed by the potential benefits of the research.[1196] Such research may subject to further restrictions under the Common Rule or state law, as discussed in Chapter I.

3. Audit and Evaluation Activities. Patient identifying information may be disclosed in the cursory review of records on the program premises for audits by any federal, state or local government agency that provides financial assistance to the program or is authorized by law to regulate its activities or third party payors who regulate or provide financial assistance to the program. Copies of records containing patient identifying information may be taken by qualified auditors if they agree to protect the information in accordance with the regulations.[1197] If copies are requested, as always, proper documentation is critical. Information may be disclosed for the purposes of Medicare or Medicaid audit or evaluation.[1198]

[1195] 42 C.F.R. 2.51(c)
[1196] 42 C.F.R. 2.52
[1197] 42 C.F.R. 2.53
[1198] 42 C.F.R. 2.53(c)

4. <u>Law Enforcement.</u> Additionally, limited information may be disclosed without a patient's authorization to law enforcement when it is directly related to crimes or threats of crimes on the program premises or against its personnel.[1199] Such disclosure is limited to the circumstances of the incident and the patient's status, name, address, and last known whereabouts.

7. *Court Order Authorizing Disclosure and Use*

The federal law and regulations permit disclosure of patient identifying information pursuant to a court order, after a court of competent jurisdiction has made a finding of *good cause*.[1200] A court order under these regulations may authorize disclosure of confidential communications made by a patient to a program in the course of diagnosis, treatment or referral for treatment only if:

1. The disclosure is necessary to protect against an existing threat to life or serious bodily injury, including circumstances which constitute suspected child abuse and neglect and verbal threats against third parties.[1201]

2. The disclosure is necessary in connection with investigation or prosecution of an extremely serious crime, such as one which directly threatens loss of life or serious bodily injury, including homicide, rape, kidnapping, armed robbery, assault with a deadly weapon or child abuse and neglect.[1202]

3. The disclosure is in connection with litigation or an administrative proceeding in which the patient offers testimony or other evidence pertaining to the contents of the confidential communications.[1203]

[1199] 42 C.F.R. 2.12(c)(5)
[1200] 42 U.S.C.A. 290dd-3(b)(2)(C), 42 U.S.C.A. 290ee-3(b)(2)(C), and 42 C.F.R. Part 2, Subpart E
[1201] 42 C.F.R. 2.63(1)
[1202] 42 C.F.R. 2.63(2)
[1203] 42 C.F.R. 2.63(2)

A court order alone does not compel disclosure. A subpoena must be issued as well in order to compel disclosure.[1204]

A court order under this section may authorize:

1. Disclosure for purposes other than criminal investigation or prosecution by any person having a legally recognized interest in the disclosure;

2. Disclosure for investigating or prosecuting a patient if the crime involved is extremely serious such as one that causes or directly threatens loss of life or serious bodily injury;

3. Disclosure for investigating or prosecuting a program or a person holding the records; and

4. The placement of an undercover agent or informant in a program as a employee or patient of the program.

8. Security

Records not in use must be maintained in a secure room, locked file cabinets, safe or other similar container. A facility must adopt written procedures regulating and controlling access to and use of

---

[1204] 42 C.F.R. 2.61 of the Regulations provides some examples:

(1) A person holding records subject to these regulations receives a subpoena for those records. A response to the subpoena is not permitted under the regulations unless an authorizing court order is entered. The person may not disclose the records in response to the subpoena unless the court of competent jurisdiction enters an authorizing order under these regulations.

(2) An authorizing court order is entered under these regulations, but the person authorized does not want to make a disclosure. If there is no subpoena or other compulsory process, or a subpoena for the record has expired or been quashed, that person may refuse to make the disclosure. Upon the entry of a valid subpoena or other compulsory process, the person authorized to disclose must disclose unless there is a valid, legal defense to the process other than the confidentiality restrictions of these regulations. (Emphasis added.)

patient's records. Programs discontinued or taken over by other programs must generally purge identifying information from or destroy patient records. Written patient authorization to transfer records vitiates this obligation. Special procedures apply where retention of the record is required by law.

9. *Enforcement of These Regulations*

The Department of Justice has the sole responsibility for prosecuting violations of this statute,[1205] in contrast to HIPAA which is enforced by the Office of Civil Rights within HHS.[1206] Any violation of these regulations should be reported to the United States Attorney for the jurisdictional district in which the violation occurs. Any violation of these regulations by a methadone program should be directed to the regional offices of the Food and Drug Administration. Violation of any provision of the statute can bring fines of not more than $500.00 in the case of a first offense and not more than $5,000.00 in the case of each subsequent offense.

A violation of the statute does not create a private cause of action for a patient.[1207] However, the patient may have a cause of action for violation of civil rights if the person who improperly obtains the protected records is a government employee, such as a police officer.[1208]

[1205] 42 C.F.R. 2.5

[1206] 45 C.F.R. 160.306

[1207] Doe v. Broderick, 225 F.3d 440, 453 (4th Cir. 2000) citing Ellison v. Cocke County, Tenn., 63 F.3d 467 (6th Cir. 1995)

[1208] Doe v. Broderick, 225 F.3d 440, 453 (4th Cir. 2000)

I.   HIV-Positive Patient

1. Consent to HIV Testing

a. Informed Consent for HIV Testing

Virginia law establishes the general rule concerning the consent required before a Human Immunodeficiency Virus (HIV) test can be performed:[1209] The rigors of the statute were softened in 2008 to a position more consistent with other medical tests. A provider must inform the patient that the test is planned, provide information about the test and tell the patient that he has the right to decline the test. If it is declined, the provider must note that fact in the patient's chart.

A licensed practitioner, including nurses, must advise every pregnant patient that HIV testing is recommended and that she will receive an HIV test as part of a routine prenatal test unless she opts-out.[1210] Refusal by a patient must be documented in the woman's medical record. Oral or written information on HIV, interventions to reduce HIV transmission from mother to infant and the meaning of test results must be offered to prenatal patients.

A person who has a confirmed positive test for HIV must be afforded the opportunity for individual face-to-face disclosure of the test results and appropriate counseling, which must include the meaning of the test results, the need for additional testing; the etiology, prevention and effects of AIDS; the availability of health care, mental health care and social services; the need to notify any person who

---

[1209]   Va. Code 32.1-37.2.A
[1210]   Va. Code 54.1-2403.01

may have been exposed; and the availability of assistance through the Department of Health in notifying such people.[1211]

b. Deemed Consent

There are several situations under which Virginia law states that an individual has *deemed to have consented* to HIV testing.

i) Exposure of a Health Care Provider or Patient

Whenever a health care provider, or any person employed by or under the direction of the health care provider, is directly exposed to body fluids of a patient in a manner that may transmit HIV, the patient whose body fluids that were involved in the exposure shall be deemed to have consented to testing for HIV infection.[1212] The patient is also deemed to have consented to the release of the test results to the health care worker who was exposed.[1213] Unless it is an emergency situation, a health care worker must inform a patient of this statute prior to providing health care services that create a risk of such exposure. *Health care provider* was defined in a 1994 amendment of the statute to include volunteers at the scene of an emergency or en route therefrom.[1214]

The *deemed consent* statute goes both ways. Whenever a patient is directly exposed to body fluids of a health care provider in a manner that may transmit HIV, the health care provider is deemed to have consented to testing for infection with HIV, and the release of the test results to the patient who was exposed.[1215]

[1211] Va. Code 32.1-37.2.B
[1212] Va. Code 32.1-45.1(A); also see above "Impaired Health Care Providers," above. This statute was amended in 1993 to include Hepatitis B or C viruses as well.
[1213] Va. Code 32.1-45.1.A
[1214] Va. Code 32.1-45.1.D
[1215] Va. Code 32.1-45.1.B

ii) Anonymous Testing

When an individual seeks the services of a facility offering anonymous testing for HIV, he is deemed to have consented to the test.[1216] The theory behind this position is that the anonymity of the patient would be lost if the facility required a written consent form signed by the patient.

iii) Diagnostic Blood Specimens

An individual is deemed to have consented to HIV testing when blood specimens are obtained for routine diagnostic procedures, and are tested in order to conduct sero-prevalence studies of HIV infection, if such studies are designed to prevent any specimen from being identified with any specific individual.[1217] The policy decision is that the need for research and epidemiological information greatly outweighs a patient's privacy interest. The privacy interest is not compromised since there is no way to trace the blood specimen back to the individual.

iv) Blood Donation

An individual is deemed to have consented to HIV testing any time he donates or sells his blood.[1218]

c. Testing of Persons Arrested for A Crime Involving Assault

In Virginia, as soon as practicable following the arrest of an individual charged with any crime involving sexual assault, offenses against children, or assault and battery in which the victim was exposed to the suspect's bodily fluids, he may be requested to submit to testing for HIV or hepatitis.[1219] The request is made by the Commonwealth's

---

[1216]   Va. Code 32.1-37.2.A.i
[1217]   Va. Code 32.1-37.2.A.ii
[1218]   Va. Code 32.1-37.2.A.iii
[1219]   Va. Code 18.2-62.A

Attorney after consultation with the victim. If the defendant refuses, a closed hearing will be conducted in front of a judge to determine if there is probable cause to believe that the defendant committed the crime with which he has been charged.[1220] Upon a finding of probable cause, the court *must* order the accused to undergo a test for HIV or hepatitis.[1221]

If an individual is convicted of any crime involving sexual assault or offenses against children, the court *must* order the individual to undergo the test upon the request of the Commonwealth's Attorney.[1222] A hearing is not necessary. The Virginia Code also provides for mandatory testing for HIV and hepatitis C of persons convicted of prostitution, crimes against nature and drug offenses indicating intravenous use.[1223] The results of the test are confidential.[1224]

In the event that a test is determined to be positive, confirmatory tests must be performed.[1225] The results are confidential.[1226] However, the Department of Health *must* disclose the results to the victim(s) and offer counseling.

The results of these tests are not admissible as evidence in any criminal proceeding.[1227] However, the statute does not preclude the use of these results in a civil suit. The costs of the tests are paid by the Commonwealth and taxed as part of the cost of the criminal proceedings.[1228]

[1220] Va. Code 18.2-62.A

[1221] Va. Code 18.2-62.A

[1222] Va. Code 18.2-62.B

[1223] Va. Code 18.2-346.1

[1224] Va. Code 32.1-36.1

[1225] Va. Code 18.2-62.C

[1226] Va. Code 32.1-36.1

[1227] Va. Code 18.2-62.C

[1228] Va. Code 18.2-62.C

d. Testing in Institutional Settings: Prisons and Psychiatric Institutions

Virginia does not currently screen all correctional inmates or institutionalized psychiatric patients; however, mass screening has been studied by the General Assembly.[1229] Several states require HIV testing for all inmates.[1230]

e. Disclosure to School Authorities

There is no requirement that school authorities be informed of a child that is HIV-positive. However, Virginia law requires the Board of Education and the Board of Health to promulgate guidelines for school attendance for children who are HIV-positive.[1231]

f. Insurance

Insurers may require applicants for life or accident and sickness insurance coverage to be tested for the presence of HIV infection.[1232] Whenever an applicant is requested to take an HIV test, the use of such test must be revealed to the applicant and his written consent must be obtained. The consent must provide an explanation of the meaning of the HIV-related test, and must disclose:

1. The types of individuals or organizations that will receive a copy of the test results;

[1229] See Report of the Security of Human Resources on Senate Joint Resolution 90 (1987) and Screening Prisoners for AIDS (1987)

[1230] See, e.g., Ga. Code 42-5-52.1(b); Idaho Code 39-604

[1231] Va. Code 22.1-271.3. See Acquired Immunodeficiency Syndrome: Virginia Department of Health Recommendations for Day Care Center Attendance (November 1985)

[1232] See Rules Governing Underwriting Practices and Coverage Limitations and Exclusions For Acquired Immunodeficiency Syndrome (AIDS), Commonwealth of Virginia State Corporation Commission Bureau of Insurance (effective May 1, 1990)

2. The types of individuals or organizations which will have access to the applicant's insurance files;

3. The types of individuals or organizations which will keep the test information in a data bank or other file;

4. That if the applicant requests the names of the specific individuals or organizations named under subsections (1), (2) or (3) in connection with his or her application, the information will be provided to the applicant;

5. The name and address of the individual to be notified of the HIV test results; and

6. That if the person does not designate a person or physician as provided above, face-to-face counseling is available through the Virginia Department of Health.

Insurers must maintain strict confidentiality regarding HIV-related test results or the diagnosis of a specific sickness or medical condition derived from such tests.

Insurers are allowed to deny coverage where the applicant is diagnosed as HIV-positive or as having AIDS, where this finding is based on two positive ELISA tests and one positive Western Blot.

g. Anatomical Gifts

A gift of all or part of a human body authorizes "any examination necessary to ensure medical acceptability of the gift for the purposes intended."[1233] This language is sufficiently broad to include HIV testing, and the information is critically important to the recipient. Knowing sale or donation of HIV-positive blood, body fluids, organs or tissues can lead to conviction of a Class 6 felony.

[1233] Va. Code 32.1-290.1(F)

2. Mandatory Reporting Requirements

a. Living Patients

A physician must report the identity of any patient who has tested positive for exposure to HIV to the local health department.[1234] In addition, a physician or a lab director has a duty to report the identity of a patient diagnosed or reasonably suspected to be HIV-positive to the Board of Health.[1235] The statute does not define the term "reasonably suspects." A physician does not have a duty to notify any other third party and is protected from civil liability.[1236]

b. Deceased Patients

Upon transferring custody of any deceased patient to a mortician, a hospital, nursing home, home for adults, or correctional facility must, at the time of transfer, notify the mortician if the patient was known to have had, immediately prior to his death, an infectious disease that may be transmitted through exposure to any bodily fluids.[1237] This, of course, includes HIV.[1238]

All information received by any person practicing funeral services or his agent regarding the fact that a dead body that he has received harbors an infectious disease must be kept confidential.[1239]

3. Confidentiality of HIV Test Results and Treatment

The issue of confidentiality of medical information is critical when

---

[1234] Va. Code 32.1-36.C; Regulations for Disease Reporting and Control, Amendment 4, Virginia State Board of Health, 3.1.D (28 Mar. 1990)

[1235] Va. Code 32.1-36.A

[1236] Va. Code 32.1-36.C

[1237] Va. Code 32.1-37.1; 12 Va. Admin. Code 5-90-90.F

[1238] See Regulations for Disease Reporting and Control, supra, 3.2.F

[1239] Va. Code 54.1-2807.1

the medical record contains a diagnosis of HIV or AIDS. Aside from the interest that an individual always has in the confidentiality of his medical record, individuals with HIV have other concerns. The early victims of HIV were predominantly homosexual men, and information that an individual had AIDS or tested HIV-positive was frequently thought, correctly or incorrectly, to reveal his sexual preferences. Since this group is often the subject of discrimination, it became apparent very early that confidentiality, to the extent of total anonymity, was necessary. Today, one of the fastest growing populations of individuals with HIV is intravenous drug users, another group which is unpopular and often discriminated against.

Although HIV is more accepted today, individuals with HIV still receive special legal protection. The principal battleground for AIDS-related legislation puts the confidentiality concerns of an individual infected with HIV against the needs of interested others, such as spouses, lovers, epidemiologists, insurance companies, exposed health care workers and fellow needle users, to know the HIV status of the individual.

Virginia law provides strong, but not complete, confidentiality protection for the diagnosis or treatment of HIV-positive individuals. Countervailing interests that outweigh a patient's right of privacy can be grouped into three categories:

1. The interest of the HIV-positive patient in receiving the appropriate medical treatment;
2. The interest in collecting public health information; and
3. The interest of others to be protected from exposure and infection.

Virginia law allows, but does not require, a physician to disclose the results of a patient's HIV test result to certain individuals.[1240] These individuals include:

[1240] Va. Code 32.1-36.1

1. The subject of the test or his legally authorized representative.

2. Any person designated in a release signed by the patient or his legally authorized representative.

3. The Department of Health.

4. Health care providers for the purpose of consultation or providing care and treatment to the patient.

5. Health care facility staff committees that monitor, evaluate or review programs or services.

6. Medical or epidemiological researchers for use as statistical data only.

7. Any person allowed access to such information by *court order*. (A subpoena alone is insufficient.)

8. Any facility that procures, processes, distributes, or uses blood, other body fluids, tissues or organs.

9. Any person authorized by law to receive such information.

10. The parents of the patient, if the patient is a minor.

11. The spouse of the patient.

12. Health departments outside Virginia for the purposes of disease surveillance and investigation.

A physician has no duty to notify any third party, other than the local health department, that a patient is HIV-positive or has AIDS.[1241] By statute, no cause of action arises where a physician fails to warn others that the patient is HIV-positive or has AIDS.[1242] There is no duty on the part of a blood collection agency or tissue bank to notify any other person, except to the Department of Health, of the reported test results.

[1241] Va. Code 32.1-36.C
[1242] Va. Code 32.1-36.C

4. Civil/Criminal Penalties for Violation of AIDS Confidentiality Laws

Unless otherwise stated, a person willfully violating the statutes protecting the confidentiality of HIV test results is guilty of a Class 1 misdemeanor (not more than twelve months of jail and not more than $2,500 fine).[1243] A person refusing, neglecting or failing to obey these statutes may be compelled to do so by injunction, mandamus, imposition of a civil penalty, or appointment of a receiver.[1244] An individual refusing, neglecting or failing to obey an injunction, mandamus or other remedy is subject to a civil penalty not to exceed $10,000 for each violation. Each day of the violation is considered a separate offense.

Violation of this statute is found where "a person willfully or through gross negligence [makes] an unauthorized disclosure."[1245] Violators are prosecuted by the Attorney General or the Commonwealth's Attorney and a civil penalty of not more than $5,000 can be imposed. Violators are also subject to suit by the individual who is the subject of the unauthorized disclosure. The patient may initiate an action to recover actual damages, if there are any, or $100, whichever is greater. The individual may also be awarded reasonable attorney's fees and reasonable court costs.

Nonetheless, a person making a report or disclosure as required or authorized by law is immune from civil liability or criminal penalty *unless* it is proven that the individual acted with gross negligence or malicious intent.[1246]

[1243] Va. Code 32.1-27.A
[1244] Va. Code 32.1-27.B
[1245] Va. Code 32.1-36.1
[1246] Va. Code 32.1-38

J.   Mammography

Federal statutes and regulations now articulate how results of mammography must be handled.[1247] The interpretation of a mammogram must contain one of the following categories in its conclusion:[1248]

1. *Negative*: nothing to comment upon (if the radiologist is aware of clinical findings or symptoms, despite the negative assessment, these must be explained)

2. *Benign*: also a negative assessment

3. *Probably Benign*: finding(s) has a high probability of being benign

4. *Suspicious*: finding(s) without all the characteristic morphology of breast cancer but indicating a definite probability of being malignant

5. *Highly suggestive of malignancy*: finding(s) has a high probability of being malignant

6. *Incomplete*: need additional imaging evaluation (the reasons why no assessment can be made must be stated)

All women who have a mammogram must be notified in writing about the results. A summary of the mammography report must be in easy-to-understand language and provided to the patient within thirty days.[1249] A *suspicious* or *highly suggestive of malignancy* assessment should be communicated to the patient and her referring physician "as soon as possible."[1250] The FDA interprets this

---

[1247] Mammography Quality Standards Act of 1992 and Mammography Quality Standards Reauthorization Act of 1998, 42 U.S.C.A. 263b

[1248] 21 C.F.R. 900.12(c)(1)(iv) and (v)

[1249] 21 C.F.R. 900.12(c)(2)

[1250] 21 C.F.R. 900.12(c)(2) and (3)(ii)

as ordinarily within five business days. Results of less concerning studies must be provided to the referring physician as soon as possible but not later than thirty days after the study.[1251] Self-referred patients should receive the easy-to-read summary, as well as the physician's report.[1252] The facility also must maintain a system for referral of patients who do not have a physician.[1253] If the results are unclear or incomplete, the FDA recommends that the facility communicate with the patient as soon as possible to avoid delays in follow-up care. The exact language of the report to patients and the system for doing so are left to the facility's discretion.

Legislation passed by the General Assembly in 2012 and revised in several subsequent years requires the following language in a letter to the patient if it applies:[1254]

> YOUR MAMMOGRAM DEMONSTRATES THAT YOU MAY HAVE DENSE BREAST TISSUE. DENSE BREAT TISSUE IS VERY COMMON AND IS NOT ABNORMAL. HOWEVER, DENSE BREAST TISSUE CAN MAKE IT HARDER TO FIND CANCER ON A MAMMOGRAM AND MAY ALSO BE ASSOCIATED WITH AN INCREASED RISK OF BREAST CANCER
>
> THIS INFORMATION IS GIVEN TO YOU TO RAISE YOUR AWARENESS. USE THIS INFORMATION TO TALK TO YOUR DOCTOR ABOUT YOUR OWN RISKS FOR BREAST CANCER. AT THAT TIME, ASK YOUR DOCTOR IF MORE SCREENING TESTS MIGHT BE USEFUL BASED ON YOUR RISK.
>
> A REPORT OF YOUR MAMMOGRAPHY RESULTS HAS BEEN SENT TO YOUR REFERRING PHYSICIAN'S OFFICE,

---

[1251] 21 C.F.R. 900.12(c)(3)(i)
[1252] 21 C.F.R. 900.12(c)(2)(i)
[1253] 21 C.F.R. 900.12(c)(2)(ii)
[1254] Va. Code 32.1-299

AND YOU SHOULD CONTACT YOUR PHYSICIAN IF YOU HAVE ANY QUESTIONS OR CONCERNS ABOUT THIS REPORT.

Federal regulations require that an original mammogram, not a copy, be sent to the patient's physician, medical institution or the patient on the patient's request.[1255] This may be a temporary or permanent transfer. The facility is entitled to retain the original medical record and forward a copy. The charge for providing a film or medical record is limited to "the documented costs associated with this service."[1256]

[1255] 21 C.F.R. 900.12(c)(4)(ii)
[1256] 21 C.F.R. 900.12(c)(4)(iii)

K. Medical Information in the Legal System

1. Civil Litigation

The health care provider and medical information manager are frequently called upon to assist in civil litigation. Knowledge of the basic rules will make for more efficient handling of such requests.

a. Subpoena

A subpoena requires an individual to appear at a particular time and place to give testimony. This may either be for a discovery deposition or at trial. If the person being subpoenaed is requested to bring medical records, documents or other tangible items, this is called a subpoena duces tecum. Most common for the medical information manager is where a subpoena duces tecum demands the production of medical records at an attorney's office during pretrial discovery. A health care provider can be held in contempt of court for failure to comply with a subpoena duces tecum.[1257]

Virginia law now requires that the following be made a part of any request for a subpoena and sent to a patient representing himself or who is not a party to the action:

NOTICE TO PATIENT

> The attached Request for Subpoena means that (insert name of party requesting subpoena) has asked the court to issue a subpoena to your doctor or other health care providers (names of health care providers

---

[1257]   See Bellis v. Commonwealth of Virginia, 241 Va. 257 (1991)

inserted here) requiring them to produce your medical records. Your doctor or other health care provider is required to respond by providing a copy of your medical records. If you believe your records should not be disclosed and object to their disclosure, you have the right to file a motion with the clerk of the court to quash the subpoena. You may contact the clerk's office to determine the requirements that must be satisfied when filing a motion to quash and you may elect to contact an attorney to represent your interest. If you elect to file a motion to quash, it must be filed as soon as possible before the provider sends out the records in response to the subpoena. If you elect to file a motion to quash, you must notify your doctor or other health care provider(s) that you are filing the motion so that the provider knows to send the records to the clerk of court in a sealed envelope or package for safekeeping while your motion is decided.[1258]

A request for a subpoena to a health care provider also must contain the following language:

NOTICE TO PROVIDERS

IF YOU RECEIVE NOTICE THAT YOUR PATIENT HAS FILED A MOTION TO QUASH (OBJECTING TO) THIS SUBPOENA, OR IF YOU FILE A MOTION TO QUASH THIS SUBPOENA, SEND THE RECORDS ONLY TO THE CLERK OF THE COURT WHICH ISSUED THE SUBPOENA USING THE FOLLOWING PROCEDURE: PLACE THE RECORDS IN A SEALED ENVELOPE AND ATTACH TO THE SEALED ENVELOPE A COVER LETTER TO THE CLERK OF COURT WHICH STATES THAT CONFIDENTIAL HEALTH CARE RECORDS ARE ENCLOSED AND ARE TO BE HELD UNDER SEAL PENDING THE COURT'S RULING ON THE MOTION TO QUASH THE

[1258] Va. Code 32.1-127.1:03.H.1

SUBPOENA. THE SEALED ENVELOPE AND THE COVER LETTER SHALL BE PLACED IN AN OUTER ENVELOPE OR PACKAGE FOR TRANSMITTAL TO THE COURT.[1259]

As one can see from the above language, the current Virginia statutes intend to protect the privacy of patients and provide a mechanism to achieve that goal.

To comply with HIPAA,[1260] Virginia has also adopted a requirement that a health care provider should not respond to a subpoena until the attorney issuing or requesting the subpoena certifies that no motion to quash has been filed by the patient or other party to the lawsuit. The certification is issued fifteen days or more after the request for the subpoena. Once the certification is received, the health care provider is obligated to provide the records by the date on the subpoena or within five days, whichever is later.[1261]

Trial attorneys and health information managers often strongly debate what should be included in the provider's response to a subpoena. Many information managers have adopted the philosophy that only the personal records of the provider subpoenaed, not those of other providers collected in the file, will be divulged. Trial attorneys believe that all the records requested in the subpoena must be produced. This author agrees adamantly with the latter position. The recipient of the subpoena should not edit what documents will be produced. The attorney quite frequently needs to have all of the records in the health care provider's possession. This is because the issues being considered may include:

1. What did the health care provider have available and rely upon while rendering care to the patient?

[1259] Va. Code 32.1-127.1:03.H.2
[1260] See 45 C.F.R. 164.512(e)
[1261] Va. Code 32.1-127.1:03.H.4 and 5; 45 C.F.R. 164.512(e)(1)

2. What other health care providers has the patient seen? (Patients often fail to remember many of the doctors and hospitals providing care) and

3. Is there more than one version of a health care provider's records?

Despite the use of large "Not to be redisclosed" stamps, an information manager has a duty to fully disclose all records in her possession if requested.[1262] The only exception to this is drug and alcohol rehabilitation records, as discussed elsewhere in this text.

A party subpoenaing records is required to provide copies of the documents to other parties upon request, provided that a requesting party pays reasonable copying costs.[1263]

A subpoena issued by a state court other than Virginia is generally not valid in Virginia. The out-of-state litigant must obtain a subpoena issued by the appropriate Virginia court.[1264] Curiously, the Virginia Attorney General has stated that a health care provider should honor Virginia subpoenas even if the health care provider is licensed or located outside the Commonwealth where the records sought are of a party to a Virginia lawsuit.[1265] The out-of-state health care provider must move to quash the subpoena. The Court would determine whether the health care provider had *minimum contacts* to be subject to the court's jurisdiction. If not, then the Virginia litigant could obtain the records under the Uniform Foreign Depositions Act.[1266]

[1262] One should be mindful that in other settings, one is obligated to maintain the confidentiality of medical records regardless of how the records came into the health care provider's possession. See Va. Code 32.1-127.1:03

[1263] Va. Code 8.01-417

[1264] See Va. Code 8.01-411 et seq.

[1265] 1992 Op. Va. Att'y Gen. 14 (discussing Va. Code 8.01-413 and determining that the fee limitation set forth therein also applied to out-of-state health care providers)

[1266] Va. Code 8.01-411 et seq.

RODNEY K. ADAMS, ESQUIRE

b. Authentication of Documents

In any Virginia state court case where a health care provider's original medical record is admissible, copies of the medical record are admissible in their place, so long as the copies are sufficiently legible and are properly authenticated.[1267] A health care provider whose records are subpoenaed may comply with the subpoena by mailing properly authenticated copies of the medical record to the clerk whose court issued the subpoena.[1268] However, in practice, the medical record copies are usually mailed to the attorney who sought to have the subpoena issued. The court may later enter an order requiring the production of the original record where the copies are not adequately legible or concerns arise over variations among copies.

Medical records are generally admissible under the business records exception to the hearsay rule. In other words, records kept in the regular course of the health care facility's business and recorded in the regular routine of the facility are admissible despite the fact that they are hearsay. However, this exception is limited to factual entries in the medical record. The opinions and conclusions of providers recorded in hospital records are not admissible under this exception.[1269] Medical records and reports can be admitted far more liberally in general district court.[1270]

A ruling on the admission or rejection of radiology studies is a matter that rests within the sound discretion of the court.[1271] X--rays are only admissible when properly authenticated.[1272] An x--ray is properly authenticated where it is shown that it is of the person involved in the case, that it was made by a competent technician, and that it accurately portrays the condition of the person's body. Medical bills,

[1267] Va. Code 8.01-413
[1268] Va. Code 8.01-413.A
[1269] Neeley v. Johnson, 215 Va. 565 (1975)
[1270] Va. Code 16.1-88.2
[1271] Lugo v. Joy, 215 Va. 39 (1974)
[1272] Meade v. Belcher, 212 Va. 796 (1972)

once properly authenticated, are not hearsay, and are admissible into evidence.[1273] Whether the medical bills are reasonable is a question for the finder of fact.[1274]

c. Fees for Providing Copies of Records

The party requesting a subpoena or on whose behalf one is issued is responsible for the *reasonable charges* of a healthcare provider in maintaining, retrieving, reviewing, preparing, copying and mailing requested medical records.[1275] The following fee structure is the maximum allowable fees for providing records in response to a subpoena.

Per Page Fee

For the first 50 pages	50¢ per page
For pages in excess of 50	25¢ per page
From microfilm	$1.00 per page
Search, Handling, Shipping & Postage	$10.00

The fee for providing radiology images or electronic versions of medical records is not articulated beyond "reasonable charges." This fee structure cannot be exceeded by an independent medical copy retrieval service.[1276]

No schedule is set as to what fee may be charged for copying

[1273] Walters v. Littleton, 223 Va. 446 (1982)

[1274] Walters v. Littleton, 223 Va. 446 (1982)

[1275] Va. Code 8.01-413. The fee structure for *pages* applies to paper documents and computer generated documents. A federal appeals court reviewing a California trial court, for example, held that the fees charged to a law firm can be different than those charged to an individual. Webb v. Smart Document Solutions, No. 05-56282 (9th Cir. 8/27/07). Records being provided in response to a subpoena are not within HIPAA.

[1276] Va. Code 8.01-413.E. The fee structure may also apply to an out-of-state health care provider. See 1992 Op. Va. Att'y Gen. 14 discussing Va. Code 8.01-413

subpoenaed records in federal court. The witness is only obligated to produce the originals at a designated time and place. However, it is usually more efficient for everyone to mail copies to the requesting party. The reasonableness of a copying fee can be addressed by hearing before the federal district court, and likely the state statute will be followed.

2. Workers' Compensation

From the time an employee is injured through the end of when the employee claims compensation under the Virginia Workers' Compensation Act[1277], the employee, if requested by his employer or by the Industrial Commission, must submit to an examination by a physician.[1278] Under worker's compensation, the physician-patient privilege is waived with respect to any communications between this physician and the injured employee for conditions believed to be related to the injury. These communications are admissible in any action at law or any hearing before the Industrial Commission.[1279]

The mandatory *medical report* required under the Virginia Workers Compensation Act can be the attending physician's notes and reports.[1280] The American Medical Association has taken the position that the patient-physician privilege is maintained for conditions unrelated to the employment injury.[1281] However, the Virginia Court of Appeals has held that the physician/patient privilege is waived when a patient seeks care for a work-related injury. This includes all medical records that may be held by the treating physician.[1282] This is in contrast to the *minimum necessary* standard under HIPAA.

[1277] Va. Code 65.2-1 et seq.

[1278] Va. Code 65.2-607

[1279] Id. Also see Va. Code 65.2-604

[1280] Va. Workers Compensation Commission, Rule 3, 16Va. Admin. Code30-50-50 (previously cited as Rule 4.2)

[1281] AMA Opinion 5.09

[1282] Wiggins v. Fairfax Park Ltd. Partnership, 22 Va. App. 432, 440 (1996) (illustrates how refusal to produce records can lead to not being paid

What a healthcare provider may charge for providing medical records in a workers' compensation matter is vaguely described as "at no cost except for a nominal copying charge."[1283] An effort in 2007[1284] by the Commission to enact regulations that would delineate a fee schedule was not completed.

Where an employee is believed to have died from a work-related event, the Industrial Commission or the employer may demand that an autopsy be performed. Obstruction or interference with the autopsy can be punished by contempt of court.[1285]

3. Involuntary Commitment Hearing

A health care provider must disclose any and all records regarding a patient that is the subject of an involuntary commitment hearing to a magistrate or district court judge, a guardian ad litem, or the patient's attorney.[1286] The court conducting the hearing must make and retain a tape or other recording of the proceedings for three years.[1287] If the patient or his attorney requests, the medical records, reports and court documents must be kept confidential by the court and released only for good cause shown.[1288] Copies of the relevant medical records should be released to the admitting facility if requested by the treating physician or the facility director.[1289] The involuntary commitment order is reported to the Central Criminal Records Exchange for use in determining a person's eligibility to possess a firearm.[1290]

---

for worker's comp medical services)
[1283] 16 Va. Admin. Code 30-50-50. Rule 3
[1284] (website accessed 12/6/2011): http://townhall.virginia.gov/L/GetFile.cfm?File=E:%5Ctownhall%5Cdocroot%5C126%5C2497%5C4370%5CAgency Statement_WCC_4370_v1.pdf
[1285] Va. Code 65.2-607
[1286] Va. Code 37.2-804.2
[1287] Va. Code 37.2-818.A
[1288] Va. Code 37.2-818.B
[1289] Va. Code 37.2-818.C
[1290] Va. Code 37.2-819

A state facility[1291] or other facility[1292] may discharge a patient who does not meet involuntary commitment criteria after the CSB formulates a discharge plan. A facility, a CSB, and providers may exchange information required to formulate a discharge treatment plan, with or without the patient's authorization.[1293] Where a patient is unable to pay for medications, the CSB may provide them.[1294]

4. Criminal Investigation / Prosecution

Often police will arrive unannounced and inquire about whether a patient is present in a facility or about information on a patient. A healthcare provider must maintain the usual standard of confidentiality in the face of such inquiries. Police are not entitled to any more information than other lay people in the absence of a search warrant, court order, or statutory exception. This can be challenging to explain to a pushy, armed officer. Resistance is likely to bring threats of arrest for obstructing justice and other crimes. The courts do not tend to be supportive of healthcare providers in confrontations between an officer and a provider. For example, a federal judge in Louisiana found that an officer acted reasonably in arresting a hospital aide who mistakenly believed that HIPAA barred police from interviewing a domestic abuse victim and dismissed the aide's lawsuit for false arrest.[1295]

a. When Police Ask If An Individual Is A Patient

As to whether an individual is present in a facility, a facility may maintain a directory of patients that includes the patient's name, location in the facility and the patient's condition in general terms.[1296] This is commonly exemplified by directory information available

---

[1291] Va. Code 37.2-837
[1292] Va. Code 37.2-838
[1293] Va. Code 37.2-839
[1294] Va. Code 37.2-843
[1295] Maier v. Morgan Green, W. D. La. No. 06705, 3/30/07
[1296] 45 C.F.R. 164.510(a)

to a hospital switchboard operator. A patient must be given the opportunity to object to being identified in the directory, which is to be used in response to a specific inquiry. Gone are the days of broadcasting a list of who is in the hospital during the morning farm report on the radio. As discussed in more detail below, a healthcare provider can generally respond to a request by an officer as to whether an individual is present in a facility. Likewise, a provider can respond to a query of whether an individual is a patient of the practice.

The primary exception to being able to identify whether an individual is a patient is when a provider is an alcohol or substance abuse rehabilitation program receiving federal funds.[1297] A facility which provides general medical care is not viewed as a qualified program unless it has either (1) an identified substance abuse unit or (2) personnel who are identified as providers of diagnosis, treatment or a referral for treatment and whose primary function is the provision of those alcohol or drug abuse services.[1298] Facilities that provide blood alcohol tests for the sole purpose of providing evidence to law enforcement authorities regarding a person's intoxication do not fall under the current regulations.

The Center for Substance Abuse Treatment of HHS has articulated guidance that appears to loosen the strict interpretation of not identifying anyone who may be enrolled or sought enrollment in a rehabilitation program. "Part 2 permits a substance abuse treatment program to disclose information about a patient if the disclosure does not identify the patient as an alcohol or drug abuser or as someone who has applied for or received substance abuse assessment or treatment services."[1299] This is a more practical

---

[1297] Residential methadone treatment facilities in Virginia must comply with these federal regulations on confidentiality regardless of funding source. Rules and Regulations for the Licensure of Residential Facilities, 7.38

[1298] 42 C.F.R. 2.11

[1299] "The Confidentiality of Alcohol and Drug Abuse Patient Records Regulation and the HIPAA Privacy Rule: Implications for Alcohol and

approach to the situation where a program is part of a larger entity such as a health care system.

As a general rule for rehabilitation programs, disclosure of any information related to a patient is prohibited, even the fact that the person is currently a patient, has been a patient in the past, or has sought evaluation or treatment. The response to requests for this information should be simply that the release of this information is protected by the federal statutes. No further explanation is required. Also, "the restrictions on disclosure of information apply whether the holder of the information believes that the person seeking the information already has it, has other means of obtaining it, is a law enforcement or other official, has obtained a subpoena, or asserts any other justification for a disclosure or use not permitted by these regulations."[1300] Any disclosure permitted under a regulation must be limited to that information which is necessary to carry out the purpose of the disclosure.

b. When Police Ask For Information About A Patient

With consent of the patient, or one who is granted authority to release the records on his behalf, a healthcare provider is at liberty to fully cooperate with an investigation. Death of a patient does not terminate the obligation to maintain confidentiality. The right to authorize disclosure passes in the same manner as under the Healthcare Decisions Act.[1301]

HIPAA does not expand law enforcement access to a patient's information. The disclosure under HIPAA is permissive.[1302] A provider

---

Substance Abuse Programs," US Dept. of Health & Human Services, Substance Abuse and Mental health Services Administration, Center for Substance Abuse Treatment, www.samhsa.gov, June 2004, p. 10, citing 42 C.F.R. 2.11 and 2.12(a)

[1300]   42 C.F.R. 2.13

[1301]   Va. Code 32.1-127.1:03.B; *Agent* is defined in the Health Care Decisions Act, Va. Code 54.1-2981 et seq.

[1302]   *See* 45 C.F.R. 164.512 (b) (1)

may disclose limited information without the patient's authorization. The disclosure of confidential information without a patient's consent must be limited to no more than name, address, date and place of birth, social security number, ABO blood type and Rh factor, type of injury, date and time of treatment, date and time of death, and a description of distinguishing physical characteristics.[1303] A subpoena or other judicial process is required for disclosure of additional information such as DNA characteristics, fluid samples, lab results, dental records, etc.[1304] As recently lamented by the Governor's Commission, mental health records are not accessible by government agencies without subpoena or warrant authority.

Emergency medical service agencies are authorized to disclose pre-hospital patient care reports to police officers on request when 1) the patient is the victim of a crime; or 2) when the patient is in the custody of an officer and has received emergency medical care or has refused it.[1305]

Disclosure of information to officers (or others) where a patient is incapacitated or otherwise unable to give authorization is contingent on a determination by the healthcare provider that the disclosure is in the patient's best interest.[1306] Confidential information about a crime victim generally can only be released with the authorization of the victim.[1307] When consent cannot be obtained in an urgent situation, balancing of a patient's privacy rights and law enforcement interests come into play. Where a patient is believed to be the victim of a crime and is unable to authorize the healthcare provider to disclose information to the police, a three-prong test is applied:[1308]

    1. The law enforcement official represents that such information is needed to determine whether a violation of

---

[1303] 45 C.F.R. 164.512 (f) (2)(i); Va. Code 32.1-127.1:03.C.28
[1304] 45 C.F.R. 164.512 (f)(2)(ii)
[1305] Va. Code 32.1-116.1 (A)
[1306] 45 C.F.R. 164.510(a) (3) (B)
[1307] 45 C.F.R. 164.512(f) (3)(i)
[1308] 45 C.F.R. 164.512(f) (3) (ii)

law by a person other than the victim has occurred, and such information is not intended to be used against the victim;

2. The law enforcement official represents that immediate law enforcement activity that depends upon the disclosure would be materially and adversely affected by waiting until the patient is able to agree to the disclosure; and

3. The disclosure is in the best interests of the patient as determined by the healthcare provider, in the exercise of professional judgment.

In other words, when the victim is incapacitated, such information *may* be disclosed if the police represent that the information will not be used against the victim, the information is needed to determine whether another person broke the law, the investigation would be materially adversely affected by waiting until the victim could agree, and the healthcare provider believes that disclosure would be in the best interest of the patient.[1309] The difficult situation arises where a healthcare provider does not believe that disclosure would be in the best interest of the patient.

In 2008, the General Assembly attempted to address perceived problems in mental health law and procedure. In doing so, the General Assembly passed legislation now requiring a healthcare provider, upon request, to disclose mental health records of minors to police officers and others in the setting of involuntary commitment proceedings.[1310] The disclosure is to be "limited to information necessary to protect the officer, the minor or the public from physical injury or to address the healthcare needs of the minor." The officer is not permitted to use the information for any other purpose, disclose it to others or retain it. Though of dubious strength, the General Assembly states that a health care provider is immune from civil liability, including under HIPAA.

[1309] Id.
[1310] Va. Code 16.1-337.B

In 2010, the General Assembly expanded the provisions of the *Psychiatric Treatment of Minors Act*[1311] to permit CSB *or its designee* performing an evaluation, preadmission screening or monitoring of a minor to receive information regarding that minor's care and treatment by a health care provider.[1312] Lawmakers believed that gaps existed in essential channels of communication that affected the continuum of care and took legislative action to fill them. In addition to a CSB designee, the Act permits notification of a minor's parent of information directly relevant to such parent's involvement with the minor's mental health care, including the minor's location and general condition unless the health care provider has actual knowledge that the parent is prohibited by court order from contacting the minor. [1313]

Healthcare providers have an unequivocal obligation to report observations of neglect or abuse of a vulnerable patient, such as child abuse[1314] and elder abuse. [1315]

HIPAA also alerted the medical community to unusual exceptions to confidentiality of medical information such as activities under the National Security Act[1316] and for the protection of the President and other high ranking government officials.[1317]

c. When a Crime Occurs On the Premises

When a crime is believed to have occurred against a healthcare provider or on the premises of a facility, the above listed information may be disclosed to police.[1318] Even in substance abuse rehabilitation

---

[1311] Va. Code 16.1-335, et seq.

[1312] Va. Code 16.1-337.B

[1313] Id.

[1314] Va. Code 63.1-248.3; 45 C.F.R. 164.512(b)(1)(ii)

[1315] Va. Code 63.2-1606; 45 C.F.R. 164.512(c)

[1316] 45 C.F.R. 164.512(k) (2)

[1317] 45 C.F.R. 164.512(k) (3)

[1318] 45 C.F.R. 164.502 (j) (2); 45 C.F.R. 164.512(f)(5); Va. Code 32.1-127.1:03.C.30

programs subject to 42 C.F.R., Part 2, the identity of a patient suspected of committing a crime on the premises may be disclosed to the police for prosecution.[1319] Such disclosure is limited to the circumstances of the incident and the patient's status, name, address, and last known whereabouts.

d. When a Patient Makes a Threat

A healthcare provider may have an affirmative duty to notify the police if a patient makes a specific threat. Stated differently, a Virginia healthcare provider[1320] must take steps to protect a foreseeable victim of violence by the provider's patient.[1321] This can be accomplished by:

- seeking civil commitment of the patient,

- making reasonable efforts to warn the foreseeable victim (or parents of a minor who is at risk),

- making reasonable efforts to notify the local police,

- attempting to prevent physical violence by the patient until police can be summoned and takes custody of the patient, or

- rendering therapy in the session with the patient until the professional reasonably believes that the patient no longer has the intent or ability to carry out the threat[1322]

A healthcare provider is not granted any right to detain a patient, but is given immunity from liability for breaching confidentiality, for

---

[1319] 42 C.F.R. 2.12(c)(5)

[1320] *Mental health provider*, as used in the statute, is defined broadly to cover almost every licensed healthcare professional and does not limit its definition by requiring that the healthcare provider be engaged in rendering mental healthcare services at the time. Va. Code 54.1-2400.1 (A)

[1321] Va. Code 54.1-2400.1; 45 C.F.R. 164.512(j) (1) (I)

[1322] Va. Code 54.1-2400.1.C

failing to predict dangerous behavior in the absence of an explicit threat, and for not taking any steps other than those enumerated.[1323]

e. When Police Ask For Information about a Patient of a Student Health Service

The federal Family Educational Rights and Privacy Act,[1324] commonly referred to as FERPA, protects the privacy of a student's educational records by limiting funding for those educational institutions who do not comply with the federal statute.

Under FERPA, a *student* is any person with respect to whom an educational agency or institution maintains educational records or personally identifiable information, but does not include a person who has not been in attendance at such agency or institution.[1325] FERPA applies to any public or private agency or institution which is the recipient of funds under any applicable federal program.

The information that is covered by FERPA includes "records, files, documents, and other materials which contain information directly related to a student and are maintained by an educational agency or institution or by a person acting for such agency or institution."[1326] However, *educational records* do not include:

1. "Instructional, supervisory, administrative personnel and educational personal in sole possession of the maker thereof and which are not accessible or revealed to any other person except a substitute. These are some times referred to as "desk files";

[1323] Va. Code 54.1-2400.1.D; 45 C.F.R. 164.512(j) (1) (i)
[1324] 20 U.S.C.A. 1232g; 34 C.F.R., Part 99
[1325] 20 U.S.C.A. 1232g (6)
[1326] 20 U.S.C.A. 1232g (a) (4); *Student* is presumed to be a minor unless specifically stated otherwise. Also see 34 C.F.R. 99.3

2.   Records maintained by a law enforcement unit of the educational agency or institution that were created by that law enforcement unit for the purpose of law enforcement;

3.   Records of employees that are made and maintained in the normal course of business which relate exclusively to such person in that person's capacity as an employee and are not available for use for any other purpose; or

4.   Records on a student who is eighteen years of age or older, or is attending an institution of postsecondary education, which are made or maintained by a physician, psychiatrist, psychologist, or other recognized professional or paraprofessional acting in his professional or paraprofessional capacity, or assisting in that capacity, and which are made, maintained, or used only in connection with the provision of treatment to the student, and are not available to anyone other than persons providing such treatment, except that such records can be personally reviewed by a physician or other appropriate professional of the student's choice."[1327]

Educational records are also not allowed to be released without the written consent of a minor student's parents specifying the records to be released, the reasons for such release, and to whom they should be released. The school must also send a copy of such records to be released to the student's parents and the student if desired by the parents. However, records are allowed to be released without the consent of the parents under a few minor exceptions. These exceptions include releasing records when requested by:

1.   Other school officials, including teachers within the educational institution or local education agency, who has been determined by the agency or institution to have legitimate educational interest-including the educational interest of the child for whom consent would otherwise be required;

[1327]   20 U.S.C.A. 1232g (4) (B) (i) – (iv)

2. Officials of other schools or school systems in which the student seeks or intends to enroll (students must be notified of transfer and receive copy of record if requested, and have an opportunity for a hearing to challenge content of the records);

3. Authorized representatives of the Comptroller General of the United States, including those for law enforcement purpose, the Secretary or State educational authorities;

4. State statutes specifically allow release to state and local authorities. If such statute was adopted before November 19, 1974, the records must also concern the juvenile justice system and the system's ability to effectively serve such student. If the information is specifically allowed to be reported or disclosed pursuant to State statute adopted after November 19, 1974, the records must also concern the juvenile justice system and the system's ability to effectively serve such student prior to adjudication and the recipients of such information disclose in writing that the records will not be disclosed to anyone else except those allowed under state law without the parent's consent.

5. Parents of a dependant student;[1328]

[1328] A *dependant student*, as defined under section 152 of the Internal Revenue Code of 1986 means, with respect to any taxpayer for any taxable year, an individual:

who bears a relationship to the taxpayer described in paragraph (2),

who has the same principal place of abode as the taxpayer for more than one-half of such taxable year,

(i) who has not attained the age of 19 as of the close of the calendar year in which the taxable year of the taxpayer begins, or

(ii) is a student who has not attained the age of 24 as of the close of such calendar year.

(D) who has not provided over one-half of such individual's own support for the calendar year in which the taxable year of the taxpayer begins. 26 U.S.C.A. 152

6. In connection with an emergency, if knowledge of such information is necessary to prevent health or safety of student or other persons, subject to regulation of the Secretary;

7. Such information is furnished in compliance with judicial order, or pursuant to any lawfully issued subpoena;

8. The student is over the age of eighteen or attending an institution of post secondary education in which case the student's consent must be obtained.[1329]

Indirectly FERPA, as amended by the Protection of Pupils' Rights Amendment (PPRA), limits the release of health information by not allowing children to be "subject to any survey, analysis or evaluations that reveal information concerning mental or psychological problems of the student or of the student's family, illegal, anti-social, self incrimination or demeaning behavior without the prior consent of the student or with a minor, without the parent."[1330]

School officials do not need parental consent to disclose education records to a third party in an emergency situation if the third party needs to know the information in order to protect the health or safety of the student or another individual.[1331] Healthcare providers working in a school system have a *duty to warn* under Virginia law, as discussed elsewhere in this text.

Applying the discussion above, a healthcare provider working in an educational facility operates under almost identical parameters to that of other healthcare providers. FERPA merely reinforces that the privilege of confidentiality transfers from a parent to a student at the age of majority. A healthcare provider should follow the roadmap set forth above when contacted by law enforcement as to a student.

[1329] 20 U.S.C.A. 1232g (b) (1) (A) – (J)
[1330] 20 U.S.C.A. 1232h
[1331] 34 C.F.R. 99.31(a)(1) and 99.36

f. Grand Jury Subpoena

As part of the criminal indictment process, a health care provider may receive a subpoena from a grand jury to produce records related to a patient. Compliance with that subpoena should be in a fashion similar to those received for civil litigation matters.[1332]

g. Medicare / Medicaid Investigation

Under the Health Insurance Portability and Accountability Act of 1996 (HIPAA), federal investigators have obtained powerful tools to ferret out fraud and abuse of Medicare or Medicaid programs. These include civil investigative demands, authorized investigative demands, and inspector general subpoenas. Such requests must be accompanied by a statement that the information requested is relevant and material, specific and limited in scope, and de-identified information cannot be used.[1333]

i) Civil Investigative Demands

Civil Investigative Demands (CIDs) are subpoenas issued by the Department of Health and Humans Services for documents or testimony about False Claims Act violations.[1334] These can be issued before claims are brought, and the U. S. Attorney is given broad discretion.[1335]

ii) Authorized Investigative Demands

Authorized Investigative Demands (AIDs) can be issued to assist federal prosecutors who are investigating "any act or activity involving a federal health care offense."[1336] Interestingly, this does not include seeking evidence for solely violations of the Anti-

---

[1332] 45 C.F.R. 164.512(f)(1)(ii)(A)-(B)
[1333] 45 C.F.R. 164.512(f)(1)(ii)(C)
[1334] 31 U.S.C.A. 3733
[1335] 31 U.S.C.A. 3733(a)
[1336] 18 U.S.C.A. 3486

Kickback Act.[1337] The criterion for issuance is to seek relevant records. Probable cause does not have to be shown.[1338] This is a very low threshold and gives a very broad reach. Production of documents can be demanded within 500 miles of the U. S. Attorney's office[1339] and within a reasonable time period.[1340] Compelling testimony under AIDs is limited to requiring the record custodian to give testimony about production and authentication of the documents.[1341]

iii) Inspector General Subpoenas

Inspector General Subpoenas (IG Subpoenas) are issued under the authority of the Inspector General Act of 1978. They can be used only to compel production of documents. The only testimony that can be elicited pursuant to an IG Subpoena is to authenticate the produced records. Some courts have held that probable cause must be demonstrated in order to compel production of a target physician's personal records.[1342]

h. Search Warrants

A search warrant is a written order, signed by a judge or magistrate, directing a law enforcement officer to search a specific place for specific persons or items to be seized as described in the search warrant. No warrant is to be issued omitting the essentials, and no general warrant for the search of a place is proper.[1343] If not served within fifteen days, the warrant is void and should not be

[1337] The Anti-Kickback Act is 42 U.S.C.A. 1320a-7b. The definition of federal health care offense is found at 18 U.S.C.A. 24(a)
[1338] U. S. v. Bailey, 228 F.3d 341 (4th Cir. 2000)
[1339] 18 U.S.C.A. 3486(a)(3)
[1340] 18 U.S.C.A. 3486(a)(2); US Attorney's Manual, Section 9-22.202(3)
[1341] 18 U.S.C.A. 3486(a)(1)(B)(ii)
[1342] In re Subpoenas Duces Tecum Nos. A99-0001, A99-0002, A99-0003 and A99-0004, 51 F. Supp. 2d 726 (W.D. Va. 1999), affirmed 228 F.3d 341 (4th Cir. 2000)
[1343] Va. Code 19.2-54

honored. Va. Code 19.2-56 and 19.2-57 set out in detail the process to be followed in executing a search warrant.

The medical information manager should keep in mind that federal alcohol and substance abuse rehabilitation regulations may override a search warrant.[1344]

i. Subpoena

Just as in civil cases, a health care provider can be subpoenaed to testify at the trial of a criminal matter. The patient-physician privilege historically did not exist at criminal law in Virginia.[1345] However, a health care provider continues to have a duty to protect the confidences of those who are not a party to a trial.[1346]

If release of medical information appears inappropriate, a patient or health care provider, through counsel, should file a Motion to Quash pursuant to one of the recognized privileges for physician-patient,[1347] psychologist-patient,[1348] or minister-confessor confidentiality.[1349] A provider can also seek to invoke therapeutic privilege, as discussed above. In hearing a Motion to Quash, the judge should determine if good cause is shown for the release of the information over the patient's objection by considering:

1. The particular purpose for which the information was collected;

[1344] 42 C.F.R., Part 2

[1345] Gibson v. Commonwealth, 216 Va. 412 (1975)

[1346] In a case of first impression, the Virginia Court of Appeals held that a patient, including a victim, is entitled to notice of her records being subpoenaed even in a criminal case. Hairston v. Commonwealth, 5 Va. App. 183 (2007)

[1347] Va. Code 8.01-399; but see In re Grand Jury Subpoena John Doe, No. A01-209, (E.D. Va. 4/18/2002) VLW 002-3-151

[1348] Va. Code 8.01-400.2. Also see Jaffee v. Redmond, 518 U.S. 1, 116 S. Ct. 1923 (1996) interpreting Rule 501, Federal Rules of Civil Procedure

[1349] Va. Code 8.01-400

2. The degree to which the disclosure of the records would embarrass, injure, or invade the privacy of the individual;

3. The effect of the disclosure on the individual's future health care;

4. The importance of the information to the lawsuit or proceeding; and

5. Any other relevant factor.[1350]

A judge may require the government, as a condition for obtaining a provider's records, to give notice to each of the patients.[1351] A subpoena for substance abuse rehabilitation records, of course, must comply with the federal regulations for such records.[1352]

5. Prisoners

A prison warden may have access to the *minimum necessary*[1353] amount of confidential information in order to provide health care to the prisoner; for the health and safety of the prisoner, other inmates, officers or employees; or for the administration and maintenance of safety, security and good order of the facility, including law enforcement on the premises of the facility.[1354] While generally a health care provider can rely on the representation of the officer as to what is *minimally necessary*,[1355] the provider is not absolved of being vigilant on behalf of the patient. For example, the provider should verify the identity and authority of an officer before disclosing information.[1356]

[1350] Va. Code 32.1-127.1:03.H.4.
[1351] See United States v. Sutherland, 143 F. Supp. 2d 609, 612 (W.D. Va. 2001)), aff'd, 362 F.3d 923 (7th Cir. 2004)
[1352] Va. Code 32.1-127.1:03.H.4 citing 42 C.F.R. Part 2, Subpart E. See Alcohol & Substance Abuse Rehabilitation, above
[1353] *Minimum necessary* is defined in 45 C.F.R. 164.502(b) and 164.514(d)
[1354] 45 C.F.R. 164.512(k)(5)
[1355] 45 C.F.R. 164.514(d)(3)(iii)(A)
[1356] 45 C.F.R. 164.514(h)

L. Disposition of Medical Records

Managing the documents accumulating daily is one of the most onerous tasks of a medical information manager. Being able to efficiently utilize available storage space is vitally important. Therefore, appropriate retention and destruction policies are key to the effective operation of a medical information service. Strict adherence to such policies will also foreclose accusations that records were destroyed for ulterior motives.

1. *Retention of Medical Records*

Inpatient institutions must keep a record of each person admitted or confined to the facility.[1357] Hospitals,[1358] outpatient hospitals,[1359] and nursing homes[1360] must retain records for the following periods under state regulations:

Adult patients:	5 years after discharge
Minor patients:	5 years after reach age 18
Birth and death information:	10 years

Pathology reports must be maintained for at least ten years under Medicare's Conditions of Participation.[1361]

Home health agencies and hospices must retain records for a

[1357] Va. Code 32.1-274; 42 C.F.R. 482.24 (Medicare)
[1358] 12 Va. Admin. Code 5-410-370; 42 C.F.R. 482.24(b)(1); also see American Hospital Association, Statement on Preservation of Patient Medical Records in Health Care Institutions (1990).
[1359] 12 Va. Admin. Code 5-410-1260.C
[1360] Virginia Nursing Home Regulation 24.5, et seq.
[1361] 42 C.F.R. 493.1109

minimum of five years.[1362] State agencies[1363] must retain medical records for the following duration:

Adult: 10 years from last treatment or contact

Minor or incompetent: the later of 5 years after majority or competency; or ten years from last contact

Deceased patient: 5 years from date of death

Recent Board of Medicine regulations require that a physician retain medical records for six years from the last encounter.[1364] Immunization records must be maintained until a child reaches age 18. A practitioner is required to advise patients by posting a sign or other means of how long records will be retained.[1365]

No state statute specifies how long radiology studies must be retained. However, the above guidelines are a good rule of thumb. Medical records and films of mammograms must be retained for "not less than five years, or not less than ten years if no additional mammograms of the patient are performed at the facility."[1366]

Viewed from a different perspective, the federal statute of limitations for fraud and abuse actions is five years for criminal charges[1367] and six years for civil allegations.[1368] HIPAA requires that a patient's amendment to medical records or the provider's refusal to amend the records must be retained for six years.

OSHA requires that employee injury records be retained for five

---

[1362] 12 Va. Admin. Code5-381-280 (2008)
[1363] Va. Code 42.1-79.1
[1364] 18 Va. Admin. Code 85-20-26
[1365] 18 Va. Admin. Code 85-20-26.E
[1366] 21 C.F.R. 900.12(c)(4)(i)
[1367] 42 U.S.C.A. 3282
[1368] 42 U.S.C.A. 1320a-7a(c)(1)

years. Records of employee exposure to blood-borne pathogens must be maintained for thirty years.[1369]

The Department of Health has adopted the National Fire Protection Association guidelines for storage and retrieval as a state regulation for hospitals.[1370] All licensed organizations and professionals must provide for the safety and retrieval of medical records. Medical records may be stored by electronic, microfilm, or other media.[1371] If an unalterable image is created, the original paper version may be destroyed.

2. Disposal of Records

Proper disposal of medical records is an important concern of a medical information manager. If an outside service is used, it should agree to maintain the confidentiality of all records and assure that all records are completely destroyed and disposal occurs in a proper fashion. A business associate agreement should be part of a contract with a document-destruction service. The U.S. Environmental Protection Agency recommends destruction by shredding and recycling.[1372]

3. Closure, Sale or Relocation of Practice

Virginia law regulates the procedure for a professional who closes, sells or relocates his practice with regard to patient records.[1373] This legislation reflects the position of the American Medical Association,[1374] but the statute applies to all practitioners who

---

[1369] 29 C.F.R. 1904.6
[1370] Va. Hospital Regulations 208.7
[1371] Va. Code 54.1-2403.2 and 32.1-127.1:01
[1372] 40 C.F.R. 246
[1373] Va. Code 54.1-2405.A, which is cited by the Board of Medicine in its regulations, 18Va. Admin. Code85-20-26
[1374] AMA Opinions 7.03 and 7.04

are licensed, registered, or certified by the Department of Health Professions.

Before transferring patient medical records as part of closing, selling or relocating[1375] a practice, the practitioner must notify current patients[1376] by mail at their last known address and by newspaper publication that, if a patient desires, the records will be sent to any like-regulated practitioner of the patient's choice or to the patient. Written authorization is not required from a patient to transfer medical records maintained by a selling corporation upon sale of its assets to a purchasing corporation.[1377] The notice must also disclose any fee for providing the records or copies to the patient or his new practitioner. The fee must not exceed the actual costs of copying and mailing the records. In contrast, a separate Virginia statute says that the fee may be as set forth above under Va. Code 8.01-413.[1378] A practitioner closing or selling his practice can retain copies of his medical or prescription records.[1379]

4. *Retention of Other Business Records*

A health care enterprise will generate many records in addition to patient care data. Below is an outline of how to approach managing retention of such documents.[1380]

- <u>Organizational Documents</u>. The Organization's articles of incorporation, by-laws and IRS Form 1023, Application

---

[1375] *Relocation* is defined as moving a practice more than 30 miles from its original location or moving outside Virginia. Va. Code 54.1-2405.B

[1376] *Current patient* is defined as a patient being seen within the last two years. Va. Code 54.1-2405.B

[1377] See 1998 Va. AG LEXIS 35, interpreting Va. Code 32.1-127.1:03 and 54.1-2405

[1378] See Va. Code 54.1-111.C

[1379] Va. Code 54.1-111.C

[1380] This outline is adapted from one created by Andrew White, a corporate law partner at LeClairRyan who often serves health care clients.

for Exemption[1381] should be retained permanently. IRS regulations require that the Form 1023 be available for public inspection upon request.

- Tax Records. Documents concerning payroll, expenses, proof of contributions made by donors, accounting procedures, and other documents concerning the Organization's revenues should be retained for at least seven years from the date of filing the applicable return.

- Employment Records/Personnel Records. State and federal statutes require the Organization to keep certain recruitment, employment and personnel information. The Organization should also keep personnel files that reflect performance reviews and any complaints brought against the Organization or individual employees under applicable state and federal statutes. The Organization should additionally keep in the employee's personnel file all final memoranda and correspondence reflecting performance reviews and actions taken by or against personnel. Employment applications should be retained for three years. Retirement and pension records should be kept permanently. Other employment and personnel records should be retained for seven years. Retention of employee health records is discussed elsewhere.

- Board and Board Committee Materials. Meeting minutes should be retained in perpetuity in the Organization's minute book. A clean copy of all other Board and Board Committee materials should be kept for no less than three years by the Organization.

- Press Releases/Public Filings. The Organization should retain permanent copies of all press releases and publicly filed documents under the theory that the Organization should have its own copy to test the accuracy of any document a

---

[1381] IRS Form 1023 applies to non-profit organizations

member of the public can theoretically produce against the Organization.

- <u>Legal Files</u>. Legal counsel should be consulted to determine the retention period of particular documents, but legal documents should generally be maintained for a period of ten years.

- <u>Marketing and Sales Documents</u>. The Organization should keep final copies of marketing and sales documents for the same period of time it keeps other corporate files, generally three years.

- An exception to the three-year policy may be sales invoices, contracts, leases, licenses, and other legal documentation. These documents should be kept for at least three years beyond the life of the agreement.

- <u>Contracts</u>. Final, execution copies of all contracts entered into by the Organization should be retained. The Organization should retain copies of the final contracts for at least three years beyond the life of the agreement, and longer in the case of publicly filed contracts.

- <u>Correspondence</u>. Unless correspondence falls under another category listed elsewhere, correspondence should generally be saved for two years.

- <u>Banking and Accounting</u>. Accounts payable ledgers and schedules should be kept for seven years. Bank reconciliations, bank statements, deposit slips and checks (unless for important payments and purchases) should be kept for three years. Any inventories of products, materials, and supplies and any invoices should be kept for seven years.

- <u>Insurance</u>. Expired insurance policies, insurance records, accident reports, claims, etc. should be kept permanently.

- <u>Audit Records</u>. External audit reports should be kept permanently. Internal audit reports should be kept for three years.

M. Appendix

1. *Guidance for Risk Managers in Light of Va. Code 8.01-399 and HIPAA*

In managing the potentially conflicting laws and regulations, a risk manager may consider the following approach to investigating incidents in a health care facility in light of Va. Code 8.01-399 along with the HIPAA regulations,[1382]

Va. Code 8.01-399 does not come into play until a lawyer is retained or litigation is initiated.[1383] The statute also exempts "operations of a health care facility or health maintenance organization or in order to comply with state or federal law."[1384] This is consistent with the HIPAA regulations.[1385] With this in mind, a risk manager should undertake a thorough investigation of an incident and make such reports as may be required by Joint Commission, regulations and hospital policy. Peer review, sentinel event investigation, and other inquires may go beyond just one physical facility or other artificial boundary in health care. The confidentiality of such reports continues to be hotly debated in pre-trial discovery.

Once counsel is retained to defend a hospital against a claim or lawsuit, the risk manager should work with the defense attorney to prepare the defense. Va. Code 8.01-399 and HIPAA permit a free exchange of medical information between the health care provider and defense counsel as to the *plaintiff's health care at issue* in the

---

[1382] 42 C.F.R. 164.502(a), 504(e), 506(c), 508(a) and 512(e)
[1383] Fairfax Hospital v. Curtis, 254 Va. 437, 443 (1997) quoting Pierce v. Caday, 244 Va. 285, 290 (1992)
[1384] Va. Code 8.01-399.F
[1385] 42 C.F.R. 168.504(e), 506(c) and 520

case.[1386] Careful attention needs to be focused on the key words of *plaintiff* and *health care at issue*. Defense counsel should only be provided with medical records of the actual plaintiff (or in the case of a wrongful death, the decedent) related to the course of care that is the subject of the litigation. For example, a hospital suffered the consequences of releasing the mother's obstetrical records to defense counsel and its nursery nurse in a lawsuit alleging wrongful death of an infant due to suffocation in the neonatal unit.[1387] Additional records that are identified as potentially relevant within the health care system should be obtained by defense counsel through subpoena or patient authorization.

In situations where different defense counsel are retained to represent separate parties within the health care system, the more prudent course would be for the risk manager to provide only the records of the entity or individual being defended by the attorney to that defense counsel. Additional records can be obtained through a request for production, subpoena, or patient authorization. The Archambault[1388] case suggests that defense attorneys are free to collaborate and share information, even when representing health care providers who are being deposed but are not parties.

Va. Code 8.01-399.D.1 explicitly permits a lawyer, or his agent, to communicate with the health care provider and "that practitioner's employers, partners, agents, servants, employees, co-employees or others" for whom the practitioner may be liable or who may be liable for the practitioner's care. Thus, the risk manager and attorney are free to interview any of the health care system's employees involved in the health care at issue. On the other hand, the risk manager should refrain from interviewing or obtaining records from physicians and others who are not health care system employees.

[1386] Va. Code 8.01-399.D.1 and F. See Fairfax Hospital v. Curtis, 254 Va. 437, 443 (1997)

[1387] Fairfax Hospital v. Curtis, 36 Va. Cir. 35 (Fairfax Cir. Ct. 1995) upheld on appeal 254 Va. 437 (1997)

[1388] Archambault v. Roller, 254 Va. 210 (1997)

2. HIPAA resources

The following web sites provide information from the federal government on complying with HIPAA:

Office of Civil Rights, The Privacy Rule, and frequently asked questions: http://hhs.gov/ocr/hipaa

Substance Abuse & Mental Health Services Administration: http://www.hipaa.samhsa.gov

Center for Medicare and Medicaid Services:
http://cms.gov/hipaa/hipaa2/default.asp
http://www.cms.hhs.gov/hipaa/hipaa2

The Security Rule, 45 C.F.R. Part 160 and Part 164:
http://www.cms.hhs.gov/hipaa/hipaa2

III. Medical Malpractice Litigation

One of the most troubling events likely to occur in a physician's career is being sued by a patient or her family for medical malpractice. Not to discount the distress caused by this attack on the professional's emotions, much of the stress stems from not knowing how the legal process works. Exaggerated stories in medical journals and the press further exacerbate the problem. This chapter is intended to give an overview of how medical malpractice actions proceed under Virginia law.

A. Commencement of A Lawsuit

1. *Plaintiff's Initial Pleading: Complaint*

The patient starts a lawsuit in Virginia by filing a Complaint in a Circuit Court. Formerly this initial pleading was called a Motion for Judgment. The patient, now assuming the title of plaintiff, must set forth in a Complaint why the court has jurisdiction; that the health care provider, now called defendant, was negligent; that the plaintiff was injured; and that the negligence of the defendant proximately caused the injuries suffered by the plaintiff. The plaintiff must also set forth a demand for damages, i.e., how much money is wanted. Most plaintiffs will demand the statutory limit in medical malpractice actions.[1389]

[1389] The medical malpractice cap is increasing, as set forth in the below table. Va. Code 8.01-581.15

July 1, 2008, through June 30, 2012 $2.00 million
July 1, 2012, through June 30, 2013 $2.05 million
July 1, 2013, through June 30, 2014 $2.10 million
July 1, 2014, through June 30, 2015 $2.15 million
July 1, 2015, through June 30, 2016 $2.20 million
July 1, 2016, through June 30, 2017 $2.25 million
July 1, 2017, through June 30, 2018 $2.30 million
July 1, 2018, through June 30, 2019 $2.35 million
July 1, 2019, through June 30, 2020 $2.40 million
July 1, 2020, through June 30, 2021 $2.45 million
July 1, 2021, through June 30, 2022 $2.50 million
July 1, 2022, through June 30, 2023 $2.55 million
July 1, 2023, through June 30, 2024 $2.60 million
July 1, 2024, through June 30, 2025 $2.65 million
July 1, 2025, through June 30, 2026 $2.70 million
July 1, 2026, through June 30, 2027 $2.75 million
July 1, 2027, through June 30, 2028 $2.80 million
July 1, 2028, through June 30, 2029 $2.85 million
July 1, 2029, through June 30, 2030 $2.90 million
July 1, 2030, through June 30, 2031 $2.95 million

(Some plaintiffs have been embarrassed by demanding an amount less than what a jury is willing to give them. A plaintiff is not allowed to recover more than is demanded.) Some plaintiffs are not deterred by the statutory cap on damages and will ask for many millions of dollars. The demand in a Complaint usually has little or no impact on the amount that a jury awards or for which the parties settle.

A plaintiff, by filing a medical malpractice action, is presumed to have had an expert review the case and the expert found merit to the allegations.[1390] A plaintiff, if requested by a defendant, must certify that a physician has found merit to the claim asserted by the plaintiff. If the plaintiff fails to do so, the Court should impose sanctions and may dismiss the case with prejudice.

The Complaint must be filed in a court that has jurisdiction. Usually this is the county or city where the parties live and the medical care took place. However, a plaintiff can file suit in any jurisdiction where a defendant lives or regularly conducts business. For example, the location of the registered agent for a physician's corporation may be sufficient contact to maintain jurisdiction.

The alleged negligence does not have to be pled with much specificity in Virginia. The Complaint need only put the defendant on notice of the event in question. One tactic that a defendant can employ is to move for a Bill of Particulars requesting specificity.

2. Responsive Pleadings by Defendant

Within twenty-one days after being served with a Complaint, a defendant must enter an appearance and file a responsive pleading. This can be in the form of an Answer, a Demurrer, a Special Plea, or

---

The constitutionality of the cap has been upheld on several occasions. For example, see Pulliam v. Coastal Emergency Services of Richmond, 257 Va. 1 (1999)

[1390] Va. Code 8.01-20.1 (personal injury cases) and 8.01-50.1 (wrongful death cases)

other responsive pleading. If the defendant fails to appear within twenty-one days, a Default Judgment can be entered against the defendant and the only issue remaining to be decided by the court is the amount of damages the defendant will be ordered to pay. Needless to say, a malpractice insurer may be reluctant to pay a default judgment if the default is due to a physician's procrastination. This is why it is so important that a physician's malpractice insurance company know as soon as possible that the physician has been served. Failure to notify a malpractice insurer in a timely manner may leave the physician personally liable for a malpractice judgment.

A physician's medical malpractice insurer will work with the doctor to obtain the services of a medical malpractice defense attorney. Rarely is a physician's personal or business attorney appropriate to defend a malpractice case. Medical malpractice defense is highly specialized.

a. Answer

An Answer, formerly called a Grounds of Defense in Virginia, is a response to plaintiff's Complaint. The physician's attorney will file this for the physician. Typically, a defendant admits the fact that the health care provider was duly licensed to practice in Virginia. Beyond that, careful attention must be paid to admitting only what is known to be factually correct and undisputed.

b. Demurrer

When a plaintiff has filed a Complaint that a defendant believes is insufficient either due to a lack of facts pled or due to a lack of a remedy at law, defendant may file a Demurrer. This is known as a Motion to Dismiss in most other courts. The Demurrer will set forth why the defendant contends that the Complaint is insufficient and should be dismissed. If the Complaint is found to be insufficient, the plaintiff usually will be given the opportunity by the Court to file an Amended Complaint to cure the defect.

c.　Affirmative Defenses

Affirmative defenses are often included as part of a defendant's response to the plaintiff's Complaint. These usually include allegations that the defendant was not negligent, the plaintiff was not injured due to any negligence, the plaintiff caused or contributed to his injury, the plaintiff failed to mitigate his damages, and so on. A defendant must present evidence at trial to prevail on any of these affirmative defenses. Many of these, if proven, will preclude plaintiff from recovery. Others will limit the recovery.

d.　Special Plea

A Special Plea may be filed by a defendant where the plaintiff's cause of action is barred by law. The two most common examples are the statute of limitations and sovereign immunity. The statute of limitations provides that in most cases, a plaintiff must file suit within two years of the last medical care rendered by the defendant health care provider.[1391] Sovereign immunity is available to full-time employees of the state, such as interns and residents.[1392] Curiously, academic faculty members are not given such immunity in most circumstances.[1393] Virginia also grants immunity to a physician that treats a patient for free in an emergency and no prior physician-patient relationship existed.[1394]

3. Medical Review Panel

Once a lawsuit has been filed against a health care professional, either the plaintiff or the defendant can request a Medical Review Panel within thirty days of the defendant appearing.[1395] A Medical

---

[1391]　Va. Code 8.01-243

[1392]　Lawhorne v. Harlan, 214 Va. 405 (1973) overruled by First Virginia Bank-Colonial v. Baker, 225 Va. 72 (1983)

[1393]　James v. Jane, 221 Va. 43 (1980)

[1394]　Va. Code 8.01-225; also see the federal Volunteer Protection Act, 42 U.S.C.A. 14501et seq.

[1395]　Va. Code 8.01-581.2

Review Panel is composed of two health care providers and two attorneys appointed by the Supreme Court of Virginia. A Circuit Court judge presides over the proceedings. The panel members review written submissions by the parties and the medical records. They may hear oral testimony and other evidence in determining whether a breach of the standard of care occurred and whether the patient was injured by the deviation, if any. An oral hearing must be specifically requested by one of the parties. If not requested, the panel can render its decision on the written submissions and medical records.[1396]

The opinion of a Medical Review Panel is strictly advisory. It does not mandate any result in resolving the lawsuit. It can be submitted as evidence to the jury at trial,[1397] and it is usually very persuasive. However, it is does not replace the requirement of expert testimony, and it is not binding on the jury.

The enthusiasm for medical review panels has waned among patients, physicians and attorneys. Physicians have been reluctant to serve on medical review panels because of the trivial payment for their time. Defense attorneys have avoided volunteering to be panel members because plaintiffs will perceive them as being pro-physician. If the defense attorney finds adversely to the physician, the medical malpractice insurer may not send any work to the attorney or his law firm. Perceiving that they do not receive as favorable of a reception as before a jury, many plaintiffs refuse to participate in the proceeding. This gives them the opportunity to argue that the medical review panel's opinion was based solely on the defendant's story. Defendants often elect not to request a medical review panel because it gives plaintiff a free opportunity to obtain all of the information about the defense theories and expert witnesses. Few plaintiffs are deterred by an adverse medical review panel opinion.

[1396]   Va. Code 8.01-581.5
[1397]   Va. Code 8.01-581.8

4. *Virginia Birth-Related Neurological Injury Compensation Act*

Infants who suffer catastrophic neurological injury during the birth process can be compensated through the Birth-Related Neurological Injury Compensation Program if a treating physician or hospital was a participant in the Program.[1398] Obstetrical patients must be advised by physicians and hospitals of their participation or non-participation in the Program.[1399] Any party involved in a civil action against a health care provider raising allegations of negligence can request that the matter be referred to the Workers' Compensation Commission to determine if the child qualifies.[1400] Insurance companies and self-insured entities are required to report to the Program any claims alleging such negligence. The Program will inform the injured child's parents or guardians of the program and eligibility requirements. The report is not admissible at trial and does not imply liability.[1401]

Unfortunately, many plaintiff attorneys actively try to dissuade families from seeking compensation through the Program. Many physicians and hospitals do not participate in the Program because they have not seen any utility from it. Unless a child fits into the narrow criteria of eligibility, the Program cannot provide compensation. Due to the Program being under significant financial stress, the Program has aggressively opposed several applications. All of this has led to a well-intentioned initiative that has done little to protect children or health care providers.

[1398] Va. Code 38.2-5000, et seq.

[1399] Va. Code 38.2-5004.1

[1400] Va. Code 8.01-273.1 Professional corporations of participating physicians are included in the program. HB398 (2000) reversed the decision in <u>Fruiterman & Assocs. PC v. Waziri</u>, 259 Va. 540 (2000)

[1401] Va. Code 38.2-5004.1

B. Discovery

Discovery is the formal process by which lawyers gather information pertaining to a lawsuit. The amount of this varies from case to case and depends on the style of the lawyers involved as well as the goal of each lawyer. Litigants in medical malpractice cases rarely leave many stones unturned.

A defendant healthcare provider should never be communicating directly with a plaintiff's attorney. All contact should be through defense counsel.

1. Interrogatories

Interrogatories are written questions exchanged between the parties to be answered by the other.[1402] This initial volley of interrogatories allows each party to gather background material, either prior to the deposition of the parties or to supplement other discovery. Routinely, plaintiffs ask health care providers about their credentials, medical malpractice claim history, hospital privileges, and the identity of any witnesses who have knowledge of pertinent facts or who may be called at trial.

These written questions must be answered within twenty-one days. Failure to do so can result in fines or other sanctions by the court.

2. Notice to Produce

A Notice to Produce is a request by one party to another party to produce particular documents in the party's possession that may

---

[1402]   Va. Sup. Ct. R. 4:8

be relevant to the litigation.[1403] Requests for production are usually drafted very broadly and can be burdensome. Unfortunately, the test is whether the request is for documents that may be admissible at trial or that may lead to information that may be admissible. A Notice to Produce is different from a subpoena. A subpoena is a request to an individual who is not a party to a lawsuit to produce documents or appear to testify, either at deposition or trial.

Prior to the production of documents, a physician's attorney will review all of the documents for objections. These objections are quite limited and usually fall under one of four categories: attorney work product; attorney/client privilege; health care provider/patient privilege; and peer review privilege.

3. *Depositions*

A deposition is where a party's attorney can ask questions of a witness under oath.[1404] A witness can be either a party or anyone with pertinent information. Questions posed during a deposition are usually quite wide ranging. Questions may be intended to elicit facts or they may be focused on getting witnesses to commit to a certain set of facts, to which they will be held at the later trial. The questions are asked in the presence of a court reporter that records the testimony verbatim. A deposition may also be videotaped.

Objections may be made during a deposition by any attorney in attendance on behalf of a party. However, the witness still must answer any questions posed, despite an objection, unless he follows his attorney's advice not to do so. If a witness refuses to answer a question, regardless of the circumstances, the party taking the deposition can either terminate the deposition at that point or leave that line of questioning and reserve the right to continue those questions later. A judge will then rule on whether or not the question was proper.

[1403] Va. Sup. Ct. R. 4:9
[1404] Va. Sup. Ct. R. 4:5

Preparation is essential before a deposition. The deposition is the most critical piece of trial preparation. The plaintiff's attorney will want to judge a physician's credibility, her demeanor, and her knowledge of the facts. The physician will be questioned as to actions by other health care providers and herself. Familiarity with the issues of the lawsuit and the medical records will make a physician more at ease during the deposition and reduce any embarrassing misstatements. A physician must keep in mind that she can be cross-examined at trial using any inconsistencies between her deposition testimony and trial testimony.[1405] Early, thorough preparation is the only way to avoid embarrassment. A defendant should prepare as she would for a Board examination.

In preparing for a deposition, a physician needs to consider the following:

1. Her medical records;
2. The medical records of other health care providers;
3. Plaintiff's Complaint;
4. Any deposition transcripts available;
5. Pertinent interrogatory responses by the physician;
6. Pertinent interrogatory responses by plaintiff or other defendants;
7. The plaintiff's theory of the case, if disclosed; and
8. The defense theory of the case

At the end of a deposition, the court reporter will ask if the witness wishes to "reserve signature, or waive." The person testifying has the right to review the transcript and correct any errors on an *errata sheet*, or she may waive this right. The better practice is to reserve signature.

[1405] Va. Code 8.01-403

4. *Requests to Admit*

A party can request an opponent to admit that a statement is true or that a document is authentic.[1406] These are known as Requests to Admit. The procedure is intended to dispose of routine evidentiary issues in an effort to speed up a trial. However, parties have increasingly tried to use Requests for Admission as a trap for the unwary by requesting the opponent to concede the major points of a trial. The danger here is that if objections or denials to Requests for Admission are not made within twenty-one days, the Requests may be deemed to have been admitted. Therefore, a timely response is of the utmost importance.

5. *Expert Witnesses*

A vital component of any medical malpractice defense is the use of expert witnesses.[1407] Each party is allowed to call expert witnesses who can testify on the standard of care, the alleged injury, and the relationship of the two (proximate cause). Failure to do so may be fatal to a party's case.[1408] Other experts may testify as to economic damages and prognosis. The performance of expert witnesses is crucial in persuading a jury.

In most medical malpractice cases, a deadline will be set by which expert witnesses must be identified. Each party must state the names, specialties, and opinions of the experts intended to be called at trial.[1409] Shortly thereafter, the depositions of the experts will be taken.

At trial, experts will be called to explain a defendant's actions. They

---

[1406] Va. Sup. Ct. R. 4:11
[1407] Va. Code 8.01-581.20
[1408] Raines v. Lutz, 231 Va. 110 (1986)
[1409] Va. Sup. Ct. R. 4:1(A)(4)

may be cross-examined by medical textbooks, articles and other literature.[1410] Experts can also rely on such information.[1411]

A defendant physician is likely to be frustrated by the testimony of plaintiff's expert witnesses. The Supreme Court of Virginia, while requiring an active clinical practice,[1412] does not require that an expert be in the same specialty as the defendant. For example, a gynecologist was permitted to testify against an ER physician on performing a pelvic examination.[1413] An expert is not required to have done the exact procedure at issue.[1414] The experience and expertise of an expert can be considered by the jury in weighing her opinion, but it will not be determinative of whether the expert is allowed to testify.

A defendant physician's involvement is extremely important with regard to expert witnesses. It can make the difference in winning or losing the case. A defendant may know potential experts from professional meetings or the current literature. He may be able to identify medical literature that disagrees with the contentions of plaintiff's experts. A physician's active assistance will help his attorney to excel in defending the case.

A treating physician may be asked to serve as an expert witness in a personal injury action stemming from an auto accident, slip and fall, medical care or other event involving his patient. A physician should carefully evaluate the whole picture before agreeing to be an expert witness. Does he have the requisite expertise to render an opinion? Does he have adequate information on which to base an opinion?

[1410] Hopkins v. Gromovsky, 198 Va. 389 (1956)
[1411] Va. Code 8.01-401.1
[1412] Hinkley v. Koehler, 269 Va. 82 (2005)
[1413] Sami v. Varn, 260 Va. 280 (2000)
[1414] Wright v. Kaye, 267 Va. 510 (2004)

C. Trial

In Virginia, trial of a medical malpractice action will usually be scheduled within one year of a physician being served with the lawsuit. Trials in Virginia move very quickly, lasting usually less then a week.

1. Motions in Limine

Before trial, a hearing may be held on any Motions in Limine. These are motions by the parties on evidentiary issues that they anticipate will come up during trial. Usually they are brought as an effort to keep out evidence that would be highly prejudicial and not probative of the issues. For example, a patient's business practices may be considered highly prejudicial and would not be probative of any issue in the trial. The judge would hear argument by both sides and enter a ruling. Motions in Limine are very important as a way of both sensitizing the judge to the issues in the case and building a framework within which the trial will be held.

2. Jury Selection

In Virginia, civil cases, including medical malpractice actions, can be tried before a jury of seven people or before a judge alone. Juries are usually considered preferable for defendants. In addition to the seven jurors, one or more alternate jurors may be selected if the trial is anticipated to last more than a few days.

Voir dire is the process by which the judge and the attorneys question jurors for potential bias.[1415] For better or for worse, Virginia judges are increasingly limiting the depth of questioning that can be conducted

---

[1415] Va. Code 8.01-358; <u>Davis v. Sykes</u>, 202 Va. 952, 956 (1961)

by counsel. Typical questions for potential jurors includes such things as being represented by one of the attorneys involved in the case, being related to one of the parties, or some other situation that would affect the impartiality of the juror.[1416] An unlimited number of jurors can be struck *for cause,* i.e. obvious bias. However, Virginia judges are reluctant to dismiss a potential juror *for cause* if she says that she can be impartial. After questioning of the potential jurors, each side will dismiss three individuals from the panel of thirteen potential jurors. No explanation need be given for the *strikes.*

3. *Opening Statements*

As with other steps of the trial, plaintiff will go first in making an opening statement. This is a speech by plaintiff's counsel to the jury that is intended to outline the facts that plaintiff's attorney believes will be proven during the trial, i.e. what the evidence will show. Defendants have an opportunity to make an opening statement after plaintiff's opening statement. Opening statements differ from closing statements in that argument of law and the evidence by an attorney are not to be made in the opening statement. However, they are vital components of the closing statement.

4. *Plaintiff's Case*

The plaintiff presents evidence first during a trial. This is because the plaintiff has the burden of proving his case is more likely than not. The plaintiff must prove three elements: the defendant was negligent; the plaintiff was injured; and the plaintiff's injuries were proximately caused by the defendant's negligence. In a medical malpractice action, almost all of this evidence must come through treating physicians or expert witnesses. If the plaintiff fails to produce any evidence on one of these three points, a judge should grant a directed verdict in favor of the defendant. In practice, this almost

---

[1416] Cantrell v. Crews, 259 Va. 47 (2000)

never occurs. Occasionally, the judge strikes a particular issue, but the case is usually allowed to continue toward jury deliberation.

The plaintiff may call a defendant physician as an *adverse witness*. A clever plaintiff's attorney may, in fact, call the doctor as the first witness of the trial. This is an attempt to catch the defendant at her most vulnerable. The plaintiff's lawyer hopes that the physician has not prepared to be cross-examined and that she will be nervous from being in the unfamiliar confines of a courtroom. The doctor will not have heard the testimony of the plaintiff's experts or anyone else. For these reasons, a defendant needs to work closely with her attorney before trial.

5. *Defendant's Case*

Theoretically, the physician as a defendant does not have the burden of proving that he was not negligent; the plaintiff was not injured; or the plaintiff's injuries were not related to the physician's negligence. However, in practice, it is extremely important for a defendant to offer an alternative explanation to the jury. Frequently, this becomes a battle of the experts as to who is more believable on these three key points.

The defendant's case is extremely important in that it allows the jury the opportunity to observe the physician and her demeanor and relate to the defendant in a personal way. If the physician is prepared, caring and reasonable; a jury is often willing to give the benefit of the doubt to the physician.

Usually, the focus of the defense will be on the physician's compliance with the standard of care under the circumstances. Occasionally, the defendants will present evidence as to the extent of the injuries or damages. However, usually this is not a good tactic because the jury may assume that the physician is conceding liability.

6. Rebuttal Evidence

A growing trend is that the plaintiff will seek to put on additional evidence after the defendant has completed her case. While this is supposed to be limited to new matters raised by the defendant, few judges seem willing to limit a plaintiff from retrying his case. This can be highly prejudicial to the defendant.

7. Jury Instructions

Jury instructions are the statements of law read to the jury at the conclusion of the trial by which the jury is to make its decision.[1417] The statements of law are intended to be the framework in which the jury considers the evidence. The evidence must support a jury instruction.[1418] Likewise, a jury instruction should not unduly emphasize a particular piece of evidence.[1419] Experienced trial attorneys debate the importance of jury instructions. One school of thought is that a jury does what it believes is fair, based on the jurors' preconceptions of justice. This makes jury instructions superfluous. The other school contends that the jury instructions are crucial in guiding the jury in its decision-making. The latter school of thought is most effectively illustrated during closing argument where the jury instructions are used as part of the presentation by applying the facts to the instructions.

One of the principle roles of jury instructions is creating points to be considered on appeal by the unsuccessful party. Jury instructions may be accepted or rejected based on what the judge's opinion of the evidence has been. Further, wording of the instructions can be prejudicial or a misstatement of the law in some circumstances. This often is the focus of arguments on appeal.[1420]

[1417] Atwell v. Watson, 204 Va. 624 (1963)
[1418] Van Buren v. Simmons, 235 Va. 46, 51 (1988)
[1419] Owens-Corning Fiberglas Corp. v. Watson, 243 Va. 128 (1992)
[1420] Clohessy v. Weiler, 250 Va. 249 (1995) cited in Rosen v. Greifenberger, 257 Va.373, 381 (1999)

8. *Closing Argument*

Closing argument is where the attorneys bring together the law and the evidence as they see them.[1421] The plaintiff's counsel will speak first. The defense counsel then has an opportunity to speak, followed by a rebuttal argument from the plaintiff's counsel. The importance of closing argument is that it is a means of summarizing all of the evidence that has been brought forward and apply it to the law. Counsel may argue any inferences and deductions that can be fairly drawn from the evidence.[1422] What may have appeared to be obscure points can be highlighted in the closing for better or worse from the physician's perspective.

9. *Jury Deliberations and Verdict*

After closing arguments, the jury retires to the jury room to deliberate. The jurors may take the exhibits with them.[1423] Due to the random nature of jury selection, the dynamic of the group is unpredictable. Some juries will immediately agree on a verdict. Others will consider the evidence in great detail before reaching a verdict.

The verdict of a Virginia jury must be unanimous. In other words, all seven jurors must agree on what the verdict should be. If the jurors are not able to agree after an appropriate length of time, the impasse is known as a *deadlocked jury* or *a hung jury.* The judge will then declare a mistrial and another trial with a new jury will be scheduled.

A verdict in Virginia is known as a general verdict. That is, the jury does not itemize the dollars it is awarding. The jury will return a verdict either in the defendant's favor or for the plaintiff in a specific dollar amount. For example, the dollar amount is not apportioned among

---

[1421] Va. Code 8.01-379

[1422] Burr v. Va. Railway & Power Co., 151 Va. 934 (1928)

[1423] Va. Code 8.01-381

defendants. No further detail is permitted. The only circumstance in which more detail is forthcoming is where special interrogatories are submitted on specific questions. For example, in wrongful death cases, one of the beneficiaries may be barred from recovering due to his contributory negligence. If that is the case, the jury must find specifically that the beneficiary was negligent and reduce the award accordingly.

10. Post-Trial Motions

Post trial motions are usually not successful, but are routinely made. The party that does not prevail usually will request that the jury be polled to determine that the verdict is unanimous. The losing party will also frequently ask that the judge set the verdict aside as being against the weight of the evidence. A new trial may be sought. In the alternative, the losing party may ask that the jury verdict be set aside and judgment entered in favor of the losing party. This is also called *judgment not withstanding the verdict* (JNOV) from the Latin term *non obstante verdicto*.

A judge may also hear motions as to whether an award to the plaintiff was too low or too high. If the verdict is outside the range of what he believes to be fair, he may order the parties to accept his determination of the appropriate amount or face a new trial.[1424] When he reduces the award, this is known as *remittitur*. When he increases the award, this is known as *additur*. In medical malpractice cases, the judge must reduce the verdict if the jury's award is in excess of the statutory cap.

11. Appeals

Appeals in Virginia can usually only be taken after a verdict has been returned. For example, a judge's order that a hospital turn over an incident report to the plaintiff would usually not be appealable until

---

[1424] Va. Code 8.01-383

after a jury verdict is returned. This results in Virginia having very little case law on discovery disputes. It gives a Virginia judge almost complete discretion in how a matter will be handled before trial. The Supreme Court of Virginia will intervene only in the most abusive of situations. Once a verdict has been returned, the high court will reverse only if it believes that the verdict would have been returned in favor of the losing party, had the appropriate course been taken.

The Supreme Court of Virginia does not hear every appeal that is sought. One must petition the court to hear an appeal. The court refuses the majority of cases at that point. Those cases that are heard by the court may be considered because of the novelty of the question presented or the desire of the court to make a statement.

D. Reporting Requirements after Settlement or Adverse Verdict

Unfortunately, settling a lawsuit or suffering an adverse verdict is not the end of the process for a physician. She must complete the following tasks:

- Advise the Virginia Board of Medicine. A professional liability insurer is required to make a report within thirty days of a settlement or judgment.[1425] However, a physician also has an obligation to report. Usually this will be handled by the insurer, but a physician needs to assure that it has been done. Only one report is required.

- Update the web page maintained by the Virginia Department of Health Professions (Virginia Practitioner Profile System) within thirty days.[1426] A physician is required to keep her web page up to date, including any settlements or adverse verdicts. The Board requires that the amount of payment be disclosed. While this information is kept confidential by the Board, a physician needs to assure that the agreement in a settlement provides for such disclosure.

- Disclose in applications for credentials with hospitals or health insurers. Often the bylaws of a hospital medical staff require that information regarding a claim, demand, or lawsuit be disclosed during the renewal process. However,

---

[1425] Va. Code 54.1-2909(A)(2) and (3).

[1426] Va. Code 54.1-2910.1; 18 Va. Admin. Code 85-20-280; see "physician information project" on https://www.vahealthprovider.com/edit/default.asp Settlements for less than $10,000 do not have to be reported unless there has been another settlement or judgment against the practitioner in the past 12 months. Va. Code 54.1-2910.1

some hospitals and third-party payors mandate that the physician advise them at the time of event.

A professional liability insurance company has its own reporting requirements in Virginia. For example, an insurer must report *any* payment on behalf of a physician to the Board of Medicine.[1427] This reporting requirement is stricter than to the National Practitioner Data Bank (NPDB),[1428] which has a few exceptions to reporting of settlements. A physician does not have an obligation to report a settlement to the NPDB.[1429] However, a physician would be well served to request that she and her attorney be permitted to draft the report to NPDB that will be submitted by the insurance company. A physician is not required to make a report to NPDB if she personally paid a settlement, but she will still be required to make a report to the Board of Medicine.

The Board of Medicine is likely to investigate the circumstances of a settlement or adverse verdict. The process for this is discussed in Chapter V. In addition, the Board of Medicine must now require a physician to undergo a competency assessment when three medical malpractice claims of $75,000 or more are paid in a ten year period.[1430]

[1427] Va. Code 54.1-2909

[1428] NPDB is contained within the Health Care Quality Improvement Act, 42 USC 11131 et seq. The requirement for entities, not individuals, to report is contained in 45 C.F.R. § 60.7. Additional information is available at www.npdb-hipdb.com.

[1429] Am. Dental Ass'n v. Shalala, 3 F.3d 445 (D.C. Cir. 1993)

[1430] Va. Code 54.1-2912.3

IV. Health Care Employment Law

Health care presents several unique situations for employment law. This chapter is intended to briefly introduce the topics that frequently arise in health care. Unfortunately, employment law quickly changes in light of new statutes and court decisions.

A. Pre-Employment Screening

1. Testing for Use of Illegal Drugs

Pre-employment drug testing continues to be very fashionable. However, a health care employer should undertake such testing with care. The courts recognize pre-employment drug testing for illegal drugs as "searches" in constitutional terms when conducted by governmental entities.[1431] As such, where an employer conditions employment on a drug test, it is necessary that the prospective employee's privacy expectations do not outweigh the employer's interests.[1432] For instance, a court struck down a Florida city's policy of testing "suspicionless" applicants for illegal drugs because the city could not articulate a "special need" for the tests.[1433] The court noted that while the United States Supreme Court has held that "there are few activities in our society more personal or private than the passing of urine," there are types of employment where it would be reasonable to condition employment on a routine, uniform drug test. Only in cases where the "risk to public safety is substantial and real or where public safety is genuinely in jeopardy" may suspicionless drug testing be considered reasonable.[1434]

A lawyer who refused to provide a urine sample for the Department of Justice challenged the constitutionality of the policy.[1435] The court

---

[1431] See, e.g., Knox Cty. Educ. Ass'n v. Knox Cty. Bd. of Educ., 158 F.3d 361 (6th Cir. 1998); Baron v. City of Hollywood, 93 F. Supp. 2d 1337 (S.D. Fla. 2000)

[1432] Knox Cty. Educ. Ass'n v. Knox Cty. Bd. of Educ., 158 F.3d 361 (6th Cir. 1998)

[1433] Baron v. City of Hollywood, 93 F. Supp. 2d 1337 (S.D. Fla. 2000)

[1434] Chandler v. Miller, 520 U.S. 305, 323, 117 S. Ct. 1295, 137 L. Ed. 2d 513 (1997)

[1435] Willner v. Thornburgh, 928 F.2d 1185 (D.C. Cir. 1991)

found that the lawyer's privacy expectations were significantly diminished by the Department's need to screen prospective employees. The court noted that applicants already supplied the Department with written information that was of a highly confidential nature and that the drug testing policy, uniform as it was, was merely intended to confirm or validate what the applicant had provided in writing.[1436]

Similarly, a group of teachers challenged a school board's post-offer drug-testing policy.[1437] Initially, the court had to determine whether teachers held safety-sensitive positions. The test for whether employees held safety sensitive positions was whether the employees engaged in duties fraught with risks of injury to others that even a momentary lapse of attention could have disastrous consequences.[1438] The court reasoned that teachers, who were the subjects of the board's pre-screening policy, held safety-sensitive positions since they were routinely entrusted with the care of children and teenagers.[1439] The drug-testing policy was upheld because the teacher's privacy interests were significantly diminished by the very nature of the work they performed.[1440] The only questions that the court felt were at issue was whether the policy was uniform, whether the applicants were given reasonable notice of the test, and whether the overall policy was reasonable. The court found that it was.[1441]

[1436] Willner v. Thornburgh, 928 F.2d 1185 (D.C. Cir. 1991)

[1437] Knox Cty. Educ. Ass'n v. Knox Cty. Bd. of Educ., 158 F.3d 361 (6th Cir. 1998)

[1438] Knox Cty. Educ. Ass'n v. Knox Cty. Bd. of Educ., 158 F.3d 361, 377 (6th Cir. 1998)

[1439] Knox Cty. Educ. Ass'n v. Knox Cty. Bd. of Educ., 158 F.3d 361, 378 (6th Cir. 1998)

[1440] Knox Cty. Educ. Ass'n v. Knox Cty. Bd. of Educ., 158 F.3d 361, 384 (6th Cir. 1998)

[1441] Knox Cty. Educ. Ass'n v. Knox Cty. Bd. of Educ., 158 F.3d 361, 384 (6th Cir. 1998)

The Federal Procedures for Transportation Workplace Drug Testing[1442] were promulgated pursuant to the Omnibus Transportation Testing Act of 1991.[1443] The statute is focused primarily on truck drivers.

The U.S. Court of Appeals, Fourth Circuit, has held that a laboratory can be held liable to an employee for negligently performing or reporting drug tests in the employment setting.[1444]

2. Testing for Genetic, Physiologic & Disease Conditions

Pre-employment medical testing is allowed under current law. However, employers must comply with the Americans with Disabilities Act (ADA)[1445] as to timing and substance. An applicant can be required to submit to a medical examination only after a conditional job offer has been made.[1446] Testing for illegal drugs is not a "medical examination" under the ADA.[1447] In contrast, testing for alcohol can only be done after a conditional offer of employment has been made.[1448] The test must be "job related and consistent with medical necessity." All entering employees must be subject to the same examination regardless of disability.

For example, a federal appellate court held that an employer could not turn away a prospective employee because a job may jeopardize his health. The ADA does not permit an employer to shield people from high-risk occupations.[1449] "Congress concluded that disabled

---

[1442] 49 C.F.R. 40

[1443] Codified as amended in scattered sections of 45 & 49 U.S.C.A.

[1444] Cooper v. Lab. Corp. of Am. Holdings, 150 F.3d 376 (4th Cir. 1998)

[1445] 42 U.S.C.A. 12112(d)

[1446] 42 U.S.C.A. 12112(d)(3)

[1447] 42 U.S.C.A. 12114(d)(1)

[1448] 42 U.S.C.A. 12112(3)

[1449] Echazabal v. Chevron USA, Inc., 226 F.3d 1063 (9th Cir. 2000), rev'd sub nom. Chevron U.S.A. Inc. v. Echazabal, 536 U.S. 73, 122 S. Ct. 2045, 153 L. Ed. 2d 82 (2002) (The applicant suffered asymptomatic, chronic active

persons should be afforded the opportunity to decide for themselves what risks to undertake."[1450] Curiously, this contradicts the current regulations of the Equal Employment Opportunity Commission (EEOC). The U.S. Supreme Court attempted to reconcile this conflict by holding that with regard to the direct threat defense under the ADA, a court must decide whether an employer based its decision on a reasonable medical judgment that relies on the most current medical knowledge and the best available objective evidence, and on an expressly individualized assessment of the individual's present ability to safely perform the essential functions of the job, reached after considering, among other things, the imminence of the risk and the severity of the harm portended.[1451]

Covert testing of employee blood samples for pregnancy, venereal disease and sickle-cell trait was found to be a violation of employee civil rights under Title VII of the Civil Rights Act because it singled out blacks and women for additional testing. Consenting to a general medical examination "does not abolish one's privacy rights not to be tested for intimate, personal matters involving one's health - nor does consenting to giving blood or urine samples or filling out a questionnaire."[1452]

Current employees cannot be required to undergo medical examination (which includes drug and alcohol testing) unless the examination is shown to be "job related" and "consistent with business necessity."[1453] For example, mandatory disclosure of all

---

hepatitis C. Chevron concluded that the exposure to toxins at the refinery might damage the applicant's liver.)
[1450] Echazabal v. Chevron USA, Inc., 226 F.3d 1063 (9th Cir. 2000), rev'd sub nom. Chevron U.S.A. Inc. v. Echazabal, 536 U.S. 73, 122 S. Ct. 2045, 153 L. Ed. 2d 82 (2002)
[1451] Chevron U.S.A. Inc. v. Echazabal, 536 U.S. 73, 122 S. Ct. 2045, 153 L. Ed. 2d 82 (2002)
[1452] Norman-Bloodsaw v. Lawrence Berkeley Lab., 135 F.3d 1260 (9th Cir. 1998)
[1453] 42 U.S.C.A. 12112(d)(4)

drugs used by an employee was found to be over-reaching,[1454] where prescription drug use was permitted only to the extent reported to the employee's supervisor. However, an employer can defend such a program on the basis that it is intended to screen out individuals that pose a direct threat to the health and safety of other individuals in the workplace.[1455] An employee must not be discriminated against solely because of past drug use.[1456] A current drug user, as opposed to a recovering addict, can be disciplined or terminated.[1457] Interestingly, alcoholism is distinguished in the ADA. Alcohol use is not automatically denied protection under the ADA.[1458] Whether related to drug or alcohol use, an employer may hold an employee "to the same qualification standards for employment or job performance and behavior that such entity holds other employees, even if any unsatisfactory performance or behavior is related to the drug use or alcoholism of such employee ..."[1459]

3. *Americans with Disabilities Act*

The Americans with Disabilities Act[1460] (ADA) provides that health care organizations are prohibited from discriminating against disabled individuals.[1461] A prospective employee is protected under the ADA if she meets three criteria: (1) that she is physically or mentally impaired to the extent that the disability (2) "substantially

---

[1454] Roe v. Cheyenne Mountain Conference Resort, Inc., 124 F.3d 1221 (10th Cir. 1997)

[1455] 42 U.S.C.A. 12113(b)

[1456] See Scott v. Beverly Enterprises-Kansas, Inc., 968 F. Supp. 1430, 1440 (D. Kan. 1997); E.E.O.C. v. Exxon Corp., 1 F. Supp. 2d 635 (N.D. Tex. 1998), aff'd, 202 F.3d 755 (5th Cir. 2000)

[1457] 42 U.S.C.A. 12114(a) and (b); 42 U.S.C.A. 12210(b); Scott v. Beverly Enterprises-Kansas, Inc., 968 F. Supp. 1430, 1438 (D. Kan. 1997); Nielsen v. Moroni Feed Co., 162 F.3d 604, 610 (10th Cir. 1998)

[1458] Mararri v. WCI Steel, Inc., 130 F.3d 1180, 1184–5 (6th Cir. 1997)

[1459] 42 U.S.C.A. 12114(c)(4)

[1460] 42 U.S.C.A. 12101 et seq.

[1461] John Walker Smith, *Hospital Liability*, 16.01[1]

limits one or more of the major life activities" [1462] or has a record of impairment or is regarded as having impairment[1463] and yet, (3) despite the impairment, the individual would be able to perform "the essential functions of the employment position."[1464] A prospective employee must not only be disabled, she must be "qualified" to trigger the ADA. A person is "qualified" if she can perform the essential functions of the desired job. For instance, a person would be "qualified" under the ADA if she could perform a requisite aspect of the job that was highly specialized and which only a select group of people could perform.[1465]

The ADA applies to all public and private entities with fifteen or more employees. Full-time as well as part-time employees are to be counted when considering whether a facility must comply with the ADA.[1466] In contrast, the federal Rehabilitation Act of 1973 does not contain a minimum-employee definition and may apply to all employers.[1467]

The ADA requires that facilities make *reasonable accommodations* for protected employees. Examples of "reasonable accommodation" include (1) making the facility usable by individuals with disabilities; (2) job restructuring; (3) initiating modified or part-time work schedules; (4) reassigning a disabled person to a vacant position; (5) acquiring or modifying equipment or devices; (6) adjusting or modifying examinations, training materials or policies; and/or (7) providing qualified interpreters or readers.[1468] An employer's duty to make reasonable accommodations to disabled individuals extends to all employment decisions, not just hiring and promotion decisions.[1469]

[1462]   42 U.S.C.A. 12102(8)

[1463]   42 U.S.C.A. 12102(2)

[1464]   42 U.S.C.A. 12111(8)

[1465]   29 C.F.R. 1630.2(n)

[1466]   *See* Smith, *Hospital Liability,* at 16.02[a]

[1467]   29 U.S.C.A. 504; Schrader v. Fred A. Ray, M.D., P.C., 296 F.3d 968 (10th Cir. 2002)

[1468]   *See* Smith, *Hospital Liability,* at 16.01[2]

[1469]   *See* Smith, *Hospital Liability,* at 16.01[2]

For example, the ADA's prohibitions against discrimination apply to (1) recruitment, advertising and job application procedures; (2) hiring, upgrading, and rehiring; (3) rates of pay; (4) job assignments; (5) leaves of absence, and; (6) any other term or condition of employment.[1470]

The ADA prohibits employers from conducting medical examinations prior to the time an individual is offered employment, including having an individual complete a form listing potential disabilities he may have.[1471] An employer may, however, state the attendance requirements of the job and ask the individual if he can meet them.[1472] The ADA does allow post-offer examinations and may condition the job offer on passing the examination, provided the employer require all other prospective employees in the same job classification to take the same examination. The employer must also keep all medical data confidential, and is prohibited from using the medical information to discriminate against the applicant.[1473]

A jury found that a hospital failed to make reasonable accommodations for an obstetrical nurse who began experiencing diabetes-related health problems and requested scheduling changes.[1474] The hospital refused to modify and/or reduce the nurse's consecutive on-call days, and specifically required a doctor's excuse when the nurse was forced to remain home due to nausea. When the nurse failed to timely provide a doctor's note, the hospital fired her. The appeals court determined that the jury could reasonably infer that the nurse's discharge was proximately caused by the hospital's unlawful discrimination under the ADA.[1475]

The ADA does not cover people with physical impairments, such as bad eyesight or high blood pressure that can be corrected with

---

[1470]   29 C.F.R. 1630.4
[1471]   56 Fed. Reg. 35750
[1472]   56 Fed. Reg. 35750
[1473]   42 U.S.C.A. 12102(c)(3)
[1474]   McCall v. Myrtle Beach Hosp., Inc., 122 F.3d 1062 (4th Cir. 1997)
[1475]   McCall v. Myrtle Beach Hosp., Inc., 122 F.3d 1062 (4th Cir. 1997)

medication or devices such as eyeglasses. [1476] For detailed guidance on complying with the ADA, see "Enforcement Guidance: Disability-Related Inquires and Medical Examinations of Employees under the Americans with Disabilities Act.[1477] Also see, "Policy Guidance on Executive Order 13145: To Prohibit Discrimination in Federal Employment Based on Genetic Information."[1478]

The ADA requires an employer to accommodate an employee's disability. While the health care employer must balance accommodation against patient safety. For example, a nurse's forty-pound lifting restriction was not a disability within the meaning of the ADA. This was despite the hospital's 75-pound lifting requirement for all staff nurses. The hospital offered her other jobs, but the nurse went to work for another health services company. "The major life activity of working 'does not mean working at a particular job of that person's choice.'"[1479] A nurse suffering rheumatoid arthritis was unable to fulfill the essential functions of her job in a nursing home and therefore her employer did not violate the ADA in terminating her employment.[1480]

In a similar fashion, a medical school was not required to keep a student who repeatedly acted unprofessionally.[1481] The school was not required to accommodate his diagnosis of attention deficit hyperactivity disorder and anxiety disorder. The U.S. Court of Appeals held that the school's decision on enrollment was entitled to significant deference.

[1476] Sutton v. United Air Lines, Inc., 527 U.S. 471, 119 S. Ct. 2139, 144 L. Ed. 2d 450 (1999), overturned due to legislative action (2009); Murphy v. United Parcel Serv., Inc., 527 U.S. 516, 119 S. Ct. 2133, 144 L. Ed. 2d 484 (1999)

[1477] EEOC Guidance 915.002 (7/27/00)

[1478] EEOC Guidance 915.002 (7/26/00)

[1479] Brunko v. Mercy Hosp., 260 F.3d 939 (8th Cir. 2001) citing Wooten v. Farmland Foods, 58 F.3d 382 (8th Cir. 1995)

[1480] Stafne v. Unicare Homes, 266 F.3d 771 (8th Cir. 2001)

[1481] Halpern v. Wake Forest University Health Sciences, ___ F.3d ___ (2012), VLW 012-2-048

4. *Criminal Conviction History*

Virginia health care facilities must screen job applicants to avoid hiring or retaining persons with a record of *barrier crimes*.[1482] Certified nurse aide training programs must provide a copy of the Virginia law requiring a criminal history check for employment in certain health facilities and a list of crimes that bar employment in that field.[1483] This must be provided prior to or upon enrollment in the training program.

Beginning in 2016, applicants for licensure as a practical nurse or registered nurse must submit fingerprints and undergo a criminal background check by the Department of Health Professions.[1484]

5. *Credit Reports*

An employer may feel that a consumer credit report is an appropriate part of screening job applicants. The Fair Credit Reporting Act[1485] requires an employer to:

1. Provide a separate written notification to the applicant or employee that the information is being sought;

2. Obtain written consent; and

3. Notify the applicant or employee that he has the right to request additional information and a summary of rights prepared by the Federal Trade Commission.

Requests for medical information, or employment decisions based

---

[1482] Hospitals: 42 C.F.R. 482.13(c)(3) and Va. Code 32.1-126.02; Nursing homes: Va. Code 32.1-126.01; Home care organizations: Va. Code 32.1-162.9:1; Assisted living facilities: Va. Code 63.2-1720; Children's residential facilities: Va. Code 37.2-408.1

[1483] Va. Code 22.1-326.1

[1484] Va. Code 54.1-3005.1

[1485] The Fair Credit Reporting Act, 15 U.S.C.A. 1681 *et seq.*

on information received through such a report, impose additional requirements under the Fair Credit Reporting Act.[1486]

6. *Social Media Accounts*

An employer can't require a current or prospective employee to provide access for the employer to social media accounts.[1487] For example, an employer cannot demand an employee's username and password or require that a manager be added to an employee's contacts. However, access to social media can be required as part of a formal investigation. An employer is not prohibited from viewing an employee's social media that is open to the public.

7. *References*

A current or former employer, who upon request by a person's prospective employer, provides information about the person's professional conduct, reasons for separation or job performance, including information contained in any written performance evaluations, is immune from civil liability under Virginia law.[1488] This assumes that a former employer is not acting in bad faith or with reckless disregard for whether the information is false. Conversely, punitive damages may be awarded against the employer if it acts in bad faith or with reckless disregard. Despite this statute, an employer should carefully consider what objective information to release when discussing a former employee.

[1486] The Fair Credit Reporting Act, 15 U.S.C.A. 1681 *et seq.*
[1487] Va. Code 40.1-28.7:5
[1488] Va. Code 8.01-46.1

B. Infectious Disease

1. *Bloodborne Pathogens Standard*

Before Medicare compliance programs became all the rage in health care, clinicians were already under a mandate for compliance programs from the federal Occupational Safety and Health Administration (OSHA)[1489] and its state equivalent, Virginia Occupational Safety and Health (VOSH) for bloodborne pathogens.[1490] As this is one of the most important federal employment directives facing health care providers, it will be discussed in some detail. Much to the surprise of most health care providers, this has been the law since 1992. Even more surprising to the health care provider may be VOSH's directive that all alleged violations are to be presumed to be "serious."[1491]

The Bloodborne Pathogens Standard applies to any employer who has one or more employees with occupational exposure to blood or other potentially infectious materials, including saliva. OSHA defines "employee" to include part-time, temporary and probationary workers. The health care provider (physician, dentist, etc.) is also considered an employee of his own professional corporation.

a. Exposure Control Plan

Every employer is required to have a written exposure control plan

---

[1489] Virginia is in OSHA's Region 3, which is headquartered at The Curtis Center-Suite 740 West, 170 S. Independence Mall West, Philadelphia, PA 19106-3309, Telephone (215) 861-4900

[1490] US Occupational Safety and Health Administration, 29 C.F.R. 1910.1030 (12/6/91); VOSH Program Directive 02-400 (6/1/92). Virginia adopted a federal identical standard.

[1491] VOSH, Occupational Exposure to Bloodborne Pathogens: Final Rule, p. vii

designed to eliminate or minimize employee exposure to bloodborne disease.[1492] The plan must contain:

1. An *exposure determination*; and
2. How and what schedule the office is implementing the mechanisms of compliance listed below.

An *exposure determination* must be prepared by each employer that includes a list of job classifications in which:

1. All employees in the job classification have occupational exposure; and
2. Some employees in the job classification have occupational exposure. For each of the jobs in this category, the employer must also list the tasks and procedures in which *occupational exposure* occurs.

Occupational exposure is defined as "reasonably anticipated skin, mucosal, eye, or parenteral contact with blood or other potentially infectious materials, that may result from the performance of an employee's duties."[1493]

The plan must be accessible to employees. It must be updated at least annually and whenever necessary to reflect changes in the facility's practice.

b. Mechanisms of Compliance

The exposure control plan must be a detailed set of policies and procedures for the office staff. OSHA will be looking not only for the written documents but that the staff is knowledgeable of their contents.

[1492]   29 C.F.R. 1910.1030(c)(1)
[1493]   29 C.F.R. 1910.1030(b)

i)   Universal Precautions

The facility's policy should be explicit that universal precautions must be observed to prevent contact with blood or other potentially infectious materials.[1494] Where the determination is difficult as to whether a substance is potentially infectious, the health care provider is to presume that it is.

ii)   Engineering and Work Practice Controls

The employer must study the work place and institute engineering and work practice controls that eliminate or minimize employee exposure.[1495] Where the occupational exposure cannot be completely eliminated, personal protective clothing must be used. OSHA has a very detailed list of work place habits that are either mandated or prohibited.[1496]

iii)   Personal Protective Equipment

When there is occupational exposure, the employer must provide, at no cost to the employee, *appropriate personal protective equipment*.[1497] This may include gloves, gowns, lab coats, face shields, masks, eye protection, mouthpieces, resuscitation bags, etc. Personal protective equipment is *appropriate* only if it does not permit potentially infectious material to pass through or to reach the employee's clothes, undergarments, skin, eyes, mouth or other mucous membranes under normal circumstances of use.

Appropriate personal protective equipment in the appropriate sizes must be readily accessible at the worksite or is issued to the employees.[1498] This includes a responsibility on the employer to provide alternatives to those who may have latex allergies. The

---

[1494]   29 C.F.R. 1910.1030(d)(1)
[1495]   29 C.F.R. 1910.1030(d)(2)
[1496]   29 C.F.R. 1910.1030(d)(2)(iii) through (xiv)
[1497]   29 C.F.R. 1910.1030(d)(3)(i)
[1498]   29 C.F.R. 1910.1030(d)(3)(iii)

employer also has the responsibility to clean, launder, or dispose of this equipment at no cost to employees.[1499] Likewise, the employer must repair or replace equipment to maintain its effectiveness at no cost to the employee.[1500] As one would anticipate, the federal regulations require that a garment must be removed as quickly as possible after penetration by potentially infectious materials[1501] and before leaving the work area.[1502]

The obligation is on the employer to ensure that the employee uses appropriate personal protective equipment.[1503] The only exception is when the employee temporarily and briefly declines to use personal protective equipment when "under rare and extraordinary circumstances, it is the employee's professional judgment that in the specific instance its use would have prevented the delivery of health care or public safety or would have posed an increased hazard to the safety of the worker or co-worker."[1504] If this happens, the circumstances must be investigated and documented in order to determine whether changes can be instituted to prevent future occurrences. An employer is not required to justify its adherence to a federal safety regulation when an employee presents a personal waiver to that regulation.[1505]

iv) Housekeeping

(A) Cleaning & Decontamination Schedules

The employer must ensure that the work area is maintained in a clean and sanitary condition. This includes the responsibility of drafting and implementing written schedules for when and

---

[1499] 29 C.F.R. 1910.1030(d)(3)(iv)
[1500] 29 C.F.R. 1910.1030(d)(3)(v)
[1501] 29 C.F.R. 1910.1030(d)(3)(vi)
[1502] 29 C.F.R. 1910.1030(d)(3)(vii)
[1503] 29 C.F.R. 1910.1030(d)(3)(ii)
[1504] 29 C.F.R. 1910.1030(d)(3)(ii)
[1505] Albertson's, Inc. v. Kirkingburg, 527 U.S. 555, 119 S. Ct. 2162, 144 L. Ed. 2d 518 (1999)

how decontamination will be conducted.[1506] The regulation has further specific details of how and when decontamination is to be performed.[1507]

(B) Infectious Waste

OSHA has very stringent requirements for the discarding of needles, scalpels, and other *sharps*[1508] as well as other potentially contaminated waste.[1509]

(C) Laundry Requirements

Contaminated laundry must be bagged or containerized at the location where it was used.[1510] It cannot be sorted or rinsed in the work area and must be transported with appropriate labeling. Laundry personnel must be decked out in protective gloves and other appropriate personal protective equipment.

v) Hepatitis B Vaccination

The employer must make Hepatitis B vaccination available to employees who have occupational exposure at no cost and at a reasonable time and place.[1511] Post-exposure evaluation and follow-up must also be available to all employees who have had an exposure incident at no cost to the employee.

Hepatitis B vaccination must be made available to an employee within ten days of initial assignment to a job with occupational exposure.[1512] The only exceptions are when the employee has previously received the vaccine, antibody testing reveals that the employee is immune,

---

[1506]   29 C.F.R. 1910.1030(d)(4)(i)
[1507]   29 C.F.R. 1910.1030(d)(4)(ii)
[1508]   29 C.F.R. 1910.1030(d)(4)(iii)(A)
[1509]   29 C.F.R. 1910.1030(d)(4)(iii)(B)
[1510]   29 C.F.R. 1910.1030(d)(4)(iv)
[1511]   29 C.F.R. 1910.1030(f)(1)
[1512]   29 C.F.R. 1910.1030(f)(2)

or the vaccine is contraindicated for medical reasons. If an employee refuses vaccination, the employer must assure that the employee signs a statement documenting this.[1513]

The employer is responsible for providing a copy of the OSHA regulation to the health care professional[1514] performing the Hepatitis B vaccination.[1515] In turn, the health care professional must provide a written opinion to the employer, who must provide it to the employee, as the advisability of the employee receiving the vaccination and whether the employee received the vaccination.[1516]

vi) Post Exposure Evaluation

If exposure occurs, the employer must make a confidential medical evaluation available to the employee immediately.[1517] The employer must also document:

1. The route and circumstances of the exposure; and

2. The source individual unless identification is infeasible or prohibited by state or local law.

The source individual's blood must be tested as soon as feasible after consent is obtained in order to determine Hepatitis B virus (HBV) and Human Immunodeficiency Virus (HIV) status.[1518] If the source individual is known to be infected with HBV or HIV, the study does not need to be repeated. The results must be made available to

---

[1513] The form for refusal of Hepatitis B vaccine is set forth in Appendix A of 29 C.F.R. 1910.1030

[1514] *Licensed health care professional* is defined by 29 C.F.R. 1910.1030(b) as a person whose legally permitted scope of practice allows him or her to independently perform the activities required by 29 C.F.R. 1910.1030(f) Hepatitis B Vaccination and Post-exposure Evaluation and Follow-up.

[1515] 29 C.F.R. 1910.1030(f)(4)(i)

[1516] 29 C.F.R. 1910.1030(f)(5)(i)

[1517] 29 C.F.R. 1910.1030(f)(3)

[1518] 29 C.F.R. 1910.1030(f)(3)(ii)(A). A patient is deemed to have consented to such testing under Va. Code 32.1-45.1(A)

the exposed employee, and the employee must be informed of the applicable laws and regulations concerning disclosure of the identity and infectious status of the source individual.

To establish a baseline, the employee's blood is to be collected as soon after an exposure incident as feasible and consent can be obtained.[1519] If the employee agrees to have blood drawn but does not consent to HIV testing, the sample must be preserved for ninety days in case the employee changes his mind. The employee must be provided with post-exposure prophylaxis (if medically indicated), counseling, and evaluation of reported illnesses.

The employer also must provide the following to a health care professional treating an employee after an exposure incident: [1520]

1. A copy of the OSHA regulation;

2. A description of the exposed employee's duties as they relate to the exposure incident;

3. Documentation of the route(s) of exposure and circumstances under which exposure occurred;

4. Results of the source individual's blood testing, if available; and

5. All medical records relevant to the appropriate treatment of the employee including vaccination status which are the employer's responsibility to maintain.

The treating health care professional must provide a written opinion for post-exposure evaluation and follow-up within fifteen days of completing the evaluation including at least the following information: [1521]

[1519] 29 C.F.R. 1910.1030(f)(3)(iii)
[1520] 29 C.F.R. 1910.1030(f)(4)(ii)
[1521] 29 C.F.R. 1910.1030(f)(5)(ii)

1. The employee has been informed of the results of the evaluation; and

2. The employee has been told of any medical conditions resulting from exposure to infectious material that may require further evaluation or treatment.

All other findings or diagnoses are to be kept confidential and not included in the report.

vii) Labeling

OSHA regulations mandate the use of red bags or containers for potentially infectious waste.[1522] Alternatively, *biohazard* labels, as specified in the regulation, may be used.

viii) Training & Information

Employers must provide training programs at no cost and during working hours for all employees with potential occupational exposure.[1523] This must be done at the time of employment and annually thereafter. Additional training must occur when changes are made in workplace tasks or procedures. The training should be at an appropriate educational level and in an appropriate language for the employees.

The training program, at a minimum, must cover: [1524]

1. A copy of the OSHA regulations on bloodborne pathogens;

2. A general explanation of the epidemiology and symptoms of bloodborne diseases;

3. An explanation of the modes of transmission of bloodborne pathogens; an explanation of the employer's exposure

---

[1522] 29 C.F.R. 1910.1030(g)(1)
[1523] 29 C.F.R. 1910.1030(g)(2)
[1524] 29 C.F.R. 1910.1030(g)(2)(vii)

control plan and the means by which the employee can obtain a copy of the written plan;

4. An explanation of the appropriate methods for recognizing tasks and other activities that may involve exposure to blood and other potentially infectious materials;

5. An explanation of the use and limitations of methods that will prevent or reduce exposure including appropriate engineering controls, work practices, and personal protective equipment;

6. Information on the types, proper use, location, removal, handling, decontamination and disposal of personal protective equipment;

7. An explanation of the basis for selection of personal protective equipment;

8. Information on the hepatitis B vaccine, including information on its efficacy, safety, method of administration, the benefits of being vaccinated, and that the vaccine and vaccination will be offered free of charge;

9. Information on the appropriate actions to take and persons to contact in an emergency involving blood or other potentially infectious materials;

10. An explanation of the procedure to follow if an exposure incident occurs including the method of reporting the incident and the medical follow-up that the employer is required to provide for the employee following an exposure incident;

11. An explanation of the signs and labels and / or color coding required for medical wastes; and

12. An opportunity for interactive questions and answers with the person conducting the training session.

ix) Record Keeping

(A) Company Records

The healthcare practice or facility should maintain the following records to document that it is in compliance with the Bloodborne Pathogen Standard:

1. The OSHA regulations;

2. Its Exposure Control Plan;

3. Records indicating when and how the Exposure Control Plan was updated;

4. Documentation that the cleaning and decontamination schedule was followed;

5. Employee medical records, as discussed below; and

6. Training records, as discussed below.

(B) Medical Records

The employer must maintain the following records for each employee with occupational exposure for at least the duration of employment plus thirty years: [1525]

1. Name and social security number of the employee;

2. A copy of the employee's hepatitis B vaccination status including the dates of all the hepatitis B vaccinations and any medical records relative to the employee's ability to receive vaccination;

3. A copy of all results of examinations, medical testing, and follow-up procedures for exposure incidents;

4. The employer's copy of the health care professional's written opinions as described above; and

---

[1525] 29 C.F.R. 1910.1030(h)(1)

5. A copy of the information provided to the health care professional either as part of administering vaccinations or treating an employee after an exposure incident.

These records must be maintained as confidential. The records are only to be released with express written consent of the employee or to OSHA inspectors.[1526]

(C) Training Records

The employer must keep records of the following information about bloodborne pathogens training programs for three years from the date when the training occurred:

1. The dates of the training sessions;
2. The contents or a summary of the training sessions;
3. The names and qualifications of persons conducting the training; and
4. The names and job titles of all persons attending the training sessions.

The training records must be made available on request to an employee, employee representatives, or OSHA.[1527]

2. Infection of a Health Care Provider

A health care employer is faced with a serious dilemma when an employee has a bloodborne illness. Several conflicting statutes need to be considered. For example, the Americans with Disabilities Act prohibits discrimination solely on the basis of disease status. On the other hand, the health care provider has a duty to protect

---

[1526] 29 C.F.R. 1910.1030(h)(1)(iii) and (3)(iii)
[1527] 29 C.F.R. 1910.1030(h)(3)(ii)

patients from exposure to contagious diseases.[1528] Before action is taken, the prudent health care provider will seek assistance from an experienced health care attorney.

[1528] For example, the US Court of Appeals found that a Georgia dental practice did not violate the ADA by discharging a hygienist after finding out he was HIV-positive. His HIV-status was "a significant risk to the health or safety of others that cannot be eliminated by reasonable accommodation." Waddell v. Valley Forge Dental Associates Inc., 276 F.3d 1275 (11th Cir. 2001), cert. denied 535 US 1096 (2002)

C. Sexual Harassment

An employee who suffers sexual harassment may seek redress under state or federal laws.

1. *Virginia Human Rights Act*

The Virginia Human Rights Act applies to employers with more than five but fewer than fifteen employees.[1529] It states that:

It is the policy of the Commonwealth of Virginia:[1530]

1. To safeguard all individuals within the Commonwealth from unlawful discrimination because of race, color, religion, national origin, sex, pregnancy, childbirth or related medical conditions, age, marital status, or disability, in places of public accommodation, including educational institutions and in real estate transactions; in employment; to preserve the public safety, health and general welfare; and to further the interests, rights and privileges of individuals in the Commonwealth; and

2. To protect citizens of the Commonwealth against unfounded charges of unlawful discrimination.

If an employee is improperly discharged for any of the enumerated reasons, the employee may seek back pay for up to one year and attorney's fees (not to exceed 25% of the back pay awarded).[1531]

[1529]   Va. Code 2.2-3903
[1530]   Va. Code 2.2-3900
[1531]   Va. Code 2.2-3903.C

2. Federal Statutes

In reviewing sexual harassment allegations under Title VII (the federal statute prohibiting sexual harassment), the U.S. Court of Appeals, Fourth Circuit, requires that allegedly sexually harassing comments made between hospital coworkers be *severe or pervasive* and must create a *hostile working environment*.[1532] Whether conduct is *severe or pervasive* requires examination of all of the circumstances, including "the frequency of the [sexual conduct]; its severity; whether it is physically threatening or humiliating, or a mere offensive utterance; and whether it unreasonably interferes with an employee's work performance."[1533]

There are generally two types of sexual harassment about which an employee may complain: *quid pro quo* harassment and *hostile environment* harassment.[1534] *Quid pro quo* harassment involves a situation in which an employee will typically complain that a supervisor asked for sexual favors in exchange for a job benefit. Under the *hostile environment* standard, an employee may allege that a co-worker exhibited sexually harassing conduct with frequency. An employer can raise an affirmative defense that 1) it exercised reasonable care to prevent and correct promptly any sexually harassing behavior, and 2) the plaintiff employee unreasonably failed to take advantage of any preventive or corrective opportunities provided by the employer or to avoid harm otherwise.[1535] The U.S. Supreme Court has held that an employer's claim that it should be immune from liability because the employee failed to follow a particular grievance procedure would be "substantially stronger if [the employer's] procedures

---

[1532] Pesso v. Montgomery General Hospital, 1999 US App. LEXIS 10207 (relying on Oncale v. Sundowner Offshore Servs., Inc., 523 U.S. 75, 118 S. Ct. 998, 140 L. Ed. 2d 201 (1998)

[1533] Pesso v. Montgomery General Hospital, 1999 US App. LEXIS 10207 (quoting Harris v. Forklift Sys., Inc., 510 U.S. 17, 114 S. Ct. 367, 126 L. Ed. 2d 295 (1993))

[1534] Smith, *Hospital Liability*, §16.02[2]

[1535] Faragher v. City of Boca Raton, 524 U.S. 775, 118 S. Ct. 2275, 141 L. Ed. 2d 662 (1998); Burlington Indus., Inc. v. Ellerth, 524 U.S. 742, 118 S. Ct. 2257, 141 L. Ed. 2d 633 (1998)

were better calculated to encourage victims of harassment to come forward."[1536] An employer can be vicariously liable for actionable sexual harassment caused by a supervisor.[1537]

Generally, since the EEOC Guidelines were issued, an employer may be held liable for the sexual harassment of a non-supervisory employee if the employer knew or should have known of the conduct (unless it immediately acted upon the incident).[1538] Likewise, while there is no clear guidance in Virginia with respect to sexual harassment by patients, the EEOC Guidelines provide that "an employer may ... be responsible for the acts of non-employees ... where the employer knows (or its agents or supervisory employees) knows or should have known of the conduct and fails to take immediate and appropriate corrective action."[1539] Generally, courts will weigh such factors as the extent of control by the employer and any legal responsibility the employer had over the non-employee.

In an analogous setting to health care facilities, a restaurant was held liable for sexual harassment of employees by patrons.[1540] A "crude and rowdy" customer had grabbed the waitress earlier in the evening, prompting the waitress to complain to the manager twice. It was not the first time that the customer had behaved badly. The manager ordered the waitress to continue to wait on the customers. The court said that the manager should have asked a male waiter to serve the men, waited on them himself, or asked them to leave the restaurant. This line of reasoning has serious implications for the health care setting where patients are often offensive to staff, either intentionally or due to a disease process.

[1536] Meritor Sav. Bank, FSB v. Vinson, 477 U.S. 57, 72, 106 S. Ct. 2399, 91 L. Ed. 2d 49 (1986)

[1537] Faragher v. City of Boca Raton, 524 U.S. 775, 118 S. Ct. 2275, 141 L. Ed. 2d 662 (1998); Burlington Indus., Inc. v. Ellerth, 524 U.S. 742, 118 S. Ct. 2257, 141 L. Ed. 2d 633 (1998)

[1538] Scott v. Sears, Roebuck & Co., 798 F.2d 210 (7th Cir. 1986), Barrett v. Omaha Nat. Bank, 726 F.2d 424 (8th Cir. 1984)

[1539] 29 C.F.R. 1604.11(e)

[1540] Lockard v. Pizza Hut, Inc., 162 F.3d 1062 (10th Cir. 1998)

D. Religious Consideration

1. State Action

Traditionally the courts have regarded private hospitals as institutions that could adopt whatever rules they wished with respect to staff so long as the action was not capricious or was without malice.[1541] If state action can be established – if it is shown that a hospital is a government facility or receives a sufficient amount of federal funding – the facility must extend equal protection to all staff members. What constitutes state action? The U.S. Court of Appeals, Fourth Circuit, and a few other jurisdictions have held that the receipt by a hospital of federal funds entitled physicians seeking staff appointments to equal protection of the law and due process.[1542] Generally, however, mere receipt of federal funding alone is not in itself sufficient to constitute acting under the color of the state by a private hospital; it is usually considered an element in determining whether a hospital may have a quasi-public status.[1543] The mere fact that the hospital industry is heavily regulated will not turn a private hospital's action into state action. Moreover, even if a private hospital were deemed a state (government) hospital for purposes of religious consideration and accommodation, a discharged worker would have a tough time

---

[1541] See, e.g., Moore v. Andalusia Hosp., Inc., 284 Ala. 259, 224 So. 2d 617 (1969) (holding that staff hirings at a private hospital was solely within the discretion of the hospital and a refusal to hire was not subject to judicial review); Hoffman v. Garden City Hosp.-Osteopathic, 115 Mich. App. 773, 321 N.W.2d 810 (1982) abrogated by Feyz v. Mercy Mem'l Hosp., 475 Mich. 663, 719 N.W.2d 1 (2006)

[1542] Sams v. Ohio Val. Gen. Hosp. Ass'n, 413 F.2d 826 (4th Cir. 1969); Simkins v. Moses H. Cone Mem'l Hosp., 323 F.2d 959 (4th Cir. 1963) (allegations of racial discrimination)

[1543] Manning v. Greensville Mem'l Hosp., 470 F. Supp. 662 (E.D. Va. 1979); Greenspan v. Nat'l Med. Care, Inc., 485 F. Supp. 311 (E.D. Va. 1980)

prevailing due to a complex, multi-tiered body of First Amendment law involving public employees.[1544]

2. *Considering Religion in Hiring*

With respect to whether an employer may take a prospective employee's religious convictions into account when determining whether to hire her, the U.S. Supreme Court is quite clear: "a court may not allow preferential hiring or promotion consideration for any particular race, religion, or other group."[1545]

3. *Religion in the Workplace*

A private employer's duty to accommodate an employee's religious beliefs is governed by Title VII of the Civil Rights Act of 1964. While there is a duty to accommodate, it is a very "weak" duty. Basically, any significant hardship on the employer all but nullifies the obligation to accommodate the employee's religious beliefs.[1546] For example, the U.S. Supreme Court ruled that a major airline did not violate the civil rights of an employee whose religious beliefs prohibited him from working Saturdays. The airline had initially made reasonable accommodations, when the employee was in a junior position and no problems for the airline arose; however, once the employee was transferred to a senior position that required he work on Saturdays, the one day of the week on which the critical duties of his job were undertaken, the airline discharged him. The Supreme Court ruled that to require the airline to bear more than a minimum cost in order to give the employee Saturdays off would be an undue hardship. To require an employer to discriminate against some employees

---

[1544] See Waters v. Churchill, 511 U.S. 661, 114 S. Ct. 1878, 128 L. Ed. 2d 686 (1994)

[1545] Local 28 of Sheet Metal Workers' Int'l Ass'n v. E.E.O.C., 478 U.S. 421, 106 S. Ct. 3019, 92 L. Ed. 2d 344 (1986)(applying Title VII)

[1546] See Trans World Airlines, Inc. v. Hardison, 432 U.S. 63, 97 S. Ct. 2264, 53 L. Ed. 2d 113 (1977), Ansonia Bd. of Educ. v. Philbrook, 479 U.S. 60, 107 S. Ct. 367, 93 L. Ed. 2d 305 (1986)

in order to enable others to observe their Sabbath was not the purpose of the anti-discrimination laws.[1547]

Nevertheless, some courts have recognized that there are two theories under which an employee may make out a case based on religious discrimination: religious accommodation and disparate impact.

a. Religious Accommodation

In a religious accommodation case, an employee can establish a claim even though she cannot show that other (unprotected) employees were treated more favorably or cannot rebut an employer's legitimate, non-discriminatory reason for her discharge. This is because an employer must at least attempt to accommodate an employee's religious expression or conduct even if, absent the motivation, the conduct or expression would supply a legitimate ground for discharge.[1548] For example, an employee who is terminated for refusing to work on Sundays can maintain an accommodation claim even if other non-religious employees were also fired for refusing to work on Sundays.[1549]

The U.S. Court of Appeals, Fourth Circuit ruled that a religious practice of expressing one's faith in a manner that was patently invasive and distressing was not the sort of conduct an employer was legally required to accommodate. In that case, the plaintiff wrote letters to co-workers telling them of their sins and encouraging them to seek forgiveness from God.[1550] Similarly, a court ruled that a nurse communicating her pro-life convictions to a patient about to undergo an abortion would not be the sort of religiously-motivated conduct a hospital is legally required to accommodate.[1551] The plaintiff in that

---

[1547] Trans World Airlines, Inc. v. Hardison, 432 U.S. 63, 90, 97 S. Ct. 2264, 53 L. Ed. 2d 113 (1977)

[1548] Chalmers v. Tulon Co. of Richmond, 101 F.3d 1012 (4th Cir. 1996)

[1549] Chalmers v. Tulon Co. of Richmond, 101 F.3d 1012 (4th Cir. 1996)

[1550] Chalmers v. Tulon Co. of Richmond, 101 F.3d 1012 (4th Cir. 1996)

[1551] Benson v. Sentara Hosp., 1997 US Dist. LEXIS 684 (1997)

case was a Christian who refused to provide treatment for abortion patients. The hospital transferred the nurse to other patients whenever an abortion patient was about to come under her care. The court simply found that the nurse acted unprofessionally, not that the hospital discriminated against her because of her religion.[1552] In a similar case, the U.S. Court of Appeals, Third Circuit, found that a hospital offered reasonable accommodation of a nurse's religious objection to participating in activities that could result in abortion by offering a transfer to the neonatal intensive care unit.[1553] The hospital was found to have acted reasonably in terminating her employment when she refused to accept the transfer after thirty days.

b. Disparate Impact

Under disparate impact, an employee must prove that the employer treated her differently than other employees because of her religious beliefs. A plaintiff employee may prevail if she demonstrates that she was performing her job satisfactorily and presents evidence that a reasonable inference could be drawn that the discharge was discriminatory.[1554]

For example, a court held that an employer did not unlawfully discharge a Jewish employee who claimed he was discriminated against for observing Rosh Hashana and Yom Kippur.[1555] The plaintiff employee failed to prove at trial that he was working satisfactorily at the time of his discharge, that the employer replaced him with someone outside the protected group (in this instance, a non-Jewish employee), and that from the evidence one could reasonably infer that the discharge was discriminatory.[1556]

[1552] Benson v. Sentara Hosp., 1997 US Dist. LEXIS 684 (1997)
[1553] Shelton v. Univ. of Med. & Dentistry of New Jersey, 223 F.3d 220 (3d Cir. 2000)
[1554] Lawrence v. Mars, Inc., 955 F.2d 902 (4th Cir. 1992)
[1555] Lawrence v. Mars, Inc., 955 F.2d 902 (4th Cir. 1992)
[1556] Lawrence v. Mars, Inc., 955 F.2d 902, 905–906 (4th Cir. 1992)

E. Workplace Monitoring

Monitoring of employees has become a quite delicate issue as the means of doing so becomes more *sub rosa* and employees have become more sensitized to the issue. The Fourth Amendment prohibition against unreasonable search and seizure generally does not apply to actions taken by private employers.[1557] To have a protected privacy interest, the employee must have a reasonable expectation of privacy.[1558] For the employer, the better course is to delineate what areas or activities may be monitored.

Employers have a legitimate interest in the efficient operation of the workplace, "and one attribute of this interest is that supervisors may monitor at will that which is in plain view within an open work area."[1559] Workplace monitoring will more often than not be held legal where the employer "acted overtly in establishing the video surveillance."[1560] This puts employees on clear notice from the outset that their actions within the work area will be exposed to the employer's sight. As one court commented that, "when all is said and done, employees must accept some circumspection of their liberty as a condition of continued employment."[1561]

Federal courts outside of Virginia have considered whether an

---

[1557] Simmons v. Sw. Bell Tel. Co., 452 F. Supp. 392 (W.D. Okla. 1978), aff'd, 611 F.2d 342 (10th Cir. 1979); Jackson v. Metro. Edison Co., 419 U.S. 345, 95 S. Ct. 449, 42 L. Ed. 2d 477 (1974)

[1558] Vega-Rodriguez v. Puerto Rico Tel. Co., 110 F.3d 174, 178 (1st Cir. 1997); United States v. Simons, 29 F. Supp. 2d 324 (E.D. Va. 1998), aff'd in part, remanded in part, 206 F.3d 392 (4th Cir. 2000)

[1559] Vega-Rodriguez v. Puerto Rico Tel. Co., 110 F.3d 174, 179 (1st Cir. 1997)

[1560] Vega-Rodriguez v. Puerto Rico Tel. Co., 110 F.3d 174, 179 (1st Cir. 1997)

[1561] Vega-Rodriguez v. Puerto Rico Tel. Co., 110 F.3d 174, 179 (1st Cir. 1997) See also I.N.S. v. Delgado, 466 U.S. 210, 104 S. Ct. 1758, 80 L. Ed. 2d 247 (1984)

action based on invasion of privacy can proceed by determining whether the employer's behavior is considered outrageous. For example, secret surveillance of the entrance door to the ladies' locker room with a video camera did not meet this standard. The court held that the means chosen by the employer purported to document the dereliction of duty by a male supervisor and a female employee was the "least indiscriminate possible for achieving a lawful and important objective."[1562] In contrast, videotaping fashion models while they undress for no legitimate business purpose is actionable.[1563]

While the U.S. Supreme Court held that a government physician on suspension had a reasonable expectation that his office would not be searched,[1564] the Court laid out a balancing test to be applied where an employer wishes to use surveillance of its facility and/or employees. In essence, an employee's expectation of privacy must be assessed in the full context of the particular employment situation.[1565] For instance, one court found no reasonable expectation of privacy against video surveillance of an unenclosed locker area not sealed from view.[1566] Another jurisdiction found no reasonable expectation of privacy in an unlocked desk located in an open and accessible area.[1567]

An employee who does not share his office may have an expectation of privacy, but he does not have an expectation of privacy as to the contents of his computer hard drive.[1568] Use of the Internet on company time, the U.S. Court of Appeals, Fourth Circuit wrote,

[1562] Brazinski v. Amoco Petroleum Additives Co., 6 F.3d 1176 (7th Cir. 1993)
[1563] Doe by Doe v. B.P.S. Guard Servs., Inc., 945 F.2d 1422 (8th Cir. 1991)
[1564] O'Connor v. Ortega, 480 U.S. 709, 107 S. Ct. 1492, 94 L. Ed. 2d 714 (1987)
[1565] Vega-Rodriguez v. Puerto Rico Tel. Co., 110 F.3d 174, 178 (1st Cir. 1997)
[1566] Thompson v. Johnson Cty. Cmty. Coll., 930 F. Supp. 501 (D. Kan. 1996), aff'd, 108 F.3d 1388 (10th Cir. 1997), and aff'd sub nom. Boyer v. Johnson Cty. Bd. of Cty. Comm'rs, 108 F.3d 1388 (10th Cir. 1997)
[1567] O'Bryan v. KTIV Television, 868 F. Supp. 1146, 1159 (N.D. Iowa 1994), aff'd in part, rev'd in part, 64 F.3d 1188 (8th Cir. 1995)
[1568] United States v. Simons, 206 F.3d 392 (4th Cir. 2000)

gives rise to no legitimate expectation of privacy. However, in this court decision, the employer had previously instituted a policy that specifically prohibited accessing unlawful material and advised employees that the employer would be conducting electronic audits that could identify websites visited by an individual.

Whether an employee has a reasonable expectation of privacy as to the contents of his locker has split the courts of several states. For example, the Maryland Court of Appeals ruled that a warrantless search of an employee's locker by his employer, with police participation, was reasonable and did not violate the Fourth Amendment.[1569] The Texas Court of Appeals reached the opposite conclusion.[1570]

An employer should move cautiously in this area as the law is evolving by both statute[1571] and court decisions.[1572] Some courts have ruled that an employer may be overly intrusive when it monitors without any valid business reason.[1573]

[1569] Faulkner v. State, 317 Md. 441, 564 A.2d 785 (1989)
[1570] K-Mart Corp. Store No. 7441 v. Trotti, 677 S.W.2d 632 (Tex. App. 1984), writ refused NRE sub nom. Trotti v. K-Mart Corp. No. 7441, 686 S.W.2d 593 (Tex. 1985)
[1571] See The Omnibus Crime Control & Safe Streets Act of 1968 (known as "The Federal Wiretap statute"), 18 U.S.C.A. 2510-2522; The Electronic Communications Privacy Act of 1986, 18 U.S.C.A. 2701-2711; The Virginia wiretap statute mirrors the federal law. Va. Code 19.2-61 et seq
[1572] See Andersen Consulting LLP v. UOP, 991 F. Supp. 1041 (N.D. Ill. 1998)
[1573] See Berry v. Funk, 146 F.3d 1003 (D.C. Cir. 1998); Sanders v. Robert Bosch Corp., 38 F.3d 736, 741 (4th Cir. 1994)

F.   Workplace Violence

When violence occurs in the health care workplace, federal workplace violence guidelines, accreditation standards, and common law duties will be used to measure the facility's performance. An employee is granted immunity from civil liability that might result from his truthfully reporting a co-worker's threatening conduct making one reasonably apprehensive of death or bodily injury.[1574]

1. Occupational Safety & Health Administration

The general rule under the Occupational Safety and Health Act of 1970 is:

> [Each employer] shall furnish to each of his employees employment and a place of employment which are free from recognized hazards that are causing or are likely to cause death or serious physical harm to his employees.[1575]

If violence causes the death of an employee, the health care provider must notify the Occupational Safety & Health Administration (OSHA) within eight hours. OSHA must also be advised if three or more employees are injured seriously enough to require hospitalization.[1576] OSHA may fine a health care provider when violence presented a recognized hazard but the provider failed to minimize the risk of the hazard. "An unabated recognized hazard" can leave the facility liable.[1577]

[1574]   Va. Code 40.1-51.4:5

[1575]   29 U.S.C.A. 645(a)(1)

[1576]   29 C.F.R. 1904.8(a)

[1577]   For example, see "Psychiatric Hospital in Chicago Cited by OSHA for Workplace Violence," 23 OSHA Rep. (BNA) No. 22, p. 646 (10/27/93)

Focusing on the health care industry, OSHA issued its *Guidelines for Preventing Workplace Violence for Health Care & Social Service Workers*[1578] in 1996. OSHA did not mince words when it stated its position:

> For many years, health care and social service workers have faced a significant risk of job-related violence. Assaults represent a serious safety and health hazard for these industries and violence against their employees continues to increase.[1579]

OSHA expects a health care provider's safety program to include: [1580]

1. Management commitment and employee involvement;

2. Worksite analysis;

3. Hazard prevention and control; and

4. Safety and health training

2. Medicare and Accreditation Standards

State surveyors, under HCFA authority, may investigate incidents of violence as "in response to allegations of substantial noncompliance."[1581] This is especially true when a patient's safety is at issue.

The Joint Commission decided in 1996 not to create new standards for workplace violence prevention.[1582] However, it does require a

---

[1578] OSHA, Guidelines for Preventing Workplace Violence for Health care and Social Service Workers (1996) ("Guidelines")

[1579] Guidelines, p. 1

[1580] Guidelines, note 16

[1581] 42 C.F.R. 488.7(a), 488.1

[1582] "Hospital Accreditation Panel Won't Add A Workplace Violence Standard," 2 <u>Workplace Violence Rep.</u> No. 12, p. 4 (12/96)

hospital[1583] and a home health care agency[1584] to have a security management plan and now lists workplace violence as a Sentinel Event.[1585]

[1583] Joint Commission, 1997 Hospital Accreditation Standards, EC.1.4 at 185-186 (1997)

[1584] Joint Commission, 1995 Accreditation Manual for Home Care, EC.1.2 at 345 (1995)

[1585] See Joint Commission, Sentinel Event Alert, Issue 45: Preventing violence in the health care setting

G. Protection of Whistle-Blowers

Virginia is generally an employment-at-will state. That is, an employee may be terminated at anytime unless an express contract is to the contrary.[1586] However, narrow "public policy" exceptions to the at-will doctrine have been recognized. For example, an employee was able to state a cause of action where her employment was terminated after she exposed the efforts by directors of a bank to rig a shareholder vote to merge bank corporations.[1587] The Supreme Court of Virginia cited with approval several cases from other states that held causes of action arose from being fired in retaliation for insisting that an employer comply with statutes.[1588] However, the Supreme Court later explained that it did not create a general cause of action for "retaliatory discharge."[1589] The exception to the at-will employment doctrine is limited to discharges that violate public policy underlying laws designed to protect property rights, personal freedoms, health, safety, or welfare of people in general.[1590] Based on this guidance from the Supreme Court, one circuit court judge has held that a nursing home employee stated a cause of action where she alleged that she was terminated for cooperating with a

---

[1586]   Miller v. SEVAMP, 234 Va. 462, 465 (1987)

[1587]   Bowman v. State Bank of Keysville, 229 Va. 534 (1985)

[1588]   For example, Sheets v. Teddy's Frosted Foods, Inc., 179 Conn. 471, 427 A.2d 385 (1980) (at-will employee fired in retaliation for his insistence that his employer comply with state food labeling laws); Sabine Pilot Serv., Inc. v. Hauck, 687 S.W.2d 733 (Tex. 1985) (employee discharged for refusal to perform illegal act); Harless v. First Nat. Bank in Fairmont, 162 W. Va. 116, 246 S.E.2d 270 (1978) (bank employee discharged in retaliation for his efforts to require employer to comply with state and federal credit protection laws).

[1589]   Miller v. SEVAMP, 234 Va. 462, 465 (1987)

[1590]   Miller v. SEVAMP, 234 Va. 462, 467-68 (1987); Mitchem v. Counts, 259 Va. 179 (2000)

state investigator.[1591] A health care employer must also be mindful of whistle-blower protection available to employees under federal fraud and abuse statutes, discussed in Chapter VI. In contrast, a federal court of appeals rejected a wrongful discharge lawsuit by a former hospital safety manager who claimed she was fired after speaking out on the quality of internal air at the hospital and other concerns. Her confrontational and inflexible approach was not cured after being advised to do so.[1592]

[1591] Seay v. Grace Jefferson Home, 1992 WL 884536 (Va. Cir. Ct. 1992)
[1592] Craven v. Univ. of Colorado Hosp. Auth., 260 F.3d 1218 (10th Cir. 2001)

H. Employment Contracts for Health Care Professionals

In drafting an employment contract between a physician and a practice, one ought to approach it in a manner similar to a pre-nuptial agreement with an eye toward what happens if the relationship does not continue in bliss. One needs to pay equal attention to defining the relationship between the parties while the physician is practicing with the group as well as to what will occur when the physician decides to leave or is asked to leave the group. Both parties need to consider what is reasonable in either situation.

1. Who Can Employ Physicians?

Licensed professionals can form many different business entities in which to render professional services. For example, a physician could practice in a corporation, a professional corporation, a limited liability company, a limited liability partnership, a general partnership, or a sole proprietorship. Usually a provider will be best served by forming a corporation or limited-liability entity. Determining the one best for a particular situation requires the assistance of both an attorney and an accountant who are experienced in health care management.

Unlike many states, Virginia law does not appear to prohibit a physician from being directly employed by a non-professional corporation.[1593] However, the agreement must provide "authority for the physician to exercise control over diagnosis and treatment of patients, and to exercise professional judgment that is not improperly influenced by commercial or lay concerns and that does

---

[1593]   1992 Va. Atty Gen. Op. DL-8 interpreting Va. Code 54.1-2900 et seq. Also see Va. Code 54.1-111.D, amended by HB 605 (2008)

not alter physician-patient relationship".[1594] In contrast, dentists and optometrists are prohibited from being employed by a non-professional corporation.[1595] Professional corporations are permitted to use independent contractors to render professional services.[1596]

2. Non-Compete Clauses

A non-compete clause is a common effort to prevent a physician from leaving a practice and starting a competing practice. Virginia courts will enforce a non-compete agreement if it is limited in scope and reasonable. However, courts often look for ways to void it.[1597] "Since the restraint sought to be imposed restricts the employee in the exercise of a gainful occupation, it is a restraint of trade, and it is carefully examined and strictly construed before the covenant will be enforced."[1598] For example, one court held that a non-compete agreement would not be enforced because it was silent as to the scenario of where the contract simply expired and was not renewed.[1599] Another court found that an agreement not to practice medicine at all after leaving the employer was over broad.[1600] Prohibiting an anesthesiologist from practicing in a county may be too broad where the employer's practice is limited to a single hospital.[1601]

Virginia courts will consider the following factors in determining if a non-competition agreement will be enforced:[1602]

[1594] 1992 Va. Atty Gen. Op. DL-8
[1595] Va. Code 54.1-3205 and 54.1-2716
[1596] HB1863 (2003) amending Va. Code 13.1-546 and 13.1-1107, which reversed Palumbo v. Bennett, 242 Va. 248, 251 (1991) citing Va. Code 13.1-546
[1597] Modern Environments Inc. v. Stinnett, 263 Va. 491 (2002)
[1598] Clinch Valley Physicians, Inc. v. Garcia, 243 Va. 286, 289 quoting with approval Linville v. Servisoft of Va., 211 Va. 53, 55 (1970)
[1599] Shenandoah Chiropractic, Inc. v. Berman, 40 Va. Cir. 297 (1996)
[1600] Alexander v. Shah, 51 Va. Cir. 527 (1995)
[1601] Statkus v. Loudoun Anesthesia Associates, L.L.C., 42 Va. Cir. 35 (1996)
[1602] Blue Ridge Anesthesia and Critical Care v. Gidick, 239 Va. 369 (1990)

1. Is the restraint, from the standpoint of the employer, reasonable in the sense that it is no greater then is necessary to protect the employer in some legitimate business interest?

2. From the standpoint of the employee, is the restraint reasonable in the sense that it is not unduly harsh and oppressive in curtailing his legitimate efforts to earn a livelihood?[1603]

3. Is the restraint reasonable from the standpoint of a sound public policy?[1604]

A non-competition agreement is justified, in the opinion of the Supreme Court of Virginia, when an employee is in personal contact with his employer's customers. The employee need not have access to confidential information or trade secrets of his employer.[1605] No explicit consideration needs to be paid to an employee in return for signing a non-compete agreement. For example, the Court has held that mere continuation of at-will employment after signing a non-compete agreement was sufficient consideration.[1606]

An employee subject to a non-compete agreement may be in violation of such a contract by aiding a spouse in conducting a competing business.[1607] This includes the use of joint marital assets to fund the spouse's company. Diverting the employer's contracts to the spouse's corporation may be viewed as a common law conspiracy justifying the imposition of a constructive trust in favor of the employer.[1608]

[1603] Modern Environments Inc. v. Stinnett, 263 Va.491 (2002)

[1604] Paramont Termite Control Co. v. Rector, 238 Va. 171, 174 (1989) citing Roanoke Eng. Sales v. Rosenbaum, 223 Va. 548, 552 (1982)

[1605] Blue Ridge Anesthesia & Critical Care, Inc. v. Gidick, 239 Va. 369, 372 (1990) citing Paramont Termite Control Co. v. Rector, 238 Va. 171, 175 (1989)

[1606] Paramont Termite Control Co. v. Rector, 238 Va. 171, 176 (1989)

[1607] Rash v. Hilb, Rogal & Hamilton Co. of Richmond, 251 Va. 281 (1996)

[1608] Rash v. Hilb, Rogal & Hamilton Co. of Richmond, 251 Va. 281, 287 (1996)

3. *Use of Employer's Information*

A physician cannot use confidential information obtained during his employment to set up a competing practice:[1609]

> The usual rule is that a former employee, after termination of his employment, may compete with his former employer, the only restraint being that he may not use the confidential information or trade secrets obtained from the former employer, appropriating, in effect, to his competitive advantage what rightfully belongs to his employer.[1610]

This translates into the principal that a physician is not entitled to solicit patients for his future employer before the end of his current employment.[1611] He is allowed to solicit patients after he leaves the employment, particularly those recalled from memory.[1612] Covert copying of a patient list for use after leaving to open a competing practice has been found by a trial court to be conversion[1613] and a compensable injury to the employer.[1614] Obviously, valuation of a patient list is challenging.

The determination of whether specific conduct taken prior to resignation breaches a fiduciary duty requires a case-by-case analysis.[1615] The right to make arrangements to resign, including plans to compete with employer, is not absolute. The policy of free competition must be balanced with the integrity and fairness attached to the relationship between employer and employee.

[1609] Nida v. Bus. Advisory Sys., Inc., 44 Va. Cir. 487 (1998); Restatement (Second) of Agency 393 (1958), Comment a.

[1610] Cmty. Counselling Serv., Inc. v. Reilly, 317 F.2d 239, 244 (4th Cir. 1963)

[1611] Restatement (Second) of Agency 393 (1958), Comment e.

[1612] Peace v. Conway, 246 Va. 278 (1993); Restatement (Second) of Agency 396 (1958) and Comment b

[1613] *Conversion* in civil law is analogous to theft at criminal law

[1614] Sci. Enterprises, Inc. v. George, 47 Va. Cir. 9 (1998)

[1615] Feddeman & Company, CPA v. Langan Associates, 260 Va. 35 (2000)

Willful and malicious efforts to interfere with an employer's practice by departing physicians can result in an award of treble damages. In one case, two physicians were found liable to a physician who owned several dialysis centers for treble damages when they undertook to damage his practice and develop their own.[1616]

From a departing physician's perspective, a practice must not attempt to interfere with the new practice of departing physicians. For example, several physicians were allowed to proceed toward trial with their lawsuit where their former practice and other defendants allegedly said that the physicians "abandoned their patients" and that there were "concerns about their competence."[1617]

The better course for a physician leaving a practice is for her to do so on the best terms possible. Hopefully, the employment agreement will give the practice and the physician a road map of how the separation will occur. Both parties need to do their best to leave emotions aside and work toward an amiable parting.

[1616]   Greenspan v. Osheroff, 232 Va. 388 (1986)
[1617]   Fuste v. Riverside Health care Ass'n, Inc., 265 Va. 127 (2003)

V. Licensure, Medical Staff Privileges & Insurance

A. Professional Licensure

1. Defining the Practice of Medicine

What constitutes the practice of medicine is difficult to define. The Virginia Code describes the practice of medicine as "the prevention, diagnosis and treatment of human physical or mental ailments, conditions, diseases, pain or infirmities by any means or methods."[1618] The Attorney General has pointed out that the key element of the statute is for a diagnosis that requires 'the exercise of independent medical judgment."[1619] *Surgery* was defined by the General Assembly in 2012 as "structural alteration of the human body by the incision or cutting into of tissue for the purpose of diagnostic or therapeutic treatment of conditions or disease processes by any instrument causing localized alteration or transposition of live human tissue, but does not include the following: procedures for the removal of superficial foreign bodies from the human body, punctures, injections, dry needling, acupuncture, or removal of dead tissue. For the purposes of this section, incision shall not mean the scraping or brushing of live tissue."[1620] *Surgery* is limited to physicians, podiatrists, dentists, nurse practitioners, physician assistants under the supervision of a physician or podiatrist, licensed midwives in the performance of episiotomies during childbirth, and one action pursuant to the orders and under appropriate supervision of a physician, podiatrist or dentist.[1621]

In practice, defining the limits between physicians, nurses and other health care providers has become increasingly blurred. The

---

[1618]   Va. Code 54.1-2900
[1619]   The Honorable Phoebe M. Orebaugh, 1990 Va. Op. Atty. Gen. 203, citing Att'y Gen. Ann. Rep.: 1989 at 281, 282; 1984-1988 at 172, 173
[1620]   Va. Code 54.1-2400.01:1.A
[1621]   Va. Code 54.1-2400.01:1.B

Department of Health Professions (DHP) has shown little interest in drawing bright lines. For example, many hospitals now have medical information lines staffed by nurses. A nurse often conducts "telephone triage" in a physician's office. Pursuant to statute, collaborative agreements between a physician and a pharmacist can now be made.[1622]

2. *Licensure*

The criteria for licensure of a health care professional are set forth by statute and regulation. Interpretation of the criteria can be highly subjective. This can make the licensure process particularly frustrating for a practitioner who does not have a traditional American education and training experience. For example, foreign medical graduates may be far more carefully scrutinized than the lowest achiever in an American medical school.

Interns and residents holding temporary licenses may be employed by hospitals, medical schools or other organizations operating graduate medical education programs.[1623]

Beginning in 2007, administrators of assisted-living facilities are required to be licensed by the Board of Long-Term Care Administrators (previously known as the Board of Nursing Home Administrators).[1624]

The General Assembly passed legislation in 2005 for the Board of Medicine to license Certified Professional Midwives (CPM).[1625] This is a category separate and apart from nurse practitioners certified as

---

[1622] 18 Va. Admin. Code 110-40-10 through 70, under authority of Va. Code 54.1-3300.1

[1623] Va. Code 54.1-2961

[1624] SB1183 (2005) amending Va. Code 54.1-3100 *et seq.* Regulations governing assisted living administrators can be found at 18 Va. Admin. Code 95-30-10

[1625] HB 2038 and SB 1259 (2005) enacting Va. Code 54.1-2957.7 *et seq.*

nurse midwives. As part of the political compromise, the legislation also provides immunity to physicians, nurses, pre-hospital emergency personnel and hospitals for negligent acts committed by a CPM.

Beginning in 2016, applicants for licensure as practical nurses or registered nurses must submit fingerprints and undergo a criminal background check.[1626]

3. Application

Application for a practitioner's license must be made to the appropriate Board within the Department of Health Professionals (DHP). Usually, this is a routine matter. However, those who have trained abroad or have something unusual in their background may be asked to appear before a panel of Board[1627] members to discuss the situation.

4. Renewal

Renewal of a practitioner's license is usually a matter of merely assuring that the Board has the professional's current address and paying the appropriate fee. However, as part of the movement toward informing consumers about practitioners, a physician must report and make available the following information:[1628]

1. Medical school & graduation date;

2. Graduate education;

[1626] Va. Code 54.1-3005.1

[1627] "Board" is used throughout this chapter to indicate the Board of Medicine. However, the Boards of Nursing, Dentistry, Veterinary Medicine, Nursing Home Administrators and other professions operate in a similar manner.

[1628] Va. Code 54.1-2910.1. The Board of Medicine has been charged with promulgating regulations for this consumer program. This report will also include information about medical malpractice settlements or awards.

3. Specialty board certification or eligibility for certification;

4. Number of years in active, clinical practice;

5. Any hospital affiliations

6. Medical school faculty appointments and peer-reviewed publications;

7. Location of offices and percentage of practice time at each;

8. Access to translating service;

9. Whether the physician participates in Medicaid;

10. Any disciplinary actions required to be reported to the Board;

11. Conviction of any felony; and

12. Other information related to the competency of the physician.

A physician licensed in Virginia is obligated to keep his physician profile current on the Board of Medicine's web site. A physician needs to be diligent to update the information at least once a year. If a patient requests, a physician or podiatrist must inform the patient of how to access the Board of Medicine physician profile.[1629]

Pursuant to a statutory mandate, the Board has adopted regulations to ensure continuing competency.[1630] This includes continuing education,[1631] testing and other requirements that would address ethical practice, appropriate standard of care, patient safety, application of new medical technology, appropriate communication with patients and knowledge of the changing health care system. For license renewal, a physician, chiropractor or podiatrist must complete 60 hours of continuing education within the immediate prior two years.[1632] Thirty of these hours must be Type 1 activities, and 15 of the Type 1 hours must be in face-to-face activities. Of the

[1629] Va. Code 54.1-2910.01
[1630] Va. Code 54.1-2912.1
[1631] 18 Va. Admin. Code 85-20-235. Continued competency requirements for renewal of active license
[1632] 18 Va. Admin. Code 85-20-235

thirty Type 2 hours, a practitioner must include activities on ethics, standards of care, patient safety, new medical technology and patient communication. Certification of completing the required CME is to be done on a form provided by the Board.[1633] The Board will also accept evidence of specialty recertification or an AMA Physician Recognition Award.[1634] The practitioner must retain records of CME activities for six years.[1635] The Board may grant an extension for meeting these requirements for up to one year if good cause is shown.[1636] The Board may also exempt a practitioner from all or some of these requirements for circumstances beyond the practitioner's control.[1637] The Board must assess the competency of a physician who has settled three medical malpractice actions of greater than $75,000 each in a ten year period.[1638]

A physician who is not actively practicing may apply for an inactive license.[1639] The Board is quite adamant that one holding an inactive license is not allowed to perform any service for which an active license is required.[1640] Reinstatement of an inactive or lapsed license of more than two years but less than four years may occur after the appropriate application, payment of fees, and certification of meeting the continuing education requirements for the number of years that the license has been inactive or lapsed.[1641] If one's license has been inactive or lapsed for more than four years, the physician must pass the Special Purpose Examination (SPEX).[1642]

[1633] See Va. Board of Medicine, "Board Briefs," #59, Winter 1999. The form is also available at http://www.dhp.state.va.us/medicine/medicine_forms.htm#CME

[1634] Va. Board of Medicine, "Board Briefs," #59, Winter 1999

[1635] 18 Va. Admin. Code 85-20-235.C

[1636] 18 Va. Admin. Code 85-20-235

[1637] 18 Va. Admin. Code 85-20-235

[1638] Va. Code 54.1-2912.3

[1639] 18 Va. Admin. Code 85-20-236

[1640] 18 Va. Admin. Code 85-20-236; also see Va. Board of Medicine, "Board Briefs," #59, Winter 1999

[1641] 18 Va. Admin. Code 85-20-240

[1642] 18 Va. Admin. Code 85-20-240.C

5. *Enforcement Actions*

Under continued public and political pressure, the Department of Health Professions (DHP) takes every complaint it receives very seriously. Therefore, a health care provider should be very careful in responding to any inquiry by DHP, regardless of how spurious the complaint may appear. To do otherwise is to risk even more scrutiny. The list of "unprofessional conduct" is described by statute.[1643] The Board construes this quite broadly and will sanction a physician for activities that are clearly not part of practicing medicine, e.g. tax evasion or sexual harassment of hospital employees.[1644] Defaults on educational loans will result in suspension of professional licensure.[1645] The Board has the authority to summarily suspend or restrict a physician's license.[1646]

In limited circumstances, the Board may offer a Confidential Consent Agreement (CCA) for situations involving minor misconduct where there is little or no injury to a patient or the public and little likelihood of repetition by the practitioner.[1647] For example, a CCA may be used when a physician fails to update her Physician Profile in a timely manner.

a. Investigation

When DHP receives a *complaint*, the Department staff undertakes an investigation. DHP is also now routinely investigating all settlements

---

[1643] Va. Code 54.1-2915; the court will give deference to an agency in interpreting its regulations, such as the definition of "unprofessional conduct." Leonard v. Va. Board of Veterinary Medicine, unpublished, 2015 WL 10990105 (Va. 2015)

[1644] See Board of Medicine Regulations, 18 Va. Admin. Code 85-20-10 *et seq.* Other states have upheld such broad interpretation of "unprofessional conduct." For example, see Bd. of Physician Quality Assur. v. Banks, 354 Md. 59, 729 A.2d 376 (1999)

[1645] Va. Code 54.1-2400.5

[1646] Va. Code 54.1-2408.1

[1647] Va. Code 54.1-2400(14); see Board of Medicine, Guidance Document 85-23 adopted October 9, 2003

and adverse verdicts in medical malpractice actions. Much of this information is received from mandatory reports made by insurers, hospitals and other entities. No matter how specious or vindictive an allegation may appear to a practitioner, DHP will look into the matter. Any person who makes a voluntary report to DHP is granted civil immunity.[1648]

A practitioner should always take any inquiry by a DHP investigator quite seriously and experienced counsel should be consulted. The Department may not tell the health care provider that is being interviewed whether she is the target of the investigation. However, a complaint or report and any supporting documentation should be provided to the licensee before she is interviewed, unless it would materially obstruct a criminal or regulatory investigation.[1649]

Berating, ignoring or otherwise challenging an investigator should be avoided. Failure to cooperate can result in administrative sanction as well as criminal prosecution.[1650] Likewise, a health care provider should be able to expect an investigator to behave in a courteous, truthful, and otherwise professional manner. Counsel for the practitioner may be needed to intercede and reduce friction between the health care provider and the investigator. One who is the target of an investigation is well advised to always be represented by counsel when meeting with a DHP investigator.

Information received, developed or maintained by any health regulatory board in connection with a possible disciplinary

---

[1648]   Va. Code 54.1-2400.6 and 54.1-2400.8; See Hatten v. Campbell, (Rockwell, J.) (Chesterfield Cir. Ct. 6/5/2006) (respiratory therapist survived demurrer under statute by alleging sufficient facts that the report was made in "bad faith")

[1649]   Va. Code 54.1-2400.2

[1650]   Va. Code 54.1-111.A.7; 18 Va. Admin. Code 85-20-105; See Hill v. Commonwealth, 2006 Va. App. LEXIS 16 (2006) (Couple convicted of failing to cooperate with warrantless search related to their manufacture of goat cheese).

proceeding is kept strictly confidential. Such confidential information may be disclosed only: [1651]

1. In a disciplinary proceeding or in a subsequent trial or appeal of an action or order;

2. To licensing authorities for a health profession;

3. To hospital committees concerned with granting, limiting or denying hospital privileges if a final determination regarding a violation has been made;

4. Pursuant to an order of a court of competent jurisdiction;

5. For research or educational purposes, if personally identifiable information has been removed;

6. To the Health Practitioners' Intervention Program with the Department in connection with health practitioners who apply to or participate in the Program; or

7. To law enforcement or regulators for further investigation[1652]

Of importance to a practitioner, confidential information received, maintained or developed by any board, or disclosed by a board to others, should "in no event" be disclosed in discovery or used as evidence in medical malpractice actions or other lawsuits arising out of the provision of or failure to provide services.[1653] However, orders and notices of the health regulatory boards are available to the public.[1654] A Board must notify a complainant of hearing dates and disposition.[1655]

If a physician has three judgments or settlements of more than

---

[1651] Va. Code 54.1-2400.2.A. The limited disclosure was clarified or broadened, depending on one's perspective, in 2009 to allow investigators to review documents with fact witnesses to refresh their recollection. Va. Code 54.1-2400.2.H, added by HB 1852 (2009)

[1652] Va. Code 54.1-2400.2.E and F

[1653] Va. Code 54.1-2400.2.B

[1654] Va. Code 54.1-2400.2.G

[1655] Va. Code 54.1-2400.2

$75,000 each in medical malpractice actions within ten years, the Board must require the physician to undergo a competency evaluation.[1656]

b. Obligation of Health Care Providers and Others to Report

A hospital and other licensed facilities must report to the Department of Health Professions about any licensed individual with regard to impairment, misconduct, disciplinary action or resignation while under investigation.[1657] When the chief executive officer or chief of staff becomes aware in his official capacity, he must report a situation within thirty days. The report must be made within five days of admission or commitment for substance abuse or psychiatric disorder.[1658] The controversial aspect of this amendment is the requirement that any disciplinary action taken or *begun* against a practitioner must be reported to DHP within thirty days of notifying the practitioner. He must be given an opportunity to review the report, and he may submit a separate statement. Failure to report to DHP may result in a civil penalty up to $25,000.

Every licensed or certified provider who treats a practitioner must report to the Department of Health Professions when a practitioner is being treated for a mental disorder, chemical dependency or alcoholism, unless prohibited by federal law or the treater makes a determination that the professional is competent to continue practice or would not constitute a danger to himself, his patients or the public.[1659] Anyone who makes a report, whether mandatory or

---

[1656] Va. Code 54.1-2912.3
[1657] Va. Code 54.1-2400.6
[1658] Caution should be taken when a healthcare provider is enrolled in a federally-funded substance or alcohol abuse rehabilitation program. Va. Code 54.1-2400.6.E provides that information protected under 42 CFR, Part 2 should not be divulged.
[1659] Va. Code 54.1-2400.7

not, is granted immunity from any civil liability unless the report was made in bad faith or malicious intent.[1660]

The presidents of professional organizations are required to report disciplinary actions taken against any member that is licensed by the Board of Medicine for conduct that causes or is likely to cause injury to a patient, a breach of professional ethics, incompetence, moral turpitude, or substance abuse.[1661] Reports must be made within thirty days. If a society receives a complaint against a member, it may request that the Board of Medicine investigate in lieu of the society. Failure to report may result in a civil penalty of up to $5,000.

Any person licensed by the Department of Health Professions,[1662] presidents of medical societies, health care institutions, malpractice insurance carriers and health maintenance organizations must report the following matters to the Board of Medicine within thirty days: [1663]

1. Any disciplinary action;
2. Any malpractice judgment;
3. Any settlement of a malpractice claim; and
4. Any evidence that indicates a reasonable probability that a person may be incompetent, has engaged in misconduct that causes or is likely to cause injury, has engaged in unprofessional conduct or may be mentally or physically unable to practice safely.

The requirements of this section are deemed to have been met if a report is made to the National Practitioner Data Bank and notice of the report is provided to the Board of Medicine. Likewise, a provider does not need to submit an additional report if she is aware that

---

[1660] Va. Code 54.1-2400.8

[1661] Va. Code 54.1-2908

[1662] This includes the provider who is the subject of the investigation, disciplinary action, malpractice settlement, etc.

[1663] Va. Code 54.1-2909

the matter has already been reported to the Department. Failure to make a report may result in a civil penalty up to $5,000.

c. Informal Conference

The Board will notify a practitioner that an informal conference has been scheduled and the allegations that will be considered.[1664] In response to consumer pressure, the Board must also notify the complainant of the hearing dates and disposition.[1665] An informal conference can be requested due to any concern of a Board member. This may be nothing more than a desire to obtain further information. Occasionally the forum is used by a Board member to convey a message to the practitioner. The professional is entitled to all of the information to be relied upon by an Informal Conference Committee. Often overlooked, even by counsel, is the right of the practitioner to also submit information to the committee. The better approach is to do this by a written submission provided to the Board in sufficient time that the committee members can receive it along with the investigator's information. (The Board has recently begun setting a deadline for submission of exhibits prior to the hearing.) This will present both sides of the issue to the committee before an adverse first impression is formed and reinforced by time. A practitioner should take steps well ahead of an informal conference to assure that his professional life is in order. Are CMEs up to date? Can corrective actions be taken to reassure the Board that a prior situation will not happen again?

Traditionally an Informal Conference Committee was composed of three Board members. None of the members need be of the same profession as the practitioner. In 2004, the General Assembly granted authority to the Board to delegate some informal fact-finding proceedings to "agency subordinates," which is defined as a single Board member, Board staff, or other qualified individual.[1666] Board

---

[1664] Va. Code 2.2-4019
[1665] Va. Code 54.1-2400.2
[1666] Va. Code 54.1-2400

regulations limit the types of cases to be heard by a subordinate to profiling, CME, advertising, defaults on student loans, failure to provide medical records and compliance with previous Board orders.[1667]

At the informal conference, a practitioner, or his counsel,[1668] are usually invited to give an opening statement. The professional's goal should be to articulate as concisely as possible what actually occurred during the incident(s) in question. If the practitioner has already made corrective changes, this should be explained to the committee. Committee members and the adjudication specialist[1669] will then often ask questions of the provider. The practitioner should prepare with counsel for these questions.

Expert witnesses may be called by the Board[1670] and/or by the physician to assist in evaluating the care at issue. For the physician, this can be a difficult challenge to confront. Experts are usually fellow physicians who should be presumed to have the best intentions but may not know all of the facts or may hold a philosophy at odds with the practitioner. This requires intensive preparation to know all of the facts of the case, be able to quickly draw the expert's attention to the document containing the fact and be agile in using reputable medical literature to challenge the expert's opinions. To do this well, one needs the skills of an experienced medical trial attorney.

[1667] 18 Va. Admin. Code 85-15-10 et seq.

[1668] Under the Administrative Procedures Act, parties may be accompanied by counsel for both informal and formal proceedings. Va. Code 9-6.14:11 and 14:12(C). This consistent is with "well-defined public policy." See Com. v. Edwards, 235 Va. 499 (1988). Likewise, one can contend that a physician should have a right to counsel during questioning by a Board investigator.

[1669] An adjudication specialist is often a paralegal or other non-lawyer who acts like a prosecutor in presenting the case to the informal conference committee

[1670] Va. Code 54.1-2925

Under the Virginia Administrative Process Act,[1671] a professional is entitled to know what the allegations are against him and upon what information will be relied. This is a very important point that is often overlooked by committee members as they inquire on unrelated matters. Counsel, as gently as possible, needs to steer the committee member back to the allegations as charged and the articulated information. This can be extremely challenging as a strong-willed committee member heads down a path of questioning and only becomes more zealous when he meets resistance.

At the end of an Informal Conference, the committee will go into a closed session to determine its recommendation. The committee will usually recommend that the practitioner should be fully exonerated of the charges or that corrective action is necessary. For example, the committee may recommend that a monetary fine be imposed; the professional's license be suspended or terminated; the professional be placed under the supervision of another professional; the professional attend a specified continuing education course; the professional participate in the Health Practitioners Intervention Program; or such other remedy as the committee deems appropriate for the situation. The recommendation will be offered to the professional in the form of a consent order, which will include findings of fact. If the physician refuses to agree to the committee's conclusion, then the matter will be considered by the full Board for action. Occasionally the committee will decide that it has insufficient information to make a recommendation and refer the matter to the full Board for consideration.

The Virginia General Assembly enacted an informal dispute resolution procedure for nursing facilities.[1672]

d. Hearing

If a practitioner does not accept the recommendation of the Informal

[1671]   Va. Code 2.2-4000 et seq.
[1672]   Va. Code 32.1-126

Conference Committee or if the Committee feels it necessary, the Board will hear the allegations against a practitioner. This is usually conducted in a fashion similar to a trial with witnesses and exhibits being introduced by the Board and by the practitioner. The Board considers all of the evidence independent of the Informal Conference Committee's findings or proposed corrective action. Depending on the seriousness of the charges against the practitioner, an Assistant Attorney General may prosecute the case on behalf of the Commonwealth. A second Assistant Attorney General will be present to provide the Board with legal advice. (The Attorney General rationalizes that no conflict of interest is present by segregating the Assistant Attorneys General into separate divisions.) Unlike a trial, strict rules of evidence are not followed. This is dangerous, as hearsay and other flimsy evidence can be considered by the Board. Witnesses testifying at a hearing are immune from liability for what they say before the Board.[1673] The practitioner has the right to be represented by an attorney, and the Board must comply with the Administrative Procedures Act. The Board usually invites statements by the practitioner, or her counsel, at the beginning and end of the hearing. After hearing all the evidence, the Board deliberates in a closed session to draft findings of fact and an order.

e. Legal Remedies

Historically, the health care provider had little remedy in Virginia courts against adverse DHP decisions. Such review by a trial court was limited to assuring that the Board followed the Administrative Process Act,[1674] the agency did not make a procedural error that was not harmless, and the Board had sufficient evidentiary support for its findings of fact.[1675] The court did not conduct a trial *de novo*.

[1673] Lindeman v. Lesnick, 268 Va. 532 (2004); also see Va. Code 8.01-581.19:1

[1674] Virginia Administrative Procedures Act, Va. Code 2.2-4000 et seq.

[1675] Hurwitz v. Bd. of Med., 46 Va. Cir. 119 (1998) citing Johnston-Willis, Ltd. v. Kenley, 6 Va. App. 231, 242 (1988); Goad v. Virginia Board of Medicine, 40 Va. App. 621 (2003); Abofreka v. Virginia Board of Medicine, 2007 Va. App.LEXIS 304 (2007); In a rare win for the practitioner, the Court of

This means that the court solely looked at the factual record as set forth in the agency proceedings. The court functioned solely as an appellate tribunal.[1676] For example, the Board's decision to deny licensure to a physician who did not do sufficient rotations in an approved residency program would not be reversed on grounds that due process was denied.[1677] The court could reject an agency decision under the substantial evidence test only if the court concluded, after reviewing the record as a whole, that reasonable minds would necessarily reach another conclusion.[1678] Similarly, the Court of Appeals held that any errors committed by an informal hearing were moot once the matter was considered at a formal hearing.[1679] If sufficient evidence was contained in the record, a Board's decision would not be reversed.

In 2013, the standard for review by a circuit court was modified to become: When the decision on review is to be made on the agency record, the duty of the court with respect to issues of fact shall be limited to ascertaining to determine whether there was substantial evidence in the agency record upon which the agency as the trier of the facts could reasonably find them to be as it did to support the agency decision. The duty of the court with respect to the issues of law shall be to review the agency decision de novo.[1680]

Appeals reversed a Board of Dentistry order but the court then ruled that its decision was not to be published. Zurmati v. Virginia Board of Dentistry, Record No. 1250-07-4, 6/17/2008. The Court of Appeals reversed a trial judge who held that a Board improperly interpreted its own regulation. Virginia Board of Veterinary Medicine v. Leonard, unpublished (11/12/14)

[1676] Hurwitz v. Bd. of Med., 46 Va. Cir. 119 (1998) citing School Board of County of York v. Nicely, 12 Va. App. 1051, 1062 (1991).

[1677] Last v. Virginia State Bd. of Med., 14 Va. App. 906, 421 S.E.2d 201 (1992) applying Va. Code 54.1-2930(4)

[1678] Avante at Lynchburg v. Teefey, 28 Va. App. 156 (1998) citing Va. Code 9-6.14:17 and Virginia Real Estate Comm'n v. Bias, 226 Va. 264, 269 (1983)

[1679] John Doe, DDS v. Virginia Board of Dentistry, 51 Va. App. 136 (2008)

[1680] Va. Code 2.2-4027

A suspended or revoked healthcare provider is not permitted to practice while an appeal is pending.[1681]

The U.S. District Court has held that a physician cannot use a federal civil rights action under 42 U.S.C.A. § 1983 (West) to block the Board of Medicine from making a report to the federal Healthcare Integrity and Protection Data Bank (HIPDB).[1682] Likewise, the Supreme Court of Virginia stated that a physician does not have a right to appeal the Board's decision to make the report.[1683] The issue of whether a report is appropriate should be taken up directly with HIPDB.

6. *Physician Extenders*

a. Nurse Practitioners, Nurse Midwives, & Nurse Anesthetists

The General Assembly dramatically overhauled the statutory framework for nurse practitioners in 2012. The strict restrictions that were rarely followed in practice have been lifted. The new statute reads as follows:[1684]

> A. As used in this section:
>
> "Collaboration" means the communication and decision-making process among members of a patient care team related to the treatment and care of a patient and includes (i) communication of data and information about the treatment and care of a patient, including exchange of clinical observations and assessments, and (ii) development of an appropriate plan of care, including decisions regarding the health care provided, accessing and

---

[1681] Va. Code 54.1-2408.3

[1682] Giannoukos v. Harp, 369 F. Supp. 2d 715 (E.D. Va. 2005)

[1683] Giannoukos v. Virginia Board of Medicine, 44 Va. App. 694 (2005)

[1684] Va. Code 54.1-2957 (2016)

assessment of appropriate additional resources or expertise, and arrangement of appropriate referrals, testing, or studies.

"Consultation" means the communicating of data and information, exchanging of clinical observations and assessments, accessing and assessing of additional resources and expertise, problem-solving, and arranging for referrals, testing, or studies.

B. The Board of Medicine and the Board of Nursing shall jointly prescribe the regulations governing the licensure of nurse practitioners. It shall be unlawful for a person to practice as a nurse practitioner in the Commonwealth unless he holds such a joint license.

C. Except as provided in subsection H, a nurse practitioner shall only practice as part of a patient care team. Each member of a patient care team shall have specific responsibilities related to the care of the patient or patients and shall provide health care services within the scope of his usual professional activities. Nurse practitioners practicing as part of a patient care team shall maintain appropriate collaboration and consultation, as evidenced in a written or electronic practice agreement, with at least one patient care team physician. Nurse practitioners who are certified registered nurse anesthetists shall practice under the supervision of a licensed doctor of medicine, osteopathy, podiatry, or dentistry. Nurse practitioners appointed as medical examiners pursuant to § 32.1-282 shall practice in collaboration with a licensed doctor of medicine or osteopathic medicine who has been appointed to serve as a medical examiner pursuant to § 32.1-282. Collaboration and consultation among nurse practitioners and patient care team physicians may be provided through telemedicine as described in § 38.2-3418.16. Practice of patient care teams in all settings shall include the periodic review of patient charts or electronic health records and may include visits to the site where health care is delivered in the manner and at the frequency determined by the patient care team.

Physicians on patient care teams may require that a nurse practitioner be covered by a professional liability insurance policy with limits equal to the current limitation on damages set forth in § 8.01-581.15.

Service on a patient care team by a patient care team member shall not, by the existence of such service alone, establish or create liability for the actions or inactions of other team members.

D. The Board of Medicine and the Board of Nursing shall jointly promulgate regulations specifying collaboration and consultation among physicians and nurse practitioners working as part of patient care teams that shall include the development of, and periodic review and revision of, a written or electronic practice agreement; guidelines for availability and ongoing communications that define consultation among the collaborating parties and the patient; and periodic joint evaluation of the services delivered. Practice agreements shall include a provision for appropriate physician input in complex clinical cases and patient emergencies and for referrals. Evidence of a practice agreement shall be maintained by a nurse practitioner and provided to the Boards upon request. For nurse practitioners providing care to patients within a hospital or health care system, the practice agreement may be included as part of documents delineating the nurse practitioner's clinical privileges or the electronic or written delineation of duties and responsibilities in collaboration and consultation with a patient care team physician.

E. The Boards may issue a license by endorsement to an applicant to practice as a nurse practitioner if the applicant has been licensed as a nurse practitioner under the laws of another state and, in the opinion of the Boards, the applicant meets the qualifications for licensure required of nurse practitioners in the Commonwealth.

F. Pending the outcome of the next National Specialty Examination, the Boards may jointly grant temporary licensure to nurse practitioners.

G. In the event a physician who is serving as a patient care team physician dies, becomes disabled, retires from active practice, surrenders his license or has it suspended or revoked by the Board, or relocates his practice such that he is no longer able to serve, and a nurse practitioner is unable to enter into a new practice agreement with another patient care team physician, the nurse practitioner may continue to practice upon notification to the designee or his alternate of the Boards and receipt of such notification. Such nurse practitioner may continue to treat patients without a patient care team physician for an initial period not to exceed 60 days, provided the nurse practitioner continues to prescribe only those drugs previously authorized by the practice agreement with such physician and to have access to appropriate physician input in complex clinical cases and patient emergencies and for referrals. The designee or his alternate of the Boards shall grant permission for the nurse practitioner to continue practice under this subsection for another 60 days, provided the nurse practitioner provides evidence of efforts made to secure another patient care team physician and of access to physician input.

H. Nurse practitioners licensed by the Boards of Medicine and Nursing in the category of certified nurse midwife shall practice in consultation with a licensed physician in accordance with a practice agreement between the nurse practitioner and the licensed physician. Such practice agreement shall address the availability of the physician for routine and urgent consultation on patient care. Evidence of a practice agreement shall be maintained by a nurse practitioner and provided to the Boards upon request. The Boards shall jointly promulgate regulations, consistent with the Standards for the Practice of Midwifery set by the American College of Nurse-Midwives, governing such practice.

A nurse practitioner[1685] is permitted to prescribe Schedule II through VI controlled substances and devices.[1686] However, this is limited by the written or electronic practice agreement between the nurse

---

[1685] Licensure of nurse practitioners is established by Va. Code 54.1-2957 et seq. Regulations for practice are at 18 Va. Admin. Code 90-30-10 et seq.

[1686] Va. Code 54.1-2957.01.A; 18 Va. Admin. Code 90-40-40; The schedule of controlled substances is set forth in Federal Controlled substances Acts, 21 USC 812. Also see Va. Code 54.1-3303. Dispensing by a nurse practitioner is allowed only where the supervising physician is authorized to dispense. 18 Va. Admin. Code 90-40-120. NP prescribing authority was expanded as of 7/1/03 to include up to Schedule III.

practitioner and a patient care team physician[1687] and the formulary promulgated by the Board of Nursing and Board of Medicine.[1688] The written practice agreement must contain a description of prescriptive authority, an authorization for categories of drugs and devices, and the signature or name of the patient care team physician.[1689]

A nurse practitioner must disclose to the patient at the initial encounter that he is a nurse practitioner.[1690] A patient care team physician is limited to serving in that role to not more than six nurse practitioners at one time.[1691] The prohibition of a nurse practitioner not being allowed to establish a separate office unless practicing as a certified nurse midwife or employed in health clinics funded by the government or nonprofit organizations was stricken in the 2012 reforms.[1692] Legislation in 2004 extended the authority of nurse practitioners to sign forms routinely signed by a physician. However, this authority must be incorporated within the protocol with the collaborating physician.[1693] The authority to render medical advice to emergency medical personnel acting in an emergency situation was extended to nurse practitioners by the General Assembly in 2012.[1694] In 2015, the General Assembly added provisions for a restricted volunteer license for nurse practitioners.[1695]

A certified nurse anesthetist must practice within the Guidelines and

---

[1687] Va. Code 54.1-2957.01.A; 18 Va. Admin. Code 90-30-120.A; 18 Va. Admin. Code 90-40-90

[1688] Va. Code 54.1-2957.01.C

[1689] 18 Va. Admin. Code 90-40-90.C

[1690] Va. Code 54.1-2957.01.E.1; 18 Va. Admin. Code 90-40-110

[1691] Va. Code 54.1-2957.01.E.2; 18 Va. Admin. Code 90-40-100

[1692] Va. Code 54.1-2957.01; 18 VAC 90-40-100.2; HB2656 (2005) established a pilot program for certified nurse midwives to practice more independently in underserved areas.

[1693] Va. Code 32.1-50 and 32.1-60; 18 Va. Admin. Code 90-30-120

[1694] Va. Code 54.1-2901, as amended by HB346 (2012)

[1695] Va. Code 54.1-3011.01

Standards of the American Association of Nurse Anesthetists and under the supervision of a physician, podiatrist or dentist.[1696]

Beginning in 2006, a certified nurse midwife may practice in collaboration and consultation with a physician.[1697] A certified nurse midwife is required to practice in accordance with the Standards for the Practice of Nurse-Midwifery, American College of Nurse-Midwives.[1698] Legislation passed in 2005 provides for the licensure of Certified Professional Midwives.[1699]

b. Physician Assistants

A physician assistant (PA) may prescribe Schedule II through VI controlled substances or devices if authorized by the Board of Medicine. To obtain approval, a PA must provide evidence of a written protocol with a physician or podiatrist who will provide direction and supervision,[1700] successfully pass the NCCPA exam and complete a minimum of thirty-five hours of training acceptable to the Board of Pharmacology.[1701] The formulary for PAs established by the Board of Medicine is identical to that of nurse practitioners described above.[1702] Each prescription by a PA must bear the names of the supervising physician as well as the PA.[1703] A physician can supervise up to six physician assistants.[1704] A PA must wear

---

[1696] 18 Va. Admin. Code 90-30-121
[1697] Va. Code 54.1-2957 and 54.1-2901.A.31 as amended by SB0488 (2006); 18 Va. Admin. Code 90-40-100.A.4
[1698] 18 Va. Admin. Code 90-30-120.D
[1699] Va. Code 54.1-2957.7 et seq. as enacted by HB2038 (2005) & SB1259 (2005)
[1700] Va. Code 54.1-2952.1.A; 18 Va. Admin. Code 85-50-101
[1701] Va. Code 54.1-2952.1; 18 Va. Admin. Code 85-50-130
[1702] Va. Code 54.1-2952.1.C; 18 Va. Admin. Code 85-50-140
[1703] 18 Va. Admin. Code 85-50-160
[1704] Va. Code 54.1-2952.A

identification when seeing patients that clearly identifies that he is a physician assistant.[1705]

In contrast to the regulations for nurse practitioners, a physician supervising a PA must see and evaluate any patient presenting for the same complaint twice in a single episode of care and having failed to improve significantly. A physician must be involved similarly for at least every fourth visit for a continuing illness.[1706] Invasive procedures must be done under direct physician supervision unless the supervising physician has observed the PA perform the procedure three times or more and certifies that the PA is competent.[1707] In an institution, a PA may not render care to a patient unless the physician responsible for the patient has signed the protocol to act as a supervisor. In other words, a physician assistant is not permitted to render independent health care.[1708] In 2005, the scope of practice for a PA in the emergency department was broadened to permit a PA to practice in the ER so long as he remains under the supervision of his employing physician or entity, whether or not the physician is in the facility.[1709] In 2011, the General Assembly enacted a broadly worded statute that says a physician assistant's signature can be accepted whenever a physician's signature is required by law or regulation.[1710] In 2012, a physician's assistant became authorized to use fluoroscopy after completing training and successfully passing an exam.[1711]

[1705] 18 Va. Admin. Code 85-50-115.A.3; Interestingly, another regulation only requires that the PA disclose his status to the patient. 18 Va. Admin. Code 85-50-160
[1706] 18 VAC 85-50-110.1
[1707] 18 Va. Admin. Code 85-50-110.2
[1708] 18 Va. Admin. Code 85-50-115.A
[1709] Va. Code 54.1-2952
[1710] Va. Code 54.1-2952.2
[1711] Va. Code 54.1-2952.C

7. *Other Health Care Professionals*

A patient may utilize a doctor of physical therapy without a physician referral for up to thirty days.[1712] A physical therapist that does not hold a doctorate may perform a one-time evaluation but no treatment in the absence of a physician referral. Otherwise, a referral is required from a physician, nurse practitioner or physician's assistant.

The practice of acupuncture is defined by statute and regulated by the Board of Medicine.[1713] Prior to performing acupuncture, an acupuncturist must obtain written documentation that the patient had received a diagnostic examination from a physician, osteopath, chiropractor, or podiatrist with regard to the ailment or condition to be treated.[1714]

Podiatrists are permitted to perform surgery under general anesthesia only in hospitals or ambulatory surgical centers.[1715] The definition of podiatry was enlarged in 2011 to include diagnosis and treatment of lower extremity ulcers.[1716]

Delegation of nursing tasks and procedures by a registered nurse are regulated by the Board of Nursing.[1717] A nurse may delegate only in accordance with a plan for delegation adopted by the entity responsible for client care.[1718] The delegating nurse must assess the patient and the unlicensed person[1719] and supervise the delegated tasks.[1720] Certain tasks cannot be delegated.[1721]

[1712] Va. Code 54.1-3482
[1713] Va. Code 54.1-2956.9
[1714] Va. Code 54.1-2956.9
[1715] Va. Code 54.1-2939
[1716] Va. Code 54.1-2900
[1717] 18 Va. Admin. Code 90-20-420 et seq
[1718] 18 Va. Admin. Code 90-20-430
[1719] 18 Va. Admin. Code 90-20-440
[1720] 18 Va. Admin. Code 90-20-450
[1721] 18 Va. Admin. Code 90-20-460

A registered professional nurse, licensed nurse practitioner, graduate laboratory technician "or other technical personnel who have been properly trained" are permitted to render services within the scope of their usual professional activities, which includes the taking of blood, giving intravenous infusions and intravenous injections, and the insertion of tubes when performed under the orders of a physician, a nurse practitioner or a physician assistant.[1722]

[1722] Va. Code 54.1-2901

B. Telemedicine

Telemedicine is thriving in Virginia. The medical schools boast of their ability to serve rural communities over the Internet and have even provided anesthesia services from Richmond to a patient in Ecuador. One health care system has received national recognition for its e-ICU services where an intensivist oversees a number of ICU units from a remote command center using video observation as well as other monitors. Several health care systems are now advertising direct-to-consumer video-conference physician appointments.

While the economic efficiency of telemedicine at present is still somewhat unclear,[1723] the Governor and General Assembly have lauded this new technology. A statute passed in 1999 required the Commissioner of Health to report annually to the Governor and General Assembly on the status of telemedicine initiatives by agencies in the Commonwealth.[1724] The report was to include at least:

1. A summary of telemedicine initiatives by agencies of the Commonwealth;

2. An analysis of the cost-effectiveness and medical efficacy of health services provided using telemedicine;

3. Recommendations regarding any improvements needed in current telemedicine initiatives; and

4. Identification of additional opportunities for use of telemedicine to improve access to quality health care

---

[1723] See Whitten et al., "Systematic review of cost effectiveness studies of telemedicine interventions," British Medical Journal 324:1434-1437 (15 June 2002)
[1724] Va. Code 32.1-19.1

and to health professions education for citizens of the Commonwealth.

The annual reporting statute was repealed in 2004.[1725] The final report issued by the Commissioner was in 2003.[1726] The study, performed by George Mason University for VDH, focused almost entirely on the technical infrastructure needed for improving delivery of telemedicine in the Commonwealth. Moving forward, the Department of Health hosted the Virginia Telehealth Initiative Consensus Conference on May 26, 2005 and it continues to facilitate the development of telemedicine.

In contrast, the General Assembly and Board of Medicine have been restrained in promulgating statutes or regulations specifically focused on telemedicine. Perhaps wisely, they have chosen to not step into this evolving field yet. For example, an insurer must provide coverage for healthcare provided through telemedicine services, which is defined as:[1727]

> the use of electronic technology or media, including interactive audio or video, for the purpose of diagnosing or treating a patient or consulting with other health care providers regarding a patient's diagnosis or treatment. "Telemedicine services" does not include an audio-only telephone, electronic mail message, facsimile transmission, or online questionnaire.

Likewise, the required collaboration and consultation among nurse practitioners and patient care team physicians may occur through telemedicine.[1728]

[1725] SB 278 (2004)

[1726] http://leg2.state.va.us/DLS/H&SDocs.NSF/4d54200d7e28716385256ec100 4f3130/48f8571f5c43015785256cfc0057d4c0?OpenDocument

[1727] Va. Code 38.2-3418.16

[1728] Va. Code 54.1-2957

The Federation of State Medical Boards issued Model Guidelines for the Appropriate Use of the Internet in Medical Practice[1729] in April 2002. In the absence of precise boundaries, a health care professional must consider at least the following issues before participating in telemedicine.

1. *Licensure*

Virginia does not have a discrete provision for out-of-state physicians to participate in telemedicine care of Virginia patients. The conservative interpretation is that a physician caring for a patient via telemedicine in Virginia should be licensed by the Commonwealth.[1730] Virginia law does provide that a non-Virginia physician can consult with a Virginia physician in the care of a patient.[1731]

In 1996 the Federation of State Medical Boards accepted the report of its Ad Hoc Committee on Telemedicine, entitled a "Draft Model Act to Regulate the Practice of Medicine Across State Lines."[1732] The model statute would provide for special licensure of physicians that practiced in the state only via telemedicine or other communication devices (such as radiology, EKG, etc.). It also has exceptions for the only occasional interloper (occurs less than once a month, involves fewer then ten patients a year, or comprises less than one percent of the physician's practice) or in providing emergency treatment. The act also would not apply to physician-to-physician consultation.

[1729] Report of the Special Committee on Professional Conduct and Ethics, FSMB, April 2002 http://www.fsmb.org/pdf/2002_grpol_use_of_internet.pdf
[1730] This position is adopted in "Telemedicine Licensure Report," Office for the Advancement for Telehealth, Health Resources & Services Administration, US Dept of Health and Human Services, June 2003
[1731] Va. Code 54.1-2952.1
[1732] http://www.fsmb.org/pdf/1996_grpol_Telemedicine.pdf

The Young Lawyers Committee of the American Bar Association proposed a federal statute:[1733]

> Notwithstanding any state law to the contrary, a physician licensed to practice medicine or surgery in any state is permitted to engage in the diagnosis, evaluation, or treatment of a patient in any state via interstate communication using electronic signals, telephonic devices, or fiber optics, provided that the physician is in consultation with a physician licensed in the state where the patient is located; and provided further that the consulting physician licensed in the patient's state retain the ultimate decision-making authority for the patient's care

Supporting the same principle, the Center for Telemedicine Law[1734] pointed out that the U.S. Congress has already taken steps to set a federal standard to regulate what has traditionally been controlled by individual states. For example, the Mammography Quality Standards Act of 1992 allows the Food & Drug Administration to set national standards for mammography facilities, staffing, and practices. Likewise, the Health Insurance Portability and Accountability Act of 1996 (HIPAA) has dramatically shifted the regulation of patient privacy from the state to the federal level.

2. Prescriptive Authority

Legislatures continue to wrestle with the potentially conflicting problems of off-shore pharmacies. Some dispensers are willing to provide any prescription medication with little or no physician

---

[1733] ABA, Young Lawyers Division, health Care Law Committee, "Recommendation and Report to the Assembly of the Young Lawyers Division," January 1998

[1734] "Telemedicine Licensure Report," Office for the Advancement for Telehealth, Health Resources & Services Administration, US Dept of Health and Human Services, June 2003

authorization. A few have their own physician who will write a prescription. On the other hand, many American patients, especially senior citizens, have found better prices for expensive drugs through Canadian pharmacies.

Virginia requires that a prescription must be written only in a *bona fide* physician/patient relationship.[1735] A *bona fide* physician/patient relationship can be established under the statute by means of electronic transmission, but the statute does add that physical examination should be performed by the prescribing physician or a consulting physician. A Virginia pharmacist may fill a prescription of an out-of-state physician if the prescription complies with Virginia law.[1736] The prescribing physician must be licensed in the United States.

3. Credentialing

The medical staff by-laws of most hospitals and other health care entities require that before a physician can provide services in a facility, he must be admitted to the medical staff. While courtesy privileges for visiting professors and other dignitaries have usually been a formality, the routine use of off-shore radiology or other diagnostic specialties to cover night time services has become quite problematic. Most professional societies have endorsed continuation of local facility credentialing even for telemedicine.

4. Liability

As an experienced physician knows, having less then hands-on interaction with a patient in a controlled environment, e.g. the office or the hospital, limits the data on which a physician can base a decision. No matter how good a patient believes that she can

---

[1735] Va. Code 54.1-3303.A
[1736] Va. Code 54.1-3303.D citing to Va. Code 54.1-3400 et seq. (drug control act)

describe her symptoms and give a precise history, it is still not as helpful to the clinician as being able to directly examine the patient. To its credit, telemedicine adds video to the daily experience of physician-patient telephone conversations. Obviously a physician needs to proceed with caution.

Patients are increasingly communicating with physicians by e-mail. Many patients (like law firm clients) assume that they will receive an immediate response to an inquiry. Patients must be reminded as to the potential for messages not to be received, that emergent services are not appropriate for this media, and a physician reply may not occur for an extended period of time. Physicians expose themselves to increased liability if they attempt to diagnose and treat over e-mail. Lacking the sensory aids of hearing a patient's voice and being able to interact in real time make e-mail a poorer communication device then a telephone call.

The distant physician in a telemedicine arrangement needs to be very clear with the patient and any local health care providers as to what roles are being assumed by each party. A problem seen often in medical malpractice cases is a break down in communication, particularly as to who will be handling what aspect of subsequent care. This is likely to be exacerbated by telemedicine.

The Virginia cap on damages in medical malpractice actions applies to physicians who are licensed in the Commonwealth.[1737] This creates an interesting potential for an out-of-state physician rendering services via teleconference to be exposed to unlimited exposure while his Virginia colleague is protected. Conversely, a Virginia physician rendering services to an out-of-state patient is not likely to be protected by the Virginia damages cap if the patient did not physically come to Virginia. A physician may be hailed into the

---

[1737]   Va. Code 8.01-581.1

court of the jurisdiction where the patient resides even though the physician has never physically been in the jurisdiction.[1738]

A physician should carefully review his professional liability insurance policy to determine if telemedicine is included within the policy's terms. Many policies have probably not been updated to consider this issue but may be explicit as to the geographic region in which coverage is provided.

5. Informed Consent

Telemedicine creates added facets to the informed consent conversation between a physician and patient. Would a reasonable physician disclose that a) the effectiveness of rendering telemedicine services for the patient's condition has not been fully determined; b) the evaluation process (and potentially interventional process) is limited by not having hands-on capability by the distant physician; or c) the physician has limited experience rendering telemedicine?

6. Privacy and Confidentiality

As in the academic medicine setting, a telemedicine patient must consent to more then merely a distant physician being able to observe the encounter. Other health care providers as well as video technicians may need to participate.

Most health care centers are very attuned to maintaining confidentiality of medical records. Telemedicine creates a new challenge in protecting the privacy of the Internet encounter. Appropriate Internet privacy safeguards must be in place. If the encounter is recorded, how and where will the data be stored? The

---

[1738] For example, a Fairfax Circuit Court judge held that a Maryland company that transmitted MRI and CT images to Virginia radiologists for interpretation could be sued in Virginia. Citing Peninsula Cruise, Inc v. New River Yacht Sales, Inc, 257 Va. 315 (1999), the defendant's contacts were sufficient to assert jurisdiction.

patient should be advised at the beginning of the encounter as to who will be observing and whether the encounter is going to be recorded.

7. *Reimbursement*

Medicare and Medicaid have moved to pay physicians for rendering medical care via telemedicine. (Curiously, they still do not pay physicians for the daily burden of responding to telephone calls from patients desiring diagnosis and treatment.) Private insurers have moved more slowly, but became compelled to pay for telemedicine services in 2010.[1739]

[1739] Va. Code 38.2-3418.16, as enacted by SB 675 (2010)

C. Medical Staff Privileges

A medical entity, whether a hospital, nursing home, health maintenance organization or other entity, holds most of the cards in determining who may participate in the entity's activities. State and federal statutes give broad protection to the entity for peer review and quality assurance activities. The goal is for an entity to carefully screen practitioners, admit only those who practice "quality" medicine, and limit the practice of those who do not meet the efficiency and quality goals of the organization. This determination is almost solely in the eye of the entity. However, potential avenues of seeking judicial oversight are discussed below. Equally importantly, immunities available to individuals participating in peer review activities are also discussed below. Even the wrongly accused physician has little recourse in the Virginia courts.

In light of the stacked deck, a prudent physician should take an inquiry or corrective action by a credentialing entity very seriously. A well-reasoned response to such matters is very important. A physician will often benefit from assistance by an experienced health care attorney early in the process.

1. Legal Remedies for the Practitioner

Virginia statutes and court decisions provide very little relief for a physician who suffers denial, suspension or restriction of his privileges. If a hospital fails to provide the reasons for such action in writing, the physician can seek an injunction from the Circuit Court "prohibiting any such further violation."[1740] The statute is rather vague as to what this phrase means. It appears that the hospital need only provide a reason in writing that states its action was

---

[1740]   Va. Code 32.1-134.1

related to "standards of patient care, patient welfare, violation of the rules and regulations of the institution or staff, the objectives or efficient operations of the institution, or the character or competency of the applicant, or misconduct in any hospital."[1741] The court apparently will not examine the merit of the hospital's contention or its procedure, and the statute does not create a cause of action for the physician.[1742] Federal courts are also likely to dispose of a physician's lawsuit in the early pleading stage.[1743] The court decisions do not find a distinction between the refusal to grant privileges and the suspension of privileges. The Supreme Court of Virginia stated:

> When the trustees of a private hospital, in their sound discretion, exclude a doctor from the use of the facilities of the hospital, the courts are without authority to nullify that discretion by injunctive process. There are no constitutional or statutory rights of the doctor, or his patients who wish to be treated in the hospital by him, which warrant such interference.[1744]

Economic credentialing, as defined by the American Medical Association, is the "use of economic criteria unrelated to quality of care or professional competency in determining qualifications for initial or continuing medical staff memberships or privileges."[1745]

[1741] Va. Code 32.1-134.1

[1742] Medical Center Hospitals v. Terzis, 235 Va. 443, 446 (1988)

[1743] For example, see Velo v. HCA Health Services of Va., Inc., unpublished, (J. Hudson), (E.D.Va, 11/14/2002) that ruled as a matter of law the physician could not plead a cause of action under the Sherman Act or HCQIA. Also see Wahi v. Charleston Area Med. Ctr., Inc., 562 F.3d 599 (4th Cir. 2009)

[1744] Khoury v. Community Memorial Hospital, 203 Va. 236, 245 (1962), cited with approval in Medical Center Hospitals v. Terzis, 235 Va. 443, 446 (1988)

[1745] AMA, Economic Credentialing: Can Physicians and Hospitals Find Common Ground, 1993

Rarely is economic credentialing overtly identified as a factor in granting or limiting privileges. However, hospitals and surgeons are under pressure from data that shows high-volume practices have improved outcomes over low-volume practices. This is likely to lead to efforts to sideline low-volume practitioners at a hospital.

a. Due Process

A government entity is required to provide due process to citizens. Arguing that a hospital, by accepting federal or state funds, is therefore a government agency has been rebuffed by the Supreme Court of Virginia.[1746] The state will not interfere with the internal affairs of a private corporation.[1747] "There are no constitutional or statutory rights of the doctor, or of his patients who wish to be treated in the hospital by him, which warrant such interference."[1748] Thus, the court will not consider whether a physician was given a fair hearing.[1749]

b. Equitable Estoppel

The Supreme Court of Virginia has not given much comfort to a physician trying to preserve medical privileges under a theory of *equitable estoppel*. The physician must show that he has acted in reliance on an action or statement of the other party. The court has not found such a case in hospital staff privileges termination to date.[1750]

c. Antitrust

In Virginia, suing under a theory of antitrust law violation is often

---

[1746] Khoury v. Community Memorial Hospital, 203 Va. 236, 244 (1962)
[1747] Khoury v. Community Memorial Hospital, 203 Va. 236, 245 (1962)
[1748] Khoury v. Community Memorial Hospital, 203 Va. 236, 245 (1962); also see Brooks v. Arlington Hosp. Ass'n, 850 F.2d 191, 198 (4th Cir. 1988)
[1749] Khoury v. Community Memorial Hospital, 203 Va. 236, 245 (1962)
[1750] See Khoury v. Community Memorial Hospital, Inc., 203 Va. 236, 243 (1962)

discussed but rarely successful for a physician in a medical staff credentialing dispute. The two primary federal antitrust statutes under which private causes of action may be brought are the Sherman Act and Clayton Act.

i)   The Sherman Act

To prove a Sherman Act, Section 1, claim, a plaintiff must prove: [1751]

1. That the conspiracy produced adverse anticompetitive effects with the relevant product and geographic market;

2. That the objects and conduct pursuant to the conspiracy were illegal; and

3. That the plaintiff was injured as a proximate result of the conspiracy

The U.S. Supreme Court held that a New Orleans hospital did not create an illegal tying arrangement under Section 1 by entering into an exclusive anesthesia contract.[1752] Competition would not be harmed because the hospital did not possess sufficient market power (only 30% of the parish's residents seeking hospital treatment went to the hospital). Likewise, the U.S. Court of Appeals, Fourth Circuit, recently concluded that an exclusive services contract for radiology services at a hospital did not violate Section 1 as there was inadequate evidence to show that the hospital engaged in exclusive dealing, a group boycott or conspiracy to restrain trade.[1753]

[1751] Higgins v. Med. Coll. of Hampton Roads, 849 F. Supp. 1113 (E.D. Va. 1994) citing Advanced Health-Care Servs., Inc. v. Radford Cmty. Hosp., 910 F.2d 139, 144 (4th Cir. 1990)

[1752] Jefferson Par. Jefferson Par. Hosp. Dist. No. 2 v. Hyde, 466 U.S. 2, 104 S. Ct. 1551, 80 L. Ed. 2d 2 (1984) abrogated by Illinois Tool Works Inc. v. Indep. Ink, Inc., 547 U.S. 28, 126 S. Ct. 1281, 164 L. Ed. 2d 26 (2006)

[1753] Imaging Center Inc. v. Western Maryland Health Systems, 4th Cir., No. 04-2177, unpublished 12/13/05

To prove a Sherman Act, Section 2, claim, a plaintiff must prove that the defendant(s) have: [1754]

1. Possession of monopoly power in a relevant market;

2. Willful acquisition or maintenance of that power in an exclusionary manner; and

3. Causal antitrust injury

For a short time, Virginia doctors seemed to be able to pursue a Sherman Act antitrust claim against hospitals and medical staffs. The U.S. Circuit Court of Appeals, Fourth Circuit, held that a hospital and a medical staff would be considered distinct for purposes of conspiring together.[1755] However, on rehearing by the full panel of the appeal judges, that decision was reversed. The court went to great lengths to describe how rarely a credentialing matter would give rise to an antitrust claim:

> This case illustrates well the dilemma that hospitals face when they consider disciplining a physician by altering his admitting privileges. On the one hand, if the hospital failed to discipline a physician against whom documented complaints were legion, the efficiency of the entire institution could be affected and the hospital could even be exposing itself to malpractice liability. Yet, if the hospital takes corrective action, it and its medical staff face the prospect of a disgruntled physician bringing an antitrust suit against them.
>
> In our view, the antitrust laws were not intended to inhibit hospitals from promoting quality patient

---

[1754] Higgins v. Med. Coll. of Hampton Roads, 849 F. Supp. 1113 (E.D. Va. 1994) citing Advanced Health-Care Servs., Inc. v. Radford Cmty. Hosp., 910 F.2d 139, 147 (4th Cir. 1990)

[1755] Oksanen v. Page Mem'l Hosp., 912 F.2d 73 (4th Cir. 1990), opinion superseded on reh'g, 945 F.2d 696 (4th Cir. 1991).

care through peer review nor were the laws intended as a vehicle for converting business tort claims into antitrust causes of action. While we cannot say that no peer review decision would ever implicate the Sherman Act's concern for competition, this assuredly is not such a case. Page Memorial simply took measured steps to discipline an imperious physician. In taking these actions, Page Memorial and its medical staff have violated neither federal nor state law. The judgment of the district court is therefore AFFIRMED.

As will be discussed below, the Health Care Quality Improvement Act of 1986[1756] even further dims the hopes of physicians to recover damages under antitrust laws.[1757]

ii)   The Clayton Act

The Clayton Act[1758] prohibits the following anticompetitive practices:

1. Forming trusts by two companies with interlinking boards of directors

2. Fixing prices in agreement with other businesses offering competing products

3. Making agreements with other businesses to control the supply, and thus the price, of a product

4. Abusing power to gain or maintain a monopoly

The Clayton Act is most often used in relation to price fixing. However, occasionally one or more of the listed anticompetitive actions will arise in the health care arena.

[1756]   42 USC, Chapter 117
[1757]   See Imperial v. Suburban Hosp. Ass'n, Inc., 37 F.3d 1026 (4th Cir. 1994)
[1758]   15 U.S.C.A. § 12

d. Breach of Contract

In looking at a suspension of physician privileges, a Virginia court may assume that the by-laws constitute a contract between the physician and the hospital. Unfortunately for the physician, the by-laws usually provide that the final appeal is to the hospital's board of directors and that the board's decision is binding on the physician.[1759]

The Supreme Court of Virginia, in considering an action by a physician that was not appointed to a hospital staff, wrote, "We will assume, for the purposes of this appeal only, without so holding, that a contract would have come into existence if the board of trustees had, in fact, appointed Dr. Khoury to the staff."[1760] In a subsequent opinion, the court once again assumed that a contract existed.[1761] The Supreme Court of Virginia has declined to review a trial court's decision finding that hospital bylaws do not create a contract.[1762] In contrast, the courts of other states have reached the conclusion that hospital by-laws can form an implied contract by the actions of the hospital and the physician. For example, the Connecticut Supreme Court wrote:

> The hospital changed its position by granting medical staff privileges and the plaintiff physician has likewise changed his position in doing something he was not previously bound to do, i.e., to 'abide' by the hospital medical staff bylaws. Therefore, there is a contractual relationship between the hospital and the plaintiff.
>
> ...

[1759] See Medical Center Hospitals v. Terzis, 235 Va. 443, 445 (1988)

[1760] Khoury v. Community Memorial Hospital, 203 Va. 236, 242 (1962)

[1761] Medical Center Hospitals v. Terzis, 235 Va. 443 (1988). However, the court found that a provision of the by-laws specifically precluded judicial review. Also see Brooks v. Arlington Hosp. Ass'n, 850 F.2d 191 (4th Cir. 1988) (court assumed that hospital bylaws constitute a contract between hospital and privileged physician)

[1762] Miranda v. Norton Community Hospital, Record No. 961013, (7/30/96)

It is crucial to understand that the medical staff
bylaws, per se, do not create a contractual relationship
between the hospital and the plaintiff but because of
the undertakings of the plaintiff and the hospital and
because the hospital has a duty to obey its bylaws,
the bylaws have now become 'an enforceable part of
the contract' between the hospital and this physician
to whom it has given privileges at the hospital.[1763]

A recent decision of the U.S. Court of Appeals, Fourth Circuit, held
that a physician's employment contract obligation to abide by the
employer hospital's by-laws may give rise to a breach of contract
claim against the hospital where the hospital was alleged not to have
followed the by-laws in suspending the physician's privileges.[1764]

The Ohio Supreme Court, in reviewing the many decisions from
other states, observed that, "The cases holding that a hospital is
bound by its staff bylaws base their decisions on the reasoning that
if the hospital is not bound by the bylaws, then essentially the bylaws
would be meaningless."[1765] In reviewing a case applying Maryland
law, the U.S. Court of Appeals, Fourth Circuit, has held that whether
or not an implied contract exists between the physician and a

---

[1763] Gianetti v. Norwalk Hosp., 211 Conn. 51, 63, 557 A.2d 1249 (1989) holding
modified by Batte-Holmgren v. Comm'r of Pub. Health, 281 Conn. 277,
914 A.2d 996 (2007) citing Pariser v. Christian Health Care Sys., Inc.,
816 F.2d 1248, 1251 (8th Cir. 1987); Adler v. Montefiore Hospital Assn.
Of Western Pennsylvania, 453 Pa. 60 (1973), cert. denied, 414 U.S. 1131
(1974). The Tennessee Court of Appeals has followed this decision.
Alfredson v. Lewisburg Comm. Hospital, 1989 Tenn. App. LEXIS 746
(1989)
[1764] Wuchenich v. Shenandoah Memorial Hospital, 2000 U.S. App. LEXIS
11557 (4th Cir. 2000) (unpublished opinion)
[1765] Bouquett v. St. Elizabeth Corp., 43 Ohio St. 3d 50, 52, 538 N.E.2d 113
(1989)

hospital based on the bylaws is a question of fact for the jury to determine.[1766]

If a court concludes that a contract, express or implied, existed, then the court generally would have the authority to address enforcement of the contract.[1767] However, the Supreme Court of Virginia has held that:

> [w]e are of the opinion that when the trustees of a private hospital, in their sound discretion, exclude a doctor from the use of the facilities of the hospital, the courts are without authority to nullify that discretion by injunctive process. There are no constitutional or statutory rights of the doctor, or of his patients who wish to be treated in the hospital by him, which warrant such an interference.[1768]

In a later opinion, the Supreme Court of Virginia held that a provision of the by-laws precluded judicial review where the hospital followed the procedures set forth in the by-laws.[1769] (The Court's language suggests it is analyzing a contract.) Curiously, the Supreme Court of Virginia has been willing to entertain the question of whether terms of an employee manual change the employment relationship from "at will" to "for cause" termination.[1770] As one Circuit Court interpreted, an employee manual may have constituted a binding promise.[1771] Unfortunately, physicians have not been given such protection.

[1766] Sibley v. Lutheran Hosp. of Maryland, Inc., 871 F.2d 479, 486 (4th Cir. 1989)

[1767] Westminster Investing Corp. v. Lamps Unlimited, Inc., 237 Va. 543 (1989)

[1768] Khoury v. Community Memorial Hospital, 203 Va. 236, 245 (1962). It is important to note that no monetary damages were sought in this action. The sole remedy sought was injunctive.

[1769] Medical Center Hospitals v. Terzis, 235 Va. 443, 445 (1988)

[1770] Progress Printing Company v. Nichols, 244 Va. 337 (1992)

[1771] Ludwig v. T2 Med., Inc., 34 Va. Cir. 65, 68 (1994) citing Barger v. Gen. Elec. Co., 599 F. Supp. 1154 (W.D. Va. 1984); also see Byer v. Virginia Elec.

e. Business Torts

Terminated physicians often want to pursue actions against hospitals on theories of various business torts, such as interference with contract, interference with business expectancy, civil conspiracy, etc. The Virginia Business Conspiracy Act[1772] is an intimidating weapon for plaintiffs in that it provides for the awarding of treble damages if a defendant is found liable. The Supreme Court of Virginia has observed that many of these torts are actually the same allegation under different theories.[1773] Thus, the court is reluctant to invoke the treble damages provision. For example, a federal trial court dismissed an anesthesiologist's claim that termination by his group after a hospital reported claims of sexual harassment to the group's chairman based on the judge's finding that the allegations did not fall under the Business Conspiracy Act.[1774]

When a contract is terminable at will, a plaintiff must prove not only an intentional interference that caused the termination of the at-will contract, but also that the defendant employed *improper methods*.[1775] These are defined as including violence, threats or intimidation, bribery, unfounded litigation, fraud, misrepresentation or deceit, defamation, duress, undue influence, misuse of inside or confidential information, or breach of a fiduciary relationship.[1776] Methods also may be improper because they violate an established standard of a trade or profession; involve unethical conduct; or are sharp dealing, overreaching or unfair competition.[1777]

The Supreme Court of Virginia has not directly addressed whether any of these theories would support an action against a hospital for

& Power Co., 11 Va. Cir. 171, 177 (1988)
[1772] Va. Code 18.2-499 to 501
[1773] Simbeck v. Dodd Sisk Whitlock Corp., 257 Va. 53 (1999)
[1774] Mansfield v. Anesthesia Associates, unpublished, 2008 WL 1924029 (E.D. 2008)
[1775] Chaves v. Johnson, 230 Va. 112 (1985)
[1776] Duggin v. Adams, 234 Va. 221 (1987)
[1777] Duggin v. Adams, 234 Va. 221 (1987)

an adverse medical staff membership ruling. The Supreme Court of Virginia has declined to review a case where a trial judge held that failing to refer unassigned patients from the emergency department to the plaintiff surgeon as prescribed in the hospital by-laws did not give rise to a claim for interference with business expectancy.[1778] However, the U. S. Court of Appeals, Fourth Circuit, has given some hope to physicians that outrageous behavior resulting in termination of staff privileges can be compensated under theories of breach of contract, defamation, and tortuous interference with patient contracts.[1779] A Virginia judge granted summary judgment to a radiology group and its physicians after finding that the hospital's proposed contract rejected by the group would have violated the anti-kickback statutes.[1780]

f. Defamation

Some physicians have attempted defamation actions against hospitals that have limited their privileges. At common law in Virginia, defamatory words that are actionable *per se* are: [1781]

1. Those which impute to a person the commission of some criminal offense involving moral turpitude, for which the party, if the charge is true, may be indicted and punished;

2. Those which impute that a person is infected with some contagious disease, where if the charge is true, it would exclude the party from society;

[1778] Miranda v. Norton Community Hospital, Record No. 961013, (7/30/96). For discussion of rulings in other states, see "Annotation: Liability for Interference with Physician-Patient Relationship," 87 A.L.R. 4th 845
[1779] Wuchenich v. Shenandoah Memorial Hospital, 2000 U.S. App. LEXIS 11557 (4th Cir. 2000) (unpublished opinion); 215 F.3d 1324 (2000)
[1780] Virginia Radiology Associates v. Culpeper Memorial Hospital, (Va. Cir. Ct. opinion letter, Dec. 1995)
[1781] Great Coastal Exp., Inc. v. Ellington, 230 Va. 142, 334 S.E.2d 846 (1985) overruled by Cashion v. Smith, 286 Va. 327, 749 S.E.2d 526 (2013) citing Fleming v. Moore, 221 Va. 884, 889 (1981)

3. Those which impute to a person unfitness to perform the duties of an office or employment of profit, or want of integrity in the discharge of the duties of such an office or employment;

4. Those which prejudice such person in his or her profession or trade; and

5. All other defamatory words which, though not in themselves actionable, occasion a person special damages.

Where defamatory words that are actionable *per se* are used, damages for injury to reputation, humiliation, and embarrassment are presumed and a plaintiff is relieved of the necessity of proving the quantum of his damages.[1782] Punitive damages may also be awarded even though actual damages are neither found nor shown.[1783] However, the evidence must be clear and convincing that the defendant made the statements with "actual malice."[1784]

Pure expressions of opinion are protected by both the First Amendment to the U.S. Constitution and Article I, Section 12 of the Virginia Constitution.[1785] However, factual statements made to support or justify an opinion can form the basis of an action for defamation.[1786] The determination of whether an alleged defamatory statement is one of fact or of opinion is for the judge, not the jury, to

---

[1782] Great Coastal Exp., Inc. v. Ellington, 230 Va. 142 (1985) overruled by Cashion v. Smith, 286 Va. 327 (2013) relying on Gertz v. Robert Welch, Inc., 418 U.S. 323, 94 S. Ct. 2997, 41 L. Ed. 2d 789 (1974)

[1783] Swengler v. ITT Corp. Electro-Optical Prod. Div., 993 F.2d 1063 (4th Cir. 1993)

[1784] Swengler v. ITT Corp. Electro-Optical Prod. Div., 993 F.2d 1063 (4th Cir. 1993) citing New York Times Co. v. Sullivan, 376 U.S. 254, 84 S. Ct. 710, 11 L. Ed. 2d 686 (1964)

[1785] Williams v. Garraghty, 249 Va. 224 (1995) citing Chaves v. Johnson, 230 Va. 112, 119 (1985).

[1786] Williams v. Garraghty, 249 Va. 224 (1995)

determine.[1787] Defamation actions must be brought within one year from the date of the defamatory act.[1788]

The Texas Court of Appeals has allowed a physician's defamation claim based on a hospital's adverse action report to the National Practitioner Data Bank (NPDB) to proceed against the hospital.[1789] It further added that the single publication rule did not apply to a physician's libel claim. Thus, each transmission of the report was a new publication for statute of limitations purposes. The adverse action information provided by the hospital was contained in a single report made available to a wide audience through the NPDB. However, the confidential nature of the report meant it necessarily reached a separate and discrete audience with each dissemination by the NPDB. There was no mass publication. The physician could suffer a new and distinct injury with each republication of the report by the NPDB. No Virginia state court decision has been found on this topic, but the federal appellate court believes that Virginia would follow this line of reasoning.[1790]

g. Discrimination

Some physicians have had limited success in pursuing discrimination claims against health care institutions. For example, the Fourth Circuit of the U.S. Court of Appeals is considering whether a physician's need to find out if discrimination played a role in the termination of his privileges is outweighed by the peer review privilege.[1791]

Similarly, a state-owned hospital may regulate speech by public employees under certain circumstances. A physician in that

---

[1787] Williams v. Garraghty, 249 Va. 224 (1995) citing Chaves v. Johnson, 230 Va. 112, 119 (1985).
[1788] Va. Code 8.01-247.1; Jordan v. Shands, 255 Va. 492 (1998)
[1789] Stephan v. Baylor Med. Ctr. at Garland, 20 S.W.3d 880 (Tex. App. 2000).
[1790] See Wuchenich v. Shenandoah Memorial Hospital, 2000 U.S. App. LEXIS 11557, 2000 WL 665633, (4th Cir. 2000) (unpublished opinion)
[1791] Virmani v. Novant Health Inc., 259 F.3d 284 (4th Cir. 2001)

circumstance does not have a cause of action for retaliation for exercising his First Amendment rights.[1792]

2. Immunities for Peer Review Activity

Medical entities and individuals are cloaked with broad immunity for peer review activities by federal and state statutes. The jilted physician must show bad faith by the participants in order to obtain compensation.

a. The Health Care Quality Improvement Act of 1986

The Health Care Quality Improvement Act of 1986 (HCQIA)[1793] gives broad immunity to hospitals and physicians involved in peer review. However, this act does not address efforts by a physician to obtain injunctive relief.[1794] Several courts have gone so far as to state that a hospital does not even have to fully comply with the provisions of HCQIA to be within its protection. A good faith effort is sufficient.

To qualify for HCQIA immunity, a medical staff and hospital must provide a rudimentary due process before limiting or terminating a physician's privileges.[1795] Usually these provisions are now mimicked in a facility's medical staff by-laws. A court is rarely interested in looking at the quality of that decision process.[1796] HCQIA peer-review immunity has withstood constitutional challenges of due process and equal protection.[1797] Few leaks have been found in this umbrella

---

[1792] Braswell v. Haywood Reg'l Med. Ctr., No. 06-1360, unpublished, (4th Cir. 4/26/2007)

[1793] 42 USC, Chapter 117. The full text can be found at http://www4.law. cornell.edu/uscode/42/ch117.html#PC117

[1794] Imperial v. Suburban Hosp. Ass'n, Inc., 37 F.3d 1026 (4th Cir. 1994)

[1795] 42 U.S.C.A. § 11112

[1796] For example, see Egan v. Athol Mem'l Hosp., 971 F. Supp. 37 (D. Mass. 1997), aff'd, 134 F.3d 361 (1st Cir. 1998) (medical staff decision will not be examined even though plaintiff's experts contend that medical staff reached wrong conclusion on particular medical issues.)

[1797] Freilich v. Upper Chesapeake Health, Inc., 313 F.3d 205 (4th Cir. 2002)

of protection. In one of the rare cases finding an exception to HCQIA immunity, the Supreme Court of Nevada held that good faith reporting by a psychiatrist to outside agencies did not constitute improper conduct to form a basis for revocation of hospital privileges and HCQIA did not bar tort and contract claims.[1798]

HCQIA should also give pause to a physician plotting litigation, as many courts have held almost any action against hospitals and others for peer review to be frivolous.[1799] If an action is found by the trial court to be frivolous or in bad faith, HCQIA provides that attorney's fees and costs of the defendant hospital and peer review participants can be charged to the plaintiff.[1800]

b. Virginia Peer Review Statute

The Virginia statute[1801] gives very broad protection to a participant in peer review. It gives immunity to the participant "for any act, decision, omission, or utterance done or made in performance of his duties ..."[1802] The only exceptions to this broad protection are if the act, decision, omission, or utterance "is not done or made in bad faith or with malicious intent."[1803] It goes without saying that a physician will have a difficult time proving bad faith or malice.

The Virginia statute does not have explicit language stating that attorney's fees and cost incurred in defending an action that is frivolous or filed in bad faith will be assessed against the physician. While a judge does have discretion to award these if he believes that any action is frivolous,[1804] this is not favored in Virginia.

[1798] Clark v. Columbia/HCA Info. Servs., Inc., 117 Nev. 468, 25 P.3d 215 (2001)

[1799] See Imperial v. Suburban Hospital Association II, *unpublished opinion,* 1998 U.S. App. LEXIS 893 (4th Cir. 1998)

[1800] 42 U.S.C.A. § 11113

[1801] Va. Code 8.01-581.16

[1802] Va. Code 8.01-581.16

[1803] Va. Code 8.01-581.16

[1804] Va. Code 8.01-271.1

c. Protection from Discovery

The Supreme Court of Virginia has come out very strongly in supporting the confidentiality of the activities related to peer review. In HCA Health Services of Virginia v. Levin,[1805] the court made the first clear statements on the scope of the statute providing confidentiality for peer review activities [1806] in addressing three issues in the appeal. The mandate of confidentiality applies in all settings, not just medical malpractice cases. The privilege does not belong to the physician and therefore cannot be waived by him. The standard for showing "good cause arising from extraordinary circumstances" is quite different from being merely relevant to the litigation. Unfortunately, this high standard has often not been observed by trial judges when plaintiffs seek peer review material in medical malpractice cases.

The California Supreme Court recently prohibited testimony and a draft report of a Department of Health Professions investigator because he reviewed confidential hospital peer review materials in the course of his official duties.[1807] With the peer review privilege statutes of California[1808] and Virginia[1809] being similar and Virginia having a statute that creates a privilege for all information supplied to the Department of Health Professions as part of an investigation,[1810] the Virginia courts are likely to reach the same result.

The state law privilege from discovery may not be recognized in federal courts. No peer review privilege exists under federal common law or federal statutory law.[1811]

[1805] HCA Health Services of Virginia v. Levin, 260 Va. 215 (2000)

[1806] Va. Code 8.01-581.17

[1807] Fox v. Kramer, 22 Cal. 4th 531, 994 P.2d 343 (2000)

[1808] Cal. Evid. Code § 1157

[1809] Va. Code 8.01-581.17

[1810] Va. Code 54.1-2400. California has a broad statute that effects all official information. Cal. Evid. Code § 1040

[1811] Robertson v. Neuromedical Ctr., 169 F.R.D. 80 (M.D. La. 1996); Univ. of Pennsylvania v. E.E.O.C., 493 U.S. 182, 110 S. Ct. 577, 107 L. Ed. 2d 571 (1990); contra Wei v. Bodner, 127 F.R.D. 91 (D.N.J. 1989)

D. Professional Liability Insurance

1. Types of Insurance Policies

Medical malpractice insurance policies are generally classified as *claims-made* or *occurrence* policies. The distinction is extremely important from the perspective of purchase price and protection. *Claims-made* policies are more common and provide protection for claims identified to the insurer during the calendar period of the policy. Allegations made against a physician after the expiration of the policy are not covered by the policy unless the physician has purchased *extended coverage*, also known as *tail coverage*. *Prior acts* coverage, often called a *nose* policy, can also be purchased as part of a new policy. The important message of this discussion is that a physician will have no insurance protection under a claims-made policy if he does not purchase a contract to continue the coverage after the policy year.

Occurrence policies are not seen very often these days because the reinsurance market was almost destroyed by the long tail of liability that can arise in the United States. Lloyd's and the London insurance market were devastated by huge medical malpractice claims as well as asbestos liability. Many of the claims were on policies written more than twenty years before the claims were made.

2. Amounts of Coverage

Most insurers sell policies in multiples of $1,000,000. This is further divided between the amount of coverage per claim and in the aggregate. For example, a common policy provides $1,000,000 per claim and $3,000,000 in the aggregate. This means that up to $1,000,000 will be paid on an individual claim. Regardless of the number of claims, a total of $3,000,000 is available to cover all payments for liability under the policy. The costs of defending a lawsuit (for example, attorney's fees) are not usually calculated in determining the policy limits. In Virginia, a physician generally does not need more insurance coverage than the limit set forth by the medical malpractice cap on damages.[1812] This cap is gradually increasing for actions arising during the following dates:

July 1, 2008, through June 30, 2012 $2.00 million
July 1, 2012, through June 30, 2013 $2.05 million
July 1, 2013, through June 30, 2014 $2.10 million
July 1, 2014, through June 30, 2015 $2.15 million
July 1, 2015, through June 30, 2016 $2.20 million
July 1, 2016, through June 30, 2017 $2.25 million
July 1, 2017, through June 30, 2018 $2.30 million
July 1, 2018, through June 30, 2019 $2.35 million
July 1, 2019, through June 30, 2020 $2.40 million
July 1, 2020, through June 30, 2021 $2.45 million
July 1, 2021, through June 30, 2022 $2.50 million
July 1, 2022, through June 30, 2023 $2.55 million
July 1, 2023, through June 30, 2024 $2.60 million
July 1, 2024, through June 30, 2025 $2.65 million
July 1, 2025, through June 30, 2026 $2.70 million
July 1, 2026, through June 30, 2027 $2.75 million
July 1, 2027, through June 30, 2028 $2.80 million
July 1, 2028, through June 30, 2029 $2.85 million
July 1, 2029, through June 30, 2030 $2.90 million
July 1, 2030, through June 30, 2031 $2.95 million

The statute, of course, is subject to amendment or judicial attack at any time. Based on the General Assembly's recent history, these caps will likely stay in effect for several years.

[1812] Va. Code 8.01-581.15

3. *Common Exclusions from Coverage*

Most professional liability policies specifically exclude coverage of claims alleging an intentional tort or illegal acts. Common intentional torts are assault, fraud, and other activities that have parallel criminal sanctions. Malpractice insurers may not cover activities that are deemed experimental or unorthodox. A policy may also exclude allegations of sexual harassment or misconduct, whether lodged by an employee or patient. Defending Board of Medicine or medical staff inquiries may not be within the policy language. Policies are often silent as to coverage for participation in clinical research. Keeping in mind that insurance companies are very risk averse, a health care provider should carefully review a policy for exclusions.

4. *Other Questions that A Physician Should Ask*

A physician should carefully consider who will provide his professional liability insurance. A few considerations, for example, are:

- What is the rating of the insurance company for financial strength? A.M. Best and other companies frequently rate companies. State insurance commissions also monitor the solvency of a company.

- How long has the company been in business writing professional liability policies? Some insurers get in the professional liability business only to discover that it is much more difficult than other lines of insurance with which they are more familiar. As quickly as they got in, they get out, leaving the physician to look for a new insurer.

- How long has the insurer been writing insurance in Virginia? Currently, Virginia is viewed as a good market for insurers to be in because of the cap on damages. However, markets can turn sour. If a company has not consistently written in Virginia during down times, the physician may be left scrambling during the next market downturn.

- What is the company's renewal rate? This is a combination of taking care of the insured physicians when they are sued as well as premium prices. It also reflects, in part, the willingness of the company to renew a policy on a physician who has been sued one or more times.

- Does the policy provide for defending the physician before the Board of Medicine or in medical staff privilege actions? These administrative hearings can have a tremendous impact on the doctor's career and can be very costly to defend. The outcome may also have repercussions on any related medical malpractice lawsuits.

- How are claims handled? Does a claims representative manage them locally or somewhere else? What support services are provided when a claim is filed? Many physicians benefit from counseling services to cope with the stress of a medical malpractice action.

- Who will be the physician's lawyer if he is sued? Is the company using experienced defense counsel? Medical malpractice defense is very specialized. Does the attorney take cases to trial on a regular basis? A physician will usually prefer to have an experienced malpractice defense attorney defending the case.

- Does the insurance company have guidelines that it imposes on defense counsel? In order to contain costs, many insurers have rules (much like managed care) that set parameters for what a defense attorney will be compensated. Will any of these have an impact on the successful defense of a physician's case?

- How strongly does the insurance company defend physicians? What percentage of cases is taken to trial? Some insurers treat medical malpractice actions like "fender benders" and settle almost all of them. Others believe that a strong defense is better and take many cases to trial. Due to the tremendous impact a lawsuit can have on a physician's career, a physician needs to be sure that the company will actively defend against the allegations.

- Does the policy have a *consent clause*? This policy term requires an insurer to obtain a physician's consent before a medical malpractice case is settled.

- Will the insurer allow the physician to participate in writing the submission to the National Practitioner Data Bank if the physician agrees to settle a case? Will the insurer pay to defend the subsequent Board of Medicine investigation?

- Will the physician be required to purchase a "tail" when he retires or relocates his practice?

E. Advertising

As discussed in relation to advertising abortion services, the power of the legislature to suppress health care advertising is limited. However, an advertisement must always be true. An advertisement that is false, misleading or deceptive is considered unprofessional conduct by the Virginia Board of Medicine.[1813] In addition, the Board of Medicine requires full disclosure of fees for associated services if a physician advertises free or discounted services.[1814] If a physician advertises that he is board-certified, Virginia regulations require that the complete name of the specialty board must be stated.[1815]

A weight loss clinic is prohibited from using the words "physicians" or "doctors" in its name or advertising unless a full-time registered nurse is employed by the facility and at least one physician provides services or consultation.[1816] The only exception to this is where the clinic is operated by or in conjunction with a hospital. A physician must have primary responsibility for medical services as well as for the medical decisions relating to evaluation for appropriateness of admission of patients to the weight loss program.

Below are a few examples of regulations affecting advertising by Virginia physicians:[1817]

A. Statement specifying fee

- Must include the cost of all related procedures, services and products

B. Discounted or free service, examination or treatment

[1813] 18 Va. Admin. Code 85-20-30.E
[1814] 18 Va. Admin. Code 85-20-30.A through C
[1815] 18 Va. Admin. Code 85-20-30.D
[1816] Va. Code 18.2-502.1
[1817] 18 Va. Admin. Code 85-20-30

- Charging for any additional service, examination or treatment which is performed as a result of and within 72 hours of the initial office visit in response to advertisement is considered unprofessional

- This restriction can't be waived by agreement of patient and physician

C. Advertising of a discount on medical services

- Must disclose full fee

- Must maintain documented evidence to substantiate discounted fee

- Must make such information available to consumer on request

D. Specialty board certification

- Must disclose complete name of board when using term "board certified" or similar wording

E. False, misleading or deceptive information is prohibited

- For solo practice, presumed that physician is responsible and accountable

- For group, name of responsible & accountable practitioner must be documented and maintained for two years

F. Documentation supporting claims made in advertising

- Must be maintained and available for Board's review for two years

Physicians seeking to improve their income by expanding into areas beyond traditional medicine should be aware of the following regulations

18 Va. Admin. Code 85-20-40
Vitamins, minerals & food supplements: mandatory procedure

18 Va. Admin. Code 85-20-50
Anabolic steroids may only be prescribed for therapeutic uses

18 Va. Admin. Code 85-20-80
Solicitation or remuneration in exchange for referral prohibited

18 Va. Admin. Code 85-20-90
Pharmacotherapy for weight loss: mandatory procedure

F. Physician Contracting with Health Insurers

The Virginia "Fair Business Practice Act" describes the parameters for health insurers contracting with physicians.[1818] For example, a carrier must pay a *clean claim* within forty days of submission. A provider is given the right by statute to institute a lawsuit to recover actual damages suffered as a failure of an insurer to adhere to the Act.[1819] Gross negligence or willful conduct that results in damage to a provider will entitle the provider to treble damages.[1820] Retaliation by the carrier against a provider that invokes his rights under this Act is prohibited.[1821] A health insurer may not be protected by ERISA when sued under the Act.[1822] The General Assembly has also enacted legislation that forbids an insurer from forcing a physician to participate in all or none of the insurer's products.[1823] However, the State Corporation Commission has no power to adjudicate controversies with health insurers or managed care organizations.[1824]

Health insurers are generally prohibited from discriminating among health care providers who are licensed to perform a particular service.[1825] For example, a psychologist cannot be excluded from a managed care plan solely because he is not a psychiatrist.[1826] Likewise, a state-established group health plan may not exclude

---

[1818]   Va. Code 38.2-3407.15

[1819]   Va. Code 38.2-3407.15.E

[1820]   Va. Code 38.2-3407.15.E

[1821]   Va. Code 38.2-3407.15.F

[1822]   Valley Nursing Homes Inc. v. Group Hospitalization & Medical Services Inc. unpublished opinion (ED Va. 2002) (VLW 002-3-150)

[1823]   Va. Code 38.2-3407.10.0, amended 7/1/2000

[1824]   Va. Code 38.2-3407.B; 38.2-3407.10.P; 38.2-3407.15.K; 38.2-4209

[1825]   Va. Code 38.2-4209.D; 38.2-3407.C

[1826]   Blue Shield of Virginia v. McCready, 457 U.S. 465, 102 S. Ct. 2540, 73 L. Ed. 2d 149 (1982);

a physician solely on the basis of a reprimand or censure from the Board of Medicine so long as the physician otherwise meets the plan criteria.[1827] The *any willing provider* laws state that a health insurer cannot exclude any health care provider who is willing to meet the terms and conditions set forth by the insurer.[1828] However, an insurer can limit the number and types of "preferred providers."[1829]

Health insurers are prohibited from requiring by contract that a health care provider not render medical services that a health care provider knows to be medically necessary and appropriate.[1830] *Gag clauses* are not only generally prohibited,[1831] but contracts "shall permit and require the provider to discuss medical treatment options with the patient."[1832] Utilization review standards and appeals are set forth by statute.[1833]

Females age 13 and older have a right of direct access to a participating obstetrician-gynecologist for an annual exam and routine services incident to an annual exam.[1834] Obstetrical inpatient services coverage, copayment, deductible, limits and coinsurance factors must be "no less favorable than for physical illness generally."[1835] Breast reconstruction after a mastectomy must be covered by an insurer.[1836] The State Corporation Commission will handle appeals by patients of decisions by HMOs denying care in excess of $300. An expedited review is available for final adverse health coverage decisions.[1837] A health insurer that bundles or down codes claims must disclose the practice to a provider. An insurer is also required to

---

[1827] Va. Code 2.1-20.1.F
[1828] Va. Code 38.2-4209.C
[1829] Va. Code 38.2-3407.A; 38.2-4312.E
[1830] Va. Code 38.2-3407.10.N; 38.2-4209.F; 38.2-4312.F
[1831] Va. Code 38.2-3407.10.J
[1832] Va. Code 38.2-3407.10.K
[1833] Va. Code 32.1-137.7 et seq. and 138.6 et seq.
[1834] Va. Code 38.2-3407.11
[1835] Va. Code 38.2-3407.16
[1836] Va. Code 38.2-3418.r
[1837] Va. Code 38.2-5902 and 5905

disclose its bundling or down coding policies and its claims payment dispute process.[1838]

Virginia has little, if any, court guidance on the relationship between health insurers and providers. Some courts of other states have shown a willingness to referee disputes between physicians and managed care companies. For example, the California Supreme Court affirmed an appeals court ruling that, despite a "without cause" termination provision, an insurer could not terminate a provider's participation without first granting him a fair hearing.[1839] The New Hampshire Supreme Court concluded that an HMO's decision to terminate its relationship with a particular physician should be evaluated based on public interest and fundamental fairness. The HMO's decision should comport with the covenant of good faith and fair dealing and may not be for a reason that is contrary to public policy.[1840]

Virginia has given health care providers a new tool to stem the practice of a growing few patients that keep an insurance payment intended for the health care provider. A health care provider may sue a patient for the amount of the payment, the lesser of $250 or three times the amount of the payment and any sanctions that may be imposed under Va. Code 8.01-271.1.[1841] The health care provider must first bill the patient and wait until thirty days after the patient receives the insurance payment.

In 2012, the General Assembly enacted legislation to create the Virginia All-Payer Claims Database "to facilitate data-driven, evidence-based improvements in access, quality, and cost of health care and to promote and improve the public health through the understanding of health care expenditure patterns and operation and performance of the health care system."[1842]

[1838] Va. Code 38.2-3407.15
[1839] Potvin v. Metro. Life Ins. Co., 22 Cal. 4th 1060, 997 P.2d 1153 (2000)
[1840] Harper v. Healthsource New Hampshire, Inc., 140 N.H. 770, 674 A.2d 962 (1996)
[1841] Va. Code 8.01-27.3
[1842] Va. Code 32.1-276.7:1

VI. Compliance for the Health Care Provider

A. Background of the "Fraud & Abuse" Saga

In light of a few spectacular scams and political posturing, "fraud and abuse" in health care has become a major issue confronting all health care providers. Most physicians and other providers do not have much to worry about with regard to innocent mistakes. However, the government is aggressively pursuing through criminal and civil actions those health care providers who intentionally or recklessly ignore federal statutes and regulations. In 1995 President Clinton announced the formation of a program, Operation Restore Trust that increased the government's effort to investigate and prosecute health care fraud and abuse. Attorney General Janet Reno made reducing health care fraud a priority second only to the war on drugs. The Bush and Obama Administrations have continued this crusade

An estimated ten percent of health care expenditures are lost to fraud and abuse. Jumping on the political bandwagon, Congress has appropriated a large amount of money to fight this corruption. To give the federal agencies even more incentive, the agencies are given a portion of the money they recover for operational items. Because the government estimates that every $1 spent to fight fraud returns at least $10,[1843] these efforts will not go away until the perception of health care fraud has dimmed. Unfortunately for a health care provider, the cost of successfully defending against a fraud and abuse claim can cost far more then settling.

The federal government defines *fraud* as an intentional deception or misrepresentation that the individual:

[1843] Settlements with the government are collected at http://www.ffhsj.com/quitam/recset.htm

- Knows to be false;
- Does not believe to be true; or
- Makes knowing that the deception could result in some unauthorized benefit to himself or some other person

Needless to say, the government's definition is quite broad and hard to refute. *Fraud* is often observed by the government in the form of:

- Incorrect reporting of diagnoses or procedures to maximize payments;
- Billing for services not furnished;
- Routinely waiving Medicare co-payments and/or deductibles;
- Duplicate billing for the same services or supplies;
- Misrepresentations of the identity of the patient or of the provider;
- Billing for noncovered or nonchargeable services as covered items; or
- Kickbacks to induce referrals

The government defines *abuse* as incidents or practices that are not considered fraudulent normally, but are not appropriate given the accepted medical, business, and fiscal practices of the industry. Ignorance of the law is no defense:

> An example of a provider who submits a false claim with deliberate ignorance would be a physician who ignores provider update bulletins and thus does not inform his/her staff of changes in the Medicare guidelines or update his/her billing system in accordance with changes to Medicare billing practices. When claims for non-reimbursable services

are submitted as a result, the False Claims Act has been violated.[1844]

4. The Governmental Actors

Government auditing and enforcement activities are spearheaded by the following federal entities:

- Center for Medicare & Medicaid Services (CMS);
- Medicare Carriers and Intermediaries;
- Office of the Inspector General (OIG) with the Department of Health & Human Services;
- Federal Bureau of Investigation (FBI)
- Department of Justice (DOJ)

a. The Center for Medicare & Medicaid Services (CMS)

The Center for Medicare & Medicaid Services (CMS)[1845], formerly known as the Health Care Finance Administration (HCFA), administers the Medicare and Medicaid programs. CMS contracts out with insurance companies, called Carriers for Medicare Part B claims and Fiscal Intermediaries for Medicare Part A claims, to pay and review provider claims. CMS maintains the Medicare Learning Network web site[1846] to help providers properly submit claims and receive correct payment.

b. The Medicare Carriers & Intermediaries

As the pay agents for CMS, Medicare Carriers and Intermediaries identify cases of suspected fraud based on statistical sampling and claim review. They are responsible for ensuring that providers are

---

[1844] Compliance Program Guidance for Individual and Small Group Physician Practices, Appendix A
[1845] Internet Address: http://www.cms.hhs.gov/
[1846] http://www.hcfa.gov/medlearn/default.htm

being paid correctly. If a problem appears to be innocent, the carrier or intermediary will first work with providers to correct billing errors. However, intentionally fraudulent practices are referred to the OIG.

c. The Office of the Inspector General (OIG)

The Office of the Inspector General (OIG)[1847] is a sister agency to CMS within the US Department of Health and Human Services. The OIG investigates suspected fraud and performs audits and inspections of Medicare and Medicaid providers. It has access to the files, records, and data of CMS and the Medicare Carriers and Intermediaries. The OIG may impose civil penalties (fines) on providers or administrative penalties by excluding providers from Medicare and other federal programs. It also may refer cases to the Department of Justice for criminal or civil action. The OIG sets forth its priorities each year in a work plan that it publishes.[1848]

d. The FBI and The Department of Justice

The Health Insurance Portability and Accountability Act of 1996 (HIPAA)[1849] formalized the FBI, CMS, OIG, and the Department of Justice (DOJ) partnership to fight and investigate health care fraud that was created under Operation Restore Trust. The DOJ lawyers have criminal and civil authority to prosecute those providers who defraud Medicare and other Federal health care programs.

e. The Medicaid Fraud Control Unit

Each state, including Virginia, has a Medicaid Fraud Control Unit (MFCU) organized to investigate and prosecute misconduct related to the Medicaid program. The Virginia Fraud Against Taxpayers

---

[1847]   Internet Address: http://www.cms.hhs.gov/home/outreacheducation.asp
[1848]   OIG's annual work plans can be found at http://oig.hhs.gov/publications/workplan.html
[1849]   P.L. 104-191

Act[1850] is similar to the federal False Claims Act. The Virginia MFCU is part of the Attorney General's Office. It works cooperatively with the various federal agencies to develop cases against offenders. The state and federal prosecutors may elect to proceed in state court or federal court for tactical reasons.

1. Laws Utilized By Government Investigators and Prosecutors

Government investigators have a wide range of statutes to use as a basis for investigating and pursuing a health care provider. Not infrequently the government will use criminal, civil, and administrative actions simultaneously to force a health care provider into capitulation. The following federal statues may be invoked in prosecuting a health care provider:

a. Health Care Fraud

The knowing or willful execution (or attempted execution) of a scheme to defraud any health care benefits program is prohibited.[1851] The criminal statute applies not only to federal programs but also to most other types of health care benefit programs. Penalty for violation can include:

- A fine
- Imprisonment up to 10 years
- Imprisonment up to 20 years, if violation resulted in serious bodily injury
- Imprisonment up to life, if violation resulted in death

[1850]   Va. Code 8.01-216.1 et seq
[1851]   18 U.S.C.A. 1347

b. Theft or Embezzlement in Connection with Health Care

Embezzlement, theft, or intentionally misapplying any of the assets of a health care benefit program is prohibited.[1852] Penalty for violation can include:

- A fine
- Imprisonment of up to 10 years
- If value of asset is $100 or less, imprisonment of up to one year

c. False Statements Relating to Health Care Matters

Falsifying or concealing a material fact, making any materially false statement, or using any materially false writing or document in connection with the delivery of or payment for health care benefits, items or services is a criminal act.[1853] Penalty can include:

- A fine
- Imprisonment up to 5 years

d. Obstruction of Criminal Investigations of Health Care Offenses

Preventing, obstructing, misleading, or delaying the communication of records relating to a federal health care offense to a criminal investigator or attempting to do so is a crime in itself. [1854] Penalty can include:

- A fine
- Imprisonment of up to 5 years

[1852]   18 U.S.C.A. 669
[1853]   18 U.S.C.A. 1035
[1854]   18 U.S.C.A. 1518

e. Civil False Claims Act

The Civil False Claims Act[1855] prohibits a person from knowingly presenting or causing to be presented to the federal government a false claim for payment or approval. The government does not have to prove specific intent[1856] – all that needs to be proven is that the provider acted with intentional ignorance of the truth, reckless disregard of the truth, or that his conduct established a pattern of "in-artful coding." However, every failure to comply with state or federal law is not a False Claim Act case.[1857] Penalties can include:[1858]

- A civil fine ranging from $5,500 to $11,000 per false claim
- Government may recover treble damages

Under the Patient Protection and Affordable Care Act, CMS has created a requirement that providers, suppliers and health plans report and repay *identified overpayments*[1859] by Medicare or Medicaid within sixty days or face liability under the False Claims Act.[1860] The look-back period is six years, and overpayment includes any payment that a supplier or provider is not entitled to, and is not limited to fraudulent activity.[1861] Providers continue to be responsible for the acts of their agents, such as third-party billing companies.[1862] The "60-Day Rule" has created more than a little stress among healthcare executives.

[1855] 31 U.S.C.A. 3729 – 3733; for discussion of FCA's broad reach, see Raspanti & Mackuse, "Modern False Claims Act Liability: Cradle to Grave Liability?" *Health Lawyers News*, Jan 2007, pp. 42-48
[1856] 31 U.S.C.A. 3729(b)(1)(B)
[1857] US v. University of Pittsburgh, 192 F.3d 402, 416 (3rd Cir. 1999); US v. Anton, 91 F.3d 1261, 1266 (9th Cir. 1996)
[1858] 31 U.S.C.A. 3729(a)
[1859] Defined at 81Fed. Reg. 7661
[1860] Section 6402(a) of PPACA, 42 U.S.C.A. 1320a-7k; Also see Section 1128J(d) of the Act; Medicare Part A & B: final rule published at 81 Fed. Reg. 7654-7684 (12 Feb 2016); Medicare Part C & D: 79 Fed. Reg. 29843 (23 May 2014)
[1861] 81 Fed. Reg. 7656
[1862] 81 Fed. Reg. 7666

The state version of the FCA is the Virginia Fraud Against Taxpayers Act.[1863]

f. Criminal False Claims Act

Dating back to the Civil War, federal law imposes criminal sanctions for submitting false claims to the government.[1864] It is not limited to the health care setting, but requires actual knowledge of the false claim. Failure to meet medical standards alone does not support a criminal conviction for the federal offense of healthcare fraud.[1865] Penalties can include:

- A fine up to $250,000 per false claim
- Imprisonment of up to five years (10 years for conspiracy)

g. Civil Monetary Penalties Act

Specifically targeting health care fraud, the federal government can impose civil monetary penalties for knowingly presenting or causing to be presented a claim for an item or service that was not provided.[1866] It is similar to the Civil False Claims Act. The government does not have to prove specific intent – all that needs to be proven is that the provider acted with intentional ignorance of the truth, reckless disregard of the truth, or that the conduct established a pattern of "in-artful coding." Penalties can include:

- A civil fine up to $10,000 per claim
- Government may recover treble damages
- A provider may be excluded from participation in Medicare and Medicaid.

[1863] Va. Code 8.01-216.1 et seq.

[1864] 18 U.S.C.A. 287

[1865] US v. McLean, 715 F.3d 129, 132 (4th Cir. 2013)

[1866] 42 U.S.C.A. 1320a-7b; Regulations are at 42 C.F.R. 1001.952 et seq.

h. Federal Anti-Kickback Statute

Originally enacted to hinder defense contractor kickbacks, the criminal anti-kickback statute[1867] was expanded in 1977 to include Medicare and Medicaid and in 1996 to all federal health programs (except for Federal Employees Health Benefit Plan). It prohibits the knowing and willful intent to the exchange of anything of value for referrals or the purchase and/or lease of goods or services (including professional discounts) to induce or reward referrals or generate federal healthcare program business. Penalties can include:

- A fine of $25,000 per violation
- Imprisonment up to five years per violation
- Mandatory exclusion from the Medicare and Medicaid programs and other federal health care programs
- Additional civil/administrative penalties including under the False Claims Act, civil monetary penalties and program exclusion, up to $50,000 civil monetary penalty per violation, and civil assessment up to three times the amount of the kickback.

Overpayments due to kickback schemes are subject to the "60 Day Rule" for reporting and repayment.[1868] A few safe harbors have been created to foster business conduct that may fall within the strict definition of the anti-kickback statute.[1869]

The Commonwealth prohibits a healthcare provider from soliciting or receiving any remuneration in return for referring a patient to a healthcare facility.[1870]

[1867] 42 U.S.C.A. 1320a-7b; The state version is Va. Code 54.1-2962.1 and 18.2-502
[1868] 81 Fed. Reg. 7666
[1869] 42 C.F.R. 1001.952
[1870] Va. Code 54.1-2962 and 54.1-2962.1 and 18.2-502

i. Stark Amendment

Referral of Medicare/Medicaid patients by a physician to *designated health services* with which the physician or a family member has a financial relationship is prohibited and subject to civil penalties.[1871] Likewise, a *designated health service* entity is prohibited from submitting claims to Medicare for services resulting from such a referral. The designated health services are:

- Clinical laboratory services
- Physical therapy services
- Occupational therapy services
- Outpatient speech-language pathology services
- Radiology therapy services and supplies
- Durable medical equipment and supplies
- Parental and enteral nutrients, equipment and supplies
- Prosthetics, orthotics, and prosthetic devices and supplies
- Home health services
- Outpatient prescription drugs
- Inpatient and outpatient hospital services

A financial relationship includes:

- Investments
- Compensation arrangements
- Discounts
- Other direct and indirect relationships

Federal regulations provide an exception for non-monetary gifts up to an aggregate amount of $392 for a calendar year.[1872] Some exceptions to the broad prohibition are created by statute, and a

---

[1871] 42 U.S.C.A. 1395nn; Regulations are set forth at 42 C.F.R. 411.350 et seq.
[1872] 42 C.F.R. 411.357(k)

procedure is available to seek an advisory opinion from the Office of Inspector General.[1873] Subjective intent alone is not sufficient to find a violation.[1874] However, a jury will consider whether agreements between a physician and an entity take into account the value or volume of anticipated referrals, which is prohibited. Penalties can include:

- A civil fine up to $15,000 per claim
- Amounts collected in violation of this law must be refunded promptly
- Civil assessments up to three times the amount claimed
- Potential civil False Claims Act liability

Referral to a service or facility owned, even in part, by a practitioner or a member of her immediate family, is also prohibited under Virginia law unless a specific exception is met.[1875]

j. Other Means of Prosecution

As if the foregoing list of statutes was not enough, prosecutors have traditional criminal statutes at their disposal:

- Mail fraud, 18 U.S.C.A. 1341
- Wire fraud, 18 U.S.C.A. 1343
- Conspiracy
- False statements to a Government official
- Obstruction of Justice
- Money Laundering
- RICO

[1873] 42 C.F.R. 411.370 et seq.
[1874] US v. Tuomey Healthcare System, __ F.3d __, No 10-1819 (4th Cir. 2012)
[1875] Va. Code 54.1-2410 et seq and 2964; also see Va. Code 18.2-502

2. *Private Actors*

Individuals are permitted under the False Claims Act to bring actions on behalf of the government. [1876] As the *qui tam* relator is allowed to keep 15 to 20% of the recovery plus attorney's fees, health care providers have become a juicy target. Many disgruntled former employees have enjoyed playing whistle blower. Whistle blowers are protected from retaliation by employers under federal and state laws.[1877]

3. *Mandatory Exclusion*

Individuals and entities suffer mandatory exclusion from all federal healthcare programs if convicted of the following criminal offenses:[1878]

- Fraud or any other offense related to delivery of goods or services to Medicare or Medicaid;
- Abuse or neglect of patients;
- Fraud, theft or other financial misconduct related to healthcare (felony convictions)
- Unlawful manufacture, distribution, prescription or dispensing of controlled substances (felony convictions)

Permissive exclusion is at the OIG's discretion such as a licensure suspension or revocation relating to professional competence, performance or financial integrity; providing substandard or unnecessary services; and submission of false or fraudulent claims to a federal healthcare program.[1879]

[1876] 31 U.S.C.A. 3729-3733
[1877] Va. Code 2.2-3011
[1878] 42 U.S.C.A. 1320a-7(a)
[1879] 42 U.S.C.A. 1320a-7(b)

4. The Health Care Provider's Role in Combating Fraud

A health care provider is obligated to reasonably ensure that 1) claims submitted to Medicare and other federal health care programs are true and accurate, and 2) to not receive payments or other kickbacks for referring patients or for receiving payment from Medicare. Realizing that innocent errors do occur, the OIG has repeatedly stated that it believes that most health care providers are trying to practice within the federally-mandated boundaries. However, the government has wide discretion in pursuing a health care provider. The mere cost to defend of federal criminal or civil allegations can bankrupt a physician. Therefore, a prudent health care provider should take steps to minimize her exposure to even the appearance of impropriety.

When considering the appropriate level of administrative penalties, government prosecutors will consider the existence of an effective compliance plan that was implemented before any governmental investigation. "Reckless disregard" for the law is the standard of intent that the government must prove in a false claims action.

By implementing a compliance plan on its own and by agreeing to assist the governmental investigation of its employees, some health care organizations have been able to avoid criminal prosecutions. A provider, in order to settle a Federal investigation, is often required to establish and implement a compliance plan under the direction and close control of the government. These are known as "corporate integrity agreements." Needless to say, they are often far more heavy-handed than would have been voluntarily implemented by the health care provider. The better course is to avoid the government's scrutiny.

5. Future Government Initiatives

As the easy pickings among the large health care entities are plucked, the federal agencies have turned their attention to smaller organizations and physician practices. The OIG has issued compliance guidance for physicians.[1880] The likelihood of investigators visiting a physician's office will continue to increase for the foreseeable future.

To date, the government has focused on billing and other financial issues. The enforcers have long discussed pursuing health care providers on quality of care issues.[1881] So far this has not been a priority for federal investigators even though investigating quality was the springboard for many Operation Restore Trust investigations. A few civil and criminal actions have been pursued.[1882] The challenge for both the prosecutor and defendant will be defining what the quality of care is.

[1880] See Appendix. This was issued September 25, 2000.

[1881] For example, see OIG's Compliance Guidance Program Guidance for Nursing Facilities

[1882] See US v. Chester Care Center, 1998 U.S. Dist. LEXIS 4836 (E.D.Pa. 2/4/98)

B. The Compliance Program

While a compliance program is not mandatory for a health care provider, the Federal Sentencing Guidelines[1883] look favorably on health care providers that have made a conscious effort to comply with statutes and regulations. A compliance program also reduces the likelihood of an investigation as well as, if violations are found, the level of sanctions imposed. Many practitioners also find that a successful compliance program improves the efficiency of their business, resulting in improved profitability.

1. Model Guidance Programs

The OIG has issued model compliance guidance programs for many entities including:[1884]

- Clinical laboratories
- Home health
- Durable medical equipment companies
- Third-party billing agencies
- Hospitals
- Nursing homes
- Physician practices
- Hospices
- Medicare + Choice plans
- Clinical research

[1883] U.S. Sentencing Commission Guidelines, Guidelines Manual, 8 A1.2, Application Note 3(k)

[1884] See OIG's model compliance guidance web site: http://www.oig.hhs.gov/fraud/complianceguidance.html

This chapter will discuss the physician practice model compliance guidance. It is applicable to physicians, chiropractors, podiatrists, dentists, and optometrists.[1885] The OIG also recommends it to allied health professionals such as physical therapists, psychologists, speech pathologists, and occupational therapists.[1886] More recent guidance has come from a joint effort of HHS and others.[1887]

2. *The Essential Elements*

All of the model guidance programs issued by the OIG have seven primary components:

- Written policies & procedures
- Compliance officer
- Educational programs
- Communication
- Discipline & enforcement
- Monitoring & auditing
- Response & correction

Each of these components will be discussed below. Obviously the practicality of applying such a formal program to a small physician practice is problematic.

[1885] Compliance Program Guidance for Individual and Small Group Physician Practices, footnote 1

[1886] Id., footnote 2

[1887] US Dept of Health & Human Services, Association of Healthcare Internal Auditors, American Health Lawyers Association, Health Care Compliance Association, Practical Guidelines for Health Care Governing Boards on Compliance Oversight (4/15/2015), http://oig.hhs.gov/compliance/compliance-guidance/docs/Practical-Guidance-for-Health-Care-Boards-on-Compliance-Oversight.pdf

a. Written Policies & Procedures

The primary policies and procedures for a compliance program should address:

- The organization's code of conduct; and
- Specific prohibitions on activities identified as primary exposures to the organization

The OIG suggests that a small practice might avoid drafting detailed policies and procedures by collecting Medicare carrier bulletins, Fraud Alerts, CMS directives and similar guidance documents in a binder. The practice may also meet its obligation, in part, by regularly updating its clinical forms and records to reflect changes in Medicare practices.

i) Code of Conduct

A practice's code of conduct should be specific to the organization. However, most such codes of conduct tend to be general statements about how the practice will strive to provide excellent patient care, to seek reimbursement only for actual services provided, and to comply with all laws, regulations and ethics of the medical profession.

ii) Specific to Primary Exposures

The OIG has identified the following areas as being at high risk for physicians:

1. Billing and related activities
   a. Billing for items or services not rendered as claimed
   b. Submitting claims for equipment, supplies, or services that are not reasonable and necessary
   c. Double billing
   d. Billing for non-covered services as covered

    e. Failure to provide Advanced Beneficiary Notices

    f. Knowing misuse of provider identification number

    g. Billing for unbundled services

    h. Failure to properly use coding modifiers

    i. Upcoding

2. Documentation[1888]

    a. Incomplete or illegible record

    b. Failure to state for each encounter:

       i. The reason

       ii. Relevant history

       iii. Exam findings

       iv. Prior test results

       v. Assessment

       vi. Clinical impression or diagnosis

       vii. Plan of care

       viii. Date

       ix. Identity of provider

3. Kickback / Improper Inducement

    a. Stark and anti-kickback laws violations

    b. Routine waiver of co-payment or deductible

    c. Failure to make reasonable collection efforts

    d. "Professional courtesy"

    e. Violation of teaching physician guidelines[1889]

4. Medical Necessity of Services

[1888] More complete guidelines are contained in HCFA/AMA Documentation Guidelines for Evaluation and Management Services. http://www.cms.hhs.gov/MedlearnProducts/20_DocGuide.asp

[1889] 42 C.F.R. 415.150-190

      a. Submitting claims for physician services that are not necessary

      b. DME / home health:

         i. Signing blank certificates of medical necessity (CMNs)

         ii. Signing CMNs without seeing the patient to verify the necessity

         iii. Signing CMNs for a service the physician knows is not reasonable and necessary

5. Relationships with Hospitals

      a. Patient Anti-Dumping Statute (a/k/a "COBRA" or "EMTALA")[1890]

      b. Gainsharing arrangements[1891]

The OIG has pointed out that, "[p]hysicians should remember that they remain responsible to the Medicare program for bills sent in the physician's name or containing the physician's signature even if the physician had no actual knowledge of a billing impropriety."[1892] This is of particular importance to physicians who utilize a billing agency. While the OIG has found no statutory preclusion, it strongly condemns the practice of percentage-basis contracts with billing agencies.

Whether "professional courtesy" violates fraud and abuse laws depends on:

1. How the courtesy recipients are selected; and

2. How the courtesy is extended.

If courtesy recipients are selected in a manner that takes into

---

[1890] 42 U.S.C.A. 1395dd

[1891] See OIG Special Fraud Alert, issued July 1999. http://oig.hhs.gov/fraud.html

[1892] OIG, Draft Compliance Program Guidance for Individual and Small Group Physician Practices, Appendix A

account their ability to affect past or future referrals, the kickback laws may be violated. If the courtesy is given in the form of a co-payment waiver, it may be viewed as a violation of prohibitions on inducements to beneficiaries of Federal programs. A claim submitted under either set of circumstances may violate the Civil False Claims Act.

b. Compliance Officer

A compliance officer is the individual designated to implement the compliance program and to assure that it functions well. He will be policy and procedure drafter, educator, auditor, detective, communicator, and disciplinarian. Managing this many roles is challenging in any size organization. Juggling all of these roles by an individual is almost impossible.

In a large organization, a full-time compliance officer should be hired as a high-ranking member of the organization. In-house counsel or chief financial officer is not the appropriate position to fill this important function. A compliance officer must have the ability to cause change in the organization. This author has often recommended that the compliance officer report directly to the Board of Directors.

In a small practice, a full-time compliance officer position is not feasible. The OIG agrees that the function can be split between staff members or even outsourced. However, this author disagrees with the OIG's suggestion that the office manager or billing director could be designated as compliance officer. These are the very positions that are to be audited for compliance. One would never designate the bookkeeper as the financial auditor. The better solution is to outsource, at least, the auditing functions of compliance programs in small offices. The office manager, with physician oversight, may be appropriate to handle the other facets of the compliance program. A physician should keep in mind that she is ultimately responsible for the activities of her office.

c. Educational Programs

The effectiveness of a compliance program is only as good as an organization's diligence in educating its staff. New employees should be oriented to the company's code of conduct and compliance program. An employee also should be trained as to his job responsibilities and the policies and procedures specific to his position. The OIG recommends that this occur within sixty days of starting employment. The company must provide ongoing, usually annual, education to its employees. For small practices, the OIG suggests a "compliance bulletin board." CMS provides free general fraud and abuse training through its web site.[1893] Newsletters, in-service training, and outside seminars are other examples. When a problem is detected, an important component of a compliance program is to provide remedial education to the individual(s) involved as well as to the staff as a whole.

A company needs to document that its employees have received the organization's code of conduct, its policies and procedures, and education about them. An additional step is that an employee needs to be able to demonstrate proficiency in understanding these documents. To achieve these goals, many companies have adopted pre- and post-testing after educational programs. All employees are required to acknowledge in writing that they have received the employee handbook containing general policies as well as those specific to the employee's position.

Most health care organizations that receive or make Medicaid payments of at least $5 million annually must establish and implement an education plan for their employees, managers, contractors and agents that includes written policies and detailed guidance on the False Claims Act.[1894]

[1893] http://www.cms.hhs.gov/MedlearnNetworkGenInfo/
[1894] Deficit Reduction Act of 2005, Section 6032, "Employee Education About False Claims Recovery," Pub. L. 109-171 (2006)

d. Communication

An effective compliance program must have communication at a number of levels. As discussed above, employees must be educated about an organization's policies and procedures. In addition, a company must foster a culture of compliance. An employee must understand that it is his obligation but also the company's goal to comply with statutes and regulations. He must feel comfortable bringing concerns about, for example, coding levels to the attention of his supervisor as well as the compliance officer. Various means of employee reporting are encouraged by the OIG: face-to-face reporting to a supervisor; oral or written reports to the compliance officer; and an anonymous "hotline" where messages can be conveyed to the compliance officer.

e. Monitoring & Auditing

Employees at all levels should be aware that their job performance will be reviewed for compliance with statutes and regulations. This is more easily done with regard to billing staff than with patient-care staff. However, a compliance officer is charged with assuring that all staff members are in compliance. She should construct a monitoring and auditing program that is designed to detect wrongdoing as well as to act as a deterrent. A basic guide for record review, per the OIG, is two to five records per third-party payor, or five to ten charts per physician in a practice.

The OIG does not specify how frequently audits should be performed. It leaves to a practice's judgment as to whether retrospective reviews should be conducted. A baseline audit[1895] is important to determine the weaknesses of the organization and establish benchmarks. Educational and operational efforts should be focused on any detected weaknesses. Periodic audits, performed at least annually,

---

[1895] OIG's Self-Disclosure Protocol details OIG's view of the appropriate elements of an effective investigative and audit plan. It can be found at OIG's website: http://oig.hhs.gov/fraud/selfdisclosure.html

should then be done. Audits also should be undertaken in response to complaints from employees, patients, providers, or any other source. The goal should be to ferret out any deviations, immediately address them and work to ensure that they do not occur again.

In undertaking auditing activities, a practice is well advised to work with experienced health care counsel to minimize the risk of adverse action. Use of attorney/client privilege and/or pre-submission auditing techniques may be appropriate.

f. Discipline & Enforcement

The only thing worse, in the eyes of the OIG, than not having a compliance program is having one on paper that is not functioning. This, to the government, demonstrates that a provider had knowledge of the statutes and regulations and either recklessly or intentionally ignored them.

A compliance program includes the screening of employees for criminal convictions and Medicare exclusion.[1896] While a provider is prohibited from associating with an individual or entity that has been excluded from federal programs, what a provider is supposed to do if a potential employee is found to have a criminal record is often unclear. For example, an individual with a history of violent crimes is prohibited from working in patient care positions. Is she barred from working in a billing office? Should white-collar criminals be barred from cleaning bed pans?

A compliance program should have well publicized disciplinary provisions. These need to be objectively based, but the OIG points out that a practice's disciplinary and enforcement procedures should be flexible enough to consider mitigating or aggravating circumstances. This might range from a verbal reprimand for a minor infraction to termination of employment for a serious infraction.

[1896]   The OIG maintains a list of excluded individuals and entities at http:// oig.hhs.gov/fraud/exclusions.html

g. Response & Correction

Once a deviation is detected, an organization must respond quickly and effectively. The goal should be to avoid a recurrence of the problem. In Joint Commission parlance, this would be referred to as "root cause analysis." If the problem is limited to one or a few employees, the first step is to determine why the employee took the prohibited course of action. Was he not educated in the company's policy or procedure? If so, education for him as well as any others who may be similarly situated should occur as quickly as possible. If the employee knew or should have known that the behavior was prohibited, appropriate sanctions should be imposed. If the matter is of a procedural nature, revisions to the office's systems should be undertaken. A complicated decision process must be undertaken to determine whether the incident should be reported to the OIG.

C. When a Problem is Found: The Decision of Whether to Self-Report

One of the most difficult decisions facing a compliance officer is whether to inform the government of suspicious transactions or behavior that may have resulted in overcharges to Medicare. On the one hand, a health care provider is committing a felony if it fails to disclose information "with the fraudulent intent to secure overpayment"[1897] or knowingly conceals a felony.[1898] Publicly traded companies have an obligation to disclose contingent liabilities.[1899] On the other hand, reporting of potential wrongdoing is likely to trigger a detailed investigation of an organization that may result in severe sanctions to the company and its key managers. A compliance officer wants to be sure of the facts before pulling the trigger.

Federal legislation[1900] states that if a person has received an overpayment, the person shall a) report and return the overpayment to the Secretary of HHS, the State, an intermediary, a carrier or a contractor, as appropriate; and b) notify the payer to whom the overpayment was returned in writing of the reason for the overpayment. The report and return of the overpayment must be made within sixty days after the date on which the overpayment was identified.[1901]

If overcharges can reasonably be viewed as simple mistakes or the result of mere negligence, and the government would likely have not

---

[1897] 42 U.S.C.A. 1320a-7b(a)(3)
[1898] 18 U.S.C.A. 3 and 4
[1899] For example, SEC Form 10-K
[1900] Section 6402(a) of the Patient Protection and Affordable Care Act, which is codified as 42 U.S.C.A. 1320a-7k(d)
[1901] 81 Fed. Reg. 7654-7684 (Feb. 12, 2016); Section 6402(a) of the Affordable Care Act (ACA),

have initiated a fraud action, a provider can return the overpayments and/or report the matter to the Medicare carrier or intermediary. If the matter appears to consist of fraudulent claims or reckless billing, a compliance officer should carefully consider whether disclosure to law enforcement agencies is the proper course.

The OIG has published a "Self Disclosure Protocol" for health care providers.[1902] The threshold for self-reporting, per OIG, is that matters "in the provider's reasonable assessment, are potentially violative of Federal criminal, civil or administrative laws." The OIG encourages that reports be made only after an initial assessment substantiates that a problem exists. No time limit is imposed by the OIG. Two activities are excluded from the Self Disclosure Protocol:

- Ongoing fraud (this should be immediately reported to the OIG without further investigation or efforts to quantify the problem); and
- Transactions exclusively involving overpayments or errors that do not suggest that law violations occurred (these should be reported to the federal entity that processed the claim)

In voluntarily disclosing a problem, the health care provider must conduct an internal investigation and make a financial assessment of the amount of government funds at issue. This requires use of detailed guidelines for statistical sampling[1903] and other procedures set forth by the OIG. A compliance officer must submit a certified, written report of her findings along with all supporting documentation being made available to the OIG. The self-disclosure must contain:

- A full description of the nature of the matter being disclosed, including the type of claim, transaction or other conduct

---

[1902] 42 C.F.R. 401.305; 81 Fed. Reg. 7674
[1903] These are drawn from the government-sampling program known as RAT-STATS. http://oig.hhs.gov/organization/OAS/ratstat.html

giving rise to the matter, the names of entities and individuals believed to be implicated and an explanation of their roles in the matter and the relevant period involved; and

- The reasons why the disclosing provider believes that a violation of Federal criminal, civil or administrative law may have occurred

The OIG self-disclosure protocol requires certification by a provider as to:[1904]

- The truthfulness and completeness of the information provided to the government
- The willingness of the provider to engage in a good faith effort to assist the OIG in its inquiry
- Verification of the disclosed matter; and
- The truthfulness and good faith belief in the accuracy of any estimate of overpayment

Self-disclosure has many potential risks.[1905] These include:

- Reporting to the OIG instead of to the carrier or intermediary may predispose the government to view the matter as one involving intentional or knowing false claims
- Unless very carefully done, reporting misconduct will result in a provider making "admissions" that can be used against the provider in any subsequent litigation
- Depending on the nature of the misconduct, self-disclosure may lead to criminal prosecution of the disclosing provider and its employees and agents

---

[1904] OIG, Provider Self-Disclosure Protocol, 63 Fed. Reg 58399 (Oct. 30, 1998)
[1905] This list is from an article by S. Slade, "Truth and Its Consequences: Should You Voluntarily Disclose Overbillings to Law Enforcement," ABA Health Law Newsletter, 9/2000, pp. 36-42

- Criminal prosecution resulting in a plea of guilty or *nolo contendere* or a court conviction may result in the provider being excluded from participation in federal health care programs

- If the OIG determines that false claims were made with deliberate ignorance, reckless disregard or actual knowledge of their falsity, the government may conclude that the provider is potentially liable under the civil False Claims Act for treble damages and penalties of $5,000 to $10,000 for each false claim

- Disclosure to the OIG may result in waiver of privileges, and a compromised ability to defend against a suit brought by the government or by private persons

- Publicity about the inquiry will alert private insurers, shareholders, patients, prospective whistle-blowers and others with potential claims; and

- Publicly traded companies may be obligated to report the matter as a pending legal proceeding or contingent liability in public securities filings

On the other hand, self-disclosure has many potential benefits:[1906]

- Because the provider will perform the investigation, self-disclosure can minimize the OIG's intrusion into the provider's business activities

- Because the provider will prepare the initial report, the self-disclosure process helps the provider ensure that the government's first impression of the case is based on a balanced presentation of the facts

- Self-disclosure can expedite final resolution of a matter

- If the matter is not already the subject of litigation, self-disclosure to the OIG within 30 days can reduce potential civil False Claims exposure to as low as double damages

---

[1906] Id.

- By evidencing an effective compliance program, self-disclosure usually does not result in the typical False Claim Act settlement that must include a corporate integrity agreement[1907]
- Self-disclosure before the government learns of the misconduct may persuade prosecutors to exercise leniency in deciding whether to prosecute the provider, and, if so, which charges to bring
- If a provider is criminally prosecuted for the misconduct, the self-disclosure will be a favorable consideration for the prosecutor and judge in determining the appropriate sentence under the Federal Sentencing Guidelines
- Provided that the provider is not convicted of a crime requiring mandatory exclusion from federal health care programs, self-disclosure will reduce the likelihood of exclusion; and
- Public disclosure reduces the likelihood of a *qui tam* relator filing suit or prevailing based on the disclosed conduct

In conclusion, the decision to self-disclose should be carefully considered in consultation with an experienced health care litigation attorney.

[1907] See OIG's open letter at http://www.oig.hhs.gov/fraud/docs/openletters/OpenLetter4-15-08.pdf

D. Planning for the Investigation

Being audited for compliance is a matter of playing the odds. The trigger for an investigation can range from being conveniently close to the investigator's office to being an "outlier" for a particular Medicare code to being the subject of a complaint. Regardless of why an investigation might be triggered, a health care provider should be prepared for the eventuality. Here are a few tips on how to prepare.

1. Avoid Invitations to Investigators:
   - Use appropriate advertising:
     a. Are you using any buzzwords like "Free"?
     b. What's the message that customers are receiving?
   - Police your website
     a. Everything about advertising applies to the web!
     b. Beware of contracts, links, portals, and other norms of e-commerce!
   - Train your employees
   - If you are on the cutting edge, make sure that you have backup for your positions.

2. Train Employees:
   - Proper billing, coding, & documentation: The compliance program
   - Responding to informal inquiries
   - Responding to a formal investigation

3. Inform Constituencies Who Care and Need to Know:

- Employees
- Owners / shareholders / investors
- Public
- Customers
- Referral sources
- Suppliers
- Your family

4. Consider These Other Important Factors:
   - Communicate with employees and others;
   - Keep accurate records;
   - Check out all subcontractors;
   - Stay informed of what is going on with other health care providers in your particular industry; and
   - Be cautious about requesting or accepting anything of value

5. Run Drills:
   - Audit yourself
   - Have an independent audit
   - Make sure your employees respond appropriately to customers, investigators, and reporters

6. Maintain Contact Lists

A list of individuals should be maintained for the manager on duty to contact when the first indication of an investigation appears:

- Attorney
- Crisis manager
- Liaison for investigators

The person designated to act as the crisis manager should maintain a deeper contact list:

- Senior management team
- Attorney
- Public relations consultant
- Outside billing specialist
- Insurance agent
- Liaison for investigators

E. Crisis Management During A Fraud & Abuse Investigation

1. How Health Care Providers Are Investigated

A health care provider may be advised that she is under investigation. More likely than not, she will not be directly told of the inquiry at its outset.

a. The Tactics That A Health Care Provider May See

Seeing any of the following documents should alert a health care provider that an investigation is underway. The investigation may or may not be directed at the recipient of the search warrant or subpoena.

i) Search Warrant

A search warrant is a written court order entitling law enforcement officers to search a defined area. A search warrant does not require that a recipient have advance notice of its execution. Requirements of a valid search warrant are:

- It must be signed by or on behalf of a judge or magistrate with jurisdiction over the premises to be searched
- It must be directed to a named law enforcement officer and must command him or her to search the specified premises
- It must describe the material to be seized

Outside of the courts, administrative agencies also have the right to inspect records of those who participate in government programs:

- Center for Medicare & Medicaid Services
- Office of Inspector General
- Medicare carriers and intermediaries
- State Medicaid Fraud Control Units
- State licensure agencies

Failure to grant immediate access may result in exclusion from the government programs or actions against the provider's licensure.

ii)   Subpoenas

Two types of subpoenas may be used during investigation of a health care provider:

- The routine *subpoena* is a an order directing a person to appear and to testify at a given place and time
- A *subpoena duces tecum* is an order directing a person to deliver certain documents at a given place and time

Subpoenas may be issued by:

- A grand jury
- A lawyer representing a party in a civil or criminal case
- A government agency

A health care provider should be aware of the following in regard to subpoenas:

- A subpoena must provide the recipient with time to respond;
- A recipient of a subpoena may try to convince a court or an administrative agency that the subpoena's terms are unreasonable and oppressive; and
- Noncompliance with a subpoena could result in incarceration;

iii) Audits

Federal and state agencies that may audit health care providers include:

- Internal Revenue Service
- Center for Medicare and Medicaid Services
- Office of Inspector General
- State Medicaid agency
- State Medicaid Fraud Control Unit

A health care provider may encounter the following types of audits:

- Routine, periodic audits
- Investigatory audits

Because of the emphasis on health care fraud, there is an increasing likelihood that government agencies will share audit results and recoveries with interested regulators and third-party payors.[1908]

b. The Tactics That a Health Care Provider May Not See

A health care provider may be investigated using *sub rosa* techniques such as:

- Interviews of staff off premises
- Auditing of claims data via third-party payors or other providers
- Interviews of suppliers, customers, and others

[1908] A Circuit Court judge reversed the determination of DMAS of overpayment based on the hyper technical audit of a third-party. The judge dismissed breach of contract claims and lack of documentation as arbitrary and capricious. <u>ATG Rehab v. Department of Medical Assistance Services</u>, ___ Va. Cir. ___ (J. Harris, 15th Judicial Circuit, 10/28/14), VLW 014-8-102

- Scanning web sites and advertising

2. *Responding During a Visit from Investigators*

a. Basic Rules

1. Contact your attorney and others on your contact list;

2. Do not make any statements regarding any documents, allegations, or facts related to the investigation; and

3. Be polite and courteous to the investigators.

b. Working with Employees

1. Advise employees in advance of how to respond to an inquiry from a government agency; and

2. DO NOT tell the employees not to speak with government investigators. To do so would be to invite an obstruction of justice charge.

c. Search Warrants

1. Instruct your employees to contact you immediately, even if you are not present, whenever anyone shows up with a search warrant

2. Find out who is in charge of the group executing the warrant and ask for his identification

3. Ask for a copy of the warrant and any affidavit that was submitted to the court which issued the warrant

4. Contact your attorney and provide him with all relevant information and a copy of the warrant

5. Consider sending all non-essential employees home until the search is completed

6. Have your "point-person" accompany the officers searching the premises, but do not interfere with the search

7. Be polite to the officers

8. Ask for copies of all documents that are taken, especially if patient safety is a factor

9. Because search warrants are for documents and things only, do not volunteer any information; and

10. Obtain a receipt for everything that is seized and if possible a time when everything will be returned

d. Subpoenas

1. Review the subpoena to determine:
   - When it was received
   - Who received it
   - When the document production is required; and
   - What court or agency has issued the subpoena

2. Contact your attorney and provide him with all relevant information and a copy of the subpoena

3. Discuss with your attorney whether the subpoena is an isolated request or part of a broader investigation

4. If the subpoena is part of a broad investigation, advise your employees of what is occurring

5. Determine whether an internal investigation is necessary

e. Overall Points to Remember

1. Be aware that each investigation gives rise to unique circumstances, and these circumstances must be assessed on a case-by-case basis to determine the most appropriate course of action

2. Have a plan in place for dealing with investigations, rather than waiting for an agent to knock on your office door

3. Understand the Attorney-Client Privilege:

- The attorney-client privilege protects confidential communications between a client and her attorney that occur for the purpose of obtaining legal advice.

- Discussions with an attorney do not need to be disclosed to the government.

- Where an attorney retains an accountant or outside billing company to review the billing practices of your company, the findings and communications of the accountants or billing companies that are made through your attorney are usually protected by the privilege.

F. Outline for Audit of A Medical Practice

1. Corporate Structure

Articles of Incorporation

       Confirmation of filing

       Any amendments

By-Laws

       Resolution adopting

       Any amendments

List of All Shareholders

List of All Officers

Shareholder Agreements, Buy-Sell Agreements, Voting Trusts, etc.

Minutes of all Shareholder, Director or Committee Meetings

Annual Corporate Reports / Filing Fees

Corporate Name / Fictitious Name

       Confirmation of filings

Business License for Each Jurisdiction

Tax ID Numbers for Each Entity

Tax Returns, Annual, for Each Entity, in Each Jurisdiction

2. *Finance*

Capitalization of Corporation

> Notes or Loans to/from Shareholders

> Loans and other Debt Instruments to/from the Corporation

> Liens on Property or Equipment

> Security Interests, including UCC Filings

> Loan Guarantees by the Corporation or Shareholders

Debt Collection

> Policy / Instructions for Debt Collection by Staff

> Agreements with Debt Collection Agencies / Attorneys

3. *Contracts*

Real Estate

> List of Real Estate Ownership or Other Interests

> Deeds

> Mortgages

> Owner's Title Insurance

> Leases / Rental Agreements of Corporation as Tenant

> Leases / Rental Agreements of Corporation as Landlord

Environmental Audits or Studies of Property

Real Estate Tax Payments

Equipment

Leases

Purchase / Service Agreements

License Agreements

Distributor / Royalty Agreements

Noncompetition, Nondisclosure, or Confidentiality Agreements

4. *Employment Law*

Total Number of Employees

Employee Files

Immigration Status

State & Federal Tax Withholding

Employment Application

Evaluations

Wage Documentation

Medical / Vaccination Records

Employment Agreements

Verification of Credentials for Health care Providers

State License

DEA Number

Board Certification

Hospital Privileges

Managed Care Credentials

Taxes

Federal

Income

Medicaid

Social Security

State

Income

Unemployment

Annual Reports

Worker's Comp Insurance

Notices Posted: Minimum Wage, OSHA, FMLA, EEOC

Employee Handbook

Recruitment, Selection & Hiring Policies

Reference Checking / Responding

Employee Termination Process

Civil Rights (Race or Gender Discrimination) Policies

Family & Medical Leave Act Policies

Americans with Disability Act Policies

OSHA / Blood Borne Pathogens Policy Manual

Employee Benefits

Employee Bonus / Incentive Plans

Pension, Deferred Compensation, 401(k), or Other Retirement Plans

Employee Insurance Plans, including Health, Life, Disability, Etc.

5. *Patient Care Issues / Risk Management*

A healthcare provider might consider the following outline in reviewing the compliance status of the organization:

1. Insurance Policies
   - Professional Liability
     - Corporate
     - Individual
   - Director & Officer
   - Errors & Omissions
   - Employment Practices
   - Automobile
   - Property
   - General Liability
   - Umbrella
   - Business Interruption
   - Disability
   - Health
   - Life
2. List of All Litigation, Arbitrations, Administrative or Regulatory Proceedings Involving the Company or Its Employees For the Past Five Years
3. Clinical Practice
   - Documentation of Patient Care / Prescriptions

- o Telephone Medicine
- o Chaperones with Physicians & Staff
- o On-Call Care & Documentation
- o Peer Review

4. Advertisements
5. Americans with Disabilities Act

- o Physical Access
- o Accommodation of Patients
- o Treatment Decisions

6. Interpreter Services
7. Clinical Laboratory Improvement Act
8. Bio-Hazard Waste Disposal
9. Medicare / Medicaid compliance
10. Documentation

- o Coding
- o Compliance policies

VII. Healthcare Law Resources

Code of Virginia:
http://leg1.state.va.us/000/src.htm

Virginia Administrative Code:
http://leg1.state.va.us/000/srr.htm

Virginia Health Professions:
http://www.dhp.state.va.us/

Virginia Judicial System:
http://www.courts.state.va.us/

Virginia Association of Law Libraries:
http://law.richmond.edu/vall/

HIPAA / Office of Civil Rights, US Dept. of Health & Human Services:
http://www.hhs.gov/ocr/hipaa/

Center for Medicare and Medicaid Services
http://www.cms.hhs.gov/

Office of the Inspector General, Department of Health and Human
Services
http://oig.hhs.gov/

United States Court of Appeals, Fourth Circuit:
http://www.ca4.uscourts.gov/

American Health Lawyers Association
http://www.healthlawyers.org/

CPSIA information can be obtained
at www.ICGtesting.com
Printed in the USA
BVHW03s1145060818
523690BV00001B/2/P